THEORIZING COLONIAL CINEMA

NEW DIRECTIONS IN NATIONAL CINEMAS
Robert Rushing, *editor*

THEORIZING COLONIAL CINEMA

Reframing Production, Circulation, and Consumption of Film in Asia

Edited by
NAYOUNG AIMEE KWON,
TAKUSHI ODAGIRI, AND
MOONIM BAEK

INDIANA UNIVERSITY PRESS

This book is a publication of

Indiana University Press
Office of Scholarly Publishing
Herman B Wells Library 350
1320 East 10th Street
Bloomington, Indiana 47405 USA

iupress.org

© 2022 by Indiana University Press

All rights reserved
No part of this book may be reproduced or utilized in any form or by any means, electronic or mechanical, including photocopying and recording, or by any information storage and retrieval system, without permission in writing from the publisher. The paper used in this publication meets the minimum requirements of the American National Standard for Information Sciences—Permanence of Paper for Printed Library Materials, ANSI Z39.48-1992.

Manufactured in the United States of America

First printing 2022

Cataloging information is available from the Library of Congress.

ISBN 978-0-253-05974-1 (hardback)
ISBN 978-0-253-05975-8 (paperback)
ISBN 978-0-253-05976-5 (web PDF)

CONTENTS

Acknowledgments   vii
On Romanization, Naming, and Translation   ix

Introduction: Revisioning Colonial Cinema / Nayoung Aimee Kwon and Takushi Odagiri   1

Part I   **Time and Racialized Other: Colonial Modernity and Early Cinema**

1. Time, Race, and the Asynchronous in the Colonial Documentaries of Malaya / Nadine Chan   25
2. Facing Malcontent Colonial Korean Comrades: A Typology of Colonial Cinema in Asia's Socialist Alliances / Moonim Baek   47
3. Colonial-Era Film Theory, Spectatorship, and the Problem of Internalization / Aaron Gerow   68
4. Chinese Cinema's Other: Wrangling over "China-Humiliating" Films (*ruHua pian*) / Yiman Wang   92
5. World Export: Melodramas of Colonial Conquest / Jane M. Gaines   111

Part II   **Divided Mis-en-Scène: Colonial Cinema and Cold War Afterimages**

6. Tarzan/Taishan and Other Orphans: Taiwan's Melodrama of Decolonization / Zhang Zhen   139
7. What Is an Auteur? Hŏ Yŏng / Hinatsu Eitarō / Huyung between (Post)colonial Indonesia, Japan, and Korea / Thomas Barker and Nikki J. Y. Lee   163

Part III   **Millennial Hauntings: Rising Global Asian Cinemas**

          8. Cinema's Coloniality / Takushi Odagiri   189

          9. A Hallucinatory History of the Philippine-American War: Khavn's *Balangiga: Howling Wilderness* / José B. Capino   214

         10. Millennial Vengeance: Park Chan-wook's *Agassi* (*The Handmaiden*) and the Return of Postcolonial *Japonisme* / Nayoung Aimee Kwon   242

          Index   273

ACKNOWLEDGMENTS

From conception to completion, this volume has been a multilingual and transborder collaboration with participants from around the world. Scattered as we were, the volume contributors made every effort to stay engaged and connected over the years as the project took us—together and apart—to many places, archives, workshops, and conferences, in Asia, North America, and Europe. We would like to thank those whose unwavering support made our journeys and this project not only possible but memorable and rewarding. We are grateful to those who have sponsored and helped coordinate numerous international conferences, workshops, and conversations in multiple locations and languages where many of the ideas were set in motion. At Duke University: Asian/Pacific Studies Institute, Department of Asian & Middle Eastern Studies, Program in Cinematic Arts (formally Arts of the Moving Image), Franklin Humanities Institute, Program in Literature, Global Asia Initiative, Office of the Provost, and Duke Kunshan University. We thank Yonsei University's Center for Korean Visual Culture (KOVIC), Korean Studies Forum and Institute of Korean Studies, for their generous sponsorship.

The following individuals were invaluable interlocutors through various conferences, workshops, and chance encounters: Cao Yongrong, Leo Ching, Mary Ann Doane, Mark Driscoll, Prasenjit Duara, Gregory Flaxman, Amadou Fofana, Beth Holmgren, Guo-Juin Hong, Young-suk Kim, Walter Mignolo, Debashree Mukherjee, Hoshino Noriaki, Markus Nornes, Kim Chul, Helen Lee, and Yi Youngjae. Other participants whose papers were not included in the final volume are gratefully acknowledged here for their thoughtful engagement at various stages of the collaboration: Michael Baskett, Calvin Hui, Hieyoon Kim, Hwajin Lee, and Stephen Poland. Special thanks are in order for Hyunseon Park at Yonsei University for supporting several international conferences in Seoul. We also thank Jennifer Sun, Tong Meng, Ge Wangyong, Haiyan Gao, Andrew Field, Don Snow, Xu Li, and many others at Duke Kunshan University, for welcoming us to the new campus under construction. Our visits to the Shanghai Film Museum and other archival excursions were especially memorable.

We thank Elizabeth Brown and Geof Garvey for their expert and artful editing. Everyone at Indiana University Press deserve special recognition for their unwavering professionalism and ongoing support—especially Allison Blair Chaplain, Robert Rushing, Sophia Hebert, and Rachel Rosolina for their dedication to this project. Anonymous reviewers offered invaluable constructive comments at a crucial stage of the process.

The publication of this volume has been made possible through generous grants and subventions from Yonsei University's Future-leading Research Initiative of 2015 (2016-22-0118), Academy of Korean Studies, Duke Center for International and Global Studies and Asian/Pacific Studies Institute. The following archives have been instrumental in securing access to rare images and films: Korean Film Archive (KOFA), Taiwan Film Institute (TFI), British Film Institute (BFI), National Film Archive of Japan, Sinematek Indonesia, China Film Archive, Cinémathèque Française, National Archives Malaysia, Makino Mamoru Collection, and we gratefully acknowledge them here.

This volume was completed during the COVID-19 global pandemic. Our contributors were scattered around the world and under lockdown at various stages of the production process. We would like to thank everyone for their extraordinary commitment to the project in the face of multiple challenges. We dedicate this collaboration to the memories of those who are no longer with us.

ON ROMANIZATION, NAMING, AND TRANSLATION

Chinese, Japanese, and Korean names and terms follow the pinyin, Hepburn, and McCune Reischauer romanization systems respectively unless another convention is more commonly known or used. Other language transliterations follow standard conventions. Asian names follow cultural conventions of last name, first name order unless other preferences have been indicated. All translations are by the contributors unless otherwise noted.

THEORIZING COLONIAL CINEMA

INTRODUCTION
Revisioning Colonial Cinema

Nayoung Aimee Kwon and Takushi Odagiri

Volume Abstract

This coedited volume proposes a timely retrospective on the century-long constitutive relationship of film and colonialism from the past to contemporary legacies in and of Asia. Our inquiry starts with the question, How might prior articulations about film form, theory, history, and ideology be rearticulated when we put the colonial question at the center rather than the periphery of our concerns? As a way of examining film's broader connections to colonialism, we attempt to reframe inherited perspectives by beginning our inquiries in the colonies and then looking outward. Our premise is that while prior scholarship in global film studies has made important headway in examining various aspects of colonial cinemas, scholars up to now have focused primarily on the points of view of Europe's *past* imperial histories and archives about the colonies *over there*. Furthermore, local and regional blind spots and censorship within Asia of unsavory colonial memories impeded postcolonial understanding. Newly opened archives in Asia and better channels for inter-Asian and transpacific collaborations in and beyond the region since the beginning of the millennium have given us a timely opportunity to pay renewed attention to hitherto inaccessible perspectives from the colonies themselves and to present-day repercussions and reverberations.

Various forms of devaluation, misrecognition, and censorship—both within the region and outside it—have for too long relegated local voices to the margins or repressed them to the unconscious. From the start, a deeply film-critical and film-historical concern propelling our dialogue has steered this project beyond the national borderlines of Asian cinemas and culminated in ongoing interdisciplinary and transborder collaborations as both method and object of the volume's critical and theoretical inquiry. Our collective efforts aim to critique and bridge geopolitical divides between area studies *over there* and Euro-American theory *here*—between so-called anthropos and humanitas—and to overcome such provincial and racialized hierarchies of human value and knowledge formations. That is, we attempt to bring to light various latent layers—theoretical, historical, and ethical—that have not been sufficiently examined thus far.

While keeping in mind the unequal imperial power dynamics of capital, technology, and geopolitics at the heart of cinematic circulations, this volume focuses on select case studies of ways in which film has been negotiated, translated, and transformed in the nexus of a local and global cinematic encounter, from the early days of film to current, ongoing legacies from the past to the present. We go beyond a commonly assumed duality between production and consumption to consider the distinct ways film was resignified in transcolonial contact zones by directors, writers, critics, actors, coproducers, translators, movie narrators, and spectators. In so doing, the volume pays special attention to hitherto marginalized voices and disregarded and repressed subjectivities of local and regional cultural producers and consumers in order to encapsulate a fuller and more capacious story of film's regional and global circulation.

Introduction

Theorizing Colonial Cinema offers a timely retrospective on the century-long constitutive and intimate relationship between film and colonialism. As one of many possible starting points for this capacious concern—anticipating yet more conversations to come—we focus here on several select case studies from film cultures, in and of Asia.[1] As film historian Jane Gaines significantly points out in her contribution to this volume, film scholars have long described the entangled dynamic between film and colonialism as one of simple common sense. Nevertheless, this established common sense connection between film and colonialism was too often assumed, only to be left unexamined in significant detail, or even actively repressed into the depths of disavowal. When addressed, the entanglements were too often facilely referred to in passing, left in the margins or off frame, while the focus quickly turned to other concerns deemed more central, worthy, or timely.

Our volume's premise is that although prior film studies scholarship has made important headway in examining various aspects of colonial cinematic cultures, many have been delimited by a primary focus on the point of view of Europe's past imperial histories, archives, and narratives about the colonies over there. Meanwhile, other forms of postimperial and postcolonial blind spots and censorship—both internally and externally imposed—toward unsavory colonial memories further impeded local and regional understanding.[2] Since the beginning of the millennium and with the waning of some

Figure I.1 and Figure I.2. Rare film stills recently discovered in China from the film *Fukuchi Banri* (Japanese; Pokchi Malli, Korean, Miles away from happiness, Chŏn Ch'anggŭn, 1941). The film was a transcolonial coproduction between the Manchurian Film Association (Man'ei) and Korean Film Association (Koryŏ Yŏnghwa Hyŏphoe), directed by a colonial Korean filmmaker Chŏn Ch'anggŭn working in the wartime imperial film network. The film touches on the controversial topic of colonial and wartime collaboration in the region and is still considered to be lost. (Courtesy of Korean Film Archive [KOFA].)

Cold War tensions, we have witnessed newly opened colonial archives in and about Asia and improvements in channels for inter-Asian and transpacific collaborations and translations.[3] This opportune moment has at long last given us a timely opening to pay renewed attention to little-known or rarely accessed perspectives.[4]

This volume brings into dialogue a vast transnational and multilingual network of both established and new critical voices working in many disciplines, fields, and languages, including film studies, cultural and postcolonial studies, anthropology, history, and critical area studies. Building on conversations with prior articulations, this diverse network represents a contemporary global and regional theoretical paradigm shift—away from a monolingualism of universal abstraction originating from fixed and privileged geopolitical locations. Transpacific and transborder collaborations and knowledge coproductions among scholars and archivists in Asia and elsewhere open up an ethically committed, locally grounded, multilingual, and multisited theoretical methodology of engagement. By highlighting transborder methodologies as the starting point of a theoretical framework, our collective aim is to reckon with and recenter past histories and voices. The compilation marks no less than a movement away from prior limitations of what had been counted as knowledge and human value up to and throughout the long twentieth century. It calls for an overcoming of once delimited imperial, national, and Cold War borderlines, gatekeepers, and points of view—toward a more open-minded look at the braided past and its present-day repercussions and reverberations.

The volume as a collective offers a transborder and transcolonial reframing of local and global politics of knowledge, value, and cultural production and consumption. Here a transcolonial framework is defined both spatially, across imperial-colonial-national divides, and temporally, in and beyond the colonial era, from the past to the present. This multivalent spatio-temporal theoretical framework is offered in conversation with movements in postcolonial and decolonial theories as a way to engage with and move beyond prior discursive and epistemological limits—that is, semantic and temporal assumptions of an afterness or postness on the discursive level and an overemphasis on binary assumptions of resistance, overcoming, or departures on the epistemological level. We focus instead on more complex actualities and lingering legacies, including collusions, collaborations, and internalizations, long after the official end of colonial rule.

Our methods, sites, and archives necessarily vary, but the project has been propelled and grounded by a common question: How might prior articulations about film form, theory, history, and ideology be reenvisioned and rearticulated when we put the long-repressed and disavowed colonial question at the center rather than the periphery of our concerns? In other words, how would the story of film be told differently if we squarely focused our attention from start to finish on the colonial question rather than relegate that question to a passing detour or to an afterthought?

As one way of recentering film's long and intimate—but disavowed—connections to colonialism, it was essential for us to reframe inherited perspectives that have long misrecognized the colony as primarily a static and silent object and landscape of representation fixed in a time and place far and away.[5] We begin our inquiries not from the metropolitan centers and their agents, as has been the common and dominant practice, but through site-specific and locally grounded analyses from within the colonies—including occluded or marginalized voices and subjectivities.[6]

While insisting on the colonies as our starting point of articulation, we were also careful not to reproduce prior one-sidedness by neglecting the viewpoints from the metropolitan centers. We recognize the importance of including metropolitan perspectives as participants—albeit unequal—on the flip side of film's colonial story. Neglecting either side would result in mirroring past limitations, this time from another angle, reproducing no less a myopic version of a partial story. It would render our hermeneutic and political projects incomplete, leaving the unconscious unexamined. Rather, from early on we kept a multivalent focus on interimperial, transcolonial, and—in the specific case of Asian cinematic cultures—transpacific intimacies that were always at the core of imperial relations. These relationalities need to be examined simultaneously and *together*, not divided as in the past, in order to open up future scholarship toward any true approximation of the very interlaced essence that is at the heart of film's colonial story.

The volume contributors share a premise that the intimate and central affiliation between colonialism and film had been for too long made uncommon or, to borrow Nadine Chan's term from her chapter—"asynchronous"—via competing and unequal transcolonial power in discourse formation and circulation that overly privileged one side of the equation. The dynamic was exacerbated by postimperial and postcolonial disavowals of what has been historically, morally, and politically repressed in the colonial unconscious.[7] Reasons for repression were multiple and overdetermined—after the region's sudden official dissolution of empire, former colonizers and former colonized each had their own different and competing reasons for desiring to bury their once unequally connected past histories of colonial subjugation. Our insights into the colonial unconscious of film and its transcolonial repercussions are inspired by an army of previous scholarship that has expanded ethical concerns beyond individual psychology and illuminating the broader conundrum of political and collective unconscious of modern and global societal contexts and constructs.[8]

Long-standing bias and imbalance in the epistemology—or production of knowledge—of empires have persisted despite numerous and vociferous critiques. Myriad reasons beyond injunctions and blind spots continue to discard or minimize the perspectives of the other half of the colonial divide: that of the colonized and the formerly colonized who numerically are in the majority of humanity.

The legacy of unequal distribution and access in the colonies because of the extraction of resources by imperial powers has lasting effects long after the official end of empires. That those who controlled access to the technology of knowledge—its means of production and distribution—had such limited knowledge or awareness of the cultures and languages of the peoples they colonized naturally resulted in limiting the artifacts that were deemed worthy of preservation and thus rendered legible to posterity. This monopolistic gatekeeping, wittingly or unwittingly, ensured that films and their histories were predominantly recorded and passed down in the voices and languages of imperial powers and their offspring, not those of the colonies themselves.

Various forms of devaluation, misrecognition, repression, and censorship—both within the region and outside it—have for too long relegated local voices to the margins or repressed them from externalization and driven them deep into the unconscious. As a result, the histories and archives that lay over there beyond the limited borders of Euro-American—or more precisely, North Atlantic—perspectives have rarely been documented, catalogued, or examined in depth as focused concerns in standard historiographies and theorization of film. The lacuna has been further exacerbated by severely limited conditions within the colonies themselves and then in the turmoil that followed in subsequent postcolonial contexts. Violent socioeconomic, political, and cultural deracination, instability, turmoil, partitions, and wars—many of them direct consequences of imperial policies—filled the vacuum or the open wounds left hollowed out. The sudden departures of deflated imperial powers left little room for reflection and reckoning for decades to come, long after the physical withdrawal of the colonizers.

From the start, the volume contributors were propelled by a deeply film-critical and film-historical concern beyond the national boundaries of Asian cinemas, culminating in an engaged methodology of interdisciplinary and transborder collaboration as both method and object of the volume's critical and theoretical inquiry. Our efforts aim to critique and bridge geopolitical divides between area studies over there and North Atlantic theory here and between anthropos and humanitas; and to overcome provincial and racialized hierarchies of knowledge and value formations that have persisted long after the end of official colonial rule.[9] That is, we attempt to bring to light various overdetermined layers—theoretical, historical, ethical—of long-repressed and disavowed stories that have not been sufficiently examined thus far.[10]

The limitations in film history and theory are not isolated cases, but are symptomatic of the long-lasting impact of original imperial resource plunder, compounded through reproduced transcolonial inequalities and ongoing power disparities.[11] An aspect of such limitations is elaborated in Aaron Gerow's chapter and his concept of a theory complex—that even Japanese critics did not recognize Japanese film theory for the greater part of the twentieth century. Elsewhere, in discussing the historical and ongoing phenomenon of a theory complex that has both epistemological and moral consequences, Gerow (2012) significantly mentioned Nishida Kitarō, a modern Japanese philosopher who was influential in an era when Japanese media and film theory were emerging. It bears highlighting that not only the notion of "theory" (as Gerow notes) but also that of "philosophy" was changing as they were emerging in Japan in the early twentieth century. These shifting notions were themselves transcolonial sites of encounters, translations, and transformations in (and even before) Nishida's time, a moment when the notion of film itself was also still in formation.[12] The lingering question for the twenty-first century is how a historical and ongoing phenomenon of a theory complex continues to manifest itself in the broader history of film in and beyond Japan.

In embarking on the task at hand—that of untangling film's deep and storied but still insufficiently documented connection and collusion with colonialism—we harbored no illusions that the endeavor would be easy. Where do we possibly begin to address these numerous gaps in the extant and inherited story of film's intimacy with colonialism? The intimacy seems too commonsensical to even warrant mention, and yet it has been so little documented or reckoned with in any depth, as one discovers when digging below the surface of its truisms. We contributors were impelled by a shared recognition that the work was already long overdue.

Along the way, we were emboldened and inspired by prior scholars who have made substantial headway in this direction. For example, we took inspiration from Ann Stoler's (2016) own urgent injunction to focus our attention head-on and from the outset to attempt to unearth what she terms the "uncommon sense" of as yet unexamined but significant colonial histories and archives and their contemporary manifestations. We begin by asking what methods and departures would give us an entry into tackling some of these challenges. Which threads of evidence would allow us to take into account and begin to count those neglected and devalued histories and archives—much of them too long left dormant, in debris and disarray, for decades after the collapse and evacuation of empires?

Another source of inspiration has been the important two-volume contribution edited by Lee Grieveson and Colin MacCabe, *Empire and Film* and *Film and the End of Empire* (2011a, 2011b). In many ways a long-awaited and welcome project, this was a monumental effort to make widely accessible the vast film collections in the archives of the former British Empire. It is instructive, however, for us to read that the editors, in introducing their finished product, begin the very first page of the first chapter by listing not their many achievements, but rather what they perceive to have been the major "failures" of the project (2011a, 1). One of the three major failures, according to the editors, was how their project was delimited by the boundaries of the British nation, despite the imperial or international dimension of their goals. The editors lament the limit of their focus on the films housed in the three main imperial archives in the former metropolitan center of England, namely, the British Film Institute, the Imperial War Museum, and the British and Empire Commonwealth Museum:

> It should be stressed that at every stage we were more than conscious of the international dimensions of our work and that we made every effort that we could to internationalise the perspectives on our research. Indeed, the two concluding conferences in London and Pittsburgh in July and September 2010 represented a major element in this effort. Even more crucial to that effort is the publication of the proceedings of those conferences. However, it is important to stress the national nature of our funding and the extent to which that determined our corpus. To develop fully the work begun with the catalogue and website *will require the full participation of former colonies* (2011a, 3; emphasis added).

It is sobering for us, as scholars scattered internationally and embarking on our own attempts to capture fuller stories of film and empire, to hear recent colleagues express the need to introduce their completed multivolume project with so sweeping a disclaimer. The fact that a monumental project produced as late as 2011, more than half a century after the collapse of the British Empire, would still be struggling with the basic dilemma of how to enable the "full participation of former colonies" is telling of the deep and lasting afterlives of empire that continued to haunt us as we embarked on our own collaboration.

This failure or blind spot is of course a symptom of the very legacy of empire itself: the way the once seemingly borderless expanse of territories was suddenly limited to the borders of newly formed nation-states, including funding structures. In addition, the limits to full participation are themselves symptoms of postimperial and postcolonial impasses, as well as the more global inability (or unwillingness) to reckon fully with the traumas of the past—both colonial and wartime—even more than a half century after the collapse of the empires. Six years after the publication of Grieveson and MacCabe's two volumes, the editors and contributors of the volume in hand came together in our own attempt to tackle some of the remaining challenges, albeit from a different angle.

Theorizing Colonial Cinema as a whole traces the colonial history of films of and about Asia as one point of entry into a much broader global phenomenon. Throughout, we ask what is particular or universal about the case studies we explore, always with the hope of inspiring future dialogue expanded into other parallel, contradictory, and interwoven local and regional histories. Starting as landscapes in early cinematic forms of Euro-American colonial and war documentaries and adventure reels, and extending to serving as a newly opened export market for the global circulation of silent film, the region's film cultures from their inception coincided with unequal global imperial histories. At the same time, the story of film in Asia was never merely that of one-way traffic or passive consumption from the metropoles to the colonies. Keeping in mind the unequal imperial power of capital, technology, and geopolitics at the heart of cinematic circulations, we focus on select case studies of ways in which film has been negotiated, engaged, translated, and transformed in the nexus of a local and global early cinematic encounter with lasting consequences.

Our contributors go beyond what has been a commonly assumed duality between production and consumption to consider the ways film was resignified in transcolonial contact zones by subjects such as directors, writers, critics, actors, coproducers, translators, movie narrators, and spectators. In so doing, this book pays special attention to hitherto marginalized voices and disregarded subjectivities of local and regional cultural producers and consumers in order to encapsulate a fuller and more balanced story of film's regional and global circulation. A new vantage point of the rising global prominence of Asia in the contemporary moment offers a timely opportunity to interrogate prior articulations of film's imperial imbrication in and beyond the region in new ways.

Further, our compilation takes a retrospective approach in putting the history of film in and about Asia during the era of high imperialism into conversation with the legacies of film in the contemporary era of high-velocity globalization. Throughout, we emphasize both ongoing and renewed forms of coloniality, broadly defined in configurations that have lasted into the contemporary moment. In so doing, we are careful to be self-reflexive in ways that go beyond examining these colonial affiliations as merely representing historical pastness or as a structure from the outside. Our collection, rather, focuses on more complex linkages, internalizations, mutual coproductions, and lineages of transcolonial cinematic crossroads from the past to the present. Thus, it is also important to bear in mind that coloniality as we conceive it in this volume is not a phenomenon over there of a bygone past, but one that is very much still with us here and now, in the midst of the everyday.[13] Today, each of us still lives with the phenomenon of coloniality—that is, we are all implicated through the dynamics of coloniality that continue to define our contemporary world although we may not be fully cognizant of it.

In sum, *Theorizing Colonial Cinema* ultimately calls for an ethics—not simply a politics—of colonial studies that should involve a mutual scholarly engagement that builds on relationality and reciprocity and goes beyond ideological divides between the geopolitical (area studies over there) and the theoretical (North Atlantic over here) approach to the study of colonialism.[14]

Through workshops, coauthorship, translations, citations, and conversations, our contributors have been deeply engaged with one another and the editors in developing this project as a long-standing collective effort. We are grateful to the organizers and participants of multiple international conferences and workshops where the collective ideas gathered here were conceived in collaboration and in multiple languages. Workshops were held, for example, in Durham, North Carolina, United States; Shanghai, China; Seoul, South Korea; and Kanazawa, Japan. In various configurations, we invited scholars and archivists working in and beyond Asia, as well as those with expertise in other colonial, postcolonial, and decolonial film cultures, such as Amadou Fofana, an expert on African and Francophone postcolonial and colonial cinemas; Debashree Mukherjee, a specialist in South Asian visual cultures, including late colonial Bombay cinema, among others; and Walter Mignolo, a scholar of decolonial and global cultural theories of Latin America and elsewhere. Within the contingencies of time and other limits, this version was unable to incorporate essays from many of these interlocutors, but we acknowledge their invaluable contributions and hope that the conversations begun in earlier encounters will resonate into further dialogues, collaborations, and coproductions opening toward a more expansive future inquiry. We consider this book to be one opening toward many more conversations to be continued.

This volume has three parts, each braiding conceptual themes with periodization. Part I, "Time and Racialized Other: Colonial Modernity and Early Cinema," addresses the problem of time and otherness in early cinema, spanning the period from cinema's inception in the late nineteenth century to the first half of the twentieth century. It highlights the rich original scholarship engaging with newly opened cinematic archives from Asia in recent decades. Part II, "Divided Mis-en-Scène: Colonial Cinema and Cold War Afterimages," examines both continuities and divisions from the colonial era to the subsequent Cold War. Whereas prior studies on colonial cinemas are rarely brought into dialog with the question of the Cold War, this section maps cases that link the story of film and colonialism from the era of empires to that of the Cold War to make explicit a connection that is often elided or bypassed in prior film studies. Part III, "Millennial Hauntings: Rising Global Asian Cinemas," takes a look at the genealogies of colonial cinema from the retrospective vantage of the twenty-first century. The contemporary rise of Asian cinema in the context of globalization offers us a productive way to consider the vicissitudes of colonial pasts into the present, especially in the form of the return of the repressed unconscious.

Part I

In her chapter on the temporality of the colonial documentary's relation to time, "Time, Race, and the Asynchronous in the Colonial Documentaries of Malaya," Nadine Chan delves into how celluloid technology temporally reinscribed and rearranged British Malaya's racially plural society. The connective tissues of the technology of colonial documentary—editing, voice-over, narrative suturing—according to Chan, structured how the myth of colonial historicism—or a sense of economic development and progress through colonization—converged with the mechanical unwinding of colonial cinematic time. Theorizing what she calls the "colonial race-time" of the colonial documentary, Chan critiques this process of the "rearrangement of time via an arrangement of race," in the imperial desire to capture a fixed image of the colonial hinterlands and its inhabitants as backward and primitive. As Chan cogently argues, these films can be read ironically, however, in that they went against their commissioned purpose, already rendered untimely or outdated before their transcolonial release to Malayan audiences perceived as unruly, who insisted on forging an understanding of this narrative and history on their own time and terms. Theorizing cinema's asynchronous time, chapter 1 argues that although colonial documentary films served as the very technology used to script and inscribe Malaya through racialized periodizations of modernity, film itself was in actuality reproduced as an asynchronous medium misaligned with the fractured and unruly temporalities of late colonialism, in a period when the British Empire was itself entwined in the throes of its own unraveling in Southeast Asia.

In "Facing Malcontent Colonial Korean Comrades: A Typology of Colonial Cinema in Asia's Socialist Alliances," Moonim Baek examines yet another form of temporal misalignment of unruly colonial subjects, what was then labeled as "malcontent colonial Koreans" (pullyŏng sŏnin, Korean; futei senjin, Japanese), through close readings of the iconic cinematic close-up. Turning away from the figure of the female ingenue as the dominant iconography of the close-up in Hollywood films, Baek instead turns her attention to the ubiquitous figure of the malcontent colonized male as the face of anarchic or terrorist fear. The chapter captures a moment of the failed and, therefore, uninscribed attempt to form intra-Asian socialist alliances in the face of Western imperialism in the context of the Japanese Empire. Complicating the colonizer-colonized binary, the chapter delves into the unsavory intimacies of Japan's inter-Asian imperialism in which neighboring Asian territories were colonized in mutual "cooperation" against Western imperialism. Even in the utopian long-shot and long-take efforts toward building socialist alliances across the empire, the vast and uneven—and seemingly unbridgeable—spatial divides were unwittingly captured and reproduced in cinematic and other cultural images of the primitive colonized as unruly. The untamed, anarchic, rebellious malcontents were seen as prone to primitive violence. Juxtaposing a wide-angle view and attempting to suture divisions across seemingly expansive imperial spaces, Baek hones in on the close-up of the anarchic colonized cinematic hero Na Un-kyu (1902–37) as the symbol of such unruly colonized masculinity. Unlike the safely eroticized dainty figure of the *kisaeng* female entertainer, this ubiquitous Other of colonial fantasy reveals deep-seated racialized and gendered anxieties that emerged in the imperial audience's face-to-face encounter with the colonized considered as too close for comfort by the colonizers, even though they were attempting to build alliances across the colonial divide. She further turns to the failed transcolonial exchanges between Korean and Japanese intellectuals, including film critics, such as Im Hwa and Kōriyama's negotiation of just who might be interpellated in the concept of our cinema (*wareware no eiga*) in the blurry and mobile boundaries of empire.

Aaron Gerow turns the focus inward to the psycho-social conundrum of colonial internalization in his chapter, "Colonial-Era Film Theory, Spectatorship, and the Problem of Internalization." He investigates internalization in relation to colonial film culture in the Japanese Empire as both a symptom and a critique of the colonization of the mind and as an internalized critique of North Atlantic Eurocentric aspirations to universalism. Following up on Gerow's earlier research on colonial-era Korean film, in which he problematized the subjectivity open to such internalization, this chapter investigates the relation of film theory to colonization. The chapter asks what the role of film theory was in the imperial metropole and what valences the film theory produced by colonial subjects bear in the empire. Such questions are complicated by the fact that Japanese film theory exhibited a theory complex, as discussed earlier. What was the effect on the film theory of the colonized when the theory of the colonizer itself was in a neocolonial dependency with Europe? Considering the possibility that theorizing spectatorship was one means of reflecting on the colonial theorist's own association to the metropole, Gerow analyzes a number of texts published in Japanese by writers in colonial Korea and the puppet state of Manchukuo, focusing in particular on articles written by Im Hwa and O Yŏngjin. In these, spectatorship becomes a problem for empire, as internalization is complicated by action over and against language. Furthermore, Gerow engages with Baek's identification of the complexity of the question of us and them in Im Hwa/Kōriyama Hiroshi's textual exchange about "our cinema" to further elaborate a broader theory of a theory complex that was triangulated among the West, Japan, and the empire. The effect of a push for a solution involves less internalization of the empire than, in one case, the spectator pushed toward madness, or with O imagining a new postcinema of attractions that overwhelms an externalized viewer.

Yiman Wang's chapter, "Chinese Cinema's Other: Wrangling over 'China-Humiliating' Films (*ruHua pian*)," returns to another primal scene in early cinema's transpacific circulation: early Chinese film critics' encounters with Hollywood's cinematic misrepresentation of China. Divergent viewpoints and emotions are on full display as the chapter examines the Chinese protests of the 1910s to 1930s against Western-made films that were deemed detrimental to Chinese national dignity, or face, and labeled as "China-humiliating" films (*ruHua pian*). Unlike Baek's literal references to the concept of the colonized star's close-up physiognomic features, the face here is highly metaphorical, and a symbol of esteem or reputation as part of a strategic power play in the unequal transcolonial contact. In the face of the Other, the framework of unequal power offers us a new taxonomy. China-humiliating films foregrounded the inequitable—and unjust—exchange between those who had the power to represent and those who were subjected to the power of representation, and they embody how such injustices were protested. Unlike Western-centric film historiography, which captured or prioritized one side only, here we see the dialectical propositions, or at least an attempt at dialogue. Nevertheless, failure features prominently in the chapter as well—ultimately failure to enact any change. Nevertheless, instead of assuming a binary opposition between the Western imperial forces and passive Chinese subjects, Wang examines Chinese critics' and policy makers' interactions with Western—especially American—actors, with an eye to reshaping the uneven ground of transnational media ecology and rendering it more conducive to China's emerging decolonial and nation-building projects. She argues that the contestations over China-humiliating films manifested an affective articulation of a sovereign Chinese national identity emerging in response to the onslaught of uneven colonial modernity. In the process, Wang shows how film, the emblem of modern media technology, served as an apparatus of emotional *re*education for the Chinese masses and for their Western interlocutors, albeit in different and often competing registers, within an increasingly intimate and networked transcolonial and transpacific media ecology.

Part I is rounded out by Jane M. Gaines's "World Export: Melodramas of Colonial Conquest," an important reevaluation of Hollywood's intimate links with Asian cinema from the latter's inception—something that is often elided or marginalized in most historiographies. Through Gaines's expert archival work we see how Asia features prominently as both object of mis-en-scène and methodology of critical discourse as she considers the ways in which Hollywood envisioned Otherness in terms of race and nation. The chapter further puts concepts emerging from Hollywood in dialogue with contemporary theorizations featured in the present volume and elsewhere by contributors like Aaron Gerow and Zhang Zhen. Gaines's chapter further engages with Yiman Wang's earlier works and the work of Weihong Bao, on the vernacular conjoined with modernism in Chinese cinematic discourses, as well as with Aaron Gerow's question on the centrality of the West in the original theorization of Japanese film critics.

Part II

Zhang Zhen's chapter, "Tarzan/Taishan and Other Orphans: Taiwan's Melodrama of Decolonization," considers the significance of the crossings and divisions across the synchronic framework of the postcolonial to the post–Cold War as both historic temporalities and sociocultural frameworks. Focusing on a *Taiyupian* (Taiwanese-language film) called *Tarzan and Treasure* (Liang Che-fu, dir., 1965), which was produced at the height of the Cold War, Zhang traces the historical genealogy of the figure of the orphan in postcolonial and Cold War Taiwanese cinema in relation to the representation of the "orphan of Asia" in the eponymous novel by Wu Zhuoliu

(1900–1976). The condition of Wu's orphan figure is an allegorical representation of Taiwan's intellectual repression and deformation under coloniality complicated further by the triangulation between the island and its two parent nations at war with each other. The film *Tarzan and Treasure* delineates a different orphan condition in postcolonial Taiwan—coinciding with the Cold War era—which capitalizes on the trope of orphanhood, as expressed through the character Tarzan/Taishan and offering multiple interpretations and redemptive possibilities. This and other, more action-oriented, melodramas were made at the peak of *Taiyupian* as a vibrant local and regional film industry and as Taiwan readied itself to take off as a modernized nation in the free world. Whereas the orphan figure loses his way and his mind in his futile, circuitous journey without a destination, Tarzan/Taishan was able to recover his native language and return to a state recognized by the United Nations at the time. But the stereotypical portrayal of the tribal members in the Malay forest—harking back to Nadine Chan's chapter—especially their presumed untamed sexuality, raises the issue of indigeneity in modern national identity construction in general and that of Taiwan in particular. *Tarzan*, or the Asian orphan Taishan, could serve well as a pioneer figuration for Kuan-hsing Chen's argument for "Asia as method" (or Asian studies within Asia) in the era of intensified globalization (Chen 2010). Zhang supplements Chen's view by adding that, as a historical as well theoretical practice dedicated to the social and cultural analysis of base-entities beyond intellectual politics on inter-Asian heterogeneous horizons and globally, Asia as method could be enriched substantially by revisiting film archives in the region and reexamining intermedial and transnational trajectories of the all-too-important figure of the orphan of Asia.

Thomas Barker and Nikki Lee's "What Is an Auteur? Hŏ Yŏng/Hinatsu Eitarō/Huyung between (Post)colonial Indonesia, Japan, and Korea" exemplifies the collaborative spirit of the present collection as they cut across the once-divided histories of East and Southeast Asia by writing a chapter on the fascinating figure of filmmaker Hŏ Yŏng, a.k.a., Hinatsu Eitarō, whose career spanned multiple nations and national cinemas. Hŏ/Hinatsu was a complex figure in his work as a colonial collaborator who became a postcolonial national cineaste. Japanese colonialism in East and Southeast Asia, like European empires, utilized the modern technology of cinema to create and propagate images of Japanese imperial greatness, fidelity to empire, and the benevolence of Japanese rule. Within this apparatus could be found not only Japanese citizens employed as propaganda officers and *bunkajin* (cultured or well-educated men), but also as colonial subjects enlisted to create local content for various colonial possessions. Using a pseudonym, Hinatsu Eitarō was one such filmmaker, coming from occupied Korea to Japan to study filmmaking. Later, he would return to Korea to direct the infamous propaganda film *You and I* (*Kŭdae wa Na*, Korean; *Kimi to Boku*, Japanese, 1941) before departing for occupied Java in 1942 as a *bunkajin*. After 1945, instead of returning home, Hinatsu—now known as Dr. Huyung—remained in Indonesia, joining the pro-independence movement; after independence, he directed four feature films during Indonesian national cinema's formative years before his premature death in 1952.

By tracing the life and works of Hinatsu/Huyung, chapter 7 puts into question the role of the filmmaker in sustaining colonialism and the possibility of making art and becoming an auteur in a time of colonial subjectivity. Korean history does not remember Hinatsu fondly for his collaborations with Japanese colonialism, but his trajectory after 1945 suggests that a collaborator in one context could also support postcolonial independence in another. Yet the question remains: Without a national cinema to call his own, can a filmmaker like Hinatsu ever be considered an auteur, or will he be relegated to a footnote in various national cinema histories, belonging ultimately to none of them?

Part III

If, despite Fanon's ([1952] 2008) emphasis on the "epidermal" character of colonialism, corporeal differences do not clearly distinguish "black" and "white" in the colonial relationships in Asia, what alternative concepts of coloniality can be deployed to examine intimate colonial histories within Asia and their contemporary legacies? In his chapter, "Cinema's Coloniality," Takushi Odagiri examines the contradictions within the inter-Asian colonial encounter and the limits of Fanon's original assertion about epidermalization in this context from a different angle than Gerow's chapter. One of Odagiri's claims is that coloniality may have different manifestations in various contexts; specifically it can go hand in hand with certain forms of humanism. As an illustration, Odagiri unpacks the multivalent traffic of the colonial gaze beyond the black and white color line in the former Japanese Empire, with emphasis on the particular valence of the disavowed colonial unconscious at the heart of Japanese imperialism's manifest anticolonial and humanistic foundations. The chapter begins with an examination of the quasi-documentary animation films of Seo Mitsuyo, specifically *Momotarō: Divine Warriors of the Sea* (1945), and explores Imamura Taihei's contemporaneous theoretical writings on wartime documentary and animation. Odagiri considers how the wartime documentary form was instrumental in the workings of unconscious coloniality in the Japanese Empire. Investigating Imamura's film criticism as a form of critical theory—in the sense of Brecht's and the Frankfurt School's—which predates French *cinéma vérité* and North American direct cinema by decades, Odagiri argues that both Imamura's writings and Seo's animation interrogate coloniality's unconscious that was ubiquitous in cultural representations of colonial cinema in Japan in their time. Odagiri then extends this investigation to contemporary twenty-first-century global cultures, through which he theorizes the broader significance of the unconscious (and quotidian) quality of cinema's coloniality. He asks how prior discourses on colonialism, which tend to emphasize manifest differences—of race, color, ethnicity, culture, etc.—should be rethought vis-à-vis their unconscious underside, and considers the way—when fully colonized—the colonized subject's subjugation may not be experienced on the level of conscious awareness. This rethinking of coloniality also engages with Gerow's historical observation about a theory complex and its unconscious dynamics, as well as Barker and Lee's study of a (post)colonial filmmaker's multivalent colonial subjectivity, which also reveals yet another unconscious transcolonial history.

José B. Capino's chapter, "A Hallucinatory History of the Philippine-American War: Khavn's *Balangiga: Howling Wilderness*," examines Khavn's recent experimental feature in the context of other films about the Philippine-American War (1899–1902) and the forgotten primal scene of the US emergence as an overseas empire. The war has been a recurring subject of films from both the United States and the Philippines and thus provides an indispensable case study for historical and methodological aspects of colonial cinemas in the interstices of the colony-metropole divide. In this chapter, Capino uses Walter Benjamin's notion of the dialectical image to elucidate the multiple historical resonances of mise-en-scène in Khavn's film. He discusses Khavn's film in light of studies of historical representation in cinema, the rise of digital independent filmmaking in the Philippines, and the historiography of the Philippine-American War. With its sparse plot and dialogue, *Balangiga* relies heavily on oneiric images and tableaux for its historical discourse, along with other cinematic devices and allegorical tropes identified with the avant-garde, to meditate on the disavowed longue durée of US imperialism in the Philippines and elsewhere. The unflinchingly experimental method of the film enables Capino to investigate multiple levels of representations and misrepresentations and intricate politics of the war from both sides.

In addition to the elucidation of the historical resonance of the Philippine-American War in the films of both the United States and the Philippines, Capino's study makes important conceptual interventions as well.

By dialectically investigating films from both sides of the colonial history, he avoids the methodological incompleteness (or fallacy) of existing colonial cinema studies that tend to privilege and repeat the voices and languages of imperial powers, marginalizing or silencing that of the colonies themselves. By exploring the fragmented form of abstract cinema, the chapter elucidates yet other aspects of repressive legacies of the colonial unconscious, in form and content.

Section 3 and this volume conclude with Nayoung Aimee Kwon's chapter, "Millennial Vengeance: Park Chan-wook's *Agassi (The Handmaiden)* and the Return of Postcolonial *Japonisme*," which considers another historical instance of repressed coloniality and its twenty-first-century consequences in Asia. Kwon's contribution examines the postmillennial resurgence of once-repressed colonial and wartime memories in contemporary East Asia via the case of the meteoric global rise of contemporary South Korean cinema. Unlike the ubiquity of cinematic representations from the western front from the era of the world wars, Asian films of the same historical period have not circulated widely—until recently. The chapter explores the significance of the sudden contemporary hypervisibility of such historic dramas after decades of repression. The chapter maps the history of postcolonial censorship and delimitation of past colonial memories to set the stage for a close film analysis of Park Chan-wook's *The Handmaiden (Agassi*, 2016) and its shockingly new representation of a contested transcolonial past. The chapter asks, What is the significance of the return with a vengeance of these new cinematic representations in the contemporary context of the rise of Asia? In conversation with Gerow and Odagiri's chapters, Kwon argues that ultimately an uncanny repetition with difference of the imperialist gaze—in the context of a South Korea's subimperial backdrop of shifting post–Cold War power dynamics—renders problematic the possibilities of a postcolonial subversion and critique.

Notes

1. Here we follow Joseph Garncarz's chapter in the pioneering book *Early Cinema and the "National"* (2008) and his useful formulation of national film cultures. Going beyond the common framework of national cinemas, his conception encompasses films beyond those produced within a national territory and includes production and consumption habits across borders. In this volume, "Asian film cultures" or "colonial film cultures" takes into account both production and consumption sides of films across geographic borders—within and beyond Asia.

2. See, for example, Dina Sherzer (1996) on France's belated engagement with its colonial past.

3. See Fujitani and Kwon (2012) for discussions on the third-millennium discovery of colonial- and wartime-era films from the former Japanese Empire, assumed to have been lost for more than half a century.

4. Although little examined outside local contexts until recently, the story of film and colonialism in Asia is vast and expansive and goes back to the primal scenes of exoticism captured in the

early cinematic days of Auguste and Louis Lumière and Georges Méliès. Asian cinema, like all cinema, has crossed the transcolonial divide from its inception, a crossing that was never acknowledged, and the divide between the metropole and the colony was emphasized and maintained geopolitically and ideologically. As Yiman Wang, a contributor to this volume, and others point out, the heuristic of "Asia" is neither homogeneous nor stable, first conceived in European perspectives on perceivedly exotic far-flung lands "over there," with competing and shifting significations throughout history, from both inside and outside the geographic areas thus conceived. We are here primarily focused on select cases from and about East and Southeast Asia in our volume and anticipate expanding the dialogue with collaborators in other areas in the future. See Wang (2007). In addition to Wang's and other volume contributors' important scholarship, this volume is indebted to recent groundbreaking Anglophone scholarship on Asian cinemas and transpacific connections, such as Panivong Norindr (1996), Priya Jaikumar (2005), Brian Yecies and Ae-Gyung Shim (2011), Daisuke Miyao (2013, 2020), Victor Fan (2015), Weihong Bao (2015), Hikari Hori (2017), Sangjoon Lee (2020), Debashree Mukherjee (2020), and Naoki Yamamoto (2020). See chapter bibliographies for important scholarship beyond the Anglophone context that needs to be translated.

5. For an elaboration on intimate but disavowed colonial memories, see Kwon (2015).

6. See Tom Gunning (1994) on imperialist perspectives displayed at the world's fairs that emerged in the late nineteenth century in tandem with colonial exploits and how such exhibition practices anticipate and embed early film history. Seeing black-and-white photographs and stilted images from that era may give contemporary spectators the impression that such perspectives were artifacts from a long bygone era, but they actually are rather recent. A groundbreaking PBS documentary series *Asian Americans* (2020) includes an important interview conducted recently with a woman whose own grandfather was displayed in 1904 at the St. Louis Fair in the Philippines pavilion. The interview offers us a rare glimpse into his desires and motivations for "performing." Likewise, the history that the contributors of our volume are tracing are from the living memories of our grandparents' and parents' generations, not of ancient and nameless ancestors, as well as of their legacies to our own contemporary moment.

7. These disavowals of coloniality are a phenomenon far deeper than we usually think, as Takushi Odagiri argues in his volume contribution.

8. See, for example, various key contributions from Sigmund Freud, Frantz Fanon, Friedrich Nietzsche, Walter Mignolo, Fredric Jameson, Heonik Kwon, Miriam Hansen, Theodore Hughes, E. Ann Kaplan, Dominick LaCapra, Takushi Odagiri, and Jinsoo An. See also the pathbreaking scholarship on colonial modernity such as that of the Subaltern Studies Collective, Tani Barlow and the *positions* collective, and Shin and Robinson (2001), for example. It is important to point out that the concept of the colonial unconscious has yet other layers of significance for its scopic regime in the colonial context in Asia, as several contributors show. Odagiri and Gerow both discuss in their contributions how racial visibility, or "epidermalization"—in Frantz Fanon's terms—is not as readily apparent in Asia, especially in inter-Asian colonization. Likewise, this volume interrogates a rigid conceptual dualism that still persists in colonial and postcolonial studies. In particular, we aim to move away from the still-common dualism—which stems from misconceptions, or repression, of an important and constitutive underside—to divide colonial subjects in binaries either of black or white (Fanon) or of anthropos or humanitas (Nishitani). As discussed further herein, in their joint contribution to this volume, Thomas Barker and Nikki Lee trace the multiple lives and careers of the filmmaker Hŏ Yŏng/Hinatsu Eitarō/Dr. Huyung—switching from colonial Korea to imperial Japan and postcolonial Indonesia—in the compressed temporal span of a few decades from early to mid-twentieth century. The multiple and almost schizoid identities and roles of this filmmaker totter not only between the colonial and the postcolonial, but also between the realms of the conscious and unconscious in various degrees of remembrance and forgetting via several national film histories, clearly defying a dualism of substantive hermeneutics.

9. For the age-old Western-centric construction of a racialized dichotomy between those who were deemed human and thus as producers of knowledge (the West or Westerners) and those

who were relegated to the status of anthropos (whom Stuart Hall once referred to as "the Rest"), assumed to be useful only as objects of the said knowledge producers. See Nishitani (2006) and Naoki Sakai's numerous contributions, especially Sakai (2010). For the original configuration of the West-versus-Rest dichotomy, see Stuart Hall (1996).

10. For models of such decolonizing scholarship, see Naoki Sakai and Walter Mignolo's works in the bibliography for examples.

11. Naoki Yamamoto (2020), for example, discusses the active but undervalued theoretical engagement with Japanese critics from as early as the 1910s. As Yamamoto writes in reference to Markus Nornes's observation of the state of matters even today, "anyone attending introductory courses in film theory in North American universities would inevitably have the impression that 'serious film criticism and theory are the exclusive domain of the West'" (Nornes 2003, xviii, quoted in Yamamoto 2020, 3). For cogent critiques of similar cultural capital monopolies devaluing non-Western theoretical contributions in the fields of cultural and literary studies, see Chow (2006) and Mufti (2016).

12. It is possible to consider this productive aspect of a theory complex in relation to Nishida's idea of technology (*gijutsu*) as formless forms and his critique of hylomorphism (i.e., that hylomorphism of a given social reality is conceivable only after it has been well established). For further discussions on this techno-ontological critique of hylomorphism and certain forms of humanism, see Odagiri (2020) and Simondon (2011).

13. The Italian philosopher Antonio Gramsci's pioneering works clearly illustrate this everyday quality of coloniality. Some Japanese intellectuals of the same period (e.g., Tosaka Jun) also investigate this everydayness in cultural and social science. For Tosaka Jun's discussion of everydayness, see Harry D. Harootunian (2000) and Kawashima et al. (2013). Harootunian points out that Tosaka anteceded Henri Lefebvre in his attempt to "quotidianize" philosophical thought by nearly two decades (118), and that the locus of Tosaka's critical awareness is the dual quality of everydayness, namely, of its being both repetitive and singular, which makes the everyday never complete at any moment (128). See Gramsci et al. (2011); Harootunian (2000), esp. 95–201; and Kawashima et al. (2013).

14. The pitfall of assuming that coloniality is over there, and not immediately with or within us, is to underestimate the ethical consequences of coloniality itself. See the works cited in the bibliography, which variously illustrate the ethics of everyday coloniality, as well as Miki Kiyoshi's wartime writings on humanism and everyday history (1931–32) (Miki 1966). Harootunian (2000) specifically discusses the ethics of everyday history in Miki's wartime writings.

Bibliography

Baek, Moonim, Lee Hwajin, Kim Sangmin, Yu Sŭngjin, eds. 2016. *Chosŏn Yŏnghwa ran Hao: Kŭndae Yŏnghwa Pip'yŏng ŭi Yŏksa* [What is colonial Korean cinema? History of modern film criticism]. Seoul: Ch'angbi.

Bao, Weihong. 2015. *Fiery Cinema: The Emergence of an Affective Medium in China, 1915–1945*. Minneapolis: University of Minnesota Press.

Campa de la, Romàn, and E. Ann Kaplan, eds. 1995. *Late Imperial Culture*. London and New York: Verso.

Chen, Kuan-Hsing. 2010. *Asia as Method: Toward Deimperialization*. Durham, NC: Duke University Press.

Chow, Rey. 2006. *The Age of the World Target: Self-Referentiality in War, Theory, and Comparative Work*. Durham, NC: Duke University Press.

Fan, Victor. 2015. *Cinema Approaching Reality: Locating Chinese Film Theory*. Minneapolis: University of Minnesota Press.

Fanon, Frantz. 2008. *Black Skin, White Masks*. New York: Grove Press.

Fujitani, Takashi, and Nayoung Aimee Kwon, eds. 2012. "Transcolonial Film Coproductions in the Japanese Empire: Antinomies in the Colonial Archive." *Cross-Currents* no. 5 (December). https://cross-currents.berkeley.edu/e-journal/issue-5.

Garncarz, Joseph. "The Emergence of Nationally Specific Film Cultures in Europe, 1911–1914." In Abel, Richard, Giorgio Bertellini, and Rob King. 2008. *Early Cinema and the "National."* Bloomington: Indiana University Press.

Gerow, Aaron. 2012. "Theorizing the Theory Complex." Keynote speech at the *Permanent Seminar on the Histories of Film Theories*, Ann Arbor, MI. September 27.

Gramsci, Antonio, Joseph A. Buttigieg, and Antonio Callari. 2011. *Prison Notebooks*. New York: Columbia University Press.

Grieveson, Lee, and Colin MacCabe. 2011a. *Empire and Film*. London: Palgrave Macmillan.

———. 2011b. *Film and the End of Empire*. New York: Palgrave Macmillan.

Gunning, Tom. 1994. "The World as Object Lesson: Cinema Audiences, Visual Culture and the St. Louis World's Fair, 1904." *Film History* 6, no. 4 (Winter): 422–44.

Hall, Stuart. 1996. *Modernity: An Introduction to Modern Societies*. Malden, MA: Blackwell.

Harootunian, Harry D. 2000. *Overcome by Modernity: History, Culture, and Community in Interwar Japan*. Princeton, NJ: Princeton University Press.

Hori, Hikari. 2017. *Promiscuous Media: Film and Visual Culture in Imperial Japan, 1926–1945*. Ithaca, NY: Cornell University Press.

Hughes, Theodore H. 2012. *Literature and Film in Cold War South Korea: Freedom's Frontier*. New York: Columbia University Press.

Jaikumar, Priya. 2005. *Cinema and the End of Empire: A Politics of Transition in British India*. Durham, NC: Duke University Press.

Jameson, Fredric. 1998. "Notes on Globalization as a Philosophical Issue." In *The Cultures of Globalization*, 54–77. Durham, NC: Duke University Press.

Kawashima, Ken C., Fabian Schäfer, Robert. Stolz, and Jun Tosaka. 2013. *Tosaka Jun: A Critical Reader*. Ithaca, NY: East Asia Program, Cornell University.

Kwon, Heonik. 2010. *The Other Cold War*. New York: Columbia University Press.

Kwon, Nayoung Aimee. 2015. *Intimate Empire: Collaboration and Colonial Modernity in Korea and Japan*. Durham, NC: Duke University Press.

LaCapra, Dominick. 2001. *Writing History, Writing Trauma*. Baltimore: Johns Hopkins University Press.

Lee, Sangjoon. 2020. *Cinema and the Cultural Cold War: US Diplomacy and the Origins of the Asian Cinema Network*. Ithaca, NY: Cornell University Press.

Mignolo, Walter. 2011. *The Darker Side of Western Modernity: Global Futures, Decolonial Options*. Durham, NC: Duke University Press.

———. 2000. *Local Histories/Global Designs: Coloniality, Subaltern Knowledges, and Border Thinking*. Princeton, NJ: Princeton University Press.

Miki Kiyoshi. 1966. *Miki Kiyoshi Zenshū*. Vol. 6, *Rekishi Tetsugaku, Shakai Kagaku Gairon*. [Complete works of Miki Kiyoshi, vol. 6]. Tokyo: Iwanami.

Miyao, Daisuke. 2013. *The Aesthetics of Shadow: Lighting and Japanese Cinema*. Durham, NC: Duke University Press.

———. 2020. *Japonisme and the Birth of Cinema*. Durham, NC: Duke University Press.

Mufti, Aamir. 2016. *Forget English! Orientalisms and World Literature*. Cambridge, MA: Harvard University Press.

Mukherjee, Debashree. 2020. *Bombay Hustle: Making Movies in a Colonial City*. New York: Columbia University Press.

Nishitani, Osamu. 2006. "Anthropos and Humanitas: Two Western Concepts of 'Human Being,'" Translated from the Japanese by Trent Maxey. In *Translation, Biopolitics, Colonial*

Difference. 259–73. Traces: A Multilingual Series of Cultural Theory and Translation, no. 4, edited by Naoki Sakai and Jon Solomon, Hong Kong: Hong Kong University Press.

Norindr, Panivong. 1996. *Phantasmatic Indochina: French Colonial Ideology in Architecture, Film, and Literature.* Durham, NC: Duke University Press.

Nornes, Abé Mark. 2003. *Japanese Documentary Film: The Meiji Era through Hiroshima.* Minneapolis: Minnesota University Press.

Odagiri, Takushi. 2020. "*Mental* (2008): Sōda Kazuhiro's Observational Cinema." *positions* 28, no. 2 (May): 277–309.

Rice, Tom. 2019. *Films for the Colonies: Cinema and the Preservation of the British Empire.* Oakland: University of California Press.

Sakai, Naoki. 2010. "Theory and Asian Humanity: On the Question of Humanitas and Anthropos." *Postcolonial Studies* 13, no. 4: 441–64.

Sherzer, Dina. 1996. *Cinema, Colonialism, Postcolonialism: Perspectives from the French and Francophone World.* Austin: University of Texas Press.

Shin, Gi-Wook, and Michael Robinson. 2001. *Colonial Modernity in Korea.* Cambridge, MA: Harvard University Asia Center.

Simondon, Gilbert. 2011. *Two Lessons on Animal and Man.* Translated by Drew S. Burk. Minneapolis: University of Minnesota Press.

Stoler, Ann Laura. 2016. *Duress: Imperial Durabilities in Our Times.* Durham, NC: Duke University Press.

Wang, Yiman. 2007. "Screening Asia: Passing, Performative Translation, and Reconfiguration." *positions* 15, no. 2 (Fall): 319–43.

Yamamoto, Naoki. 2020. *Dialectics without Synthesis: Japanese Film Theory and Realism in a Global Frame.* Berkeley: University of California Press.

Yecies, Brian, and Ae-Gyung Shim. 2011. *Korea's Occupied Cinemas, 1893–1948.* New York: Routledge.

NAYOUNG AIMEE KWON is Associate Professor in the Department of Asian and Middle Eastern Studies and the Program in Cinematic Arts at Duke University. She is Founding Director of the Asian American and Diaspora Studies Program and Co-director of the Andrew Mellon Games and Culture Humanities Lab.

TAKUSHI ODAGIRI is Associate Professor of Ethics and Philosophy in the Institute of Liberal Arts and Science and in the School of Social Innovation Studies at Kanazawa University.

PART I.
TIME AND RACIALIZED OTHER: COLONIAL MODERNITY AND EARLY CINEMA

PART I

1. TIME, RACE, AND THE ASYNCHRONOUS IN THE COLONIAL DOCUMENTARIES OF MALAYA

Nadine Chan

Abstract

This chapter uncovers how Malaya's racially plural society was rearranged on the very material of celluloid. The connective tissues of the colonial documentary (such as editing, voice-over, narrative structure) converged colonial historicism with the mechanical unwinding of cinematic time. Films were rendered out of date, however, even before they were released when they were unable to keep up with Malayans who insisted on forging history on their own terms. Theorizing the asynchronicity of an indexical medium, this chapter argues that although colonial documentary films scripted Malaya through racialized periodizations of modernity, film was itself an asynchronous medium misaligned with the fractured temporalities of late colonialism in Southeast Asia.

In late January 1937, the Strand Film Company arrived in Kuala Lumpur on a two-week filming expedition to document the development of the Federated Malay States and Singapore.[1] The resulting film, *Five Faces of Malaya* (Shaw 1938), told a story of Malaya's path to progress—how the arrival of modernity through colonialism transformed forests into ports of commerce and orderly plantations and interlaced tropical wilderness with roads, railways, and irrigation channels. Like other such colonial documentaries about Malaya, such as *Malaya* (British Instructional Films 1928) and *Voices of Malaya* (Ministry of Information and Central Office of Information 1948), the film maps out Malaya's journey to modernity through its narrative organization of race and ethnicity. Beginning with Malaya's indigenous and nomadic forest dwellers whose displacement by new immigrants of the capitalist economy is depicted in the film, the narrative maps a historicist trajectory of time on the racialized bodies of Malaya's inhabitants and the racial stratification of Malayan society. The connective tissues possible in the cinematic documentary apparatus—such as the editing, the structural rearrangement of sound and image, and the voice-over—facilitated large-scale imaginings of Malaya as a coherent polity by organizing and hierarchizing Malaya's various "races" as an unfolding of cinematic duration and a structuring of colonial time on the material surface of celluloid. More than simply reflecting Malaya's ethnically plural society, the colonial documentary brings it into being for audiences in Malaya, Britain, and across the globe, even if such social figurations did not exist beyond the edges of the screen.

Indeed, although the documentary presented colonial cosmopolitanism as already in motion, reality ran out of synchrony with the historicisms in the films as ongoing nationalist struggles, interracial tensions, and counter-colonial globalities upended colonial narratives of modernity. Archipelagic Southeast Asia was an asynchronous space of complex intercultural exchange, friction, and contest.[2] Malayans were unruly subjects who would not sit still before the camera, choosing instead to determine history on their own terms. The colonial documentary, in spite of itself, registers these asynchronicities. At times failing to prevent these deviant moments from infiltrating the wide-eyed lens, colonial documentaries turned out to be difficult mouthpieces of empire. As a technology that could be either a recorder of reality or a magician of possibility, the cinematic apparatus had to confront its inherently divergent potential within the colonial documentary form.

This chapter theorizes what I call the asynchronous colonial race-time of documentary films. Asynchronicity is realized in convergent and divergent forms in the colonial documentary: first in the problematic convergence between colonial historicism and documentary cinema's configurations of time and temporality and second in the divergence between the documentary claim and the world outside the frame. The first part of the chapter argues that the documentary form's time-based notions of past and futurity converge with colonial historicism's temporalities in the colonial documentary. In *Five Faces of Malaya*, such *convergent* asynchronicity is realized through the representation of Malaya's ethnic landscape as racialized periodizations of colonial modernity, that is, colonial race-time. The second part of the chapter looks at moments of *divergence* where tensions between the documentary's realist mode and colonial historicism's fictive one result in moments of textual and aesthetic rupture and friction. I examine these moments of narrative contradiction and flux, also suggested in the film's lukewarm reception in Malaya, as possibilities where the various agentive forces in the colonies resisted the temporalizing thrust of the colonial documentary's project of historicism.

Asynchronicity: Colonial Historicism and Its Convergence with Documentary Time

Scholars of the postcolonial have long written about how colonial situations reconfigure spatializations of time and rewrite periodizations of history and pastness. For instance, vernacular experiences of temporality are made to conform to the linear, homogeneous time associated with European ideas of progress and history.[3] Temporality in colonial situations is an arrangement of historical time according to a presumed "naturally existing, continuous flow"—for example, what Gyan Prakash calls colonialism's "History" with a capital H or what Dipesh Chakrabarty terms "historicism"—that which made modernity and capitalism appear global *over time*, originating first in Europe and then spreading outward, elsewhere (Prakash 1995, 4; Chakrabarty 2010, 7). In Chakrabarty's configuration, there are two histories of capital. History 1 contains "pasts posited by capital," and History 2 includes "pasts that do not belong to capital's 'life-process'" (Chakrabarty 2000, 655). Historicism works on the supposition of both historicality and futurity—colonized worlds emerge from the premodern past and must/will move forward in time toward a modern, capitalist future.

The colonial documentary is, at first glance, a machine of History 1. It bears the imprint of colonial historicism's understanding of time in its impulse to record, arrange, and narrate temporality as history and historicality. Familiar since the actuality films of the Lumières, the documentary's elemental function is "the replication of the historical real, the creation of a second-order reality cut to the measure of our desire" (Renov 1993, 25). Some of this impulse to document historical time has to do with the very indexicality of the camera, which bears witness as a chronicler of time. The documentary, in Philip Rosen's terms, is "an arena of meaning centering on the authority of the real founded in an indexical trace" (Rosen 1993, 76). Malin Wahlberg designates the trace as "an indexical sign, an existential operator interrelating image, history, and memory. . . a mark inscribed, or a photograph that bears witness of life or events in the past" (Wahlberg 2011, 119). As "an art of record," the film claims witness as a historical referent (Wahlberg 2008, 33). In collecting references of the past, the colonial documentary's realist mode fixes that past in the suppositions of historicism, in the forward narrative trajectory of historicality.

Moreover, in its mechanical compulsion to unfold linearly in time, cinematic temporalities find convergences with colonial historical time.[4] Indeed, time in the cinema operates through uncannily similar logics of forward "flow." The inevitability of twenty-three frames per second, the inescapability of the uptake of the reel by the projector, and the very fact of film as movement art that takes place in time all mean that in the cinema, time flows continuously and sweeps all within its frame along with the forward thrust of its duration. As Mary Anne Doane explains, in the late nineteenth and early twentieth centuries, cinematic technologies made possible a new access to time and its representation—"the structuring of time and contingency in capitalist modernity" (Doane 2002, 4).

Yet the logic (and paradox) of documentary poetics is that documentaries also seek to persuade—as the colonial documentaries of the Griersonian tradition certainly sought to do (Renov 1993, 26). In other words, the documentary aesthetic exists in tension between the pastness of historical reference and the futurity of persuasion. Even as it claims to document the world in its affiliation with the realist mode, the documentary is also a maker of worlds—as we shall soon see in my analysis of *Five Faces of Malaya*. The colonial documentary was the means through which multiethnic Malaya was visualized as an imagined community within the larger constellation of the British Empire.

Contextually, in the British Empire, colonial documentaries were made to evidence the continuous political legitimacy of imperialism at times when the need for intraempire cooperation was at its highest or when the entire premise of imperialism came under threat. The numerous colonial documentary films of the Empire Marketing Board in the late 1920s and early 1930s, for instance, were produced to shore up consumer preferences for empire-produced goods amid a period of market protectionism and the loss of British advantage in nineteenth-century free trade. Film became a critical player in the political economy of the British Empire because of its ability to bring a visual experience of empire to life—picturing the empire as if it always was and always will be (Chan 2013, 107–8). In that way, colonial documentaries were both documents and possibilities.

Thus, the impulse of colonial historicism shares its ambitions and contradictions with the documentary genre. Colonial documentaries converge a prescription of the real with the peculiar logics of colonial temporality. In the very mediation of the image through the camera, the screen, and the editing, the cinematic sign (what we see on the screen) is always already at a remove from its referent (what existed in the world) (Renov 1993, 26). In that slippage between the actual and the image, colonial historicism approaches a point as documentary time. The discursive conditions that give rise to "nonfiction" and its ensuing "historical" fixity are shot through with historicism's hold on past, present, and future. In colonial documentaries, the trace asynchronously bears the promise of colonial historicism and is misindexed as a historical referent for a world that has not (yet) happened. If, as Wahlberg asks, the "trace is a trace of something," an "intentional object" that functions "as inscription of the past within the present," then what is the significance when trace, document, and history become misaligned in the colonial documentary? (Wahlberg 2008, 35).

I wish to posit the idea of the asynchronous as a means of theorizing this convergence of colonial historicism and documentary time. A term used in electronics or computer programming to denote events that happen outside the main program flow, though often in parallel with it, asynchronicity can arise as a result of external events or may happen concurrently as a program executes. In an asynchronous system, a program can continue running on the basis of a projection of results, even as the computation for said results has yet to occur. The idea of the asynchronous denotes how the world within the documentary film runs in parallel though perhaps at odds with events in the world outside it. Documentary asynchronicity also captures how infrastructures of image reproduction were segregated between colony and metropole in ways that "un-sync" and disrupt the camera's perceived documentary reproduction of reality as indexical, as immediate, and as a historical referent. Indeed, as I argue, two formulations of time, history, and the future meet in the colonial documentary: the promise of colonial historicism and the historicity of documentary time converge to produce a filmic world that is out of synchrony with vernacular modernities beyond the frame.

To manage asynchronicity in a programming interface, a programmer would provide subroutines—a sequence of instructions that return a parallel program to set data, typically called a promise, that best seeks to represent the ongoing events before the computation is complete. In the way that a promise prescribes conditions in the present on the basis of an indeterminable future, the asynchronous colonial documentary embodies an intended futurity as if these conditions were already in place. Colonial documentaries were exercises in asynchronous promise—less invested in what is than in depicting what ought to be as the terms for the already presently occurring. In other words, colonial documentaries do not document the present but rather the promise, suturing the historical trace with the prescriptions of future becoming. Inhabiting a precarious space between actuality (which is arguably focused on the actual) and propaganda (which manipulates the actual to motivate social outcomes and so has that element of futurity about it), colonial documentaries sought to present the empire according to the progressions of imperial modernity and to frame dispersed peoples and territories within these historicisms.

Discussion on the documentary necessarily confronts its nature as document, but I am less invested here in questions about the accuracy of the documentary versus real life than I am in the distance, disjuncture, and "unsync" that happens between the apparatus of the colonial documentary and the conditions of colonial time. As Wahlberg argues, Bazin's argument of film as record cannot be reduced to a truth claim. Rather, the "whole aesthetic of objectivity and the development of comprehensive technologies of truth" in the documentary narrates a particular ordering of temporality in Malaya according to the promise of colonial historicism (Minh-ha 1990, 80).

Colonial Race-Time in *Five Faces of Malaya*

The historicism of Malaya's social and economic uplift finds its legitimacy through the documentary form's allegiance to the realist mode. In this section, I analyze *Five Faces of Malaya* as an example of documentary asynchronicity. In the film, the realist time of the documentary (as a record of a Malaya that supposedly *is*) converges with the futurist time of colonial historicism (a projection of a Malaya that *will be*) through the temporalizing of modernity as racialized time. In colonial race-time, the ethnic body is marked with the periodizations of European modernity. Anne McClintock has coined the term "anachronistic space" to describe how moving outward from metropole to colony meant also moving "back in time" to a place more primitive. In her figuration, colonized people "do not inhabit history proper but exist in a permanently anterior time within the geographic space of the modern empire" (McClintock 1995, 30). Colonial time is thus not merely chronological but also geographically racialized.

Narrated as a series of brief episodic glimpses of the life and customs of the five "racial" groups in Malaya, the structure of *Five Faces of Malaya* articulates the organization of ethnic labor into a plural community. Each of the five segments of the film features one of the five races that make up the territory's multiracial society, explaining how each race fulfilled (or fell short of) specific socioeconomic labor roles in the colonial Malayan economy. The Malayan government had agreed to fund the production of *Five Faces of Malaya* to promote the well-oiled social and economic machinery of Malaya, particularly its plural society. British control over the region was legitimized by the racialized plural social model, a logic by which racial groups in the polity were organized, had access to benefits (or were excluded from them), and carried out political and economic life. In the imperial imagination, European, Malay, Chinese, Indian, and indigenous peoples were specialized social groups through which the British government understood, classified, and governed society (Hirschman 1987, 567).[5] Through occupying distinct socioeconomic and political roles, the various races coexisted within the same political unit and shared an economic interdependence.[6] That a well-functioning plural society managed along racial lines could be brought together under colonial government was an essential part of what Adeline Koh describes as the foundational myth of British Malaya (Koh 2008, 19). Malaya's multiracial society was also exemplary of the new progressive and cooperative spirit of the British Commonwealth. The Balfour Declaration of 1926 and the Ottawa Conference of 1932 had initiated a cultural shift in colonial attitudes toward the globalist, intercultural ambitions of late colonial capitalism. The imagination of empire's interracial cosmopolitan family was an essential part of the Commonwealth in the 1920s and 1930s (Chan 2013; Anthony 2011b; Grieveson 2011; Constantine 1986).

The documentary film's ability to reorder the world through the editing and the narrative voice-over made Malaya's plural society possible on-screen. Likening the painter to a magician and the cameraman to a surgeon, Walter Benjamin observes how the mechanical processing of reality through the camera sutures the image closer to the real (Benjamin 1969, 232–233). If the camera was a surgeon that carved up the real with its mechanical eye, the editor was the architect who put it together mechanically. Film editing meant the physical and material reassemblage of film by hand, forming the colonial plural society on a strip of celluloid. In the ability to suture and splice, the film editor brought Malaya's plural society into being. The ubiquitous voice-overs in documentary sound films facilitated large-scale imaginings of a coherent polity by bringing images of Malaya's various races together through the sound bridge of an overarching narrative (Bloom 2017, 69). The editing and the voice-over synthesized the colonial imaginary, an asynchronous realization of a fictional futurity made manifest as already-happened documentary truth.

Most critically, the racial organization of Malaya was not only a rearrangement of the region's socioeconomic life but also the reordering of historical time along racial lines. The apparatus of the colonial documentary reorganized Malaya's racial landscape into periodizations of colonial modernity rendered on the ethnic body—a History 1 of colonial capital narrated as racialized temporalities. In *Five Faces of Malaya*, certain ethnic groups are designated as premodern, others as feudal, and yet others as modern enough. The chronicalization of race-time is structured across the duration of the film. The earliest scenes mark Malaya's primal scene, and its finale celebrates the inevitable triumph of globalness, modernity, and capitalism. First depicting Malaya's indigenous Temiars as disappearing before the advancements of colonial capital, the film portrays the customs and primary occupations of the "timeless" feudal Malays, followed by the newly immigrant Chinese, Indians, and Europeans who transform the region into one of global industry. The stadial mode of thought so critiqued by postcolonial historians—that societies presumably "move from the precapitalist to the capitalist, or from feudal to modern, [and] eventually converge on the global stage"—is made possible through the *rearrangement of time* via an *arrangement of race* through the cinematic apparatus (Majumdar 2010, 46).

Embodying the tabula rasa and untamed frontiers of colonial fantasy, the film opens with a sweeping panoramic shot of the Malayan tropical forest. A narrator announces, "This is the heart of Malaya's mountains and jungles, which for thousands of years have resisted the advancement of civilization, [and] cover the greater part of the country." Emphasizing the wildness of this landscape, the film shows us an elephant emerging from the lush forest, a tiger prowling through the dense undergrowth, and impenetrable vegetation bordering forest streams. Like the other forest inhabitants who push through the depths of the forest to appear before the camera, men with blowpipes and loincloths emerge from the thickets. Configured as part of the forest fauna, the Orang Asli (a collective term for the ethnically diverse indigenous people of Malaya that include the Temiars) are the first of Malaya's five faces to appear in the film. The camera casts an ethnographic eye on the traditional customs, hunting methods, and daily practices of the Temiars—an indigenous ethnic group in peninsular Malaysia who were semi-nomadic at the time. A group of women, in perfect choreographed symphony, dip hollowed bamboo containers into the river to collect water. Publicity material for the film featured these bare-breasted women, with the *Straits Times* running an article somewhat titillatingly titled "Aborigines of Fine Physique," thus blurring the boundaries between ethnography, entertainment, and exploitation in the film (Staples 2005, 54). (See fig. 1.1.)

By opening with scenes of Malaya's indigenous people amid its wild forest landscape, the film positions Malaya's indigene to stand in for the region's exotic origins prior to the coming of colonial modernity. The Temiars in the impenetrable forest are made to represent a primitive Malaya, a Malaya before the entry of imperial capital. In the face of encroaching modernity, with no foreseeable part to play in the modern colonial economy (at least from the point of view of the colonial government), the Orang Asli are written out of the narrative of Malaya's future. Portrayed as wondrously exotic but hopelessly impervious to capitalist reform, the Temiar are quickly dismissed as irrelevant by the end of the film, melting away into the forest before the advances of the supposedly more modern races who were better suited to wage labor and imperial subjecthood.

The work of the documentary editing in its arrangement of history according to these very logics of racialized time becomes evident as the film

Figure 1.1. Malaya's indigenous people. Still from *Five Faces of Malaya*. (Courtesy of the BFI National Archive.)

transitions structurally from its depiction of the Orang Asli to its presentation of the Malays. According to the film, the Orang Asli may have existed in the Ovidian undigested mass of preontological wilderness, but the cartographic legibility of the Malay world marks the beginning of the region's entry into colonial knowledge. The image of a Temiar house rapidly dissolves before a map of the region. The film introduces the Malays as the existing inhabitants of the land who are feudal in organization, traditional in outlook, and mild-mannered in temperament. In contrast to the Orang Asli as modernity's lost cause, the Malays neither represent a class of immigrant wage labor like the Indians and Chinese (and hence not completely a comfortable cog in the colonial economy) nor are completely beyond the possibilities of modernization. Sociologist Daniel Goh describes colonial representations of Malays as medieval: "Unlike Noble Savagery, where the natives were seen as distant in evolutionary development, Medievalism represented the natives as ready for political modernization and incorporation into colonial states" (Goh 2007, 325). Existing colonial rhetoric accorded Malays the status of the almost moderns—romantically preindustrial but with the potential for modern civilization. The Malays are first described as a people with a "love of

Figure 1.2. A young Malay bride in ceremonial dress. Still from *Five Faces of Malaya*. (Courtesy of the BFI National Archive.)

pomp" and ceremonies "adopted from the ancient rituals of India." (See fig. 1.2.) We see the sultan of Selangor at an investiture at a royal court in Penang. Adorned with gilded clothes and glittering ornaments and practicing quaint customs, the Malays are depicted as far from primitive although slow on the march toward a colonial capitalist future.

In a discussion on the making of *Five Faces*, the district officer of Klang suggested that footage of Malay life ought to represent a traditional Malaya that preceded British-borne modernity: "Malaya as it would have been but for its development as part of the British Empire."[7] Malay fishermen and farmers represented the romantic image of the simple peasant, the archetypal preindustrial-age figure untouched by the demands of modern life and industry. Images of a quaint Malay fishing village by the seaside are followed by a shot of a small fishing boat out at sea as the fisherfolk mend their nets on an idyllic beach under the shade of coconut trees. The narrator describes the inhabitants as "indolent and optimistic, satisfied by a carefree, easy life in the sun. Today, as their people have done for hundreds of years, they sit on the seashore gossiping and mending their nets." Village scenes shot in the interior regions of the state of Selangor depict "the Malays leading their timeless lives in the *kampong* (village)," harvesting and threshing rice by hand.[8]

The idea of the timelessness of Malay custom is significant here in that it signals not simply the continuity of traditional practices into the present, but also how such custom lies outside time. Not quite dead or dying in the sense that Fatimah Tobing Rony elaborates in her notion of the taxidermic, yet portrayed as paralyzed by traditions that are discounted by colonial understandings of time and history, the Malays in this part of the film are excluded from the life-affirming discourse of colonial capitalism (Rony 1996, 102). Located outside modern history as it unfolded, the Malays are represented as unaffected by current affairs and made drowsy by old ways and customs. The timeless nature of Malay subsistence labor and small-scale cultivation situates them outside the colonial formations of worthwhile labor—that is, labor oriented toward production for capital, export, and the global market.

Leaving behind Malaya's almost-moderns, *Five Faces* launches into the beginning of the capitalist modernity era as marked by the arrival of European capital and commerce. This is a critical turning point in the chronological structure of the film. A montage of relatively brief shots featuring illustrations and images of European ships and monuments are accompanied by a voice-over describing the rapid succession with which the Malay region came to meet with, and succumb to, various European imperial and commercial powers. With the Portuguese in the 1500s, the Dutch in the mid-1600s, and the British at the beginning of the eighteenth century, centuries are compressed in the nonspace between the shots. Where time previously stood still with the Orang Asli and the Malays, the film's narrative now propels the region forward into *history*—time that could now be legibly measured through the developmental narratives of modernity and capital. This transition toward colonial modernity is visually depicted through shots of Singapore's commercial wharfs, colonial architecture, and bridges.

The Chinese, Indians, and British, whom the film portrays as relative newcomers to the land, become the principal characters in this new narrative of history. The film celebrates these immigrant races as part of a new cosmopolitan Malaya that followed the arrival of colonial investment. Unlike the Malays, whom the film claims were "content with their lot in the sun and would not sweat and toil to dig riches from the ground," the Chinese and Indians exemplified the new modern Asian—hardworking wage laborers behind the success of Malaya's tin and rubber industries in the new economy. Extreme long shots feature these sweaty, laboring Chinese bodies working with and among behemoth machinery. (See fig. 1.3.) The editing seamlessly combines human toil and machine-operated work into a poem of industrial productivity. Shots of laborers digging the earth with no more than the strength of their arms are juxtaposed with the might of the excavator and

Figure 1.3. Chinese laborers heading to work at the tin mine. Still from *Five Faces of Malaya*. (Courtesy of the BFI National Archive.)

moves finally to shots of a giant tin-dredging machine. Within the landscape of the tin mine, bodily entwined with mining machinery, *Five Faces* presents the Chinese in Malaya as indispensable labor in the modern colonial economy.

Against sweeping panoramas of rubber plantations, Tamil laborers parade onto the screen. These men and women make cuts into the bark of rubber trees, catching the emerging sap in buckets and transporting the buckets to the latex-processing plant. (See fig. 1.4.) The workers silently strain, sort, and process the latex into sheets that, as the narrator describes, supplies half the world's rubber. An unsigned review of *Five Faces of Malaya* in *World Film News* derogatorily described these laborers as the donkeys who performed the hard labor that the supposedly idle Malays would not deign to do: "The Tamil was born to do Malaya's donkey work. Every job that is dirty, undesirable and monotonous is the Tamil's.... Malaya gets more and better Tamils—and needs them—for Malaya can use plenty of donkeys" (*World Film News* 1938, 55).

Portrayed as newly immigrant labor forces (and thus also obfuscating the long and complex history of Chinese and Indian immigration and capital in the peninsula even before British administration), the Chinese and Tamils

Figure 1.4. Tamil rubber plantation workers. Still from *Five Faces of Malaya*. (Courtesy of the BFI National Archive.)

are shown to be doing good work for the Commonwealth, tirelessly churning the soil to discover Malaya's latent natural riches.

These scenes not only served to publicize Malayan tin and rubber to audiences in other parts of the colony but also functioned as a means of showcasing the logic of racial management in a cosmopolitan Malaya servicing the Commonwealth's economy. Indeed, the film depicts the British, the fifth face of Malaya, as the administrative minds behind this process of modernization and who, according to the narrator, "brought [Malaya] its peace and prosperity." Contemporary newspaper reviews note how the European makes a somewhat scanty appearance in the film—appearing only in short scenes at a golf club in Kuala Lumpur and at the Singapore swimming club.[9] The omission of overbearing British presence in the film was quite likely done to soften the perception of imperialism. Indeed, *World Film News* (1938, 55) makes much out of the fact that Europeans in Malaya no longer have an imperial presence over the protectorate ("Empire builders and pioneers do not live here any more") but are part of the region's middle class, with few intentions of settling down in the country.

Yet, in spite of the relative screen absence of Europeans, British presence is made evident in the very entanglement of modernity with everyday life.

Against a montage of gleaming modern buildings, an airplane, and the gushing waters of a hydroelectric dam, the narrator describes how communication technologies have brought Malaya to within eight days of London by air. With British management, the film seems to say, Malaya has ascended to the global stage. The very existence of Malaya's plural society, the film claims, is a cosmopolitan product of modernity and imperial trade. Healthy immigration and the ensuing management of race into a modern colonial workforce were the fundamental principles behind the economic progress and modernity that the British brought to the region.

Spatializing future time in the film's final scene, the promise of ongoing modernization is portrayed as the encroachment of Malaya's laboring (the Chinese and Tamils) and capitalist (the British) groups on the indigenous way of life in the peninsula's forested interior. By the end of the film, each of the races finds its place in this fertile modern colonial economy. The journey from the depths of virgin forest where we meet Malaya's vanishing indigenous tribes, followed by the medieval (but developing) Malays, the Asian non-Malays (wage laborers and business people), and finally the Europeans (capitalists and administrators), is a journey across anachronistic space on a teleological timeline of modernity. Each race has a particular role in the plural economy and signifies a specific moment in the race-time of colonial modernity.

Documentary Frictions and Divergent Asynchronicities

All is well in Malaya—at least on the surface of celluloid. A closer look at the film, however, reveals confusing narrative frictions and contradictory dramatizations of race in the forward march of modernity. Multiple ways of imagining modern community, counternationalisms, and upswells of political passions from among the locals complicate an easy convergence between the historical time of the documentary and the historicism of colonialism. Instead, the complexity of colonial Southeast Asia in the 1930s placed divergent pressures on the History 1s of the colonial documentary. These moments of friction are particularly noticeable in the film's tension-riddled depiction of Malay society's place in colonial modernity.

As described earlier, the film first depicts Malays as idealized *padi*-cultivating peasants endemically suited to traditional cultural practice (Ghee 1984, 37). The narrator insists that the Malays made for lousy laborers; "the Malay's only clock is the sun and he is generally late on that" (*World Film News* 1938, 55). Stereotypes of lazy Malays served the purposes of colonial rhetoric that sought to project the idea of the Malays as quaint and picturesque, but ultimately incapable of ruling themselves.[10] Embedded within the discourse of the timeless fisherman and lazy native is the ethnic marginalization of Malays from an expanding colonial economy. But Malayans were not quite the docile poster people of cosmopolitan empire. Reading against the grain, various scholars have instead argued that the native's supposed indolence was a refusal to be a tool in the production system of colonial capitalism (Alatas 1977, 60; Scott 1976). Further, the formation of race-based nationalisms in the 1930s explicitly challenged the discourse of the state. Malay resistance countered the very narrative of racialized time that the colonial government was trying to envision. The Malay intelligentsia pushed back against the various forces of colonial capitalism, the growing numbers of immigrants, the economic gap between Malays and non-Malays, and the disempowerment of local Malay leaders that imperiled Malay ways of life. *Bangsa Melayu*, roughly translatable as Malay race or Malay lineage, became the political passion of the growing Malay press in the 1930s as Malay ethnic nationalism developed in the 1930s and 1940s (Reid 2010, 103–4). The concept of *Bangsa Melayu* among 1930s-era Malay nationalists was oriented toward inward, ruralist, and Islamic sentiments predicated on interethnic differentiation and opposition (Kahn 2006, 68). *Bangsa Melayu* sensibilities emerging in the Malay vernacular press consolidated into a perception of immigrants as a serious threat (Omar 1993, 17–18). Malay journalist and political activist Ibrahim Yaacob, for instance, lamented the damages to Malay culture and consciousness because of new economic forces (Milner 1994, 264). Malay sentiment on the ground was thus asynchronous with the immigrant-driven cosmopolitan-capitalist fantasy that *Five Faces* sought to construct. Instead, Malay nationalists imagined connectivity of a different kind—a Pan-Malayan *bangsa* that would unite the Malay race across state lines and an even wider pan-Malayan identity that could do so across the entire Malay Archipelago.[11] Hence, alternative forms of modernity and community populated Malay political consciousness in ways that countered the plural capitalist model of the state. The divergent agencies and asynchronous visions of modernity complicated the otherwise seemingly straightforward thrust of the colonial narrative.

In spite of the colonial documentary's effort to fashion a world out of the image of empire, the History 2s that emerge from the ground bearing alternative life-worlds and forms of modernity upset the integrity of the colonial documentary's historicist form. The case is one of divergent asynchronicity—when the convergent logics of colonial temporality and documentary historicality run hopelessly out of synchrony with lifeworlds outside the frame. The complexity of Southeast Asia, the agency of its multiple social and political forces—each with its own account of history, futurity, and temporalization—was divergent from and asynchronous with that of colonial modernity's race-time.

Perhaps because of the very inevitability of its realist mode, the colonial documentary cannot help but to witness a seepage of the history 2s into its fabricated world. These social fissures revealed themselves in the film as subtle structural and aesthetic tensions. In particular, its fragmented and confused depiction of Malays revealed conflicting ideas about Malayness in colonial modernity. Although depicting the Malays as medieval near the very beginning of the film, the Malays are then oddly described midway through the film as becoming successfully modernized. The sultans of Malaya have developed a penchant for afternoon tennis matches, the film says, and one is shown putting aside his former regalia for a sport coat and trousers. Later on, however, the film again backpedals and claims that Malay tradition and the Islamic faith remained intact in spite of the breathtaking pace of change. At its close, the film carefully reassures audiences that idyllic Malay villagers have maintained their charming old ways, since, according to the narrator, "Western ideas haven't altered old customs." The last third of the film industriously archives images, sounds, and songs of traditional Malay life. The very popular folk song "Rasa Sayang" ("love") plays on the soundtrack as a game of *sepak takraw* (a ball game involving a hollow rattan ball) and a *silat* (traditional Malay martial arts) demonstration are depicted.

The back-and-forth between imagery of the romantic timeless villager and the Malay at the cusp of modernity is highly discordant. These narrative inconsistencies led to criticism from a member of the Malayan press that the film "lacked continuity."[12] The figure of the traditional Malay and its counter-figure, the modern one, represented the conflicting racial discourses that pervaded the colonial project in the Malay world. Perceiving their role as stewards rather than colonists in the 1930s, the British were to some extent obliged to honor the tenets of indirect rule—that Malay customs, religion, and economic security would not be threatened by colonial administration. Yet neither could the film show the Malay as left behind by the tidal wave of colonial modernity. Unsullied by colonial capital and yet partaking in the push toward modernity, the figure of the Malay is a paradox in this narrative of cosmopolitan society.

Hence, in spite of the film's creation of the plural Malayan cosmopolis with its "five races," existing racial tensions strained the coherence of its narrative. Unruly populations who would not quietly abide by colonialism's historicism made it impossible for any clear-cut narrative of the colonial plural society to be easily formed. Though such textual tensions are subtle in the case of *Five Faces*, they represent the glimmers of how the medium struggled to satisfy the ambitions of the sponsoring officials to create a film that narrated the History 1 of colonial capital while attending to the divergent modernities and ethnic nationalism that muddied the suppositions of such racialized temporalizations.

Conclusion: An Asynchronous Reception

The film's starkly divergent reception histories inside and outside Malaya also suggest the asynchronicity between the film's on-screen and off-screen worlds. *Five Faces* was well received outside Malaya. After its prerelease run at the Academy Cinema in London, the film garnered an audience of two hundred thousand in about one hundred twenty theaters in Great Britain.[13] A flurry of warm reviews surrounding the film provided an intertextual tapestry that taught British audiences about Malaya's cosmopolitan society.[14] Outside theaters, the film had many private showings at universities, film societies, and world's fairs, and it was screened at the Imperial Institute, an exhibition space in London showcasing Britain's empire, well into 1949 (*World Film News* 1938). US and Canadian distributors purchased rights to *Five Faces*, and it was also distributed to American schools (*World Film News* 1938). At the onset of WWII, the British Council revised the film for world circulation and television broadcasting as part of its propaganda about the British Empire.[15]

The film's reception in Malaya, however, was far less straightforward or successful. Indeed, the possibility of asynchronous worlds inside and outside the frame complicated an easy or transparent reception of the film. The sultans of Pahang and Terengganu and the Pertuan *besar* (chief leader) of Negri Sembilan saw the rough cut of the film at a private theater in London in June 1937, but *Five Faces* only publicly premiered in Malaya two years later at the 1939 Malayan Exhibition in Kuala Lumpur, where it played to an audience of three thousand.[16] This would have been one of the first (and only) times before the Pacific War that the Malayan general public would have witnessed an on-screen articulation of Malaya as a complete and coherent entity. Yet, even at such a venue, its function as the narrative of colonial modernity was dubious. Probably for lack of sound projection facilities in the temporary *atap*-roofed building in which it was screened, the film had no audio or explanatory captions. Without the voice-over, bare images lent themselves to rescripting at the mercy of the audience. The audience filled in for the lack of narration with their own commentary, with young Malays "shouting excitedly as they recognized on the screen the regal figures of a Sultan or a demonstration of a kampong game."[17] It is unclear what alternative accounts replaced the carefully extolled narrative commentary about Malaya as the empire's cosmopolitan dream. While the audience's words have been lost from the historical record, the screening nevertheless represents a moment of divergent asynchronicity, where the narrative of the audience ran counter to colonialism's on-screen narrative. Freed from sound though not completely freed from their arrangement in the reel, the film's wild images floated apart from the documentary's narrative, tethered to the historical referent of the image though released from the meaning-making work of the narration.

After this single screening, the dearth of further publicity about the film suggested that it continued to lead a very low-key existence in Malaya. Paper trails in the archive are unclear about why the film was never made available for general or educational release in Malaya. One reason was that sound-projection facilities available in schools and other public venues in Malaya were still relatively few in the late 1930s, making the screening of the film difficult. The lengthy film was also not edited in a manner that made it amenable to a dissection into shorter instructional segments about Malaya's industries. There was also the very real possibility that the Malayan government had simply little reason to screen *Five Faces of Malaya* domestically at that time; indeed, the British may have found it strategically expedient not to do so (Bayly and Harper 2007). Before WWII, the government had no impetus to foster any sense of a Malayan-imagined community; nor was the idea one that would have seemed possible amid the rising ethnic nationalisms of the time. Malayan society was made up of people of different national origins, religions, cultures, and languages. According to historians, the Malays held loyalties to their particular sultans, and the Chinese and Indians harbored loyalties to distinct clans, dialect groups, or regions (Ratnam 1965, 5).[18] Social and political life was largely segregated into ethnic, racial, and religious communalism (Ratnam 1925, 4). Power was also divided between two groups, with political power lying largely with the Malays and economic influence with the Chinese. The idea of a coherent colony was ironically of greater promise and possibility to those outside Malaya than to Malayans themselves.

Thus, while audiences abroad were able to partake in the grand narrative of Malaya's path to modernity, local audiences in 1930s Malaya were not offered this view of history—even though it was projected for and about them. Their popularity in Britain and elsewhere presented a coherent Malaya from the outside—a version of colonial historicism and racialized time whose promise was only really tenable outside Malaya itself. The visualization of colonial historicism made possible by documentary pastness and futurity was irreconcilable with the divergent Malaya(s) that was(were) unfolding in the everyday, the vernacular, and the local. Even as colonial temporality and documentary time converged in the colonial documentary, their asynchronicity with the microhistories of the everyday suggested their ultimate irreconcilability beyond the edges of the screen.

Although I have focused my analysis on *Five Faces* in this chapter, other colonial documentaries of Malaya (e.g., *Voices of Malaya*) do similar work in their attempt to both shape and record a plural colonial society on celluloid, but they also have encountered frictions that register both the political shifts of the moment and the tensions that emerge between changing filmic forms (e.g., between traditions of British documentary film and emerging modes of instructional colonial film) and modes of address (e.g., between international and local audiences; Rice 2013, 448).[19] Riddled with out-of-date commentary to the company of footage containing various political faux pas, *Voices of Malaya*, for instance, featured ideas of late-colonial pluralism embodied with the short-lived Malayan Union that were out of synchrony with fragmented ethnic nationalisms at the brink of the Malayan Emergency. What is apparent in the colonial documentaries of Malaya is how race-time—so carefully curated on the material surface of celluloid, reveals itself to be a precarious thing vulnerable to unruly possibilities amid vernacular imaginings of alternative political futures. The apparatus of colonial documentary, as an exercise in the futurity and promise of colonial time, found itself out of synchrony with vernacular modernities beyond the frame.

Acknowledgments

I would like to thank the editors of this volume and the anonymous reviewers for their input on this chapter. A different version of this chapter received feedback at the Society of Fellows workshop series at the University of Chicago; I wish to thank Rochona Majumdar and my former Harper-Schmidt colleagues for their generous engagement.

Notes

1. Alexander Shaw—who had previously made films for the General Post Office, the Orient Line (a British shipping company), and the Ministry of Labor—directed the production in Malaya. George Noble, who would later be a cameraman in the Gold Coast Film Unit, served as the cameraman. Paul Rotha, a renowned figure during the British documentary film movement, oversaw all of Strand's productions. The company was about to shoot a series of travel films for Imperial Airways and planned to stop at Penang and Singapore en route from England to Australia (Arkib Negara Malaysia (National Archives Malaysia), File No. K.1132/1936 letter from Ralph Keane, Director of Productions of the Strand Film Company to E. Jago, from the Malayan Information Agency dated September 19, 1936). For the historical significance of this series of films, see Anthony (2011a).
2. For more on this argument, see Bernards (2015).
3. For a study of postcolonial theory in history writing, see Majumdar (2010).

4. I speak here only of the mechanical time of film, as opposed to the experience of cinema in the phenomenological, Bergsonian, or Deleuzian sense.

5. Charles Hirschman's work (1987) explains how the evolution of census making in Malaya is closely tied to the expansion of the British colonial administration.

6. It is important, though, to distinguish Furnivall-ian pluralism from any sense of political ethnic equality or democracy. Colonial understandings of pluralism did not aspire to any sense of equal citizenship until after the Pacific War. Rather, the British kept to the dictates of their treaty with the Malay rulers to uphold the preferential treatment of the Malays and sought to build up a Malay elite that would assist them in maintaining "Malaya for the Malays" (Ramakrishna 2002, 7).

7. Arkib Negara Malaysia (Malaysia National Archives). File No.: Sel. Sec. 647/1937, letter from District Officer Klang, recipient unnamed, dated January 28, 1937.

8. "Talkie Films of Malayan Life for World's Screens," *Straits Times*, January 28, 1937, 12.

9. "'Five Faces' of Malaya at holiday exhibition," *Straits Times*, August 7, 1939, 13. "Film That Should Be Shown throughout Malaya," *Straits Times*, August 8, 1939, 14.

10. The figure of the lazy native—who refuses to do productive work or organize the day according to the dictates of economic time—has long been a trope in colonial literature in Malaya.

11. Ariffin Omar identifies the Persaudaraan Sahabat Pena Malaya (The Brotherhood of Friends of the Pen) as an example of the former and the Kesatuan Melayu Muda (Union of Malay Youth) as examples of the latter in the 1930s (Omar 1993, 19–21).

12. "Film that should be shown throughout Malaya," *Straits Times*, August 8, 1939, 14.

13. "Malaya Film Screened in Britain and U.S.," *Singapore Free Press and Mercantile Advertiser*, May 27, 1940, 5.

14. Arkib Negara Malaysia (National Archives Malaysia), File No: F.S. 1364/39, FMS Report on the Administration of the Malayan Information Agency for the year 1938, No.17 of 1939, 11. A write-up about *Five Faces* in *World Film News* appreciated the accuracy of the film's portrayal of Malayan society. Unfortunately, the writer proceeded to sketch his or her views on the "Sakai," Malays, Chinese, Indians, and Europeans with the broadest and most stereotypical strokes (World Film News 1938, 55).

15. "Malaya Film Screened," 5. On the film's adaptation to television, see Arkib Negara Malaysia (National Archives Malaysia), File No: F.S. 12411/50 FMS Report on the Administration of the Malayan Information Agency for the year 1949, no. 12 of 1950, 7.

16. "Malaya on the Screen," *Straits Times*, June 3, 1937, 10; "A Film of the Malay States," *Times* [London], May 22, 1937, 10; "'Five Faces' of Malaya at Holiday Exhibition," *Straits Times*, August 7, 1939, 13.

17. "Film That Should Be Shown throughout Malaya," *Straits Times*, August 8, 1939, 14.

18. There were other divisions as well, such as whether one was Malaya- or China-born, or was English-speaking or not, and further differences in linguistic and social statuses made Malaya a place of strong communalism before the war (Ratnam 1965).

19. For an archive and analysis of colonial films that sought to remake the empire in various ways beyond the Malayan context, see Rice (2019).

Bibliography

Alatas, Syed Hussein. 1977. *The Myth of the Lazy Native: A Study of the Image of the Malays, Filipinos and Javanese from the 16th to the 20th Century and Its Function in the Ideology of Colonial Capitalism*. New York and Oxford: Frank Cass and Company Limited.

Anthony, Scott. 2011a. "The Future's in the Air: Imperial Airways and the British Documentary Film Movement." *Journal of British Cinema and Television* 8, no. 3: 301–21.

———. 2011b. "Imperialism and Internationalism: The British Documentary Movement and the Legacy of the Empire Marketing Board," In *Empire and Film*. Edited by Lee Grieveson and Colin MacCabe, 135–48. London: Palgrave Macmillan.

Bayly, Christopher, and Tim Harper. 2007. *Forgotten Wars: Freedom and Revolution in Southeast Asia*. Cambridge, MA: Harvard University Press.

Benjamin, Walter. 1969. "The Work of Art in the Age of Mechanical Reproduction." In *Illuminations*. Edited by Hannah Arendt, 217–252. New York: Schocken.

Bernards, Brian. 2015. *Writing the South Seas: Imagining the Nanyang in Chinese and Southeast Asian Postcolonial Literature*. Seattle: University of Washington Press.

Bloom, Peter. 2017. "The Language of Counterinsurgency in Malaya." In *The Colonial Documentary Film in South and South-East Asia*. Edited by Ian Aitken and Camille Deprez, 63-78. Edinburgh: Edinburgh University Press.

Chakrabarty, Dipesh. 2010. *Provincializing Europe: Postcolonial Thought and Historical Difference*. Princeton, NJ: Princeton University Press.

———. n.d. "Universalism and Belonging in the Logic of Capital." *Public Culture* 12 (Fall 2000), no. 3.: 653–678.

Chan, Nadine. 2013. "'Remember the Empire, Filled with Your Cousins': Poetic Exposition in the Documentaries of the Empire Marketing Board." *Studies in Documentary Film* 7, no. 2 (June): 105–18.

Constantine, Stephen. 1986. "'Bringing the Empire Alive': The Empire Marketing Board and Imperial Propaganda, 1926–33." In *Imperialism and Popular Culture*. Edited by John M. Mackenzie, 192–231. Manchester, UK: Manchester University Press.

Doane, Mary Ann. 2002. *The Emergence of Cinematic Time: Modernity, Contingency, and the Archive*. Cambridge, MA: Harvard University Press.

Ghee, Lim Teck. 1984. "British Colonial Administration and the 'Ethnic Division of Labor' in Malaya." *Kajian Malaysia* 2, no. 2: 28–66.

Goh, Daniel P. S. 2007. "Imperialism and 'Medieval' Natives: The Malay Image in Anglo-American Travelogues and Colonialism in Malaya and the Philippines." *International Journal of Cultural Studies* 10, no. 3: 323–41.

Grieveson, Lee. 2011. "The Cinema and the (Common) Wealth of Nations." In *Empire and Film*. Edited by Lee Grieveson and Colin MacCabe, 73–114. London: Palgrave Macmillan.

Hirschman, Charles. 1987. "The Meaning and Measurement of Ethnicity in Malaysia: An Analysis of Census Classifications." *Journal of Asian Studies* 46, no. 3 (August): 555–82.

Kahn, Joel S. 2006. *Other Malays: Nationalism and Cosmopolitanism in the Modern Malay World*. Honolulu: University of Hawaii Press.

Kinematograph Weekly. 1938. "Five Faces." *Kinematograph Weekly*, March 24.

Koh, Adeline. 2008. "Inventing Malayness: Race, Education and Englishness in Colonial Malaya." PhD diss., University of Michigan.

Majumdar, Rochona. 2010. *Writing Postcolonial History*. London: Bloomsbury Academic.

McClintock, Anne. 1995. *Imperial Leather: Race, Gender, and Sexuality in the Colonial Contest*. New York: Routledge.

Milner, Anthony. 1994. *The Invention of Politics in Colonial Malaya: Contesting Nationalism and the Expansion of the Public Sphere*. New York: Cambridge University Press.

Minh-ha, Trinh T. 1990. "Documentary Is/Not a Name." *October* 52 (Spring): 76–98.

Omar, Ariffin. 1993. *Bangsa Melayu: Malay Concepts of Democracy and Community, 1945–1950*. New York: Oxford University Press.

Prakash, Gyan. 1995. Introduction to *After Colonialism: Imperial Histories and Postcolonial Displacements*. Edited by Gyan Prakash, 3-18. Princeton, NJ: Princeton University Press.

Ramakrishna, Kumar. 2002. *Emergency Propaganda: The Winning of Malayan Hearts and Minds 1948–1958*. Richmond, VA: Curzon.

Ratnam, K. J. 1965. *Communalism and the Political Process in Malaya*. Kuala Lumpur, Malaysia: University of Malaya Press.
Reid, Anthony. 2010. *Imperial Alchemy: Nationalism and Political Identity in Southeast Asia*. New York: Cambridge University Press.
Renov, Michael. 1993. "Toward a Poetics of Documentary." In *Theorizing Documentary*. Edited by Michael Renov, 12–36. New York: Routledge.
Rice, Tom. 2013. "Distant Voices of Malaya: Still Colonial Lives." *Journal of British Cinema and Television* 10, no. 3: 430–51.
———. 2019. *Films for the Colonies: Cinema and the Preservation of the British Empire*. Oakland: University of California Press.
Rony, Fatimah Tobing. 1996. *The Third Eye: Race, Cinema, and Ethnographic Spectacle*. Durham, NC: Duke University Press.
Rosen, Philip. 1993. "Document and Documentary: On the Persistence of Historical Concepts." In *Theorizing Documentary*. Edited by Michael Renov, 58–89. New York: Routledge.
Scott, James C. 1976. *The Moral Economy of the Peasant: Rebellion and Subsistence in Southeast Asia*. New Haven, CT: Yale University Press.
Staples, Amy. 2005. "Popular Ethnography and Public Consumption Sites of Contestation in Museum-Sponsored Expeditionary Film." *Moving Image* 5, no. 2 (Fall): 50–78.
Wahlberg, Malin. 2008. *Documentary Time: Film and Phenomenology*. Minneapolis: University of Minnesota Press.
———. 2011. "The Trace: Framing the Presence of the Past in *Free Fall*." In *Cinema's Alchemist: The Films of Péter Forgács*. Edited by Bill Nichols and Michael Renov, 119–34. Minneapolis: University of Minnesota Press.
World Film News. 1938. "Five Faces: An Exclusive Note on the Making of Strand's New Film, Together with Some Observations on the Races, Customs and Love Life of the Malayans, by a Doctor Who Spent Many Years among Them." *World Film News* 3, no. 2 (May–June): 54-55.

Filmography

Elton, Ralph, and Terry Trench (Dir.). 1948. *Voices of Malaya*. Crown Film Unit. Malaya. http://www.colonialfilm.org.uk/node/2541.
Shaw, Alexander (Dir.). 1938. *Five Faces of Malaya*. Strand Film Company. London, Great Britain. http://www.colonialfilm.org.uk/node/1840.
(Director unknown) 1928. *Malaya*. British Instructional Films.

NADINE CHAN is Assistant Professor in the Cinema Studies Institute at the University of Toronto.

2. FACING MALCONTENT COLONIAL KOREAN COMRADES
A Typology of Colonial Cinema in Asia's Socialist Alliances

Moonim Baek

Abstract

This chapter examines the typology of colonial cinema in the socialist alliance between the Japanese metropole and colonial Korea. The ubiquitous figure of the "malcontent Korean *pullyŏng sŏnin*" [不逞鮮人; Japanese, *futei senjin*] that is embodied in the close-up of the movie star Na Un-kyu (羅雲奎, 1902–37) is less the appropriation of a traditional ethnic hero typecasting than a recent historical product of Japan's annexation of Korea. Unlike the infantilized, naive, and submissive images of the colonized Korean that are best exemplified in the female figure of the *kisaeng* (professional entertainer) in Korean and Japanese popular culture, the *pullyŏng sŏnin* is described as untamed, rebellious, and violent. A few Japanese socialists actively appropriated the popular image of *pullyŏng sŏnin* as their colonial comrade for their allied cultural movements, but, at the same time, they ethnographize Koreans as closer to nature, or more primitive, rather than civilized. How then can we suggest that the ethno-national inclusivity in the socialist cultural project functions when it is applied to colonial comrades? In other words, does the socialist project resolve the issue of colonial taxonomy that ghettoizes the colonized as prone to spontaneous and volatile defiance, the other side of the coin of the infantilized, domesticated image of the colonized?

A Typology of Colonial Cinema

A special issue on colonial cinema appears in the October 1930 edition of *Proletaria Eiga*, a Japanese-language magazine devoted to proletarian films. The issue features the Soviet film *Potomok Chingis-Khana* (Storm over Asia, Vsevolod Pudovkin, 1928) as its main focus. As the story of a young Mongolian man named Bair who becomes a hero to his people fighting against

British imperialism, *Potomok Chingis-Khana* foregrounds the alliances between colonized Mongolian and Russian partisans on the eastern front of the Russian Civil War in 1920. In film scholar Amy Sargeant's analysis, the film legitimates the liberation of the Mongolian people and draws on the Eurasian ideology of "the geographical extent of the Soviet empire and its ethnic inclusivity" (2000, 115) in that it appropriates the Mongolian mythology of Genghis Khan in an ethnographic description of a purportedly barren culture. The centrality of Moscow (and Vladimir Lenin) is affirmed in the process of enlightenment undergone by the protagonist Bair, a naive trapper, until he realizes the atrocities of British imperialism, especially when he receives the final words of the commander of the Russian partisans: "Listen to Moscow ... go to the Russians, they are good and strong."

The reason *Proletaria Eiga* deals with this film, however, is to focus more on the alliance between the laboring masses of the metropole and colony than on the struggle for the national liberation of the colonized. The Japanese socialist filmmaker Sasa Genjū (佐々元十, 1900–59) suggests in his contribution to the special issue that "Marxist film critics should promote the awakening of the laborer masses of the metropole and colony, and ultimately international solidarity." For Sasa, colonial cinema is defined as films "either set in the colony, or collecting materials from their colony, or describing the savage land before capitalization, or dealing with (semi) colonial nations." *Potomok Chingis-Khana* is the main focus of the special issue not because it accords with any definition of colonial cinema but rather because it proposes an alternative to it: that is, international solidarity to borrow Sasa's appropriation of a contemporary Socialist catchphrase. Solidarity, however, is to be formed by putting Moscow at the center of a concentric Communist circle that assimilates other ethnicities and nations in its periphery, although not in the exploitative manner of capitalist Western empires.

In this respect, the positionality of the agents of the Japanese socialist film movement is identified with Bair and his Mongolian people allied with Moscow on the one hand and with Moscow as the center of the Communist movement on the other—that is, it premises the leading subject position of the metropole in relation to the laboring masses of the colonies such as Taiwan and Korea. Following Sasa's perspective that the world is divided into two kinds of nations, the imperial nations and oppressed nations, Japan should be considered an imperial nation that parallels the position of the British empire in *Potomok Chingis-Khana*. But as revealed in all the articles in the special issue of *Proletaria Eiga*, in which little interest in Japan's colonies is expressed, Japanese intellectuals regarded themselves more as a center of the Asian socialist movement, an Asian version of Moscow, than as a metropole. The center-periphery dichotomy in Soviet Eurasianism is reiterated in the Japanese socialist film movement, especially when Sasa declares that colonial proletarian film movements can achieve their mission "only if they unite with proletarian film movements in developed countries."

The focus of this chapter, however, is more on the typology of colonial cinema exemplified in *Potomok Chingis-Khana* than the centrality of Japanese agency itself in the socialist alliance between metropole and colony; the latter of which is a reflection of the sixth Comintern conference in 1928 that merges the Korean Communist Party into either the Japanese or the Chinese one under the banner of "one country, one party." Just as *Potomok Chingis-Khana* under director Pudovkin presents Bair, the presumed prince of ancient lineage, incarnated in the actor Valery Inkijinoff, as a typical Mongolian, a specific popular figure presents an image of the Korean male fighter in the era of socialist alliance between Japan and Korea.

The figure of the malcontent Korean [不逞鮮人; Korean, *pullyŏng sŏnin*; Japanese, *futei senjin*] that is embodied in the movie star Na Un-kyu (羅雲奎, 1902–37), whom I will examine later in this chapter, does not appropriate a traditional ethnic hero such as Genghis Khan or Stenka Lazin inherited by Bair's character, but he is rather a recent product of Japan's annexation of Korea. Unlike the infantilized, naive, and submissive images of the colonized Korean that are best exemplified in the female figure of the *kisaeng* (professional entertainer) in Korean and Japanese popular culture, *pullyŏng sŏnin* is perceived as untamed, rebellious, and violent, even prone to assassinate the Japanese emperor or to poison Japanese civilians to death. As I will demonstrate, a few Japanese socialists actively appropriated the popular image of *pullyŏng sŏnin* as a colonial comrade in their allied cultural movement, but, at the same time, they ethnographized Koreans as closer to nature, rather than as equally civilized. How then can we describe the function of ethno-national inclusivity in the socialist cultural project when it is applied to colonial comrades? In other words, does the socialist project resolve the issue of colonial taxonomy that ghettoizes the colonized as harboring a spontaneous defiance—the other side of the coin of the infantilized, domesticated image of the colonized?

Can a *Pullyŏng Sŏnin* Liberate the Colonized and Colonizer?

Historian Jinhee Lee (2013) traces the genealogy of the *pullyŏng sŏnin* in Japanese official documents and popular media and analyzes how the construction and circulation of the racial imaginary of the *pullyŏng sŏnin* is derived from the ambiguities present in Japanese colonialism. The Japanese empire had to promote the assimilation of Koreans but needed to distinguish "bad" Koreans from "good" Koreans to discern those it perceived as enemies within. Unlike European empires, the Japanese empire had "similar looking Asians both as the colonizer and the colonized"(Jinhee Lee 2013, 120) and was thereby confronted with the task of identifying and regulating Koreans who had few or no visible physical differences from the Japanese. Lee writes, "The dilemma that Imperial Japan had to face, then, was how to identify the 'inferior' elements of the empire's subjects that were physically invisible, and preach to discipline and assimilate them while simultaneously keeping them inferior for the purpose of maintaining the hierarchical order in the empire" (Jinhee Lee 2013, 120).

As clarified in the detailed information contained in *The Source Material* of 1913 (J. Lee 2013, 133) to distinguish the physical features of Koreans, the Japanese empire tried to construct physiological knowledge about Korean bodies and faces: that Koreans have straighter posture than Japanese; less and smoother hair, less facial hair, flatter faces (*noppori gao*) than Japanese; and a flatter head in the back than Japanese (from the use of wooden pillows).[1] It seems that not only was this body of knowledge circulated among the authorities but it also was widely popularized among civilians, and it became the justification for Japanese vigilantes to identify *pullyŏng sŏnin* in the 1923 massacre immediately after the Kanto earthquake. The horrific ramifications of the term become apparent when we consider the massacre of thousands of innocent Korean migrants in Japan; the Japanese public believed *pullyŏng sŏnin* were taking advantage of the natural disaster to wreak havoc. Han Sŭng-in, a survivor who successfully escaped the massacre, writes in his memoir that he was able to safely avoid the strict observation and scrutiny of the Japanese vigilantes because his outer appearance did not match the criteria above and because his Japanese was fluent (S. Han 1973, 52–53). The massacre demonstrates that the constructed Korean typology could always be (mis)used by any Japanese expressing the colonial affects of hatred or fear of the rebellious colonized in order to exterminate Koreans. Therefore, the concept of *pullyŏng sŏnin*, applied to a wide range of Koreans—from military independence fighters in China to socialist activists in Japan—became the term not only for violent rebels who threw bombs at Japanese police stations or attempted to assassinate Japanese leaders but also for civilians seen as potential terrorists.

The *pullyŏng sŏnin* was not always understood as threatening to the Japanese empire, however; it also worked to legitimize colonialism, as officials considered *pullyŏng sŏnin* behavior to be both predictable and controllable as official dissent. Following Ashis Nandy's (2010, 11–18) analysis of the homology between childhood and the state of being colonized, which a modern colonial system almost invariably employs, the untamed, rebellious, and violent *pullyŏng sŏnin* invoke childishness insofar as they are ignorant and unwilling to learn, and thus incorrigible. Simultaneously, the *kisaeng* are childlike in that they are innocent or corrigible. The former refers to the "childishness of immature adults," which is an unlovable savagery, and the latter refers to the "childlikeness of the child," a lovable savagery. The former can be repressed by managing and controlling rebellion through strict administration and rule of law, and the latter may be reformed through modernization. Despite the quite contradictory significations of *pullyŏng sŏnin* and *kisaeng*, they are altogether the cultural products of a colonialism that is based on modern concepts of progress and social evolution and that prioritizes adult masculinity and represses primitive childhood.

Ashis Nandy (2010) suggests that rebels and anticolonialists are welcomed by empire, because they are the players of colonialism who confirm or compensate for the system itself. In other words, colonialism produces not merely models of conformity but also models of "official" dissent: even when in opposition, that dissent remains predictable and under control (xii). Thus, true opposition should be located not in the dichotomy between oppressor and oppressed, but between the two and the modernity that is inextricable from colonialism, which turns oppressor and oppressed into complementary victims. Here, the wounds that modernity and colonialism have inflicted on those in the metropole should also be considered: those categories of childhood, old age, and nonmasculinity that are traditionally immanent in empire but have been repressed in the formation of the mature adult man as the modern ideal subjectivity. In this vein, the *pullyŏng sŏnin* figure, the childish Korean, can also be a projection of those repressed within the Japanese empire, whether it is applied by the socialist project or not.

Actor and filmmaker Na Un-kyu was introduced to Japanese socialist intellectuals not as a figure of the laboring masses in the colony, but as a representative Korean who incarnated "the hidden reference of resistance" of the *pullyŏng sŏnin* and who was building a national cinema out of the huge success of *Arirang* 아리랑 (Na Un-kyu 1926) and other films. This racial imaginary is also observable in other Japanese socialist cultural productions, including a poem I will analyze in the next section; but it is film criticism that makes legible the face of the colonized through the purported transparency of the universal language of cinema.

Recognizing the Other

In the late 1920s, the Hungarian film critic Béla Balázs asserted that cinema could be an aid to anthropology and psychology in the way it elaborated group physiognomy—as though groups (Others) could be identified solely by their physical characteristics. He was so devoted to the idea that film would serve as an important measuring stick that he went as far as to call for "a comparative science of gesture and mimicry, with research into these in order to find the common fundamental forms of expressive movement" (Balázs 1952, 81). In Mary Ann Doane's (2014) analysis, Balázs's assertion evidences the fact that "cinema is bound up from the very start with a profound otherness" (Doane 2014, 119), that is, with questions of colonialism. In foregrounding the human face and its close-up as the most specific characteristic of cinema, which differs from theatrical plays, the European film theory developed by Balázs was coined by facing others, the people of the colonies. The legibility of the face becomes an anchor for knowledge, which erases the unpredictability of the faces of these others that European intellectuals encounter. Just as Balázs's theory of the face was elaborated by observing the Asian actor Sessue Hayakawa in Hollywood as presenting an "inscrutable Asianness" (Doane 2014, 118), the Japanese socialists' internationalist project was developed by making the Korean actor Na Un-kyu legible through the expression of anticolonial sentiment.

Accordingly, I would like to shed light on the response by the Korean socialist poet and film critic Im Hwa (林和, 1908–53; see fig. 2.1) to the Japanese socialist cultural productions featuring the *pullyŏng sŏnin* as a way to examine what happens when a colonized socialist senses a discrepancy within a colonial taxidermy found even in the socialist project. Is it possible for the colonized to transgress the colonial typology and to imagine an alliance of laborer masses between the colony and the metropole? I try to answer this question by dealing with two exchanges in particular: the first, Im Hwa's own poetic response to a poem by the Japanese socialist poet and critic Nakano Shigeharu (中野重治, 1902–79), which describes Korean comrades who were deported from Japan in 1929; and the second, a piece of film criticism by Im Hwa arguing against the cinematic ethnographization of the colonized, evident in a 1930 essay by the Japanese proletariat poet Kōriyama Hiroshi (郡山弘史, 1902–66). Through a comparative and cross-textual reading of these four works—two poems and two pieces of film criticism—I examine how the proletarian alliance between the Japanese metropole and colonial Korea was imagined and foreclosed and how the Korean socialist Im Hwa tried to escape from the colonial typology by revealing the colonizer's wounds and by proposing "our true cinema" of the laboring masses of the colony and the metropole alike.

Revealing the Wound of the Colonizer

Rain Falling on Shinagawa Station
for Yi Puk-man and An Ho-yŏng in celebration of ×××
[Nakano Shigeharu 1929, excerpts]
Sayonara Sin

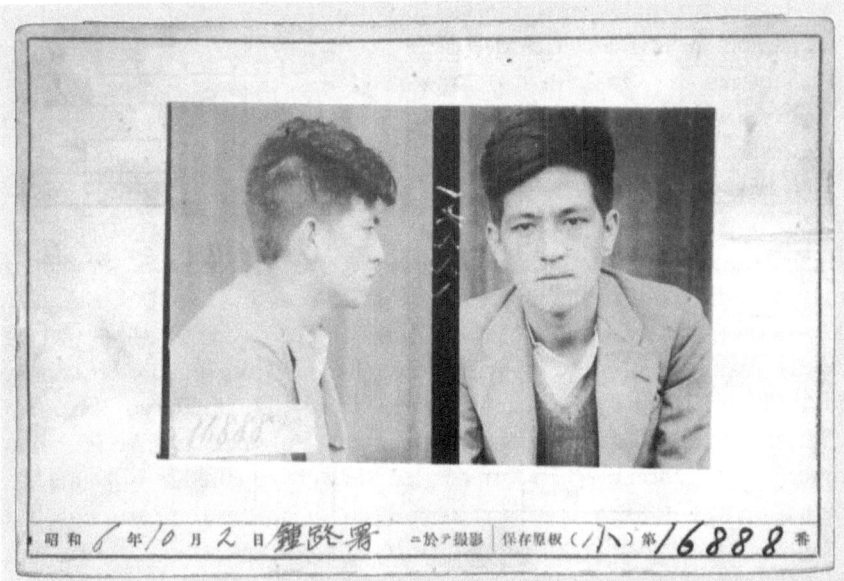

Figure 2.1. A mugshot of Im Hwa at Chongno Police Station on October 2, 1931. Im was charged with violation of the Maintenance of the Public Order Act. (*Ilche kamsi taesang inmul k'adŭ* [Japanese imperial surveillance cards]. http://db.history.go.kr /item/level.do?setId=3&totalCount=3&itemId=ia&synonym=off&chinessChar= on&page=1&pre_page=1&brokerPagingInfo=&position=2&levelId=ia_4580_3551 &searchKeywordType=BI&searchKeywordMethod=EQ&searchKeyword=%EC %9E%84%ED%99%94&searchKeywordConjunction=AND.

> Sayonara Kim
> You board the train as rain falls on Shinagawa Station
>
> Sayonara Yi
> Sayonara to the other Yi
> You return to the land of your parents
> . . . . .
> You Korean men and women
> Strong comrades to the back and bone
> Front and rear shield of the Japanese proletariat
> . . . . .
> Rush upon Tokyo via Kobe and Nagoya
> Approach his person,
> Appear suddenly before him
> Seize him

Push up against his jaw and hold it there,
Jab at his neck with your sickles
Shower your bodies with the gushing blood
In the warm joy of revenge
Cry! Laugh![2]
(*Musanja* 1929, 1; translation is mine)

Japanese writer and Communist Party member Nakano Shigeharu maintained a well-known interest in colonial Korea and kept ties with a few Korean activists. His poem "Rain Falling on Shinagawa Station" [雨の降る品川駅] was translated into Korean and published in the journal *Musanja* in 1929, which was run by the major Korean Marxist group in Tokyo. The poem, dedicated to the Korean leaders of Musanja, Yi Puk-man, and An Ho-yŏng, describes the moment when Korean activists were expelled from Japan. The expulsion was motivated by the enthronement of Japanese emperor Hirohito in 1928 and was meant to ameliorate the threatening and rebellious situation. Nakano adopts the voice of a Japanese activist who is seeing his Korean comrades off at the rainy Shinagawa station. The narrator calls his Korean comrades' last names—Sin, Kim, and Yi—to say goodbye and summons them to Tokyo to take revenge against the Japanese emperor.

As seen in the last part of the poem, the narrator asks his Korean comrades to close in on the emperor, seize him, and, finally, slash his neck. Actually, the identity behind the word *him* or *kare* here is not entirely clear. But it is widely known that "he" is the Japanese emperor, and Nakano himself explained after World War II that the three characters (represented here as x x x) erased from the dedication of the poem are enthronement [御大典]. The narrator also calls his Korean comrades the "front and rear shield of the Japanese proletariat," who could assassinate the emperor with sickles and would finally be intoxicated with the joy of victory when the emperor's blood is splattered on their bodies. The rebellious and violent image of the colonized comrades, who are the agents of vicarious revenge for the Japanese socialist activists who bear hostility to the emperor, is, I argue, an appropriation of the widely known stereotype of the *pullyŏng sŏnin*. By adopting this prevalent typology, Nakano's description capitalizes on the spontaneous rebelliousness of the colonized and sets aside the *conscience solidaire* and sense of equality between the proletariats of Japan and Korea. As the "front and rear shield of the Japanese proletariat," Nakano casts Koreans as reckless brutes who fight for the Japanese masses with their barbarous and instinctual ethnic nationalism.

Im Hwa's poem "The Pier of Yokohama under the Umbrella" has generally been interpreted as a response to Nakano's poem, reciprocating Nakano's sense of proletarian solidarity. Such readings are mainly based on the fact that the narrator is a Korean activist who is leaving Japan but promises to return and continue the struggle.

The Pier of Yokohama under the Umbrella
[Im Hwa, 1929; excerpts]

Oh my sweet love, girl of Yokohama.
Rain falls on the sea and the waves rise with the wind.
Leaving behind everything that remains
to return to the country of my mother and father,
I am afloat on the Pacific Ocean.
......
Kayo! Kayo! You must go back inside.
The siren has rung three times already and
the black uniform has pulled down my hands several times.
Now we must go: you must return and I must go.

Girl of the foreign land!
Don't shed any tears over those lads, or over me, no longer to be there in the demonstration that sweeps down the street.
Do not miss me because I will no longer be waiting behind the light pole when you leave the factory.
There will be another wave of young laborers to strengthen your heart,
and the hands of the love-deprived child-workers will be awaiting you.[3]
(*Chosŏnjigwang*, 1929. 9. translated by Ji-won Shin (David R. McCann, ed. 2004)

My focus of analysis here is how in the poem Im Hwa establishes the relationship between the Korean and Japanese activists as heterosexual lovers who have been and will continue fighting with the same goal in mind as fellow laborers. As both a lover and a comrade to his Japanese girlfriend, Kayo, the Korean activist narrator reminds her of their shared class struggle in order to comfort and encourage her. Here, the difference between the colonizer and the colonized is displaced by a parity between two people who are at once lovers and comrades. Even though the Korean man is being expelled from Japan, Korean activists remain in prison; and young Korean laborers in Kayo's factory are waiting for her care as a fellow comrade. In this case, the position of the individual Korean activist is interchangeable with other Korean comrades in Japan, and the exclusive relationship between the heterosexual couple is sublimated into interethnic proletarian solidarity. In the last part of this poem, the narrator repeatedly asks his lover, who is seeing him off in Yokohama, to go back to carry out her own mission—to continue her relationship with other Korean comrades in Japan instead of dwelling on his individual deportation. Karen Thornber (2009) writes that the narrator redefines the friendships between Koreans and Japanese as mutually beneficial relationships between politically aware cohorts, in which one party is not dehumanized for the glory of the other. But the gendered image of this interethnic, heterosexual couple invites further examination. Im relies on the masculinized figure of the *pullyŏng sŏnin* and transforms its image from one of spontaneous, instinctual action to one of a conscious, rational class struggle by gendering the Japanese comrades as dependent, emotional, and feminine.

The articulation of gender in Im Hwa's poem reminds us of the contemporaneous issue of the *pullyŏng sŏnin* couple, Pak Yŏl (朴烈, 1902–74) and his Japanese wife, Kaneko Fumiko (金子文子, 1903–26), who were arrested in 1923 for treason in Tokyo, as it foregrounds the Japanese comrade and wife of a male Korean activist. Pak and Kaneko were running an anarchist group called Futeisha (不逞社), the name of which connotes the gathering of *pullyŏng sŏnin* when they were arrested by Japanese police immediately after the Kanto earthquake. Although it is still uncertain who initially circulated the rumor that Koreans were attacking Japanese civilians in order to benefit from the chaos triggered by the earthquake, Japanese police accused the Futeisha members of treason in order to ease the anxiety of Japanese civilians and to scapegoat them so as to legitimize the massacre of thousands of Koreans by Japanese vigilantes. What made Pak and Kaneko's case unique was that they never submitted to the legal and political authorities, and for this reason, the publication of news about their interrogation and trial in the mass media was banned for two years. As is known from the "mysterious photo incident,"[4] as it was called, which describes the couple's obscene pose, embracing each other in a courtroom, they seemed to tease the legal regime of the empire as well as the mass media that yearned for such sensationalism. More interesting, however, is the attitude of Kaneko: unlike Pak's daring to negotiate with the legal authorities, she consistently revealed her passionate love for Pak and his country, Korea. The embarrassment and rage of the Japanese authorities triggered by her audacious commitment to the *pullyŏng sŏnin* reached a peak during her pregnancy while in custody. It is said that the pregnancy led to her unexpected death in prison. Officially she was reported to have committed suicide; but a rumor that she was murdered continued to circulate, as was mentioned in a recent South Korean filmic description of the events, *Pak Yŏl* 박열 (Lee Jun-ik 2017). Whether or not the rumor is true, Kaneko Fumiko's is one of the rarest and most prominent cases of comradeship intertwined with conjugal love between Japanese and Korean activists. Furthermore, Kaneko made visible the long-repressed femininity of the colonizer—something that had been eliminated from the formation of the modern subjectivity that prioritizes the masculine adult. She had to be punished by death (whether by suicide or by force), because she revealed what should stay concealed in a colonial regime; in other words, she represented the least acceptable characteristic of empire: the colonizer's wound.

The image of the Korean-Japanese *pullyŏng sŏnin* couple in Im Hwa's poem shows the paradoxical inclusivity of the colonized embracing the wound of the colonizer. The passive, dependent, emotional, and childlike character of Kayo in the poem does less to confirm the type of the aggressive, childish *pullyŏng sŏnin* than it does to evoke the radical logic of the socialist movement for mutual liberation. In other words, Im Hwa seems to identify the narrator in Nakano's poem, the Japanese primary force between the front and rear shield of Koreans, as wounded and also in need of liberation—another victim of modernity's inextricability from colonialism.

The Legibility of the Korean Face[5]

A similar Japanese description of the colonized Korean—a modification of the long-standing *pullyŏng sŏnin* figure—is also observed in as different a field as film criticism. Although Nakano's Korean comrades have no concrete faces, fellow proletarian poet Kōriyama Hiroshi's film criticism highlights a specific individual movie star, Na Un-kyu, as a representative Korean (fig. 2.2). Kōriyama published the article "Chōsen eiga ni tsuite [On Korean Cinema]" in 1930, introducing Korean cinema for the first time in the Japanese proletarian film magazine *Shinkō Eiga*. His main focus was not, however, to elucidate the proletariat film movement in Korea but to contrast the popularity of what he calls the national cinema built by Na Un-kyu in Korea with the unpopularity of Japanese proletarian films among Japanese audiences. For Kōriyama, Na is unique in that he describes the Korean farmer's agony and economic hardship under colonial exploitation with such characters as the tramp, the madman, and the wanderer who finally leaves his family, his hometown, and Korea altogether. What is more interesting, Kōriyama stresses Na's appearance as that of a typical, representative Korean and relates it to national sentiment in Korean spectatorship. He writes,

> Na Un-kyu's face is neither that of a sheikh, nor that of a villain whom we are accustomed to seeing in motion pictures. Rather, his flat face can be read as a representative of the Korean people, if you are somewhat familiar with it. Moreover,

Figure 2.2. Na Un-kyu. Courtesy of Korean Film Archive.

his severely grim face conveys the atmosphere of a dreary basement. The clear movement of his pupils, those hollow cheeks, a wide mouth and sharp teeth, a frail-looking medium build, and his talented legs that manage both mincing steps and a great pace. Consequently, he is the right man for the role of a madman in *Arirang* (1926) as well as a tramp in *P'unguna* 풍운아 (A Soldier of Fortune, Na Un-kyu,1926) and *Tŭlchwi* 들쥐 (The Field Mouse, Na Un-kyu, 1927).... I think the popularity of Na's films in Korea is a remarkable phenomenon, especially when compared to Japanese proletarian films' inferiority to commercial films in terms of their popularity. The hidden reference to resistance in Na Un-kyu's films always represents Korean people's popular sentiment.... The colonial situation of the present Korean nation will not disappear from the people's minds. The national sentiment has infiltrated deep into Korean people's sentiment, almost like an innate feeling of resistance, while it was obtained by the people of other powerful nations through the application of reason. This colonial sentiment has supported their films in spite of various technical issues, enabling them to compete with qualified foreign films in the domestic market with a strong appeal for Korean spectators. (Kōriyama 1930, 132; translation is mine.)

Na's appearance was far from that of a typical movie star, as Kōriyama describes it, and has generally been considered as evidence that his charisma derived from a unique acting talent. This opinion has been solidified through a long process of casting Na as the founder of Korean national cinema in both South and North Korean film historiography after liberation. It is Kōriyama, however, who first makes the unique move of relating Na's appearance to his apt screen personae, and through Na's national sentiment, "the hidden reference of resistance." Kōriyama finds—in such Na personae as the wanderer, the tramp, the thief, the madman, and the mute who murders the villain or commits arson to save the weak—to be allegorical figures of resistance by the colonized Korean. Redirecting opposition to Japanese rule through these allegorical figures was, he believes, a way to avoid censorship while maintaining popular appeal within the colony.

Born in Hoeryŏng in 1901, Na Un-kyu soon became a central figure in Korean cinema in the mid-1920s with his successful career not only as an actor but also as a writer and director. The decisive moment came with *Arirang*, to which he contributed his talent in acting, directing, and most of all in documenting the contemporary issue of the miserable lives of farmers. Another element that made the film a classic of colonial Korean cinema in later film historiographies was the clever management of music, in that the song "Arirang," composed for this film and based on the popular folk song of the same name, was sung not only by the characters in the film but also by the spectators at the theaters who were invited to follow the instructions in the titles. The colonial government finally banned the release of the recording of this song to preclude its circulation, because the song, colored with the sorrow of farmers, spread in popularity like an epidemic among Koreans. But the song "Arirang" had been popular even outside the peninsula during the colonial period, and today it has become such a beloved national song that it is played at public events, such as the Olympic Games, and on numerous private occasions. Although it is not clear whether colonial Koreans enjoyed the song for its national sentiment, it is true that they loved Na's film and its theme song "Arirang" even until the late colonial period; the film was awarded the best Korean silent film by five thousand Korean voters in the first and last Korean Film Festival in 1938, the year after Na's death.

For socialist intellectuals, however, Na was the most challenging figure to be overcome in order to form a socialist film culture. This was especially true in the late 1920s, when a series of socialist filmmakers and critics formed their first association, the Alliance of New Film Artists; their main targets were Na and his colleagues, whose films were growing in popularity among spectators. As I will examine later, Im Hwa, who performed the roles of young (assumed socialist) intellectuals in several socialist films and who began his career as a film critic in 1926, acidly criticized Na and his films as catering to a cheap national sentimentalism, as well as a vulgar Americanism. Na's films, for Im Hwa, gained popularity both by appealing to the defeatist grief of Koreans, as shown in the mournful tone of the song "Arirang," and by imitating American films. Spontaneous resistance to landlords and bourgeoisie, incarnated both in Na's personae (such as the madman and the tramp) and in the characters' impulsive crimes (such as arson and murder with such primitive weapons as sickles or axes), contrasted with the scientific knowledge and methods of struggle that the socialist movement needed to adopt. Na's speedy editing style, application of slapstick comedy conventions as well as swashbucklers mimicking American films (Na was known to be the Korean Richard Talmadge or Douglas Fairbanks) were also criticized as anachronistic in the transitional era when the socialist movement was emerging, anticipating cinema's effectiveness as a weapon in the fight against capitalism.

I'd like to pay special attention to the expression "flat face" that Kōriyama uses to describe Na Un-kyu. Kōriyama added that the face "can be read as a representative of the Korean people, if you are somewhat familiar with it." His comment reminds us (and Japanese readers at that time) of the typology of the Korean that I discussed in the previous section, of which flatness is crucial in identifying the faces of Koreans. Kōriyama here reaffirms the colonial taxonomy, in this case through the new technology of film that supports such physiognomic classification. Kōriyama, who had spent the years 1924 to 1928 in Korea, might have felt a sense of solidarity with the Korean subaltern, just like Nakano, when he was introducing Korean cinema to Japanese socialists for the first time. "The hidden reference of resistance" that he wanted to make legible from Na Un-kyu's appearance and screen personae might have been part of an endeavor to introduce unknown comrades in the colony to the empire's discursive visual field and, further, to inspire Japanese socialist activists to feel solidarity with their poor neighbors. But this visualization was a product of the ghettoization of the Korean body via visual anthropology. As Johannes Fabian (2002) contends, anthropology operates as a time machine, in that it is premised on notions of time that deny the contemporaneity or "coevalness" of the anthropologist and the people that he or she studies. In spite of Kōriyama's sympathetic or even envious description of the resistant hero in colonial popular culture, he interprets Na's appearance, his personae, and the audience's reception as undisciplined expressions of innate feelings, ripe for the application of reason—and control—by those more civilized.

Fatimah Tobing Rony (1996) labels the ways in which Western colonizers visualize the colonized and obsessively consume their images through visual media as "fascinating cannibalism," a term she deploys "to draw attention to the mixture of fascination and horror that the ethnographic occasions"(10). She writes, "The 'cannibalism' is not that of the people who are labeled Savages, but that of the consumers of the images of the bodies of native peoples offered up by popular media and science" (10). Kōriyama's manner of facing the colonial movie star Na Un-kyu appears not too distant from this cannibalism, in that it foregrounds the colonizer's fascination with the colonized's "innate feeling of resistance" while distancing the colonized from a contemporaneous Japanese proletarian subjectivity. Not unlike Nakano's (un)conscious appropriation of popular *pullyŏng sŏnin* figures who can assassinate the emperor with their primitive weapons, Kōriyama inadvertently excludes the colonial comrades from a coeval temporality—as well as from civilization itself.

Im Hwa's response (1930) to Kōriyama's article appeared in the same journal two months later.[6] Written in Japanese while Im Hwa was working at *Musanja* and acting as aide to its leader, Yi Puk-man, in Tokyo, Im's article exhibits perhaps the clearest vision of socialist film history in Korea up to that point. Im resolutely separates the *collateral* tendency of "presenting cheap, romantic national sentimentalism," which is represented by Na Un-kyu's films, from the *major* tendency of "producing films for proletarians and farmers," which is pioneered by a series of socialist filmmakers. On the basis of a socialist, evolutionary view of history, Im identifies the creation of the Alliance of New Film Artists in 1929 as the pivotal moment in the proletarian film movement in Korea. This is a direct criticism of Kōriyama's praise for Na as the core cinematic figure of Korean cinema in that Im declares the emergence of a new, major tendency that overcomes the reactionary characteristics of the national cinema. Incidentally, Im notes that the national cinema was increasingly abandoned as a site of class struggle in 1929, right after Kōriyama left Korea.

The most impressive moment in Im's criticism is in his repetition and problematization of Kōriyama's term "our cinema [我等の映畫]." Im intentionally borrows the term "our cinema" to indicate a broader category that included Japanese proletarian cinema, instead of following Kōriyama's practice of referring to Korean cinema as "*their* national cinema [emphasis is mine]." Kōriyama in effect distances himself from the object of Korean cinema, but Im repurposes the phrase "a cinema truly our own" to refer to cinema that includes both the Korean and Japanese laboring masses. Im writes,

> I think it is more meaningful to delineate the tendencies of Korean cinema, although this in itself is not sufficient, rather than to merely introduce the

history of Korean cinema. You Japanese readers might have realized the fact that there is cinema even in colonial Korea thanks to the introduction by someone named Kōriyama Hitoshi published in this journal, the first volume of this year. I would like, however, to share with you the more fortunate news that Korean proletarians and famers already have a "cinema truly our own" [本當の我々の映畫], not simply that found in [Kōriyama's] unusual, superficial introduction of Korean cinema. (Im Hwa 1930, 116; translation is mine.)

Im's phrasing is a somewhat confrontational way of asking Japanese socialists as well as Kōriyama personally whether the proletariat of the colonized can truly be allied with that of the colonizer. By dismantling the strong link between the signifier (that is, "our cinema") and the inferentially signified (that is, "their cinema") applied by a Japanese proletarian writer, Im trenchantly and effectively violates the unspoken rule of segregation between the Japanese and Korean proletarian movements. This was the reason for Im to publish his article in a Japanese socialist film magazine, sharing fortunate news and expecting acclamation from the Japanese "laboring masses."

What then would a cinema "truly our own," one that does not reduce the colonial comrades to a single, legible face full of national sentiment, actually look like? Although it is not clear, mainly because none of the Korean films Im mentions has survived, he seems to suggest a socialist alliance by intentionally using the term "(Soviet) montage" as a sign of a universal filmic language experimented with in Korea. He mentions the film *Honga* 혼가 (A house)—directed by Kim Yu-yŏng, one of the founders of the Alliance of New Film Artists who visited Japan to build a network with Japanese socialist filmmakers in 1930—which featured the technique of montage in 1929. First introduced in Japan through Iwasaki Akira's translation of Sergei Timoshenko's "Art of the Cinema" in 1928, montage was gaining attention in the early 1930s not only from Japanese socialists but also from Korean intellectuals. Although we are not able to see what kind of montage Im mentions in *Honga*, about which no concrete information survives, we can refer to the scenario of another socialist film, *Hwaryun* 화륜 (Flaming wheel, Kim Yu-yŏng, 1931), in which a similar montage of shots of a roaring lion, as featured in Sergei M. Eisenstein's *Bronenosets Potemkin* (Battleship Potemkin, 1925), was inserted to metaphorically describe the rage of enlightened laborers who go on strike. The laborers are rebellious, like *pullyŏng sŏnin* in a way, but they have a consciousness of their class rather than merely reacting with spontaneous, innate national feelings. Just as Eisenstein criticizes Béla Balázs's theory of the face for ignoring the "scissor" that defines cinema as an art of editing, the montage emphasizes the relations between the laborers' enlightenment and the lion's roaring; between film and society; between filmmakers and spectators; and, further, between colony and metropole—rather than ghettoizing a single face into a symbol of national sentiment.

By foregrounding the coevalness of the parallel adoption of Soviet montage, a 'universal' filmic language, by the socialist film movements in both Korea and Japan, Im cleverly transgresses the discrepancy between the colony and the metropole present in Kōriyama's introduction, despite his favorable appraisal of national sentiment in Korean cinema.

Conclusion

After a few years in a slump, Na Un-kyu's career enjoyed a second round of prosperity with the success of *Imcha ŏmnŭn Narutpae* 임자없는 나룻배 (A ferryboat without an owner, Yi Kyu-hwan, 1932), this time through the performance of an old boatman, Ch'unsam, who takes revenge against the villain who raped his daughter (fig. 2.3). The rebellious persona persists, especially when Ch'unsam tries to destroy the railroad that deprived him of his work as a boatman, using an axe, a typical primitive weapon for the *pullyŏng sŏnin*, alongside the sickle, as described in Nakano's poem. Signaling Na's return with a shaved head, which exemplifies his strenuous effort, the film also demonstrates how the assumed national sentiment was now established as one of the appealing points of Korean films in the Japanese market. Director Yi Kyu-hwan (1904–82) studied at Shinkō Kinema for three years and is known as a disciple of the Japanese director Suzuki Sigeyoshi, and his *Imcha ŏmnŭn Narutpae* foreshadowed a new era in which Korean films, with their local color, were produced for an expanding Japanese market by a new generation of filmmakers who had studied in Japan. A Korean critic appraised the film as attaining a superior level in directing and clear cinematography and as providing "a stereotype of Korean people" (Hŏ 1932) through Ch'unsam's character. Just as photographs of An Chung-gŭn, who in 1909 assassinated the first governor general of Korea, Ito Hirobumi, became a popular product for consumption among Japanese as a case of the "fascinating cannibalism" of the *pullyŏng sŏnin*, so too the national sentiment of colonized Koreans was then commodified as an export after it achieved a global standard in production value. This case suggests how malcontents may no longer pose as threatening to the oppressors at all because they become predictable and controllable through the form of the commodity, if not directly through legal regulations.

By contrast, more threatening to the empire would be to question the very basis of modernity itself, which is inextricable from colonialism. To question modernity might entail revealing the nonadult, nonmasculine aspects that

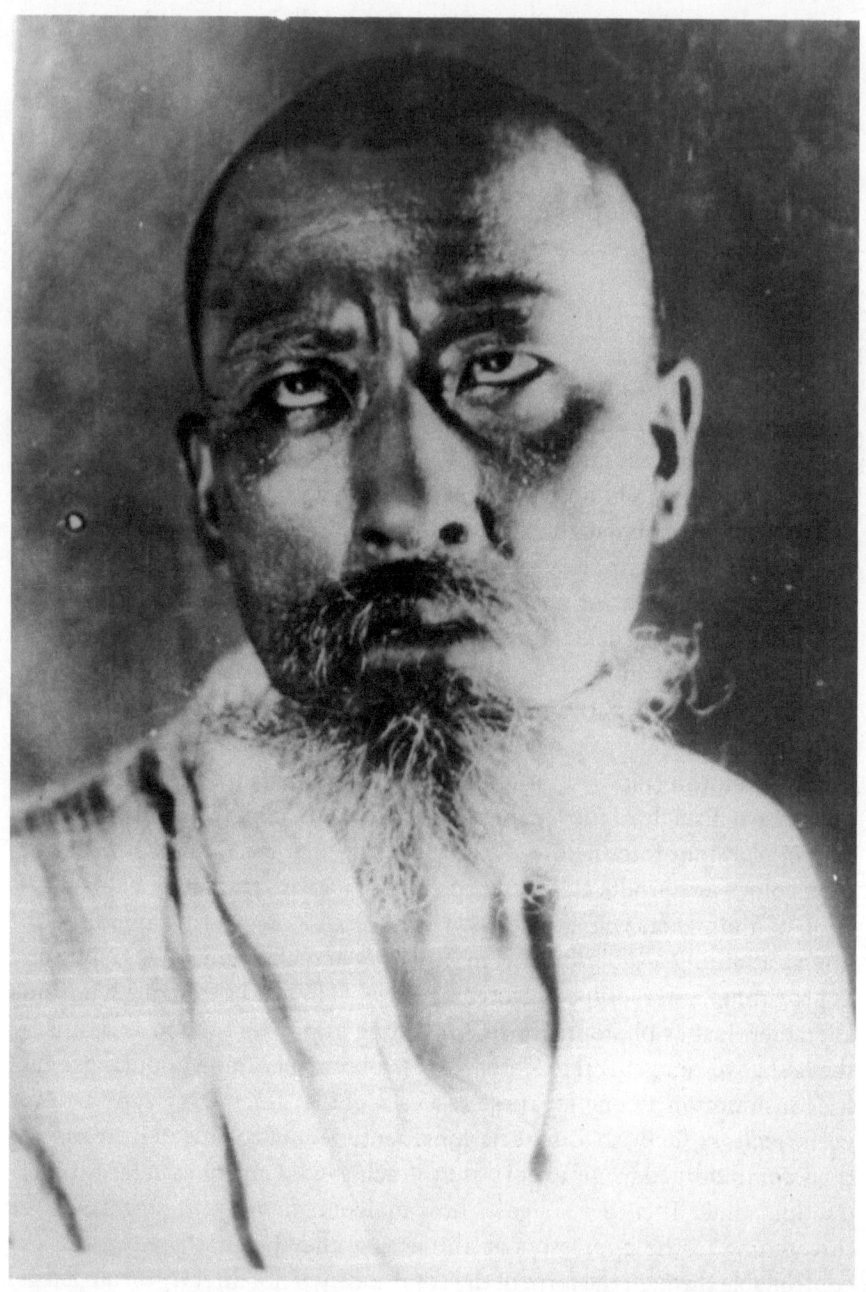

Figure 2.3. Na Un-kyu in *Imchaŏmnŭn Narutpae* (A ferryboat without an owner, 1932). Courtesy of Korean Film Archive.

are supposed to be removed from the psychology of the empire, or emphasizing a truly shared sense of belonging that is purported to obtain in the ideal of alliance or equality between the laboring masses of the colony and the metropole, all of which Im Hwa tries to argue for in his poetic and discursive response to the socialist intellectuals of Japan. For Nakano and Kōriyama, it might in part be the colonial project's positioning populations of "others" as primitive and unenlightened that created the conditions of possibility for proletarian solidarity between Japanese and Koreans. Japanese visualization of Korean comrades as *pullyŏng sŏnin*, full of rebellious national sentiment, can be interpreted as a process of confronting disparate colonial others and of claiming their own metropolitan position as the primary force of a universal movement. The difference between their portrayals and the adaptations of the *pullyŏng sŏnin* typology might have been a prerequisite condition for even beginning to approach international proletarian solidarity. If so, Im Hwa's responses to the ethnographization of Koreans by Japanese writers can be understood as not merely problematizing the ethnic and racial difference inherent in the Japanese proletarian discussion. They also challenge the very premise of modernity itself, which is still entwined with colonialism.

Notes

1. This knowledge was accumulated through the institutionalized research of anthropologists such as Torii Ryūzō (1870–1953), who conducted an extensive survey on Koreans in the 1910s.

2. Here, I translate the Korean translation of Nakano's poem, not the original Japanese version published in *Kaizō* with many censored words and phrases. The Korean translation fills in with clear expressions most of the phrases omitted in the Japanese version. According to literary scholar Han Ki-hyŏng, the reason for this discrepancy is that *Musanja* was an illegal journal not aiming for distribution in the market, while *Kaizō* was a legally distributed journal that had to be censored. It is still unclear whether Nakano himself was aware of or overlooked this restoration or supplement in the Korean translation, but it is possible that he gave his blessing to the new version because of the close relationship between Nakano and Yi Puk-man, a leader of the journal *Musanja* (K. Han 2010).

3. Im Hwa, *Chosŏnjigwang*, 1929. 9; David R. McCann, ed., *The Columbia Anthology of Modern Korean Poetry* (Columbia University Press, 2004), 45–46.

4. The "mysterious" refers to the strange fact that the photograph was circulated among a number of journalists in 1926 and then published in 1927, four years after the arrest of Pak and Kaneko, and that a few documents on how the photo was taken and how it was leaked outside the prison were circulated along with the photo. The archivist Yi Kyŏng-min (2006) examines how the incident was related to the Japanese political situation at the time, in which the oppositional party was attacking the Wakatsuki cabinet for mishandling the "high treason" of Pak and Kaneko, which resulted in a long process of political negotiations, including the prosecution and expulsion of a few personnel involved in the treason case.

5. The main argument of this section was originally included in my book (Baek 2015, 28–43).

6. Im Hwa is widely known as an influential Korean socialist poet and literary critic, though his film criticism is rarely introduced to English readership. Recently, two of his articles on late colonial Korean film, "Chosŏn Yŏnghwaron [Discourse on Chosŏn cinema I]" and "Chosŏn Yŏnghwaron [Discourse on Chosŏn cinema II]," originally published in 1941 and 1942, have been translated into English and appeared in the *Journal of Japanese and Korean Cinema* volume 11, no. 2, and volume 12,

no. 1, in 2019 and 2020. Also, my short introduction, "Im Hwa: Colonial Film Criticism in Korea," on Im Hwa's film criticism was published in the same journal in volume 12, no. 2, in 2020.

BIBLIOGRAPHY

Baek Moonim. 2015. *Im Hwa ŭi Yŏnghwa* [Im Hwa's cinema]. Seoul: Somyŏng.
Belázs, Béla. 1952. *Theory of the Film: Character and Growth of a New Art*. London: Dennis Dobson.
Doane, Mary Ann. 2014. "Facing a Universal Language." *New German Critique* 41, no. 2 (122, Summer): 111–124.
Fabian, Johannes. 2002. *Time and the Other: How Anthropology Makes Its Objects*. New York: Columbia University Press.
Han Ki-hyŏng. 2010. " 'Pŏpyŏk' kwa 'Munyŏk': Cheguk Naebu ŭi Pyohyŏnnyŏk Ch'ai wa Ch'ulp'an Sijang [The "jurisdiction" and "limits of the possibility of representation in each jurisdiction": the distinction of expressing possibility and publishing market, inside the Japanese empire]," *Minjok Munhaksa Yŏngu* vol. 44: 309–339.
Han Sŭng-in. 1973. *Tonggyŏngi Bult'altt'ae: Tonggyŏng Taejinjae Chonangi* [When Tokyo was burning: A memoir of distress during the Great Tokyo Earthquake]. Seoul: Taesŏng Munhwasa.
Hŏ Sim. 1932. "Yusin Kinema Ihoejak *Imchaŏmnŭn Narutpae* [A ferryboat without an owner: the second production of Yusin Kinema]." *Tong-A Ilbo* Sep. 14.
Im Hwa. 1929. 9. "The Pier of Yokohama under the Umbrella." *Chosŏnjigwang* vol. 87.
Im Hwa. 1930. "Chōsen eiga no shokeikō ni tsuite [On Several Tendencies in Korean Cinema]." *Shinkō Eiga* [New Cinema] 2, no. 3: 115–24.
Kim Yu-yŏng, 1931. *Hwaryun* [Flaming wheel]. Seoul: Seoul Kino.
Kōriyama Hiroshi. 1930. "Chōsen eiga ni tsuite [On Korean Cinema]." *Shinkō Eiga* 2, no. 1: 131–34.
Lee Jinhee. 2013. "Malcontent Koreans (*Futei Senjin*): Towards a Genealogy of Colonial Representation of Koreans in Japanese Empire." *Studies on Asia*, 4th ser., 3, no. 1, (March): 117–181.
Lee Jun-ik, 2017. *Pak Yŏl* [Anarchist from colony]. Seoul: Pakyŏl Culture Company.
McCann, David R., ed. 2004. *The Columbia Anthology of Modern Korean Poetry*. New York: Columbia University Press.
Nakano Shigeharu. 1929. 1. "Rain Falling on Shinagawa Station." *Musanja*.
Nandy, Ashis. 2010. *The Intimate Enemy: Loss and Recovery of Self under Colonialism*. 2nd ed. New Delhi: Oxford University Press.
Na Un-kyu, dir. 1926. *Arirang*. Seoul: Chosŏn Kinema.
Pudovkin, Vsevolod, 1928. *Potomok Chingis-Khana* [Storm over Asia]. Moscow: Mezhrabpomfilm.
Rony, Fatimah Tobing. 1996. *The Third Eye: Race, Cinema, and Ethnographic Spectacles*. Durham, NC: Duke University Press.
Sasa Genjū. 1930. "Shokuminchi eiga ni tsuite [On Colonial Cinema]." *Proletaria Eiga* 2. no. 9: 16–27.
Sargeant, Amy. 2000. *Vsevolod Pudovkin*. KINO, the Russian Cinema Series. London: Bloomsbury.
Thornber, Karen L. 2009. *Empire of Texts in Motion: Chinese, Korean, and Taiwanese Transculturation of Japanese Literature*. Cambridge, MA: Harvard University Press.
Yi Kyŏng-min. 2006. "Anakist Pak Yŏl pubu ŭi Koesajinsakŏn [The mysterious photo incident of anarchist Pak Yŏl and his wife]." *Hwanghae Munhwa* 53, 12: 331–339.

MOONIM BAEK is Professor of Korean Language and Literature at Yonsei University. She is author of *Chum A-ut: Hankuk Yŏnghwa ŭi Chŏngch'ihak* (Zoom-out: Politics of Korean cinema), *Hyŏngŏn: Munhakkwa yŏnghwa ŭi wŏnkŭnpŏp* (Figural images: Perspectives on literature and film), *Wŏlha ŭi Yŏkoksŏng: Yŏkwiro Ponŭn Hankuk Kongpoyŏnghwasa* (Scream under the moon: Korean horror film history through female ghosts), and *Im Hwa ŭi Yŏnghwa* (Im Hwa's cinema).

3. COLONIAL-ERA FILM THEORY, SPECTATORSHIP, AND THE PROBLEM OF INTERNALIZATION

Aaron Gerow

Abstract

This chapter investigates the problem of internalization, or the colonization of the mind, in relation to colonial film culture of the Japanese Empire. Following on my earlier research on colonial-era Korean film, which I argue problematizes the subjectivity open to such internalization, this chapter investigates the relation of film theory to colonization. What was the role of film theory in the imperial metropole, and what valences did the film theory produced by colonial subjects bear in the empire? Such questions are complicated by the fact that Japanese film theory exhibited what I call a theory complex, in which even Japanese did not recognize Japanese film theory. What was the effect on the film theory of the colonized when the theory of the colonizer itself was in a neocolonial relationship with Europe? Considering the possibility that theorizing spectatorship was one means of reflecting on the colonial theorist's own relationship to the metropole, I analyze a number of texts published in Japanese by writers in colonial Korea and the puppet state of Manchukuo, focusing in particular on articles written by Im Hwa and O Yŏng-jin. In these, spectatorship becomes a problem for empire, as internalization is complicated by action over and against language. The effect of a push for a solution involves less internalization of empire than, in one case, the spectator pushed toward madness or, with O, imagining a new postcinema of attractions that overwhelms an externalized viewer.

The Question of Internalization

The question of internalization of the imperial gaze of white colonizers by the nonwhite colonized in their self-perception has been central to discussions of the effects of colonialism on subjectivity and colonial societies. For example, in what has by now become a classic in the postcolonial canon, Frantz Fanon writes in *The Wretched of the Earth* from the experience of European colonization of Africa that "the colonialist bourgeoisie, by way of its academics, had implanted in the minds of the colonized that the essential values—meaning Western values—remain eternal despite all errors attributable to man. The colonized intellectual accepted the cogency of these ideas and there in the back of his mind stood a sentinel on duty guarding the Greco-Latin pedestal" (Fanon 2004, 11).

This internalization of the racialized gaze of the colonizers turned inward by the colonized toward himself, which is often inseparable from the adoption of the colonizer's ideas and values, can be as crucial to sustaining colonialism as the violence of legal or military force. The internal state of the colonized subject then becomes a significant site of analysis in considering colonial entanglements. I would like to take the opportunity in this retrospective volume to draw attention to Fanon's preferred use of the term *epidermalization* as a metonymy of this internalization and its relevance to discussing the influence of the theoretical culture of the metropole on cinema in the colonial empire.

To Fanon, the acceptance of the racist gaze and its assumptions about the inferiority of the colonized on the basis of the color of one's skin is none other than the internalization of the external epidermalization of value. With "no culture, no civilization, and no 'long historical past,'" black identity is assumed to be only the mask of whiteness that the colonized are given—their only internal being is therefore surface, skin-deep (Fanon 2008, 17). Internalization is then not simply an issue of colonial values that are internalized but also of the shape of that "internal" space within colonial spatial dynamics—the mapping of the body/surface into the psyche/internal—and of intersubjective relations.

In this chapter, I would like to speculate about what such a psychosomatic internalization of the social systems of colonial oppression might mean in the context of the Japanese Empire, when racial visibility on the surface of the skin is more nuanced or even invisible in the context of colonizing proximate neighbors within Asia, and when Japanese themselves are situated in a triangulation of Japanese imperial aggression in Asia on one side while being subjected themselves to racialized imaginations from Euro-American powers on the other. This is particularly pertinent with regard to the medium of film, which continued to have an ambivalent status within Japan arising from its apparent origin in the West.

I recently published one analysis of colonial-era Korean cinema that considered internalization of the colonizer's racism through the visual prism of film form (Gerow 2015). There I pointed to complex and sometimes contradictory formulations of internal voices in several colonial-era films to cast doubt on any assumption that Korean filmmakers simply internalized Japanese film language or the imperial voice. The next step in my research is to speculate about this internalization with regard to film theory, in particular with regard to attempts to conceptualize what cinema is and should do. There is increasing research on the complicated history of colonial cinema in East Asia, which has been foundational for my work, but few scholars have shifted the focus from analysis of the films themselves to the theory behind them (Baek 2018; Baskett 2008; Chiu 2011; Fujitani and Kwon 2012; High 2003; Hori 2017; Kim 2017; Kramer 2012; Lee 2019; Lin and Kim 2019; Misawa 2014; Taylor-Jones 2017; Yecies and Shim 2011). Because film theory has long assumed—and arguably still continues to assume—the mantle of universality, it is essential to ask what the conceptual importance of colonialism is for writing a history of film theory. My own research on Japanese film theory broaches the issue of the still-ongoing neocolonial relation between the supposedly European center of film thinking and theory produced in Japan, and so one productive avenue would be to investigate the triangulation emerging from the doubly colonized aspects of film theory: the possibility that one set of colonized subjects internalized the colonized theory of their colonized colonizer. It is in this fraught position that I contend that important questions about spectatorship can be raised.

In my article on a selection of films produced in Korea during the era of its colonization by Japan, I argued that the very forms of the texts pose intriguing questions about the problem of internalization. Although they can seem to present examples of Korean characters quite literally internalizing the voices or visions of Japanese authority, they can also problematize the assumption that there is a distinct subject with an established internal terrain open to absorbing such influence. These films from colonial Korea, I argued, offer multiple examples of complex subjectivities crisscrossed by split subjectivities and intersubjective relations that render it difficult to clearly demarcate internal and external. If colonial-era Korean cinema seems concerned with internal states and point-of-view shots, it is less because it is opening up a space to be internalized by the colonial cinematic apparatus than because it is exhibiting in complex and ambiguous ways the cracks and contradictions in the very process of internalization itself and the essential problems at the heart of colonial subjectivity.

Can we locate similar issues in film theory produced in Korea and other colonial or occupied territories? Although it is not easy to establish a correspondence between a pattern in film form and a pattern in film theory, I argue that there is a concern with spectatorship that parallels the films' obsession with gazes and internal states. Just as it is difficult to survey all colonial cinema, particularly with the lack of extant prints, I do not intend to canvass all writings on cinema in Korea, Taiwan, Manchuria, or other occupied territories; rather, I focus on several intriguing examples of discussions of spectatorship in Korea and Manchuria that were written in Japanese by colonial subjects that complicate the conception that spectators internalize imperial cinema. The question is less about the imperial gaze than it is about theorizations of how spectators work with films—and of how cinema should work on spectators. Just as they problematize the issue of colonial spectatorship, some additionally pose questions of readership through the fact they were written in Japanese. Although there are many more theoretical texts written in each native language, we can consider how the theorization of spectator internalization was both shaped and complicated by the language of the imperial metropole. Doing so can involve the "conundrum of representation" that Nayoung Aimee Kwon has described, in which "colonial cultural producers . . . necessarily and strategically were compelled to borrow the language of the hegemonic imperial Other in an attempt to voice themselves and to have the Self heard at the imperial discursive table in the language of that imperial Other" (Kwon 2015, 10).

Discussions of film language and spectator understanding become doubly problematic when voiced in the language of the colonizer. Yet, as we shall see, this fraught position can be strategic, and it can also complicate the location of language—and cinema—in the internal-external divide, particularly when the language of theory in Japanese was itself rife with fissures. Such can be the case when neither the assertion nor the denial of the nation is innocent of the imperial project, leaving the fissures in between as the space for alternative practice.

A Japanese Film Theory?

One difficulty in discussing the effect of colonialism on theories of cinema in East Asia lies in attempting to assert the existence of a national film theory espoused by the colonial power. The issue is not divorced from the difficulties of discussing the internalization of Japanese film language or style. One of the problems of researching colonial-era Korean or Taiwanese cinema in terms of the internalization of Japanese film style is that (although there may have been, as Michael Baskett has argued, an "imperial Japanese film culture" [Baskett 2008, 3]) Japanese officials, filmmakers, and critics during the war could not always agree on what Japanese film style was or was supposed to be (Gerow 2005, Gerow 2009). As scholars such as Peter B. High

(2003), Furukawa Takahisa (2003), Katō Atsuko (2003), and Hikari Hori (2017) have argued, national policy film was not clearly defined and neither did it enjoy wide public support. The existence of colonies and occupied territories sparked intense debates and anxieties over not only which Japanese films should be shown there but also eventually what Japanese films should be—whether more Hollywood in style (Mori 1942) or something different in order to wean the colonized off Hollywood (Tsumura 1942). Japanese authorities and intellectuals found Japanese cinema of poor quality, and some expressed deep anxieties about what others in the empire thought of it.[1] The choice presented colonial filmmakers with a dilemma. If they are supposedly internalizing Japanese cinema as a modern cinema, one superior to that of the colonies, they are doing so with a cinema that Japanese authorities themselves had not considered sufficient to represent the modern Japanese Empire.

In light of such issues of film form, what of film theory? Dudley Andrew has defined film theory as the effort "to formulate a schematic notion of the capacity of film," which differs from film criticism in that the latter is "an appreciation of the value of individual works of cinema, not a comprehension of the cinematic capability" (Andrew 1976, 5). Film theory is thus an ontology or epistemology of film that is often claimed as foundational against the practical knowledge of film criticism or filmmaking because it aims for abstract knowledge that has value in itself. It is not mere coincidence that the canonical histories of film theory presented in North America or Europe have overwhelmingly centered on those regions, ignoring locations such as East Asia (e.g., Braudy and Cohen 2004, Stam 2000). Even those studies supportive of Japanese cinema culture have long refrained from examining its theoretical background. Noël Burch's 1978 book, *To the Distant Observer*, might have been influential in prompting a reconsideration of prewar Japanese film, but Burch still claimed that "the very notion of theory is alien to Japan; it is considered a property of Europe and the West" (13). Burch's comment might have been one way he constructed Japanese culture as resistant to, and thus a critique of, Western logocentrism and its cinematic equivalent, the classical Hollywood cinema, but it allows him to establish a monopoly over the practice of theorizing Japanese cinema and understanding its world-historical import. Japanese theorists are largely reduced to local informants at best. The alignment of film theory with the rational and the universal can explain why it was often mapped onto orientalist hierarchies placing West over East. As Naoki Sakai (2010b) has argued, the association of theory with the West is not simply a geopolitical means of defining the West above and against the rest: "The West is particular in itself, yet it constitutes the general point of reference in relation to which others recognize themselves as particularities.... It always engages in the universal validity of how particular objects are identified. In this respect it is transcendental" (Sakai 2010b, 450).

Thus the West alone is rendered capable of both universality and particularity, which is why it can pursue both philosophy and studies of itself and others, leaving the rest in the realm of the particular, to be studied or confined to area studies as just Chinese or Indian philosophy. The question is what happens to theory when a nation among the rest becomes an imperial power. Considering theory in such a colonial context is fruitful because claims for the command of the mind (theory) over the body (practice) can both illustrate and justify imperial control at the same time that they reveal contradictions in that control to the degree such terms may be defined through the structures of Western imperial modernity.

What especially constitutes a problem for this discussion is that the absence of Japanese theorists is also evident in Japan, as very few Japanese names appear in Japanese books introducing film theory.[2] Yet theoretical discussions in Japan of what cinema is and should be also inhabited a fundamentally contradictory position, primarily because of their inferior—one could say colonized—position vis-à-vis European theory. Their inferior position is not because of a dearth of profound thinkers, which could include Tosaka Jun, Imamura Taihei, Nakai Masakazu, Osaki Midori, Gonda Yasunosuke, Sugiyama Heiichi, Nagae Michitarō, Matsumoto Toshio, Yoshida Kijū, Matsuda Masao, Yajima Midori, and Hasumi Shigehiko.

Not only do historians and theorists seem to forget film theory in Japan, but the theory that is remembered is not even considered theory. This situation has led me to spotlight the compulsion to fret over the existence of film theory in Japan—what I have called a theory complex (Gerow 2010a, Gerow 2019)—to both forget theory and remember it in a different form, to insist Japan has no film theory but still "to formulate a schematic notion of the capacity of film." It is this problem that shapes not only how the history of Japanese film theory is narrated but also how such theories are pursued. The complex itself may constitute a form of intellectual self-colonization. Film theory became, as far back as the 1910s, a process in which intellectual reformers assumed the Euro-American gaze in order to define cinema in Japan (Gerow 2010c), establishing both the hierarchy of the West's cinema and theory over Japan's, as well as their inimical relation to Japanese film and culture (Gerow 2010b).

Analyzing this work, I find that much of that theory itself, especially under the contradictions of the theory complex, is significantly self-conscious, if not self-critical. I argue that, under these neocolonial conditions, Japanese film theory often performs theory at the same time that it reflects on the possibilities of theory, exhibiting a sort of "double-consciousness" (in W. E. B. Du Bois's sense [Du Bois 1897]), in which theory is performed at the same time there is a consciousness that this performance is inadequate under the standards of the European center. The double consciousness is further complicated by the triangulation with Asia, as attempts to assume the theoretical position may not be innocent of the desire to emulate the West's theoretical command of the East through Japan's theoretical command of the rest of Asia. Even when not conscious, such reflections on theories reveal gaps and contradictions in the relationship between theory, the nation, class, and subjectivity.

In its relationship to Eurocentric theory, then, prewar Japanese film theory may internalize many of the debates that shaped Euro-American discussions of film from the 1910s to the early 1940s: including arguing for film as art, celebrating montage, and investigating the long take. But such assimilation, I argue, is not smoothly internalized, and instead produces complications and questions, manifested in several ways. One was to interrogate the imbalance in the theoretical field. Terada Torahiko, for instance, both a celebrated physicist and an avid writer on cinema toward the end of his life, criticized an absence of Japaneseness in Japanese film theory: "The theory of film art that I have seen in Japan seems often to be work divorced from the Japanese. I have come to feel it is unfortunate that apparently relatively few of the theoretical studies of cinema have looked at film through Japanese history or national character" (Terada 1961, 6:136).

Terada was one of the few to openly call for a national film theory, but even his position could seem split and doubled as he advocated in the same essay a "Japanese global film," or a form of cosmopolitan cultural nationalism. Other forms of questioning were similarly conflicted but could involve efforts to seek alternatives to the triad Japan, cinema, theory. One was to search for alternative forms of theorizing, particularly in the realm of film criticism. One of the best examples of this is Osaki Midori's concept—and practice—of "random thoughts on cinema" (*eiga mansō*), introduced in a series of essays in the early 1930s, which reconceived the relationship between film and viewer (Osaki 1998, 2:94–148).

Overall, one could argue that many Japanese film theorists, in one form or another, manifested their multifarious positionality though conceptualizing cinema itself as centered in spectatorship, where audiences are seen as producing cinema. Theorists ranging from Gonda Yasunosuke to Nakai Masakazu and Nagae Michitarō explored this possibility from different angles. One manifestation of this line of questioning, evident in theorists such as Tosaka Jun and Imamura Taihei, was to conceptualize cinema itself as a new form of theorizing. If Imamura envisioned cinema, especially documentary and animation, as a return to primitive, material forms of thought, Tosaka considered film to be a means by which the proletariat conceptualized its own ways of living, effectively becoming a new mode of philosophy.

While film theory in Japan initially developed in part to establish the authority of intellectuals over domestic film spectators deemed insufficiently modern—a sort of domestic colonial relationship—many theorists also considered how spectators shaped and understood their own modernity through cinema. This line of thought could be viewed as a manifestation of such intellectuals thinking through their own place in the intellectual world system, in which they had been forced to serve as virtual spectators of the real theory occurring in Europe. Conceptualizing spectator reception as active and intimately enmeshed in cinematic processes was one means of complicating these geopolitical dynamics by rethinking the praxis of the local.

My question, then, is how colonial subjects relate to this film theory. Was there even a perception of a body of film theory that could be termed the theory of the Japanese metropole? Does looking at theory written by colonial subjects make us rethink the nature of Japanese film theory, especially the tensions between imperial and anticolonial tendencies? Did Japanese film theory function to reinforce hierarchies within the colonies? Even if it did, can we see in the work of some Japanese theorists a model for how not just Manchurian or Korean thinkers but any non-Western intellectual may approach the problem of the Eurocentrism of theory? In that case, it may make sense when analyzing theory produced by colonial subjects to investigate moments of self-consciousness about theory or of developing the possibilities of spectator-based modes of cinematic production and thinking. Yet, rather than seeing such moments as simply repeating a Japanese example, or as being completely separate cases, might they be conceived as emerging from a doubled or triangulated version of the complex that Japanese theorists encountered, in the same way other such colonial thinkers had to face both the imperial forces of a Japan that was itself facing the imperial West, in addition to Europe itself? Or perhaps we should see such colonial subjects producing a completely different, "resistant" mode of theory?

Pursuing such questions, I believe, can help us not only complicate the concept of internalization but also relativize both Japanese film theory and the received canon of Eurocentric film theory, showing their own imperial dimensions. Although I cannot address all these questions here, I would like to introduce several cases that pose possible resolution of these issues. In the end, I will show, in Im Hwa's spectators externalizing opposition through nonlinguistic speech and in O Yŏng-jin's viewers externalization through a virtually postcinematic mode of shock, how spectatorship became a fraught locus for articulating postionality in a colonial triangulation of Japan, the colony, and the Euro-American cinematic center. As colonial spectators were believed to be mad or turned inside out, theory became less about resistance and more about facing the limits of theory itself as it imagined a spectator of pure affect, yet one with potentially unruly effects.

Japanese Film Theory and Greater East Asia

First, it is difficult to discern a clear consciousness of a singular Japanese film theory existing in either the colonies or the metropole. Although, as already mentioned, some—like Terada—could call for establishing a Japanese film theory, that call was based on a perceived lack of or inadequacy within such a theory and was one rarely voiced by others. There were continuous calls for theory, which go back to the Pure Film Movement of the 1910s and early 1920s, where *kenkyū* (study, research) placed knowledge of the essence of cinema at the core of film reform and film production. Colonial writers echoed this stance and specified the need for study and theory in order to improve the poor state of Manchurian or Korean cinema. In Manchukuo, Zhou Guoqing, for instance, stressed the crucial role of intellectuals in improving Manchu cinema (Zhou 1940, 75). Im Hwa identified theory as a defining field for Korean proletarian cinema (Im 1930, 123), and Hinatsu Eitarō (Hŏ Yŏng), the colonial Korean director of *Kimi to Boku* (You and I, 1941), cited theory as a central means of improving Korean cinema's reception in Japan (Hinatsu 1941, 51). O Yŏng-jin, citing Japanese documentary's productive relationship between theory or study and practice, advocated less the emulation of that theory than the pursuit of a similar dialectic as essential to advancing Korean film (O 1942; 1943, 40). If Na Un-kyu's summary is correct, most of this theory was foreign and largely centered on European examples (Na 1937, 102).

Theory is here largely treated as a realm of universal truths, not of national or colonial difference. Such was also the case with much of Japanese philosophy. As Naoki Sakai has argued, even Kyoto School philosophers such as Nishida Kitarō or Tanabe Hajime, who in the postwar were revived in area studies as thinkers arguing from a Japanese perspective, were in fact resolutely committed to a universalist approach to philosophy (Sakai 2010a). Miki Kiyoshi could argue for "the world of worldliness" (*sekaisei no sekai*) in part to critique both a particularist Japanese ideology and a European thought that monopolized the center to the exclusion of others (Yonetani 2005). Yet as Sakai and Yonetani Masafumi have separately argued, it is crucial to consider how the universalism of the Kyoto School itself is imbricated with particularism, for instance, providing the conceptual justification for regional consolidation under Japanese ideals, or Japan's unique ability to overcome the modern. One could find Japanese thinkers who appear to echo Edward Said's European orientalist, "for whom such knowledge of Oriental society as he has is possible only for the European" (Said 1979, 197). Takahashi Tōru, for instance, a professor of Korean languages at Keijō Imperial University, described in a 1920 introduction to Korean culture a world of philosophy mired for seven hundred years in Neo-Confucianist thought: "In Korean philosophy there is no progress, no development—it has been fossilized from the start" (quoted in Kawase 2009, 154). This is just one example of how Japanese could render colonial subjects in the same light that Europeans rendered Japanese subjects.

One could similarly investigate to what degree Japanese film theory engaged in such imperialism in thought or claimed a universal that justified Japanese power. Japanese dominated but did not completely monopolize the pages of the intellectual film journals. One can find articles by colonial subjects in even more theoretical film journals such as *Eiga hyōron* (Film criticism), but they are invariably reports on local situations. Instead of debating cinema's relationship with reality, as many of the main contributors to *Eiga hyōron* did in the late 1930s, they essentially played the role of the local informant. It was as if Japanese theorists, privileged in their access to universal issues of cinema, laid the foundations on which colonial writers were then left to offer the particulars. At the same time, it was not unusual to find Japanese elucidating the specifics of colonial film cultures.

Debates about cinema were rarely a two-way street. Several roundtable discussions (*zadankai*) on Korean cinema appeared in major journals featuring both Japanese and Korean participants, but aside from them, the conceptual playing field was generally uneven.[3] Although some of Iwasaki Akira's theoretical writings, for instance, were famously translated into Chinese by Lu Xun, works from other Asian countries rarely made it to Japan. Instead, Japanese theorists could sometimes assume the lead in teaching other Asians about their cinema. Nick Deocampo has recently unearthed the interesting case of Sawamura Tsutomu in the occupied Philippines. Later a screenwriter, Sawamura was one of the lead writers at *Eiga hyōron* in the late thirties; a graduate in aesthetics at the University of Tokyo, he was a champion of realism—but from a semiotically sophisticated standpoint that argued the socially constructed nature of cinema's relation to the real (for a discussion of his realism, see Gerow 2018). Yet Sawamura was also stationed in the Philippines during the war, helped produce the propaganda film *Tōyō no gaika* (Oriental song of victory, 1942), and, according to Deocampo, was the first person ever to delineate the conditions for Philippine cinema to become a national cinema (Deocampo 2016). In effect, a Japanese theorist was using universal standards (of national cinema) to promote a particularity (Filipino cinema) that simultaneously confirmed a particularized universality (Japanese mastery of the global phenomenon of national cinema).

The Problem of Spectators

Deocampo's example underlines how the efforts of colonial subjects to negotiate empire could not simply involve asserting a national identity against the colonial power, since the national could itself be part of imperial ideology. Asserting the national cinema against that of Japan could, ironically, become just another instance of internalization. If we are to look for the cracks and fissures in the internalization of cinema and film theory, we should do so at those points of intersection between the universal and the particular, the empire and the local. I argue the cracks and fissures crucially occur in conceptualizations of the relationship between spectators, cinema, and empire.

As I have argued elsewhere (Gerow 1999), spectatorship was a significant issue for wartime authorities in Japan, and not just in the colonies. There was real awareness that films could not ensure correct readings, even though Japanese films seemed to increasingly bear narrative forms—from voice-over narrators and intertitles to formal devices resembling those of classical Hollywood cinema—that attempted to shape and manage interpretation. Spectators were acknowledged to be capable of "changing, revolutionizing, and moving the cinema" (Yamazaki 1943, 25), which was one reason that some in charge of film regulation, such as the Information Bureau's Fuwa Suketoshi, spoke of "training" (*kunren*) spectators.[4] Local reports often foregrounded the problem of spectators in the colonies or in the puppet state of Manchukuo. Such writings could be far from celebratory and, though never going so far as to criticize Japanese imperialism itself, revealed an empire that was not smooth in its exercise of power. For instance, a special section on ethnicity in Manchurian cinema, appearing in the June 1939 issue of *Manshū eiga*, assembled pieces in Japanese by representatives of five of the puppet state's ethnicities—Japanese, Korean, Manchu, Mongolian, and Russian; the section was supposed to celebrate new efforts to represent these ethnic groups in film, ostensibly in order to emphasize their cooperation in the new nation. But the Korean representative asked that Japanese films not be shown; the Manchu representative complained that depicting ethnicities other than the majority Manchu was a waste of resources; and the Russian delegate thanked, with not a small touch of sarcasm, the supposedly multiethnic state for finally recognizing there was more than one ethnic group (Yamaguchi et al. 1939).

In more cases than not, frustrations were directed less at the state than at spectators. Take, for instance, a rather pessimistic article written by someone named Zhou Guoqing for the July 1940 issue of *Manshū eiga*.[5] Asking what Manchurian film is, Zhou complains that it is caught between two other cinemas—those of Shanghai and Japan—which have created in Manchurian spectators "a jail of preconceived ideas from which they cannot escape" (Zhou 1940, 73). Manchurian film is seen as existing between cinemas, or as an appendage of one or the other, two views that Zhou thinks are unhelpful. If Manchurian viewers possess an age-old "gloomy" (*in'utsu*) disposition, as Zhou claims, Shanghai producers take advantage of that by selling melodramas that "stimulate those emotions" and "nab the audience's worthless tears brimming with excess emotion, indecision, melancholy, and orthodoxy" (Zhou 1940, 74).

Japanese films fare not much better. While surmising that the level of Japanese cinema that Manchurian audiences could process would be only "unproductive" entertainment films, Zhou also declared that "judging from the surprising box office success of *Aizen katsura* throughout Japan, the level of film appreciation in Japan is not that high either" (Zhou 1940, 74).[6] Zhou worried that if Manchukuo produced such films, all that Manchurians would learn would be "enfeeblement and orthodoxy" (Zhou 1940, 74). Against the danger of internalizing the vulgarity of Shanghai and Japan, Zhou poses the bodily metaphor of healthiness (*kenkōsei*), proposing a healthy cinema for a new people. However, knowing that one of the trends in Japanese cinema is for bright (*meirō*) period films and comedies, Zhou refuses to equate health with surface vigor, locating it instead deeper in art and ethics. He is delicately attempting to argue for an independent Manchukuo and its cinema on the basis of an independent spectator, but he is confronted with an audience that he believes is trapped in a scorned movie culture.

Zhou was not the only one to complain of a Manchurian viewership trapped in old ways (e.g., Tan 1938), and he looked to both the youth and intellectuals as a cure for such intellectual fetters and moral debilitation. Yet, in proposing a Manchurian interiority against the internalization of Shanghai and Japan, Zhou in the end can offer only anguish and insanity as examples. The first is his own turmoil revealed in diarylike entries at the end of the article, in which he confesses his dire loneliness in attempting to defend Manchurian cinema. The second comes from his coveted savior: a new generation of film youth who "will, like a madman, throw all their energy and power—their entire life—into Manchurian cinema" (Zhou 1940, 75). Not only is the basis of a new Manchurian cinematic subjectivity thus inherently in turmoil, it also uncannily resembles the psychology of the imperial soldier devoted solely to sacrificing himself for the emperor.

Im Hwa and the Subject of Cinematic Language

If Zhou Guoquin seems to resort to the lone individual or the madman as the alternative to the universal spread of cinema, Im Hwa attempts to turn universalism back against the empire as a basis for rethinking the language used to describe motion pictures. Im was a modernist poet, critic, and cineaste who traveled to Japan in 1929 and wrote the article "Chōsen eiga no shokeikō ni tsuite" (On several tendencies in Korean cinema) for the March 1930 issue of *Shinkō Eiga*, a leftist film journal associated with the Proletarian Film League of Japan (Prokino). He would return to Korea the next year to take up a central position in the Korean proletarian cultural movement, until he, like many leftists, was arrested and renounced his politics in 1934 (Treat 2015).

As Moonim Baek does in this collection and in her 2015 book on Im Hwa (Baek 2015), Im Hwa's article (1930) can be read as a film-critical equivalent of his poetic riposte against Nakano Shigeharu's "Shinagawa Station in the Rain." A poem that ostensibly encourages Korean comrades to commit revolutionary violence, it unfortunately falls into the pattern, as John Treat describes it, "of the rampant 'left imperialism' in prewar Japan and Korea, in which erstwhile progressive Japanese intellectuals echoed their dominance of colonial counterparts by scripting for them real but usually imaginary instrumental roles in the class and national struggles of the empire: you do the killing, and at our bidding" (Treat 2015, 8).

Against this, Im's poem "The Yokohama Dock with an Umbrella" not only refuses the implicit division between Korean and Japanese proletarians of Nakano's poem, it also poses, according to Baek, the Japanese as also in need of liberation. "On Several Tendencies in Korean Cinema" can similarly be considered a response, this time to Kōriyama Hiroshi's article "Chōsen eiga ni tsuite" (On Korean cinema) a few issues earlier in *Shinkō Eiga* (Kōriyama 1930). If that piece celebrated the nationalist cinema of Na Un-kyu and not Korean proletarian film, effectively dividing it from Japanese proletarian cinema, Im aimed to describe a real Korean proletarian film that complicated such national divisions.

"On Several Tendencies in Korean Cinema" is not without its drawbacks. Essentially a history of the development of left-wing cinema in Korea, not only is its narrative teleological but it also reveals traces of mainstream Japanese film theory. A rhetoric that complains of "the ignorant masses," "primitive" film techniques, and "ignorant film theater exhibitors" and that places as much emphasis on cinematic progress as on ideological progress (Im 1930, 117–19) strongly resembles the discourse of the Pure Film Movement, which interlaced cinematic teleologies with social hierarchies. Im is likely influenced by Iwasaki

Akira, Japan's most prominent leftist film critic, who had his roots in pure film discourse. Nevertheless, Im begins the piece by stressing how imperialism operates by placing colonials at the level of the undeveloped or barbarian, a power dynamic he immediately attempts to complicate by noting that Korean cinema's late start was in part due to Japanese cinema's own state of underdevelopment. Thus, though he emulates the teleology of the dominant in Japanese film theory, he undermines Japanese pretensions to align themselves with that universal theory. Im is, in one sense, pursuing a tack similar to that of the Korean philosophers Sŏ In-sik and Pak Chi-u, who, as Yonetani Masafumi has argued, countered the universalism of Miki Kiyoshi and the Kyoto School, not by rejecting their ideas, but by turning that universalism back on Japan as a critique of fascism (Yonetani 2005, 16–18). Baek cites Im's mention of montage in Kim Yu-yŏng's *A House* as one sign of his assertion of coeval cinematic development and thus of universal alliance with, not subservience to, Japanese comrades.[7]

What is interesting from the perspective of this investigation is less Im's citation of film form than his mention of audiences. The problem with Kōriyama's article is not that it openly degrades Koreans but that it seeks to represent them through a form of projection. In some ways it resembles Noël Burch's approach to Japanese film in the way it finds in another film culture something missing in the writer's own world (in Burch's case, a popular film system that rejects the bourgeois Hollywood cinema). Although acknowledging that neither proletarian nor commercial films in Japan can claim to represent the masses, Kōriyama writes that "the rebellion hiding within Na Un-kyu's films has always managed to represent the masses" (Kōriyama 1930, 134).

The envy evident here masks his own effort to represent these Korean proletarians. The article, which, like Im's, begins with a history, spotlights the moment when "the Korean peoples had 'our own cinema' [*warera no eiga*] for the first time" (Kōriyama 1930, 132). Im is conscious of this use of the phrase "our own cinema" and contrasts it with his own: "I will inform you of the fact that the Korean proletariat and farmers have continued to truly have 'our own cinema' for some time" (Im 1930, 116). One issue is that Kōriyama uses that phrase only once and quickly shifts to a dyad of "us" and "their cinema" (*karera no eiga*) in the remainder of the piece. Beyond dividing the colonizer from the colonized, the colonizer here asserts the power to also use the term "our own cinema" in quotation marks, as if speaking for—representing—the Korean masses. Im's use of quotation marks is clearly intended to call out this abuse of representation, both quoting Kōriyama's statement and reappropriating it (through the word *truly* outside the quotation marks).

Note this is also a problem of the speech act. Kōriyama must utilize the quotation marks because, in a Japanese magazine, the ambiguous pronoun "our" alone would likely be read as referring to Japanese. Not using quotation marks for the later terms "us" and "them" confirms that the readers are intended to be Japanese, and that "our" does not include Koreans, despite their being comrades in revolution and empire. The quotation marks (called *kagikakko* and which resemble frames: 「」) frame and delimit the Korean voice for display. Im could refuse to use quotation marks, since he is Korean, although utilizing them could similarly function to avoid the implication that "our" is the "we" of Japanese readers. Im's opting for their use foregrounds their unspoken and assumed role in representation and forces especially Japanese readers to become conscious of linguistic divisions and problems of representation in speech. There is a reason this piece had to be written in Japanese for a Japanese readership, beyond simply the fact that Im was writing in a Japanese language journal read mostly by leftist Japanese comrades. It is interesting to note that the "you" in the above quotation from Im is unspoken: the polite phrase for "inform"—*tsutaete ageyō*—both implies an addressee and refuses to specify it. Unlike "our" in quotation marks, it declines to delimit and frame the subject addressed, leaving it ambiguous—in effect, it refuses to represent the other. It is possible to do so because of the structure of Japanese grammar, which Im must internalize in order to proceed with this strategy, which seeks an alternative to framing within language.

It is important that this critique of representation, especially of speech acts, ends not with speech but with action by spectators. As final proof that the Korean proletariat is not nationalist, Im cites the reaction to Kim Yŏnghwan's *The Engagement* (1929): "On the first night of the screening of *The Engagement* there was even an incident of a mass of catcalls erupting from leftist film workers in the theater. It is clear the Korean proletariat have no reason why they should neglect such reactionary films in the name of the 'national' or the 'ethnic' that Kōriyama describes" (Im 1930, 123).

While Im is not clear about the specifics of this incident, he uses it to show that Korean proletarians are not just refusing representation of the nation but are in effect refusing linguistic representation itself, foregrounding the act aspect of speech acts and preferring praxis to engagement in debate or theory. Although Im himself exhibits problems of representation (especially in degrading the mass audience), his internalization of both the Japanese language and film theory is rearticulated by a conscious critique of representation that concludes in a search for alternatives to language acts and classical spectatorship.[8]

O YŎNG-JIN, WAR, AND THE POSTCINEMATIC SPECTATOR

If it seems possible to read resistance to colonial power in Im Hwa's writings, albeit in a way that complicates the binary of internalization as cooptation versus resistance as total externalization, it is actually less possible to do so with O Yŏng-jin, who was arguably one of the more prolific colonial subjects writing about film in Japanese. O has been "considered one of Korea's most representative playwrights" (Kardoss 2002, 515) and his postliberation work described as utilizing "traditional values and local customs... to break away from western themes and subject matter" (Yoh 1998, 267). He was also involved in film production, writing scripts, producing newsreels, and assisting in distribution. Yet, although he has been described as "moving against the political trends of his time" and as being "strongly anti-Japanese and anti-communist" (Yoh 1998, 267), his collaboration with Imperial Japan during the war has been sharply critiqued by the film scholar Yi Yŏng-jae (2013, 194–95). The article "Chōsen eiga no ippanteki kadai" (General issues of Korean cinema) that O wrote for the July 1942 issue of *Sinsidae*, a culture magazine published in Korea, in fact significantly resembles the rhetoric of such Japanese intellectual war proponents in the film world as Sawamura Tsutomu and Tsumura Hideo. O enthusiastically declares Korea's membership in the empire, calling the Chōsen Film Company, created by a government-led merger of the existing film studios, the fourth Japanese film company. He proclaims it is now the age of making films for the nation, with a solid focus on relating the individual to the state.

Yet here and in later articles, the issue of the spectator provokes tensions and even a potential collapse in his vision of cinema. O can be bitingly critical of both Korean and Japanese cinema, but he often blames the problems less on systemic issues or national character than on individuals, especially their lack of spirit and theory. One genre he praises highly is Japanese *bunka eiga* (documentary culture films), which he sees as not only solidly founded in a dialectic of theory and practice, but also taking advantage of a spectator-screen relationship unique to documentary, in which "there is no distance at all between those watching and that watched" (O 1942, 100). Viewers of documentary, seeing others like themselves, perceive themselves on screen. Fiction film, however, O argues, promotes a different, critical detachment between spectator and image. He is also conscious of the centrality of audiences to the power of motion pictures. Although in the *Sinsidae* piece he is simply arguing that cinema is powerless if it does not have an audience, in a subsequent August 1944 article for *Kokumin bungaku*, he challenges film theories that locate cinema's success with the masses in factors inherent to cinema by reversing the claim and stating that cinema's power does not come from within but is externally dependent on the masses (O 1944, 32).

A November 1943 piece for *Eiga hyōron* is focused on the problem of the Korean masses, especially on the perception that there is no film, either

Japanese or Korean, that speaks to the Korean audience. Economically, "Korea has been for a long time nothing but a colony cinematically, a market for consumption" (O 1943, 38). Part of the problem, O argues, is that Japanese and American films bred in spectators an incorrect view of cinema. Although he acknowledges that early cinema anywhere relied on emulating other arts, Korean film did not progress beyond that, even falling into the pitiful position of copying Japanese films that themselves were copying American cinema—of being a colony of a neocolonized culture. He gives praise to Na Un-kyu for finally offering Koreans images of their own life but blames him for ultimately mimicking Hollywood cinema. O predictably denounces the left-wing films Im Hwa praises, dismissing them as mere propaganda; but he proceeds to argue that wartime national policy films fail for the same reason.

Having presented an ideal of spectators united with the film—and thus with the state—O's writings progressively become frustrated with the impossibility of that vision. He blames inadequacy in film theory, problems in the industry, the excessive influence of individual filmmakers' whims and tastes, and again the failure of scripts to properly tie the individual to the whole. Ultimately, it is the spectator's mentality that needs to be broken down. In the *Eiga hyōron* piece, O hopes naked realism will do that:

> Without any ostentation, exaggeration, or weapons, the naked camera must plunge into reality. Only the true life grasped in this way can manage to shake the obstinate soul of the masses. Through this, for the first time, the paradoxical viewing psychology of the masses, in which they both love cinema the most and remain cold toward it, will be defeated, and the world developed within the film will begin to appeal to the masses not as a mere fairground entertainment, but with the power of the reality closest to them. (O 1943, 41)

Through that naked and intimate reality, O argues, national-policy films should start again from scratch.

O's writings provide an alternative perspective on Japanese film theory, here posing a different view of how realist film theory, from Imamura Taihei to Sugiyama Heiichi, become dominant in Japan as it marched toward war. Realism is less the Bazinian commitment to the real than a weapon in the arsenal of the cinematic war machine aimed as much at the domestic audience. The *Kokumin bungaku* article, some nine months later, finds O even more desperate. Seeing a decline in film attendance, especially among Koreans, O throws aside the major issues of film theory—cinema's modernity, its concrete visuality, or its nature as the eighth art (to mention what he lists)—to focus solely on pleasure and attention. First complaining of the tendency in contemporary discourse to divide national-policy films from entertainment—as if the former cannot be the latter, or vice versa—he wonders what gives audiences pleasure and how pleasure can be used to spark attention to state propaganda. His answer is surprising. Instead of seeking out content that would entertain, he posits that, more than anything, "the masses . . . wish to be overwhelmed by the essential expressive power of cinema." That power is not in its modernity or visuality, but in surprise or shock (*odoroki*), in that which "deviates or transcends common sense" (O 1944, 35). His sense of what can shock is rather broad, but it involves an assault on some modes of thinking or perception. O proceeds even further in theorizing such violence toward the spectator, calling for shock therapy to bring them back into the theaters to watch national films. It is important to notice that taking this tack largely abandons the issue of the content of films. O even brushes aside films about sacrifice for the nation, in that they are now commonsense and fail to surprise or shock. Things become common, he argues, when they cease to be concrete and become concepts.

O is thus edging toward arguing against abstraction, against explanation—against meaning in some cases. Theory ends up rejecting abstract theory not for a pragmatic form of praxis, but for a mode of violence. O, however, is not necessarily outside the bounds of contemporary theory or pursuing a program of posttheory. His ideas do resonate with efforts by Imamura Taihei and others to conceive of cinema as a material, concrete form of thought. Yet in O it is a thought designed essentially to arrest spectator thought, rendering their subjectivity as pure affect. When he calls at the end for not just a focus on the concrete, but also a celebration of speed, he is both pushing for the technology of cinema to become that which overwhelms the spectator, as well as, in effect, promotes a return to the cinema of attractions—a concept Tom Gunning used to describe early cinema's focus on attention-getting spectacle over narrative (Gunning 1986).

Clearly O is not calling for a return to early cinema. In fact, he concludes that "during war . . . we are not allowed to live peacefully in the world of common sense" (O 1944, 37). His is a cinema of the present, or even the future. His declaration that cinematic perception must align with war ties his cinema of shock and surprise to Paul Virilio's wedding of cinematic attention to weaponry in *War and Cinema*. It also reminds us of the similarities drawn between the cinema of attractions and descriptions of postcinema or postclassical cinema, which Gunning has already posed (Gunning 1993). If postcinema is conceived as the breakdown of classical cinema and the resurgence of spectacle over narrative, of technological wonder over depth of content, O's theory, even if it is not purely postclassical, prompts us to consider postcinema's prehistory in war, colonialism, and imperialism, and reminds us how much our present moment is similarly an era of permanent war or a "state of exception," to borrow Giorgio Agamben's phrase (Agamben 2005).

To return to the problem of internalization, O attempted to solve the problem of an audience that has internalized what he considered incorrect modes of cinema, in part by enabling a viewership in which the spectator effectively becomes one with the film. Perhaps his writing in Japanese was another means of internalizing the screen of imperial film culture. But he is ultimately faced with a detachment he recognizes but can do nothing about: that colonial Korea remains one step removed, either as a colony of an empire that itself appears culturally colonized by Europe, or as deeply imbricated in the triangulation of Japan, Europe, and Asia. Theorizing in the Japanese language is ultimately part of that triangulation. O ultimately attempts to reduce that distance by turning the spectator inside out, rendering the internal external and reducing the spectator to a site of shock and affect in which the internalization of concepts matters less than the violent, externalized play of nonlinguistic forces—whether a viewer can be broken. In some ways, it is the corollary of Zhou's madman (Zhou 1940, 75). Even then, O's frustrations indicate this spectator might still not be moved in that way. They could still be Im's spectators, who externalize meaning through oppositional forms of movement.

Conclusion

It is not necessary here to pose all colonial film theory as presenting some mode of resistance, although their contradictions might indicate some openings in the system. In the end, they illustrate how the problem of internalization, especially when manifested in the issue of spectatorship, was both significant and a challenge even to supporters of the imperial cause. In the case of the spectator, the problem of empire and subjectivity resulted in conflicts over intersubjective relations, language and meaning, and the shape of subjectivity itself. The colonial theorists introduced here confronted the problem of internalizing Japanese film theory—if there was such a thing— either by forcing Japanese theory to confront its presumptions to universality, in effect externalizing it (an effect that colonials appropriating the Japanese language might also facilitate); or, as with O rejecting the premises of theory, by focusing on what is outside it: the battleground of the spectator's externalized body as a site that problematizes cinema itself. If Japanese theorists suffered from a theory complex, where they confronted the difficulty of assuming the mantle of theory defined by the European center, perhaps we can say that colonial theorists encountered a colonial theory complex in which they were doubly removed from theory. The rejection of theory could be a refusal of this complex, but it could simultaneously be a manifestation of the desperation of a thinker like O, attempting to be Japanese when that was impossible. As with Zhou, the colonial theory complex could border on madness.

Especially with O, the desperate effort to shape the imperial subject resulted in a figure whose inside is outside and vice versa, where war and empire affect the very surface of the subject. This could, on the level of theory, be imbricated with the complex film form I analyzed in films from colonial Korea, in which the skin of the colonial subject is "a Moebius strip, in which masks are both inside and outside the skin, masks masking masks, and the skin becoming a complexly layered boundary both internal and external" (Gerow 2015, 39). If Fanon's racialized subject internalizes the "epidermalization" of value, the value of O's colonial subject comes from externalizing what has been internalized, from becoming a surface moved by the violent contact zones of empire and media. With the elimination of distance between spectator and the body of cinema, the colonial subject is less seen by film than internalized within the imperial cinematic strip. Yet O is clearly aware that this subject can also possess another surface, neither internal nor external—another side not touched, one confoundingly out of reach. This description could also in part apply to the colonial film theorist as spectator.

Notes

1. One resident of Manchuria reported that "In the faces of those Manchurians who have come to see these films—works unbearable to watch and a disgrace to the nation—rises a strangely wry smile impossible to explain" (Watanabe 1943, 86).

2. See, for instance, the introductions to film theory written or edited by Iwasaki Akira (1956), Okada Susumu (1966), or Iwamoto Kenji and Hatano Tetsurō (1982). Of the eighteen examples of classic film theory introduced by the latter, only two—by Imamura Taihei and Asanuma Keiji—are by Japanese thinkers.

3. For more on the politics of *zadankai* featuring Korean participants, see Kwon (Kwon 2015, 131–53). High also notes how bureaucrats effectively used *zadankai* in film magazines to manage the film discursive agenda (High 2003, 82–85).

4. A word used in Fuwa's comments in a 1942 roundtable discussion entitled "Expanding and Strengthening the Audience" (Chiba et al. 1942, 50).

5. Zhou intimates he is involved in the Manchurian film industry, but because the name Guoqing 国慶 means "national celebration," it may be a pen name. Aside from noted figures such as Im Hwa, O Yŏng-jin, or Na Un-kyu, it is hard to confirm the identity of some of these colonial subjects writing in Japanese, and whether they are who they claim to be.

6. *Aizen katsura* was a hit Shōchiku melodrama directed by Nomura Hiromasa, starring Tanaka Kinuyo and Uehara Ken, that was released in several parts in 1938 and 1939.

7. Montage was not always a sign of the universal in the Japanese film world. It was popular in the late 1920s and early 1930s, at least as a concept, but some historians, such as Satō Tadao, have argued it was nothing more than a superficial fashion (see Satō 1977, 52–57). Directors such as Itami Mansaku vigorously criticized it. Theorists favored it because it solved a central problem that hounded Japanese film theory until the 1950s: how to counter Konrad Lange's argument that film

was not an art. If Lange argued that art was the creative deviation from reality, and thus that cinema cannot be an art because of its mechanical reproduction of reality, many film theorists, paralleling a tactic used by both Hugo Münsterberg and Rudolph Arnheim, endeavored to find the ways film artistically diverged from reality. Since montage promised the creation of concepts and realities not contained in the original shots, it was considered the ideal proof of cinema's aesthetic credentials. With the coming of sound and the rise of realism, however, some theorists began to not only critique montage but also question Lange's aesthetic suppositions. What is ironic, but also telling, is that, as Markus Nornes has argued, many of Prokino's statements—including, I could add, their advocacy of montage—could become the statements of wartime bureaucrats by just changing a few words (see Nornes 2003, 66–69). Montage could thus be another example of a universal used to promote Japanese imperialism.

8. It might be possible to link this to the affective realism that Irhe Sohn has discerned from Im Hwa's later writings on film, in which cinema's appeal to the audience's pathos becomes an effective means of representing what is unrepresentable in the colonial regime (Sohn 2016).

Bibliography

Agamben, Giorgio. 2005. *State of Exception*. Chicago: University of Chicago Press.
Andrew, Dudley. 1976. *The Major Film Theories*. London: Oxford University Press.
Baek Moonim. 2015. *Im Hwa ŭi Yŏnghwa* [Im Hwa's cinema]. Seoul: Somyŏng.
———. 2018. "Revisiting Colonial Cinema Research in Korea." *Journal of Japanese and Korean Cinema* 10, no. 2: 85–91. https://doi.org/10.1080/17564905.2018.1518689.
Baskett, Michael. 2008. *The Attractive Empire: Transnational Film Culture in Imperial Japan*. Honolulu: University of Hawaii Press.
Braudy, Leo, and Marshall Cohen, eds. 2004. *Film Theory and Criticism: Introductory Readings*. Oxford: Oxford University Press.
Burch, Noël. 1978. *To the Distant Observer: Form and Meaning in the Japanese Cinema*. Berkeley, CA: University of California Press.
Chiba Kichizō, Tanikawa Tetsuzō, Tsumura Hideo, Nawa Mitsumasa, Fuwa Suketoshi, Mori Iwao, Nanbu Keinosuke, and Shimizu Chiyota. 1942. "Kankyakusō no kakudai kyōka zadankai" [Roundtable on expanding and strengthening the audience]. *Eiga junpō* 43 (April 1): 48–56.
Chiu, Kuei-Fen. 2011. "The Question of Translation in Taiwanese Cinematic Space." *Journal of Asian Studies* 70, no. 1 (February): 77–97. https://doi.org/10.1017/S0021911810002950.
Deocampo, Nick. 2016. *Eiga: Cinema in the Philippines during World War II*. Mandaluyong City, Philippines: Anvil.
Du Bois, W. E. B. 1897. "Strivings of the Negro People." *The Atlantic* (August). https://www.theatlantic.com/magazine/archive/1897/08/strivings-of-the-negro-people/305446/.
Fanon, Frantz. 2004. *The Wretched of the Earth*. New York: Grove.
———. 2008. *Black Skin, White Masks*. New York: Grove.
Fujitani, Takeshi, and Nayoung Aimee Kwon, eds. 2012. "Transcolonial Film Coproductions in the Japanese Empire: Antinomies in the Colonial Archives." *Cross-Currents e-Journal* no. 5 (December). https://cross-currents.berkeley.edu/e-journal/issue-5.
Furukawa Takahisa. 2003. *Senjika no Nihon eiga: Hitobito wa kokusaku eiga o mita ka* [Japanese cinema in wartime: Did people watch national policy films?]. Tokyo: Yoshikawa Kōbunkan.
Gerow, Aaron. 1999. "*Miyamoto Musashi* to senjichū no kankyaku" [Miyamoto Musashi and wartime spetators]. In *Eiga kantoku Mizoguchi Kenji* [Film director Mizoguchi Kenji]. Edited by Yomota Inuhiko, 226–50. Tokyo: Shinyōsha.
———. 2005. "Nation, Citizenship and Cinema." In *A Companion to the Anthropology of Japan*. Edited by Jennifer Robertson, 400–414. Malden, MA: Blackwell.

———. 2009. "Narrating the Nation-ality of a Cinema: The Case of Japanese Prewar Film." In *The Culture of Japanese Fascism*. Edited by Alan Tansman, 185–211. Durham, NC: Duke University Press.

———. 2010a. "Introduction: The Theory Complex." *Review of Japanese Culture and Society* 22 (December): 1–13.

———. 2010b. "Retrospective on Japanese Retrospectives." *Undercurrent* 6. http://fipresci .hegenauer.co.uk/undercurrent/issue_0609/gerow_retro.htm.

———. 2010c. *Visions of Japanese Modernity: Articulations of Cinema, Nation, and Spectatorship, 1895–1925*. Berkeley: University of California Press.

———. 2015. "Colonial Era Korean Cinema and the Problem of Internalization." *Transhumanities* 8, no. 1 (February): 27–46. https://doi.org/10.1353/trh.2015.0001.

———. 2018. "Kaidai" [Explanatory notes]. In *Nihon senzen eiga ronshū: Eiga riron no saihakken* [Rediscovering Classical Japanese Film Theory—An Anthology]. Edited by Aaron Gerow, Iwamoto Kenji, and Markus Nornes, 629–40. Tokyo: Yumani Shobo.

———. 2019. "Theorizing the Theory Complex in Japanese Film Studies." *Journal of Japanese and Korean Cinema* 11, no. 2: 103–8. https://doi.org/10.1080/17564905.2019.1661957.

Gunning, Tom. 1986. "Cinema of Attractions: Early Film, Its Spectator and the Avant-Garde." *Wide Angle* 8, nos. 3–4: 63–70.

———. 1993. "'Now You See It, Now You Don't': The Temporality of the Cinema of Attractions." *Velvet Light Trap* 32: 3–12.

High, Peter B. 2003. *The Imperial Screen: Japanese Film Culture in the Fifteen Years' War 1931–1945*. Madison: University of Wisconsin Press.

Hinatsu Eitarō. 1941. "Naisen ryōeigakai no kōryū ni tsuite" [On the exchanges between the film worlds of Japan and Korea]. *Eiga hyōron* [Film criticism] 1, no. 7: 49–51.

Hori, Hikari. 2017. *Promiscuous Media: Film and Visual Culture in Imperial Japan, 1926–1945*. Ithaca, NY: Cornell University Press.

Im Hwa. 1930. "Chōsen eiga no shokeikō ni tsuite" [On several tendencies in Korean cinema]. *Shinkō Eiga* [New cinema] 2, no. 3: 115–24.

Iwamoto Kenji and Hatano Tetsurō, eds. 1982. *Eiga riron shūsei* [Anthology of film theory]. Tokyo: Firumu Ātosha.

Iwasaki Akira. 1956. *Eiga no riron* [Theory of film]. Tokyo: Iwanami.

Kardoss, John. 2002. "Korea." In *The Reader's Encyclopedia of World Drama*. Edited by John Gassner and Edward Quinn, 509–16. Mineola, NY: Dover.

Katō Atsuko. 2003. *Sōdōin taisei to eiga* [Cinema and the general mobilization system]. Tokyo: Shin'yōsha.

Kawase Takaya. 2009. *Shokuminchi Chōsen no shūkyō to gakuchi* [Religion and academic knowledge in colonial Korea]. Tokyo: Seikyūsha.

Kim, Dong Hoon. 2017. *Eclipsed Cinema: The Film Culture of Colonial Korea*. Edinburgh: Edinburgh University Press.

Kōriyama Hiroshi. 1930. "Chōsen eiga ni tsuite" [On Korean cinema]. *Shinkō Eiga* 2, no. 1: 131–34.

Kramer, Hanae Kurihara. 2012. "Film Forays of the South Manchuria Railway Company." *Film History* 24, no. 1: 97–113.

Kwon, Nayoung Aimee. 2015. *Intimate Empire: Collaboration and Colonial Modernity in Korea and Japan*. Durham, NC: Duke University Press.

Lee Daw-Ming, ed. 2019. *Dongtai yingxiang de juji: zaoqi Taiwan yu DongYa dianying shi* [Tracing the footsteps of motion pictures: A history of early Taiwanese and East Asian cinemas]. Taipei: Yuanliu Chuban Shiye Gufen.

Lin, Pei-yin, and Su Yun Kim. 2019. *East Asian Transwar Popular Culture*. Singapore: Springer Singapore.

Misawa, Mamie. 2014. "'Colony, Empire, and De-colonization' in Taiwanese Film History." *International Journal of Korean History* 19, no. 2: 35–70.

Mori Iwao. 1942. "Yume to hyōgen" [Dreams and expression]. *Eiga junpō* [Movie times] 43 (April 1): 4–6.

Na Un-kyu. 1937. "Chōsen eiga no genjō" [The present state of Korean cinema]. *Eiga hyōron* [Film criticism] 19, no. 1: 95–102.

Nornes, Abé Mark. 2003. *Japanese Documentary Film: The Meiji Era through Hiroshima*. Minneapolis: University of Minnesota Press.

O Yŏng-jin. 1942. "Chōsen eiga no ippanteki kadai." *Sinsidae* [New Era] 2, no. 6 (June): 95–103.

———. 1943. "Eiga to Chōsen taishū" [Film and the Korean masses]. *Eiga hyōron* [Film criticism] 3, no. 11 (November): 38–41.

———. 1944. "Gekieiga ni tsuite" [On fiction film]. *Kokumin bungaku* [National literature] 4, no. 8 (August): 31–37.

Okada Susumu. 1966. *Eiga riron nyūmon* [Introduction to film theory]. Tokyo: Hakuyōsha.

Osaki Midori. 1998. *Osaki Midori zenshū* [Complete works of Osaki Midori]. 2 vols. Tokyo: Seikōsha.

Said, Edward. 1979. *Orientalism*. New York: Vintage.

Sakai Naoki. 2010a. "Pakkusu Amerikāna no shita de no Kyōto Gakuha no tetsugaku" [The philosophy of the Kyoto School under Pax Americana]. In *"Kindai no chōkoku" to Kyōto Gakuha* [The Kyoto School and "overcoming the modern"]. Edited by Sakai Naoki and Isomae Jun'ichi, 3–28. Tokyo: Ibunsha.

———. 2010b. "Theory and Asian Humanity: On the Question of Humanitas and Anthropos." *Postcolonial Studies* 13, no. 4: 441–64. https://doi.org/10.1080/13688790.2010.526539.

Satō Tadao. 1977. *Nihon eiga rironshi* [History of Japanese film theory]. Tokyo: Hyōronsha.

Sohn, Irhe. 2016. "Imperial Ethos, Colonial Pathos: Affective Realism of Colonial Korean Cinema." *Taiwan Cinema Studies Network*, December 10. http://twcinema.tnua.edu.tw/ct/2016/12/imperial-ethos-colonial-pathos-affective-realism-of-colonial-korean-cinema/.

Stam, Robert. 2000. *Film Theory: An Introduction*. Malden, MA: Blackwell.

Tan Fu. 1938. "Eiga ni taisuru Manjin no kannen" [Ideas of Manchurians about cinema]. *Manshū eiga* [Manchurian cinema] 2, no. 8: 22–25.

Taylor-Jones, Kate. 2017. *Divine Work, Japanese Colonial Cinema and Its Legacy*. New York: Bloomsbury.

Terada Torahiko. 1960–1962. *Terada Torahiko zenshū* [Complete works of Terada Torahiko]. 17 vols. Tokyo: Iwanami.

Treat, John. 2015. "Im Hwa before and after Japan." *Trans-humanities* 8, no. 1: 5–26.

Tsumura Hideo. 1942. "Dai Tō-a eiga seisaku ni kansuru nōto" [Notes on producing Greater East Asia films]. *Eiga hyōron* [Film criticism] 2, no. 4 (April): 18–22.

Virilio, Paul. 1989. *War and Cinema: The Logic of Perception*. Translated by Patrick Camiller. London and New York: Verso.

Watanabe Hisashi. 1943. "Manshū kokkyō no eiga kankyaku" [Film audiences on the Manchurian border]. *Nihon eiga* [Japanese film] 8, no. 7 (July): 85–87.

Yamaguchi Shin'ichi, Lee Taewoo, Sun Pengfei, Jorightu, and M. Vlasov. 1939. "Manshū eiga no minzokusei" [The nationalities of Manchurian film] *Manshū eiga* [Manchurian cinema] 3, no. 6: 20–27.

Yamazaki Isamu. 1943. "Kankyaku no shinpan" [The spectator's judgement]. *Nihon eiga* [Japanese film] 8, no. 11 (November): 24–26.

Yecies, Brian, and Ae-Gyung Shim. 2011. *Korea's Occupied Cinemas, 1895–1948*. New York: Routledge.

Yi Yŏng-jae. 2013. *Teikoku Nihon no Chōsen eiga* [Korean film of the Japanese Empire]. Tokyo: Sangensha.
Yoh Suk Kee. 1998. "Korea." In *The World Encyclopedia of Contemporary Theatre*. Vol. 5, *Asia/Pacific*. Edited by Don Rubin, 257–73. New York: Routledge, 1998.
Yonetani Masafumi. 2005. "Shokuminchi/teikoku no 'sekaishi no tetsugaku'" [The "philosophy of world history" of colonies/empire]. *Nihon shisō shigaku* [Historical studies of Japanese thought] 37: 11–19.
Zhou Guoqing. 1940. "Manshū eiga no shomondai" [Various problems with Manchurian cinema]. *Manshū eiga* [Manchurian cinema] 4, no. 7 (July): 73–75.

AARON GEROW is Professor of East Asian Cinema at Yale University. He is author of *Visions of Japanese Modernity: Articulations of Cinema, Nation, and Spectatorship, 1895–1925*; *A Page of Madness: Cinema and Modernity in 1920s Japan*; and *Kitano Takeshi*.

4. CHINESE CINEMA'S OTHER
Wrangling over "China-Humiliating" Films (*ruHua pian*)

Yiman Wang

Abstract

This chapter discusses the formation of Chinese cinema culture under colonial modernity (as analyzed by Tani Barlow) by way of studying the 1910s to 1930s Chinese protests against Western-made films that were deemed detrimental to Chinese dignity and thus labeled as *ruHua pian* ("China-humiliating films"), hereafter *ruHua* films. Chinese critics of these films foregrounded the unequal relationship between those who had the power to represent and those subjected to the power of representation. Instead of assuming a binary opposition between the Western imperial forces and the Chinese subjects, I unpack the affective politics that underpinned Chinese critics and policy makers' interactions with their Western—especially American—interlocutors, which significantly intervened in the uneven ground of transnational film culture. My goal is to illuminate the complicated affective emergence of China's decolonial and nation-building projects. I argue that the impassioned debates over *ruHua* films manifested an affective articulation of sovereign identity formation in response to colonial modernity. In this process, film, the emblem of modern medium technology, served as an apparatus for channeling, educating, and regulating feelings for the Chinese and their Western interlocutors in the networked transnational media environment.

It is a well-rehearsed argument that the global dissemination of film technology and culture from its very inception at the end of the nineteenth century went hand in hand with Euro-American imperial forces' colonial enterprise of annexing foreign territories and markets, which resulted in truncating and drastically transforming the geopolitics and cultures of the regions that were subjected to various degrees and modes of colonization. The entanglement of cinema and colonialism (and coloniality, more broadly speaking) has spurred debates about the ways in which film, as a popular medium, participates in formulating local and global politics as articulated in the interconnected discourses of nationalism, decolonization, modernity, and globalization.

In this chapter, I first outline three strands of arguments that emerge from the debates on film's role in addressing and shaping the politics of coloniality, modernity, and nationalism. I then focus on a historical analysis of Chinese protests between the 1910s and the 1930s against Western-made films that were deemed detrimental to Chinese dignity and thus labeled as "China-humiliating" films (*ruHua pian*). The period from the 1910s to the 1930s witnessed two seismic transformations in China, namely (1) the dissemination and popularization of Western cinema in urban and coastal China and the emergence of a Chinese film industry, and (2) the demise of the Qing Dynasty and the founding of the Republic of China in 1911, which was soon fragmented (as a result of warlord strife) and then tentatively reunified only after the North Expedition eliminated or absorbed warlord factions in 1929. These momentous happenings make this period a critical conjuncture for excavating and tracing early film culture and its entanglement with China's nationalism in contention with coloniality.

In this context, Chinese protesters criticized what were identified as *ruHua* films so as to contest the unequal relationship between those who had the power to represent and those who were subjected to the power of representation. Yet, instead of assuming a binary opposition between Western imperial forces and Chinese subjects, I highlight the networked force field that resulted from the actual or rhetorical interactions that Chinese filmmakers, critics, and policy makers had with their Western (especially American) counterparts. It is through this networked force field that the uneven ground of transnational film media was contested and China's emerging decolonizing and nation-building projects were staged. I further argue that the impassioned debates over the *ruHua* films manifested an affective articulation and formation of sovereign racial-national identity in response to colonial modernity. In this sense, film, the emblem of modern medium technology, served as an apparatus of affective education for the Chinese and their Western interlocutors in a networked transnational force field.

Debating Film in Relation to Coloniality and Modernity

Three broad strands of argument emerge from the query into film's entanglement with colonialist and nationalist politics. The first strand sees film as part and parcel of an ideological apparatus in the service of specific economic and political agendas. The Japanese leftist critic Iwasaki Akira, for instance, published an essay in 1929, republished in 1931 (Iwasaki 1931), entitled *"Senden, sendō shudan to shite no eiga"* (Film as a means of propaganda and agitation).[1] According to the translation by Lu Xun, a pioneer practitioner of modern Chinese literature and a critic of popular culture, Iwasaki understood Western film (especially Hollywood productions) as a capitalist commodity that aimed to maximize profits and seduce and numb urban audiences by occluding class conflicts. Building on Iwasaki's criticism, Lu Xun contended that Hollywood exported films to China not to humiliate China but rather for profits, much as industrialized countries selling outmoded weaponry to backward countries (see Lu 1930). By stressing Hollywood as a weapon of global capitalist economic exploitation, Lu Xun critiqued Chinese campaigns against Western films and performers considered denigrating to the Chinese national character. The best-known examples of such campaigns include the protests against Harold Lloyd's *Welcome Danger* (1929) and Douglas Fairbanks's *The Thief of Bagdad* (1922).[2]

Instead of supporting the sentiments that rose against anything labeled *ruHua* or sentiments that were easily manipulated by knee-jerk jingoism, Lu Xun called on the Chinese to look inward to reflect on their own slavish mentality that resulted from prolonged political and economic subjugation. That mentality, he said, was characterized both by conceited belligerence and by self-denigrating reliance on Western endorsement. For Lu Xun, protesting against *ruHua* films failed to address the broader system of colonial exploitation that seeped into economic, political, and cultural domains. It also failed to understand the real danger of Hollywood, which lay not simply in its degrading portrayal of the (Chinese) Other, but, more important, in its complicity with Euro-American imperialism and colonialism. He summed up the whole package of Western exploitation of China as follows: having bred war and chaos in China by selling outmoded weaponry, the United States shipped out old Hollywood films to dazzle and befuddle Chinese audiences. When the films became even more worn out, they were shipped further inland to stupefy an even broader swath of the Chinese population (Lu 1930).[3]

Building on such economic and political critiques of Western film and its detrimental impact on peripheral and subjugated cultures and peoples, later scholars have studied the ways in which non-Euro-American cinemas have engaged with nationalism and decolonialism and their simultaneous challenge to nation-building projects. A pioneering endeavor is Dissanayake (1994), in which the contributors probe (with different degrees of success) filmic engagement with nationhood, colonialism, and postcoloniality in Japan, China, Taiwan, Korea, Vietnam, Thailand, Indonesia, India, Sri Lanka, and Australia.

Revising the critical premise that Western cinema facilitated colonialist power inequity, thus instigating the emergence of nationalist and decolonial cinema, some film scholars choose to focus on film as a global commodity and sensory medium fundamentally related to the experience of modernity in areas both within and beyond Euro-America. The most notable intervention is Miriam Hansen's (2000, 10) concept of "vernacular modernism" defined in terms of "a sensory reflexive horizon for the experience of modernization and modernity." Hansen originally developed this concept in her study of Hollywood cinema, drawing on the Habermasian "public sphere." Zhang Zhen (2005) further developed this concept in her historical study of Shanghai cinema from 1896 to 1937, paying special attention to the everyday sensory and vernacular experiences afforded by film.

This approach problematizes the reductive and determinist understanding of the film medium solely as a capitalist and colonialist tool and establishes a framework for analyzing film as a site of experiencing and negotiating modernity at the vernacular level. As I argue in my book, *Remaking Chinese Cinema* (Wang 2013), this approach risks essentializing and universalizing the sensory experience of modernity in ways that "evade colonial and subaltern politics, and thereby risk short-circuiting entrenched gender, class, and colonial power hierarchies." As will become clear in what follows, my approach to competing discourses on *ruHua* films builds on the experiential and sensory focus suggested by vernacular modernism. Yet I also reinsert colonial politics back into the discussion by mobilizing Walter Mignolo and Tani Barlow's (1997) theorization of the intertwined relationship between modernity and coloniality. Barlow uses the term "colonial modernity" to argue that modernity in the colonies and in what is conventionally called semicolonized Shanghai (and China more broadly) is inextricably bound up with global coloniality. Analogously, Mignolo (2000) calls attention to the mutual constitution of what he terms "local histories" and "global designs." He further emphasizes the importance of border thinking in negotiating the frequently conflicting local and global desires.

Both Barlow and Mignolo emphasize the power differential inherent in colonial modernity. We may best understand such politics by attending to its capillary, ground-level, and multivalent articulations (as opposed to the reductive determinism manifested in Iwasaki Akira's and Lu Xun's writings presented earlier). Such intensified attention to the ambivalent colonial power hierarchy has led to a third strand of scholarship that probes the ways in which colonialism, nationalism, modernity, and other cultural-political formations seep into (rather than comprehensively dictate) the variant and flexible uses of film—as entertainment and containment, as a "sensory reflexive horizon" for experiencing modernity, and as a tool of education, agitation, and ethno-nation building. This strand of scholarship is illustrated by the postcolonialism-inspired scholarship on colonial Korean cinema (or Joseon cinema). As summarized by Moonim Baek (2018), the rapidly growing field of Joseon cinema studies since 2000 takes a postcolonial turn and mobilizes deep and expansive archival research to shed new light on the complex and nuanced contestations and negotiations among multiple players, including Japanese settler-film businessmen, Korean filmmakers and audiences, the Japanese colonial government's regulations of film culture in Korea, Japan's expanding colonial market encompassing Manchuria and China, and the long history of importing and exhibiting films from Europe, America, and Russia in Korea. Countering the "national cinema" paradigm premised on simplistic binary opposition between the Japanese colonizer and the Korean colonized, Baek stresses the "more nuanced theoretical frameworks that incorporate transnational and transcolonial studies, which enables the tracing of conflicts existing between the colonizer and the colonized at multiple levels." In other words, the power differential undergirding film-mediated colonial modernity operated at the capillary level, seeping into multiple aspects of colonialism, modernity, and decolonialism and exceeding the binary model of colonial oppression versus nationalist resistance. It is in this context that the new and expanding film medium and the correlated discourses have offered a key site for formulating and rehearsing the contending political formations, and the medium and the discourses have in turn been shaped by the latter.

Building on these three major strands of debates on East and Northeast Asian cinemas and their relationship with colonial modernity, my article asks in what sense we might talk about colonial cinema in the Chinese context, especially in consideration of the fact that China was never colonized in the conventional sense. Its uneven and incomplete colonization (as explained in what follows) multiplied its internal and external borderlines, rendering them porous. It is therefore imperative that we trace the highly dynamic and sometimes contentious border-crossing interactions and the ways they simultaneously instigated and fractured the emerging Chinese film culture and the correlated image of China. Inspired by the postcolonial Joseon cinema studies, which takes a transnational and transcolonial perspective to foreground the complex capillary interactions between multiple domestic, settler-colonial, and Western players (including film workers, businessmen, audiences, and films that were domestically made or imported, screened, censored, or banned), I explore a specific discursive interlocution that contributed to projecting a mode of uplifting Chinese cinema. This discursive interlocution involved Chinese students, critics, practitioners, and policy makers, and their collective yet differing struggles over Western-made *ruHua* films. The struggles arose along with film's emergence and international dissemination and have periodically erupted throughout the history of Chinese reception of Western-made film and media up to the present day.[4] They agitated a vortex of discourses and practices such as open letters, appeals, protests, film burning, and censorship to engender a force field through which an uplifting Chinese cinema found expression.

Lu Xun's criticism of anti-*ruHua*-film protests as symptomatic of the slavish Chinese mentality and obsequiousness mixed with knee-jerk jingoism notwithstanding, the discourses and practices in protesting against *ruHua* films played a key role in enabling pro-China sentiments in the colonial power struggle. Meanwhile, it is important to note that the very understanding of China as one coherent geopolitical entity and as an ethnocultural identity varied significantly with the commentator's or agitator's self-positioning within and outside China. As a result, the pro-China sentiments bespoke what Raymond Williams (1977) would call a "structure of feeling" rather than a reified, homogeneous ideology. Such a structure of feeling, understood as an inchoate and preideological articulation responding to certain contradictions, registers an affective and capillary politics that have significantly shaped filmmaking and film culture in China.

In the following pages, I outline key instances of heated debates over *ruHua* films mounted by Chinese within China and overseas in the first three decades of the twentieth century. My study locates the formation of Chinese cinema and the correlated subject position at the very intersection of colonial politics and modern media technology, which was experienced at the affective level as a structure of feeling. It is through the experiential and affective interactions and contentions that (Chinese) cinema emerged as an apparatus of producing political emotions that irreversibly stitched China into the global mediascape, thus giving rise to the contested and fractured definition of Chineseness.

Sub-/Semicolonial China and the Diverse Discourses of Protest

Before exploring the intricate discourses and practices of protesting against *ruHua* films, an outline of China's idiosyncratic colonial condition is in order. Unlike colonies in South Asia, Africa, and Latin America, pre-1949 China was not exclusively colonized by any single imperialist force; nor was its sovereignty completely subsumed by a colonial government. Instead, parts of China, especially the treaty ports designated in the aftermath of China's repeated defeat by multinational Western forces, were carved up and ceded to various imperial countries that exercised extraterritorial power in their respective concessions. This condition was described by Dr. Sun Yat-sen—founder of the Republic of China—as subcolonial (*ci zhimindi*) in the 1920s. According to Sun (1928), the subcolony was even more wretched than a complete colony (such as the Japanese colonization of Korea or the French colonization of Vietnam), in that there was not a single colonizer to be held responsible for the governance and protection of the colonized subjects.[5] By the 1930s, term *ci zhimindi* was replaced by *ban zhimindi* (semicolony) and was widely adopted by socially conscious and left-leaning critics and filmmakers.

After 1949, the concept of semicolonialization was reified by the Communist government as the standard description of China's pre-1949 Republican Era with an eye to foreclosing a more nuanced understanding of its polyvalent lived experience, culture, and geopolitics and served to validate the Communist party's historical role in liberating China from Western subjugation. In the 1990s, a revisionist discourse of modernity and cosmopolitanism arose with an attempt to correct the reductive politics inscribed in the reified concept of semicolonialism.[6] This revisionist turn coincided with Miriam Hansen's (2000) "vernacular modernism" and its inspiration for the study of early Chinese cinema culture. The critique of reductive politics necessitates a more nuanced rethinking of the politics of global coloniality as illustrated in Tani Barlow's (1997) and Walter Mignolo's (2000) emphasis on colonial modernity. Following Barlow and Mignolo, I offer my study of Chinese discourses on *ruHua* films to further fine-tune our understanding of colonial politics. I do so by turning from political determinism to careful discernment of how hegemonic politics percolated into the more nebulous and affective experiences of those negotiating the polyvalent yet unequal colonial power structure.

Film, the paradigmatic Western import that quickly took root in China, serves as a particularly fruitful site for unpacking the affective workings of colonial politics. Film's mass appeal led to the quick realization by Chinese commentators both within China and overseas that it was an exceptionally impactful medium. It was soon harnessed as a stage for rehearsing, constructing, and debating the broader-scale cultural, social, and political techniques of subjectivity formation, nation building, and governance. In other words, film, from its very inception, has served as a contact zone that galvanizes multiple players to negotiate their power disparity and to carve out and contest their relative positions. Indigenous filmmaking in politically and economically compromised China emerged precisely in interacting with global film enterprises and the broader global colonial structure. An indication of the local-global entanglement is that the earliest film studios and screening venues were primarily owned and run by Westerners. An example is Benjamin Brodsky, a Russian American who launched one of China's earliest film studios, the Asia Film Company (*Yaxiya yingxi gongsi*), in 1909, which recruited Chinese as directors and actors and produced short films and travelogues in Hong Kong and Shanghai. Overall, the 1910s was a time when Chinese cinema emerged in collaboration with an international circuit of traveling cameramen, exhibitors, opportunity seekers, journalists, and missionaries who imported filmmaking equipment, technologies, and Western films to China. They ran film exhibitions and engaged with sporadic or consistent filmmaking in China by tapping the Chinese ethnography and culture and its market and resources. Coinciding with the burgeoning film culture in China, the young yet volatile Republican Chinese government (represented by the Chinese Embassy in Washington) was reported to have participated in a conference in 1916 to assure those who represented big business interests in San Francisco, Philadelphia, and New York that the government would support film production in China (*Variety* 1916). It was not until 1922 that Chinese-funded film studios started to boom, and soon they ventured into long narrative films. The collaborative yet inherently unequal Sino-Western interactions engendered the complex geopolitical force field in which Chinese cinema became both possible and circumscribed.

A distinguishing feature of this force field is the ensemble of players it involved: Western traveler-entrepreneurs in China who opened film studios and theaters, shooting footage during their travels and exhibited Western films; overseas Chinese (including students) who actively criticized Western films that purportedly jeopardized Chinese interests; and emerging Chinese filmmakers, who started to mobilize film for the nation-building project while also appealing to the masses with film's entertainment value. Finally, the nationalist Chinese government became increasingly involved in monitoring and censoring films that negatively reflected on the Chinese image. These players all shared the consensus on the critical importance of film technology and representation. Yet they occupied drastically different power positions. As I argue further on, their engagement with each other through the reiterative contentions over Western *ruHua* films demonstrated the ways in which colonialist and ethnonationalist power struggles consistently worked on the affective level, agitating a gamut of sentiments that led to shifting relative positions of the interlocutors and contenders and their flexible strategies of engagement. One of the earliest instances of

Chinese objections to American film's derogatory representation of Chinese characters was an open letter originally written in 1916 in English by a University of Iowa overseas Chinese student, Li Chow-lin (1916). This letter, purportedly addressed to all American newspapers, was soon translated into Chinese by Wang Yuxiang. According to Lee Chow-lin's diagnosis (as presented in Wang's translation), American cinema failed to refine personal life (*yuqing*) or improve social manners (*huasu*)—two lofty yardsticks traditionally applied to literature and arts and designed to enhance social morality. Instead, American cinema was accused of aggravating bad taste by producing and disseminating derogatory Chinese imagery. Li warned that if American filmmakers did not mend their ways, Chinese filmmakers might also start misrepresenting Americans, which would jeopardize the interests of American missionaries and merchants in China. The translator, Wang Yuxiang, prefaced his translation by offering a different perspective. Instead of simply blaming American filmmakers, Wang urged overseas Chinese to become self-reflective and self-disciplined and to cleanse their bad habits of opium consumption, tong wars, and poor hygiene in order to remedy their bad reputation. Such self-improvement, according to Wang, would help to stymie the derogatory representation put forward by the West. Important to note is that this critique originated in the United States and was translated into Chinese when Chinese filmmaking was at its incipient stage. Wang's translation not only disseminated the diasporic Chinese voice within China but also stimulated discussion—from Chinese within China and diasporic Chinese, urging self-uplifting as a method of resisting Western *ruHua* films. In other words, despite their shared agenda of resisting *ruHua* films, the exact methods of accomplishing the goal depended on the stance of the commentator.

Five years after Li's open letter, *Yingxi zazhi* (The motion picture review), commonly recognized as the first formal Chinese film magazine, was launched on April 1, 1921. The mission statement by the editor, Gu Kenfu, could be read as a reflection on the history of foreign investors filming in China (Gu 1621). He also reiterated Li's criticism of American films' derogatory portrayal of Chinese characters. He deplored the way Western filmmakers fetishized China's backwardness in their documentaries and their penchant to make Chinese characters seedy and subservient, causing Chinese "character bankruptcy" (*renge pochan*). Reacting against this problem, Ku outlined four goals of his magazine, two of which were to "prevent the circulation of injurious films" (*fangzhi youhai yingpian de liuxing*) and to "fight to safeguard the respectable image of China in the realm of motion pictures and theater" (*zai yingju jie shang ti women zhongguo ren zheng renge*).

Many articles published in *Yingxi zazhi* echoed Ku's mission statement by calling attention to and criticizing films that were deemed to have negatively reflected on the Chinese character. Furthermore, the writers promoted indigenous films that would correct the damage caused by Western films. In the article "Guan Tangrenjie xue'an zhi zhuiyan" (San San 1922; Thoughts on *Outside the Law*), one writer targeted *Outside the Law* (dir. Tod Browning, Universal, 1920) and *For the Freedom of the East* (dir. Ira M. Lowry, Betzwood Film, 1918) for their disrespectful portrayal of Chinese characters. The writer criticized the female lead in *For the Freedom of the East*, Lady Tsen Mei—presumed to be Chinese—for having been away and alienated from China for too long to properly represent Chinese women.[7] The character she portrayed was jilted by a Western man, which was considered a disgrace for the overall Chinese image. The writer further contended that *ruHua* films woke up the Chinese like a canon blast, catalyzing an eruption of indigenous Chinese cinema, which the writer believed must take it on itself to promote a positive image of China. In the same issue, a list of dos and don'ts that aimed to fashion a more cultivated audience specifically instructed the audience to monitor the ethics of film and report to the theater manager when the theater showed film that humiliated China (Ken 1922).

In the same year (1922), two more overseas Chinese students threw down their gauntlets to William Hays, president of the newly founded Motion Picture Producers and Distributors of America (MPPDA). Riding on the waves of the American religious groups' calls for film sanitation, T. C. Li, president of Chinese Students' Alliance in the USA, addressed "A Challenge to Mr. Will Hays" (Li 1922). Recognizing film as a powerful weapon of education, Li lamented American cinema that served as "sinister propaganda" and did "gross injustice" to "one fourth of the world's population [i.e., the Chinese]." Li concluded his challenge by urging Hays to suppress films that jeopardized "truthfulness and international friendship."

In the same issue of *Chinese Students Monthly* as Li's challenge to Hays, another article (*Chinese Students Monthly* 1922), pointed to the vicious cycle in which the American audience and film producers reinforced each other's vices, the former paying to get their minds poisoned and the latter getting paid to poison the public minds. The writer further opined that the filmic misrepresentation of China went hand in hand with the American racial prejudice against the Chinese. To uphold film's fundamental power of education, the writer concluded by tasking Hays with building a healthier and more open-minded American audience. "If the public shows a morbid taste, reform it. If the public has no good taste, create it. If the public possesses a wholesome taste, foster it."

It is not surprising that overseas Chinese students tended to be in harmony with Chinese critics and some filmmakers in protesting against *ruHua* films and enthusiastically championing a positive Chinese image for the international audience. But overseas students were also scrutinized by China-based critics who questioned the diasporic community's ability to properly represent China. Xu Hu (credited as Shu Hou in the film), a student in France who studied makeup with the comedian Gabriel Signoret, for instance, was heavily criticized for his portrayal of a Chinese character in a French film, *The Veil of Happiness* (dir. E. E. Violet, 1923, adapted from a play by the former premier of France, Georges Clemenceau). In an article that urged Chinese cinema to excavate thus-far untapped Chinese fine arts, instead of mimicking Western makeup and cinematic aesthetics, Xu Hu (like Lady Tsen Mei in the United States) was considered too Westernized to understand Chinese aesthetics.

According to a reviewer Zhang Guangyu (*Dianying zazhi*), the style of *The Veil of Happiness* was muddled. One of the Chinese male characters was inexplicably dressed like Jia Baoyu (a fictional character from *The Dream of Red Chambers*—one of the best-known Qing Dynasty novels, which chronicles the vicissitudes of an aristocratic family); women were dressed in Vietnamese costumes; a character wore a moustache evocative of Charlie Chaplin or a Japanese man. Even with a cast made up of educated overseas Chinese students, the film still managed to make Chinese a laughingstock, lamented the reviewer. Another reviewer (Xin 1926) maintained that the film contained so many errors[8] that it was not much better than Western-made *ruHua* films.

Here the reviewer assumed or expected the film to be Chinese simply because it featured a Chinese cast, disregarding the fact the play was written by a former French premier and was previously staged with a complete Caucasian cast, and that the film version was produced by a French company and French crew and was aimed at a French audience. The misapprehension led the Chinese gatekeepers to espouse the misplaced expectation that the film should offer an image of China approved by them. According to Xu Hu's account as documented in *Shen Pao* (Shanghai News) (1926), however, the fact that he offered to participate in the film and instigated the replacement of the Caucasian cast with a Chinese one was already sufficient evidence of his successful attempt to correct the Western imaging of China.

The discrepant expectations between the Chinese commentators and the overseas Chinese (despite their shared objection to *ruHua* films) indicate that the question of how to represent China under global coloniality was more than a matter of doing the right thing. For the question of what was the right thing—and who had the right to define and execute it—remained disputable. The contending definitions of the most desirable representation boiled down to the fight for the right of representation. This contention spurred bifurcated authorships, in other words, the burgeoning authorship of Chinese cinema and the rise of Chinese American filmmaking—both emerging in the 1920s. The most prominent example of the Chinese American film enterprise with a pronounced commitment to refashioning Chinese imagery is the Great Wall Film Company (*Changcheng zhizao huanpian gongsi*). Registered in Brooklyn, New York, in April 1921, the company was founded by overseas Chinese who were infuriated by two *ruHua* American films—*The Red Lantern* (dir. Albert Capellani, 1919) and *The First Born* (dir. Colin Campbell, 1921). *The Red Lantern*, set in the stereotypically xenophobic China during the Boxer Rebellion, featured a Russian émigré actress, Alla Nazimova, playing two half-sibling roles, one Eurasian, the other white. *The First Born* featured the Japanese actor Sessue Hayakawa in a Chinese role. The films aroused ire from some overseas Chinese. Apparently dismissed by what was documented as the "American central censorship committee" that claimed if the Chinese could produce their own films, and therefore that such demeaning depiction in American films would naturally disappear, these overseas Chinese decided to seek training in acting and directing in New York schools. They founded the Zhenzhen Society, dedicated to studying film and filmmaking. In 1921 they incorporated the Great Wall Film Company, procured equipment (including de Brie cameras and arc lighting equipment from the Motion Picture Apparatus Company (*Motion Picture World* 1921); and continued to study animation, cinematography, and lighting. In 1922 they made two shorts on Chinese costumes and martial arts, distributed by Urban Motion Picture Industries (Chi Hen 1927).[9]

In 1924 the founders moved the company to Shanghai, where they produced socially oriented "problem films" and genre films until 1930. They sustained the discourse of correcting Western films' injurious Chinese imagery and strove to establish themselves in the nascent filmmaking industry in China.[10] During the film company's short and still much-shrouded history, they made fiction films (initially focusing on the social problem type, later including commercial genres such as martial arts and fantasy films), newsreels, and cartoons (Chen and Xiao 2004). It is important to note that the founders maintained their US connections not only to procure state-of-the-art filming equipment but also to export their Shanghai-made films to the United States.

Their films, imported by Harold L. Lee, were shown to the diasporic Chinese communities in the Chatham Theatre in New York, a China vaudeville theater in Los Angeles, and in Chinatown in Chicago (*Film Daily* 1930). One might argue that an exclusively Chinese clientele prevented the Great Wall founders from achieving what they initially intended, which was to remedy the derogatory Western representation of China and Chinese people. Indeed, it is hard to gauge the degree to which the founders' originally expressed intent was translated into their filmmaking practice, and the efficacy of their practice. To the extent that the films' audiences were largely confined to the (diasporic) Chinese, and that Chinese protests against perceived *ruHua* Euro-American films continued from the 1920s on, one might speculate that the company's Chinese-made films had little impact on the Western depiction of China. The apparent inefficacy compelled Chinese filmmaking to continuously derive part of its raison d'être from the discourse of antihumiliation, which contributed to the decolonizing and nation-building agendas.

By the 1930s, not only politically conscious critics, filmmakers, and viewers, but also the Kuomintang-led Nationalist government participated in and sometimes escalated the campaigns to penalize and eradicate *ruHua* films. The government's increasing involvement followed shortly after its unification of China in 1928, terminating a twelve-year period of factional strife between warlords. The unification stimulated the Kuomintang (KMT) party's endeavor to implement nationwide integral, ideological, and cultural control over not only domestic filmmaking but also the domestic audience's reception of Western films. As a result, antihumiliating protests that were initially launched by individuals or local groups came to obtain the central government's official endorsement and support.

One of the most prominent antihumiliating instances was the prolonged protest against Harold Lloyd's *Welcome Danger* (1929), a protest that spread across China and also caused the removal of the film from theaters in countries such as Panama at the demand of the Chinese embassy.[11] After the *Welcome Danger* ban, a document called Regulations for Film Censorship (*Dianying jiancha fa*) was issued on November 3, 1930, to censor both domestic and foreign films, the second category later expanded to include foreign films screened in foreign concessions according to the policy revision on April 4, 1931. The number-one target of censorship, according to the regulations, was "films that damage Chinese dignity" (*yousun zhonghua minzu zhi zhunyan zhe*). A decree issued by the Film Censorship Committee (under the Ministry of Education; *Jiaoyu neizhengbu dianying jiancha weiyuan hui*), dated October 3, 1931, stated that cinema ought to be used to educate the masses and inculcate patriotism at a time of national crisis (referring to the most recent Japanese invasion into northeast China on September 18, 1931). Since film stimulates audiences viscerally, leaving indelible impressions, movie theaters were encouraged to show more films and newsreels on military training, science, and patriotic subjects. Another decree dated October 6, 1931, stated that as of October 10, new domestic films shown in domestic theaters must eliminate Western intertitles—filmed printed text—in order to privilege Chinese national integrity (*yi zhong guoti*).[12] The censorship regulations indicated the KMT government's mounting efforts to surveil foreign and domestic films with the goal of establishing a homogeneous positive public image of modern nationalist China.

Coinciding with the central government's intensifying scrutiny of *ruHua* films was the emphasis on a specific rhetoric of protest that not only identified and criticized the offending films but also threatened to burn them, thus literally annihilating the injurious image once and for all. The rhetoric (and practice) of film burning came into circulation with the 1930 *Welcome Danger* protest (mentioned earlier), when the Film Censorship Committee in Shanghai ordered the theaters showing the film to burn the prints. In 1932 Ren Chu (possibly a nationalist-minded viewer or critic) criticized a First National Pictures production, *The Hatchet Man* (dir. William A. Wellman, 1932), for exaggerating the Chinese characters' violence and urged the Chinese government to burn the film prints. In June 1932 Chinese students in Germany reported *Shanghai Express* (dir. Josef von Sternberg, 1932) as an offensive film to the Chinese Embassy in Germany and demanded that the screening be stopped. They further urged the Chinese Film Censorship Committee to confront Paramount and demand that all prints be burned. In response, the Censorship Board corresponded with Paramount, urging it to recall all overseas prints and negatives and to burn all prints of the film.

Toward a Capillary, Affective Approach to China's Cinema Culture under Colonial Modernity

The history of Chinese protests (both within China and overseas) against perceived *ruHua* films emblematized the dynamic and multipronged force field that implicated the interactions of multiple players. Players and interlocutors occupied differential positions of power as determined by the geopolitical context of colonial modernity. Negotiating their marginalized position in the global mediascape, ethnoscape, and technoscape, Chinese protesters (within and outside China) tried a range of strategies, for example, appealing to William Hays, demanding the burning of the offending films, and experimenting with redemptive China-affirmative filmmaking. The results of their strategies varied significantly.

What is important, though, is that, whether the Chinese protests took the form of an admonishing appeal or the oppositional demand for film burning, the protests consistently staged decolonial political contentions in emotional and experiential terms rather than resorting to analytical political concepts. The recurring theme in the protesting discourse was the hurt national feelings and dignity, which imposed shame on the Chinese viewer-critics and instigated their resistance to the shame. Rather than breaking away from hegemonic Hollywood, the campaigns emphasized hurt feelings and ethnonational pride, ultimately seeking to persuade their Western interlocutors to empathize with the feelings of marginalized peoples so as to design a more widely appealing cinema.

The appeal to feelings and affective experiences seemed to meet an overdue response from the Hays office. The overseas Chinese students' "challenge" to William Hays in 1922 did not seem to receive any response, but the MPPDA did eventually take measures to discourage blatant racism, if only for the purpose of securing and expanding its international market. In 1927 the MPPDA issued a set of "don'ts and be carefuls" that specifically forbade "willful offense to any nation, race or creed" and recommended "avoiding picturizing [sic] in an unfavorable light another country's religion, history, institutions, prominent people, and citizenry." In March 1930, precisely as the KMT government-sponsored campaign against *Welcome Danger* was underway, the Hays Code (the Motion Picture Production Code) was issued to monitor the production of the emerging talkies and to facilitate "a still higher level of wholesome entertainment for all the people." The code contained a section on national feelings, stressing fair representation of the "history, institutions, prominent people, and citizenry of other nations" ("Code to Govern," 410). If this caution did not eradicate *ruHua* films, its apparent response to the Chinese protests (increasingly endorsed by the KMT government) indicated a degree of success on the part of the Chinese protesters who attempted to reshape the transnational film scene to accommodate the interests of the Chinese participants. In this light, the Chinese protesters' agency consisted in their success (albeit limited) in readjusting the colonial power field.

The Chinese protester's efforts to persuade their more empowered interlocutors to transform their actions (rather than categorical antagonism) in the campaigns against *ruHua* films emblematized the subaltern strategies of negotiation under colonial modernity. Because of its technological origin in Euro-America and its almost instant dissemination across the world, film exerted both a power of amazement and an irresistible but one-way force of representation. As a result, film simultaneously fascinated the audiences who were subjected to Euro-American representation and triggered their suspicion and contestation of the use of the technology. In other words, the cultural-political environment that gave rise to the Chinese cinema culture also led to the (overseas) Chinese interlocutors' "double consciousness" (to use W. E. B. DuBois's term) or the compulsion to perceive China and themselves from the Euro-American colonialist and Orientalist perspective that was inscribed in Western cinema (and other cultural products). What this compulsive double consciousness implied was the Chinese interlocutors' simultaneous attraction to and anxiety about the power of the film medium, which resulted in two ways of addressing the perceived injurious filmic depiction of ethnonational China. One was self-uplifting (as urged by some commentators). But the approach I foreground in this study is the anti-colonial protests against *ruHua* films and the endeavors to carve out their own space in filmmaking.

The Chinese interlocutors' ambivalent reception of film (desiring it and critiquing its power at the same time) was fundamentally visceral and affective, which was in turn driven by their cultural-political interests. By appealing to feelings of hurt, shame, and pride, the ethnic Chinese commentators and the newly consolidated KMT government funneled political contentions into capillary articulations, rendering filmmaking and its spectatorship an apparatus of emotional education that strove to reshuffle the power structure under colonial modernity. Thus, to fully understand the ways in which colonial modernity shaped and undergirded Chinese film culture during the pre-1949 era, one must both go beyond political determinism and avoid depoliticization in order to retrace the affective and experiential dimension of politics.

As my study has demonstrated, the Chinese interlocutors and the government engaged their Western counterparts in a sustained and interactive process of (re)defining and producing the desirable "Chineseness" on the international stage. Through this process, the assembly of players constantly readjusted their relative positions as a gamut of sentiments was unleashed and addressed. The emergent film technology and film cultures thus became important sites for contending feelings and powers to play out during the volatile first part of the twentieth century. By underscoring the rhetoric of sentiments that enabled Chinese anticolonial self-authorship to unfold in the international film arena, my study calls for an affective approach to understanding not only Chinese cinema under colonial modernity but also the broader decolonial and nation-building politics.

Notes

1. Iwasaki Akira's essay, "*Senden, sendō shudan to shite no eiga*" ("Film as a means of propaganda and agitation") was originally published in November 1929 and was later included in his 1931 book *Eiga to shihonshugi* [Film and capitalism].

2. For an in-depth study of the affective politics of the Chinese protest against *Welcome Danger*, see Wang (2014).

3. For an earlier discussion of Lu Xun's critique of film as a bourgeoisie weapon, see Wang (2014).

4. The best-known antihumiliation case during the high socialist era is the state-sponsored campaign against Michelangelo Antonioni's *Chung Kuo/Cina* (China) (1972). Antonioni made his documentary in China at the invitation of China's premier, Zhou Enlai; the documentary was said to deliberately highlight backward aspects of China, distorting and trivializing socialist achievements. For a discussion of the film's condemnation in China and its aesthetic "visual reality" (instead of socialist realism), see Jenny Lin (2014). A more recent antihumiliating case was the protest against the Italian luxury designer fashion D & G's three short videos released on the Chinese social media network Weibo to promote its upcoming Shanghai runway extravaganza—"the Great Show"--on November 21, 2018. The videos were chastised for racism in that they feature a D & G-clad Chinese actress awkwardly attempting to eat Italian pizza, spaghetti, and cannoli with chopsticks while being mocked by a Mandarin-speaking male voice-over. The collective outcry that erupted on the internet soon led many Chinese actors and models who were invited to walk the runway to withdraw, which resulted in the cancellation of the "Great Show." The D & G products were subsequently removed from the online stores of China's e-commerce giants. For an account of this incident, see Xu (2018).

5. I do not subscribe to Sun's analysis of the conditions of complete colonization, but his diagnosis of China's unique geopolitics in relation to global colonialism is important and worth revisiting.

6. For a signal example, see Lee (1999).

7. Lady Tsen Mei, known in China as Zheng Mei (郑美), was thought to be a Chinese diplomat's daughter. Her birth name, however, was Josephine Moy. She was born in Philadelphia and raised by a Chinese American doctor. See her US passport application forms and "The Chinese Nightingale" chapter in Seligman (2012). Copies of her passport applications can be found at ancestry.com.

8. The reviewer listed these errors: the house architecture was Japanese, the interior decor was arranged in the Western fashion, the protagonist's poem was plagiarized from a Tang poem and could trick only Westerners, the calligraphy on street banners was poor, the act of kissing was not Chinese, the son was played by a Caucasian boy, and, finally, the subtitles were rendered in poor Chinese, and also were misplaced.

9. People involved in founding the film company included the overseas Chinese students Li Zeyuan (Zuliong L. Lee?) and Cheng Peilin, journalists Mei Xuechou and Liu Zhaoming, merchants Hon Sang Lum and Harold L. Lee, and possibly an American, Harry Gregin (or Grogin) (Chi Hen 1927).

10. A letter sent from the Great Wall Film Company to *Daolu yuekan* (The road construction monthly) indicated the company's origin in New York and its continuous mission to improve the Chinese imagery on the international stage. It further confirmed the company founders' lack of knowledge of China because of their overseas background, which made it difficult for them to access Chinese sceneries ("Wendu" 1924, 98–99).

11. For a detailed analysis of the ramifications of the *Welcome Danger* ban, see Wang (2014, 186–209).

12. Shanghai-made silent films routinely included English-Chinese bilingual intertitles. This linguistic hybridity is indicative of the filmmakers' acknowledgment of the film medium's Western origin and their desire to reach the demographically mixed audience both within and outside China.

Bibliography

Baek, Moonim. 2018. "Revisiting Colonial Cinema Research in Korea." *Journal of Japanese and Korean Cinema* 10, no. 2: 85–91.

Barlow, Tani. 1997. "Colonialism's Career in Postwar China Studies." In *Formations of Colonial Modernity in East Asia*. Edited by Tani Barlow, 373–411. Durham, NC: Duke University Press.

Chen Mo and Xiao Zhiwei. 2004. "Kuaihai de 'Changcheng': cong jianli dao tanta; Changcheng huapian gongsi lishi cutan" [The "great wall" that bridges the ocean: from founding to collapsing; a preliminary study of the history of the Great Wall Film Company]. *Dangdai dianying* [Contemporary film] no. 3: 36–44.

Chi Hen, ed. 1927. *Zhongguo dianying daguan* [An encyclopedia of Chinese cinema]. Shanghai: Hezuo.

Chinese Students Monthly. 1922. "The Reform of American Cinemas." *Chinese Students Monthly* 18, no. 2 (December): 6.

"Code to Govern the Making of Talking, Synchronized and Silent Motion Pictures (Motion Pictures Production Code)." 2014. In *Film Manifestos and Global Cinema Cultures: A Critical Anthology*. Edited by Scott MacKenzie, 405–16. Berkeley: University of California Press.

Dianying jiancha fa (Regulations for Film Censorship), November 3, 1930.

Dissanayake, Wimal, ed. 1994. *Colonialism and Nationalism in Asian Cinema*. Bloomington: Indiana University Press.

Film Daily. 1930. "Chinese Films Only Shown in Three Cities in the U.S., Lee Says." *Film Daily*, March 6, 1, 8.

Gu, Kenfu. 1921. "Fakan ci" [Mission statement]. *Yingxi zazhi* [The motion picture review], April 1, 10.

Hansen, Miriam. 2000. "Fallen Women, Rising Stars, New Horizons: Shanghai Silent Film as Vernacular Modernism." *Film Quarterly* 54, no.1 (Fall): 10–22.

Iwasaki, Akira. 1931. "Senden, sendō shudan to shite no eiga" [Film as a means of propaganda and agitation]. In *Eiga to shihon shugi* [Film and capitalism]. Tokyo: Oraisha.

Ken. 1922. "Yingxi guanzong zhi shijie" [Ten commandments for film audience]. *Yingxi zazhi* [Motion picture review] 1, no. 3 (May 25): 8.

Lee, Leo Ou-fan. 1999. *Shanghai Modern: The Flowering of a New Urban Culture in China, 1930–1945*. Cambridge, MA: Harvard University Press.

Lee Chow-lin. 1916. "Wei huodong xiezhen miaoxie huaqiao zhi wuzhuang zhi quanmei ge baoshu" [A Letter addressed to American Newspapers Concerning Moving Pictures' Derogatory Depiction of Overseas Chinese]. Wang Yuxiang, trans. *Liumei xuesheng jibao* [Quarterly of Chinese students in America] 3, no. 4: 167–71.

Li, T. C. 1922. "A Challenge to Mr. Will Hays." *Chinese Students Monthly* [New Haven, CT] 18, no. 2 (December): 31–32.

Lin, Jenny. 2014. "Seeing a World Apart: Visual Reality in Michelangelo Antonioni's *Chung Kuo/Cina*." *ARTMargins* 3, no. 3 (October): 21–44.

Lu Xun. 1930. "Xiandai dianying yu youchan jieji: yiwen bin fuji" [Modern cinema and the propertied classes: translation and commentary]. *Mengya Monthly* 1, no. 3 (March): 1–33.

Mignolo, Walter. 2000. *Local Histories/Global Designs: Coloniality, Subaltern Knowledges, and Border Thinking*. Princeton, NJ: Princeton University Press.

Motion Picture World. 1921. "De Brie Camera Will Shoot Chinese Pictures." *Motion Picture World*, May 7, 110.

Ren Chu. 1932. "Qing zhuyi ruHua yingpian" [Beware of a new China-humiliating film]. *Yinbo Yingkan* (Yinbo film magazine) 1, no. 3 (June 1), n.p.

San San. 1922. "Guan Tangrenjie xue'an zhi zhuiyan" [Thoughts on *Outside the Law*]. 1922. *Yingxi zazhi* (The motion picture review) 1, no. 3 (May 25), 16.

Seligman, Scott D. 2012. *Three Tough Chinamen*. Hong Kong: Earnshaw.

"Shiren wamu ji: qian Fa zongli Kelimansha bianju, Zhong liufa Zhongguo dianying mingxing zhuyan" (Veil of Happiness: Original Play by the Former French Premiere Clemenceau, Featuring Xu Hu Chinese Student Studying in France). 1926. *Shen Pao* (Shanghai News) (Mar. 11): 1.

Sun Yat-sen. 1928. *Sanmin zhuyi: The Three Principles of the People*. Translated by Frank W. Price. Shanghai: Commercial.

Variety. 1916. "Chinese Film Trust." *Variety*, September, 22.

Wang, Yiman. 2013. *Remaking Chinese Cinema: Through the Prism of Shanghai, Hong Kong, and Hollywood*. Honolulu, HI: University of Hawaii Press.

———. 2014. "The Crisscrossed Stare: Protest and Propaganda in China's Not-So-Silent Era." In *Silent Cinema and the Politics of Space*. Edited by Jennifer Bean, Laura Horak, and Anupama Kapse, 186–209. Bloomington: Indiana University Press.

"Wendu (zhailu): Changcheng huapian gongsi laihan" [Excerpt of a letter from the Great Wall Film Company). 1924. *Daolu yuekan* (Road construction monthly) 11, nos. 2–3: 98–99.

Williams, Raymond. 1977. *Marxism and Literature*. Oxford: Oxford University Press.

Xin Leng. 1926. "Shiren wamu ji zhimiu" [Errors in *The Veil of Happiness*]. *Guowen zhoubao* [News weekly] 3, no. 10: 37–39.

Xu, Yuhan. 2018. "Dolce and Gabbana Ad (with Chopsticks) Provokes Public Outrage in China." (December 1). *National Public Radio: Goats and Soda*. https://www.npr.org/sections/goatsandsoda/2018/12/01/671891818/dolce-gabbana-ad-with-chopsticks-provokes-public-outrage-in-china.

Zhang Guangyu. "Tan dianying meishu" [On the fine arts of film]. *Dianying zazhi* no. 5 (1924).

Zhang Zhen. 2005. *An Amorous History of the Silver Screen: Shanghai Cinema, 1896–1937*. Chicago: University of Chicago Press.

YIMAN WANG is Professor of Film and Digital Media at the University of California–Santa Cruz. She is author of *Remaking Chinese Cinema: Through the Prism of Shanghai, Hong Kong, and Hollywood* and guest editor of the "Asian Feminist Media" special issue of *Feminist Media Histories* volume 5, no. 1 (Winter 2019). She is currently finishing a monograph on Anna May Wong, the best known early 20th-century Chinese American screen-stage performer. Her numerous articles have appeared in journals and edited volumes.

5. WORLD EXPORT
Melodramas of Colonial Conquest

Jane M. Gaines

Abstract

This chapter begins by setting the historical stage as background to the export of US cinema to the rest of the world, a century of cultural imperialism that is too often assumed rather than documented. If other fields assume Hollywood imperialism, the history of the motion picture assumes too much on the theoretical front—for example, the postcolonial critique of uneven cultural circulation and the West's historical imagination of "the East." I then ask, "What was exported?" and examine three answers—classical Hollywood narrative, "vernacular modernism," and popular melodrama—as approaches that lend themselves to the question of the other half of the export-import equation: "What was done with the export upon arrival?" The centerpiece is a case study of a film starring Alla Nazimova called *The Red Lantern* (Albert Capellani, dir., Metro Pictures, 1919), based on the 1911 novel of the same name, that interprets the 1900 Boxer Rebellion in China from the point of view of the Western missionary. I put this film to a test of cultural confluence that considers (1) what *was already* "there" in the Chinese encounter with Western modernity, (2) what Hollywood imagined was "there" in its fantasy of the Far East, and (3) what epic narrative structures were adopted in early export blockbusters made to conquer the viewing world and that were modeled after *The Birth of a Nation* (D. W. Griffith, dir., 1915). That these films can be viewed as melodramas of race and nation makes them useful for demonstrating what film melodrama theory tells us about popular narratives recruited to rationalize newly racialized social orders coincident with colonial conquest abroad. Last, this chapter puts concepts emerging from Hollywood in dialogue with contemporary theorizations featured in this volume and elsewhere by Zhang Zhen, Weihong Bao, and Yiman Wang on Chinese cinematic discourses as well as Aaron Gerow on the question about the centrality of the West in the original theorization of Japanese film critics.

Introduction

The US motion picture industry began to plot world control just at the start of World War I, even before its European competitors had decimated each other. As early as 1914, the industry vehicle *Motography* is triumphal: "When peace reigns once more in Europe, one of the first harbingers of the return to normal living will be the reopening of the picture theaters. And their programs will be made up of American-made films. Then will come the greatest prosperity the American manufacturers have ever known. With their South American market not only established, but developed way beyond its present capacity; with the European market forced to rely almost exclusively on their productions; and with the domestic market bigger than ever, American-made films will not only lead the world—they will constitute it" (as quoted in Thompson 1985, 54). In 1916, Universal Pictures opened offices in Japan, India, and Singapore (Thompson, 204–5). Then, in 1917, it opened in China (Fu 2019, 14).

Metro Pictures and Export and Import Films, the American agent for Nazimova Films, in 1919 may also have been contemplating the East Asian market but ran into difficulty with one colonial epic, *The Red Lantern* (Albert Capellani, dir.). An adaptation of a popular 1911 novel set during the 1900 Boxer Rebellion and written by a former missionary's daughter, Edith Wherry, the extravagant production is a window into how the West imagined the rest. But, eerily, it is also an allegory of the paradox of Chinese colonial modernity: Could China modernize without westernizing, when to resist meant facing modernization by force? (See Yoshimi 2005.) As of every paradox, we will need to ask, How can this possibly be? But we will also need to ask how to account for the power of the export product as well as the enormity of the commercial campaign. Now, let's remember, the very totality of the US world film market takeover has never been in dispute. Indeed, from a market perspective, the globalization of consumer culture via moving pictures appears as a given. Yet, within film and media studies, there is as yet no consensus as to how to theorize what was exported, let alone what to say about what becomes of the import *over there* on arrival. So we have here an import-export paradox companion to that of Chinese modernity: what was exported was not the same as what was imported.[1] This chapter, more about the export than the import side of the equation, asks, What was it that Hollywood exported to the rest of the world? The corollary to which is, What does the colonial conquest epic tell us about how they *imagined* the worlds they targeted for export?

Classicism versus Melodrama versus Modernism

Of course there is the standard answer in film historiography. Studio historians and historians of style have since the 1970s assumed that between 1917 and into the 1980s, the industry exported classical Hollywood narrative film. The seminal case for this is Kristin Thompson's *Exporting Entertainment*, in which she argues that the rise of Hollywood cinema to world market dominance during World War I "has meant that for an astonishingly long period—from the mid-teens to the present, with no end in sight—a large number of films screened in most countries have been of one type: the classical Hollywood narrative film in continuity style" (Thompson 1985, ix). For several decades, the answer to what was exported was based on producers' descriptions of their films. The evidence Thompson offers is thus what major directors have said about the stylistic model they adopted in making fiction films for other national cinemas worldwide: they emulated the classical continuity style.

Within the decades after Thompson's *Exporting Entertainment*, the classical continuity style narrative has been defended and updated but also challenged, and in the following I take up the two major assaults.[2] Miriam Hansen's challenge to what is called the classicism paradigm has several prongs, but perhaps the most important for our consideration of the export is her argument that classicism is incompatible with any notion of "the modern," especially if cinema is considered the epitome of modernity. If classicism is an invocation of the ancient Greeks, she asks, would it not by definition be antithetical to the modern? Vital here, and deserving more emphasis, is the way that taking issue with classicism for its incompatibility with modernity brings the modern into relief as the opposite of the "unmodern," with all its implications for the Chinese historical narrative of the end of the nineteenth and the beginning of the twentieth century.[3]

But my interest is in juxtaposing this major challenge to classicism with a second one. Even before Hansen's direct attack on the classical paradigm, Linda Williams had challenged classicism—but from a different standpoint. To contrast the two challenges: Hansen's assault is encapsulated in "vernacular modernism," a term she coins to systematize what she calls a "first global vernacular," a theorization of the export-import question that makes a space for the local as different from but also connected to the global (Hansen 2000a, 12). Crucially, this theorization also replaces the "universal language" metaphor of the first decades of the twentieth century with a more cinematic concept: the "mass production of the senses" (Hansen 2000b, 342). Hansen's conceptualization has the advantage of addressing the export-import question directly while also replacing the stylistic specificity of classicism with a more capacious aesthetics, but Williams's challenge comes from another angle. Because, as we may know, her challenge to the dominance of the classical narrative model is simply that it *was not dominant*. No, she argues, it is not that the classical style has been dominant but that melodrama has been *the* cultural dominant, or effectively the "norm" (Williams 2001, 16–17). Following Williams, what then *was* exported? What was exported was melodrama, not classical Hollywood continuity style. To summarize these two challenges to classicism: the one finds continuity style unable to explain the newness of a new global sensorium; the other supplements that style with a tradition that, as we will see, is better studied as a modality crossing genres but also crisscrossing continents.

We may wonder, however, whether these two challenges set up a mutual exclusivity of concepts where none is required, and so let me immediately address that point. In my view, a separation of classicism as style and melodrama as mode runs into problems in a close analysis of any US popular genre film produced between 1915 and 1985. The reason is that we would still find the continuity classical style as an underlying narrative delivery system and set of editing conventions in the majority. Within the same motion picture we have both narrative continuity structure and melodrama as a rhetorical structure, most recently described as a "mode of perception and affect" that has traveled not only across centuries from the stage to the screen but also "across national cultures" (Gledhill and Williams 2018, 4). And, as I approach what I call here "melodramas of race and nation" and alternatively "melodramas of colonial conquest," we will need to posit two interdependent paradigms, really, since film melodrama largely depends on the narrative continuity system, where that system reaches an apotheosis in its delivery of melodramatic rhetoric.[4] As rhetoric, melodrama is characterized by special tenses as absolutes: "never again" or "at last," the better to encourage us to stand aghast, or to be won over. But we also cannot overlook the fact that it is narrative causality that structures situations in which the innocent is endangered and, as a consequence, must be rescued by an avenging narrative agent-character. Melodrama's rhetoric is emotional recruitment—solicitation to causes and encouragement to feelings felt on behalf of nation or home or whoever and whatever is ours. Or felt just as vehemently *against* the nations and homes of others, engendering *animosities*.

The Vernacular without Modernism

If melodrama is aligned with the heartfelt, modernism, by contrast, has been aligned with the head. Because of its career as a counteraesthetic, modernism does not exactly fit with vernacular, because, historically (as form, style, and movement), it stands adamantly opposed to all things common and popular. Easily, there are as many as four ways in which modernism is antithetical to melodrama, the lowest of forms. (See Brooks 1976 and Gledhill 1987, 5–39.) First, modernism cannot so easily shed its long-standing association with elite culture as "high modernism" or explain why there is no such term as "low modernism."[5] Second, modernism's art-historical commitment to an idea of an original work means that it "sticks up its nose" at melodrama's "plagiarizing" use of the same dramatic formulas over and over again (Gledhill 2000, 155). Third, as an antirealism, modernism has been historically skeptical of any aesthetic that is too mimetically close to its object, an attitude found in the earlier hesitation to treat still and motion photographic works as art.[6] Popular motion picture films, as we know, are automatically mimetic by virtue of the photographic and, in the mode of melodrama, are furthermore indebted to what could be called the special realism of the social. Fourth, let's not forget that modernism is both aesthetic style and an early-twentieth-century political cause, a movement of intellectuals and artists who envisioned a cultural revolution extending beyond the arts.[7] Melodrama, not so new, now seen as evolving over three hundred years, has never been a cause célèbre for either artists or intellectuals in recent decades (Buckley 2018). That is, political intellectuals aside, melodrama is the modality of the mass, its historic audience the masses, and its world, the social world of its troubled moment, which is why I once asked, "Where is the Marxism in melodrama theory?" (Gaines 2014).

Few have scrutinized the legacy of modernism as closely as Fredric Jameson, who enjoins us to see modernism as "the aesthetic ideology of the modern" (Jameson 2002, 164). Modernism is an ideology committed to the kind of formalism in which the text is immune to the social, untouched by the historical world.[8] Recall, Jameson goes on, that modernist artistic practices were not understood as modernism in their time. Modernism was not modernism until several decades after the appearance of these artistic experiments. It is as high modernism, a post–World War II Cold War American product associated with New Criticism, that the ideology emerged, he thinks (Jameson 2002, 165, 169). More important, modernism signals the end of the modern as newness. Thus, modernism is of little use to us if we are describing the modern times associated with the advent of cinema worldwide. In Jameson's historical account, those would be the same times associated with utopian newness and anticipation, with expectations that characterized the first decades of the last century and, just as significant, corresponded with the early victories of consumerism (165). Perhaps most important, modernism's immunity to the social—the text uncontaminated by the outside—situates it as quite the opposite of melodrama.[9] For, as we will see, melodrama's historical success is in its schematization of the intimate social world, a connection on which it relies. Now, to compare the relative academic standing of these three paradigms: the first two are respectable, the third not so much. Although it has been nearly forty years since Michael Walker claimed that "melodrama is arguably the most important generic root of the American cinema," until recently only a handful of scholars followed his lead (Walker 1982, 2). The melodrama-as-dominant position has to date won fewer converts than either the vernacular modernism or the narrative classicism paradigm, although new work on world melodrama suggests a shift.[10] Still, an unspoken distaste for melodrama, the lowest of modes, a historically disreputable form, seems to linger (Williams 2001, 12). To sum up: only two of our three paradigms have served to elevate motion pictures as an object of study, a reputation secured by association. As classicism elevated 1930s American cinema in its comparison with Greek theater, modernism elevates motion pictures by association with an elite avant-gardism.[11] Clearly Hansen has been aware of this issue and asks why *modernist* should apply only to the avant-garde (Hansen 2000a, 11). After all, why *should* criticality and vanguardism accrue only to high culture and never to the popular? The question does indeed turn the tables, but I would still argue that the term *modernism*, however modified by *vernacular*, leads us down the wrong political road.[12] Less politically problematic than the term *vernacular modernism*, however, is Hansen's companion formulation of a "first global vernacular," which helps us immeasurably in thinking of Hollywood export product as world-colonizing. As important, in the original theorization, the first global vernacular is also "answered" by emergent national industries, as in Hansen's example (2000a, 11) of semicolonial Shanghai in the 1930s. Thus the first-global-vernacular paradigm situates our export-import paradox in which what was exported was *not* what was imported *over there*, significantly revising the premise of one-way Western domination, as Yiman Wang has argued. Yet Wang is also concerned that vernacular modernism, even as it saw 1930s Shanghai cinema as more than a tool of Euro-American capitalist imperialism, could depoliticize exactly where the persistent politics of colonial power needs to be called out (Wang 2013, 23).

Then we should also note the response of the Chinese national industry to the West, described with the term *answer*, which, as with the word *vernacular*, returns us to the film-as-language analogy just when the field had abandoned the film grammar approach.[13] Let's note, however, that the same criticism can be leveled at Peter Brooks's (1976) concept of moral legibility used to explain melodrama's hyperbolic overstatement that clarifies forces at odds. For *legibility* too suggests linguistic decoding or language learning. Yes, motion picture melodrama relies on expression by means of words; but it also draws on a much larger repertoire of signs—acoustic as well as iconic. What is needed is a theory of expressive signs that circumvents words in the work of dichotomizing—to accuse or to exonerate, to win us over to the side of power or to stand against it. Both *vernacular* and *legibility* suggest words. But in the silent motion picture era, signification was largely wordless (Gaines 2013).[14]

Export and import, if nothing else then, is a way around language analogies. And so, "what was exported" always implies an import-receiving end, an exchange accommodated in Hansen's term *horizon of reception* (Hansen 2000a, 13). Further, the concept of horizon helps situate a "first global something" within a specific historical period. As historically specified, melodrama, too, crossing the last three centuries, has become associated with modernization, as I have said. Thomas Elsaesser (1987), Peter Brooks (1976), and, more recently, Ben Singer (2001) also suggest that melodrama evidences a capacity to respond to the most pressing social issues of modern times. Christine Gledhill concurs, adding that cinema itself constitutes a "break with past traditions" (Gledhill 2000, 232). There is a political upside and a downside here. The upside is the association of mechanical moving images with the modern insofar as that association cues us to people's aspirations. For Hansen's very term *horizon*, echoing Jameson on the first decades of the twentieth century, confirms an increased orientation toward the future that did not characterize earlier centuries.[15] But the political downside of the melodrama-and-modernity equation should give us pause if we are considering colonial cinemas. Why exactly? We need to think twice, because here is inevitably the question of *whose* modernity for *whom*. Or, as Jameson puts it, here is a "modernity for other peoples, an optical illusion nourished by envy and hope," an observation that leads him to conclude that of all the paradoxes of the term *modernity*, the "most fatal" is that "modernity is always a concept of otherness" (Jameson 2002, 211). Thus, modernity makes *the other*, by contrast, unmodern, for there would be no backward unmodern if it were not for the contrast with the forward-looking *modern*. Whether "modern motion pictures" were coincident with or contributive to changing mores and customs in urban centers from Bombay to Tehran to Shanghai is not our only interest. For the unmodern is always the implied term that refers to other peoples, a dichotomy seen in the part-Chinese Mahlee and her British half-sister Blanche in *The Red Lantern* (1919), in which the two sisters are played by the same actress—Alla Nazimova.

Perhaps the claim that cinema exported a kind of modernism is a well-intended attempt to rescue the popular mode from the too passé, the too-too close and the entirely too easy. But this is one more instance of the inconsistency in the dismissals of popular melodrama, so often said to be too effulgent *and* too shallow, too exaggeratedly overblown *and* too explicitly realist, too dated *and* too tied to the moment. In answer to this last criticism, we would say that melodrama is always becoming outmoded because it is the mode so well attuned to its social times, pulling from and then returning to it what it has drawn out while reorganizing what was found there. There is as well the attempt to update and certainly to upgrade melodrama by calling it a vernacular modernism, although this move avoids crucial differences between two paradigms. The term *vernacular modernism* is just too broad to help us describe the stylistic features and the narrative structures of the motion pictures in question, which is basic to analyzing melodrama as not only a powerfully moving mode but a political indicator.[16] But just what was it that in Hollywood *they* thought they were exporting?

The World Export: Melodramas of Colonial Conquest

Former Metro Pictures executive producer and *Red Lantern* screenwriter June Mathis (1925) credited women working as writers, producers, and directors with the worldwide commercial success of American films. What "crept in" was the "voice of the home," the "woman's viewpoint" an elusive "magic something," she thinks. Addressing our export question directly, Mathis argues that it is this "voice of the home" that resonated with global audiences and that explained what it was that made American films "supreme in the world's market" (115; see also Gaines 2018a, 158). I take this voice to be that of the functioning *melos* (Greek for music), thinking of song and attuning us to the musical strains and rhythmic patterns of melodrama. Melodrama theory has undoubted application for colonial conquest epics, those *narratives of race and nation* that echoed the structure and sensibility of that widely distributed world export *The Birth of a Nation* (D. W. Griffith, dir., 1915). There were emulators worldwide, the most notorious of which were *De Voortrekkers* (Harold Shaw, dir., South African Productions, 1916) and *The Birth of White Australia* (Phil Walsh, dir., 1928), but positing a colonial conquest genre helps us to see how many more there were (Gaines 2000; Khoo 2011). As an example, *The Red Lantern* pays subtler and more peculiar homage to Griffith's epic as adapted to a different historical narrative of territorial conflict and struggle for control over others—here others in revolt against the imposition of Western modernity. Thinking of *The Red Lantern* together with *The Birth of a Nation* further helps us to see the very Americanness of the

Figure 5.1. Frame enlargement from *A Trip to the Moon*. (Directed by Georges Méliès, France, 1902.)

racialization of a social order melodramatized as white rule over nonwhite (Carby 1992, 193–94). Or, as we will see, colonial-conquest cinema melodramatizes the defense of custom or territory as resistance to modernization in the form of revolt or tribal ferocity, which then provides justification for restoration of order by means of brutal force, whether by armed adventurers, national army, or Klan riders. A longer discussion would include two territorial-conquest films on either side of *The Birth of a Nation*, also world box-office record-breakers: *A Trip to the Moon* (Georges Méliès, dir., 1902), and *King Kong* (Merian C. Cooper, dir., 1933). (See figs. 5.1 and 5.2.) Admittedly, it sounds a bit tautological, but we cannot help but note that the world market was conquered by European and American motion pictures *about* conquest featuring the extermination of aliens on the moon and the capture of a native species from a mythical island inhabited by dark peoples.

For Paul Gilroy, reflecting on British Empire films, such moving pictures depict colonialism as "always war," Manichaean in its delirium, in Frantz Fanon's phrase (Gilroy 2011, 14–15).[17] And *delirious* decidedly describes the frenzied silent-era depictions of battlefields and armed conflict, of treachery and villainous revenge. These films, in their Manichaeism, are all about

Figure 5.2. *King Kong* poster. (Directed by Merian C. Cooper, United States, 1933.)

sides—alliances and animosities, as I am arguing. Polarization is the point in melodrama. "Signs," says Christine Gledhill, must "declare themselves" in alliance with "singular social, affective moral forces" (Gledhill 2000, 240). If colonialism is "always war," think here of the magnitudinal conflicts between victim and victimizer, colonized and colonizer, powerless and powerful, my home and your home, or our culture and yours. But it is the problematic resolution of melodrama's race wars that should interest us in the colonial conquest epic because we want to know how so many antagonisms can be stirred up only to be magically dissolved, to which we will turn in our conclusion.[18] It is not in dispute that the raw material of melodrama, the stuff that it works into drama, is drawn from the set of socially fraught situations historically specific to a given culture. Indeed, here is our point of historical entry following Foucault, who insisted that "Contradiction . . . functions throughout discourse, as the principle of its historicity." This, he goes on, is where we see the "economic and political conflict that opposes a society to itself" (Foucault 1972, 151). Here is the connection between melodrama and tumultuous times that Zhang makes by way of explaining that modality in so many national cinemas, appearing, as she says, in the "aftermath of momentous historical ruptures such as struggles for independence or decolonization and revolutions" (Zhang 2018, 87). What is remarkable about *The Red Lantern* is that the very Euro-American colonial aggression-as-modernization of China is not only configured as a race war but is partly staged inside the biracial Mahlee character as her "warring sides." What is worse, publicity urged promotion of the film as white love in opposition to Oriental hate (*Motion Picture News* 1919, 3). However, here is a conundrum with which the film has extreme difficulty right up to the last note.

And I do mean "note." For this is to call attention to a silence in the history and theory of narrative continuity where music should have figured. Once we are attuned to note and chord and tone, we refeel melodrama's structures of narrative progression: losing, striving, conquering, uniting, or separating by thrusting apart. Silent-era photoplay manuals called for "complicating action" combined with "delaying obstacles," but there would have been no on-screen action slowly delayed or hurried without at least piano accompaniment in the exhibition of motion pictures (Thompson 1998, 227, 229). Rhythmic action emphasized situations, defined as high points or crises in the early manuals Kristin Thompson analyzed in search of the origins of continuity style (236). But the historical example of the refinement of that style around 1915 is again none other than *The Birth of a Nation*, Griffith's "melodrama of black and white." It is well established in the field that Griffith's melodrama is also a model for the classical score exemplified by the Joseph Carl Breil composition that was orchestrated and performed live (Marks 1997, ch. 4). Although neither melodrama nor music figured significantly in David Bordwell and Kristen Thompson's original theorization of narrative continuity, we cannot do without either if we are to fully describe the epic of colonial conquest.[19] Just as we ask "whose modernity?" we must ask "whose music?" and to what ideological ends.

Recently, the question of silent-era cinema in China, Japan, and Korea has been addressed by another generation of scholars, all of whom help us to develop more nuanced theories of cultural conjuncture (Bao 2015; Wang 2013; Lee 2016). All concur with Aaron Gerow, who warns not to see Hollywood as a center that is then translated into a non-Western culture (Gerow 2010, 23). Thus, in the future we will likely see more work on silent melodrama as export and import in terms of confluence rather than influence. Both Zhang Zhen and Xuelei Huang confirm the arrival of D. W. Griffith's melodramas in Shanghai between 1922 and 1924, including not only *The Birth of a Nation*, but also *Intolerance* (1916), *Orphans of the Storm* (1921), and the enthusiastically received *Way down East* (1920) (Zhang 2018, 92–93; Huang 2014, 181–86). One only need compare the treacherous ice field ending of the extant *Orphan Chicks in the Snow* (Zhang Huimin, dir., Huaju Film, China, 1929) with Griffith's cross-cut frozen-river rescue of Lillian Gish to confirm a confluence of traditions. *The Red Lantern* was never exhibited in China, but this does not disqualify the film as emblematic of East-West encounter but rather shifts the question of cultural confluence from what was *there* to the corollary, as you will recall—what it was that US filmmakers *imagined was there*. Or, to how Hollywood fantasized the Far East despite the promotional hype around authenticity (Moon 2012). But, strangely enough, the very film that never arrived in the Far East urges a qualification of our export-import paradox in which what was exported was not the same as what was imported: not reception but refusal. For in the Chinese political rejection of *The Red Lantern* we have the epitome of resistant reading. Here was a motion picture product so offensive to Chinese overseas viewers living in the United States that it could not be exported to the very place that it claimed to represent so authentically. I admit to being less interested in establishing whether the film was intended for export to East Asia or to play to Western Orientalist fantasies "at home," yet, as at the outset of this chapter, I would acknowledge the US eye on the Far East as the industry projected an expansion of the world cinema market. Most important, *The Red Lantern was seen* by Chinese, not *over there*, but here in major US cities, where the film had such wide distribution. It *was seen* in the United States, where to be against it was to be *for* a new Chinese nation-building initiative—the capitalization of a business catering to a Chinese audience. Indeed, *The Red Lantern* proved to be for overseas Chinese what *The Birth of a Nation* was for angry African Americans who made the first race movies as racial uplift in reaction to that film's historical distortions (Gaines 2001, 138–44). As middle-class distancing from backwardness analogous to the race movie uplift project committed to the correction of falsehood, the Chinese overseas rejection became the rationale for another cinema. In an odd way, then, *The Red Lantern* contributed to the creation of a Chinese national film industry, as we will see.

Contradictions of Chinese Colonial Modernity: *The Red Lantern* (1919)

Rather than dismissing the strange case of *The Red Lantern*, I take it as emblematizing East-West encounter, however offensive in its portrayal of Chinese custom or retrograde in its use of the Rudyard Kipling quote "Never the twain shall meet." So, to return to June Mathis (1925) and to hold her to her word about the success of the "voice of the home" export, let's look at the motion picture that she adapted for the screen. This Alla Nazimova star vehicle, designed as a US release extravaganza and candidate for Metro Pictures new global export strategy, was handled by American Export and Import Film for Latin America and Europe, although a Paris company won the bidding for all future Nazimova productions (*Moving Picture World* 1919, 1207).[20] (See fig. 5.3.) *The Red Lantern* reached beyond Europe to Moscow but in the Asia-Pacific region only as far as New Zealand. It got no further. Japanese exhibitors turned it down.

Most damning, young Chinese intellectuals living in the United States published an editorial in the *Washington Post* objecting to the way *The Red Lantern* attributed the Boxer Rebellion to "racial antipathy between the East and the West" (Kiang, Chen, and Chang 1919; Franck 2012). It should be no surprise then that this film is indeed one of the two most notorious of the so-called "China-humiliating" films Yiman Wang discusses in her chapter. As I intimated earlier, the overseas Chinese protest against the depictions in *The Red Lantern* and in *The First Born* (Colin Campbell, dir., Hayakawa Feature Play, 1921) had their part in the formation of the Great Wall Company financed by wealthy Chinese in Brooklyn, New York (Johnson 2009, 109, Leyda 1972, 44, Chen and Xiao 2004). Astutely, in pointing to "racial antipathy," Chinese intellectuals identified the hallmark of the melodrama of colonial conquest—lightning-cut battlefield scenes enacting the clash of civilizations, racialized villainy and the corruption of innocence in Eurasian Mahlee's recruitment to the antiforeigner Boxer cause. And just as *The Birth of a Nation* is confusing about which nation was "birthed"—the imaginary

World Export 123

Figure 5.3. Advertisement for *The Red Lantern*. (Directed by Albert Cappellani, Metro Pictures/Nazimova Productions, United States, 1919.)

southern white nation of the Lost Cause or one that emerged from a united North and South—*The Red Lantern* is conflicted in its depiction of the 1900 Boxer Rebellion that attempted to oust foreigners from semicolonial China in its borrowed *Birth of a Nation* premise: race is nation.

The ways in which *The Red Lantern* uses the events of the 1898–1900 period of conflict in China are myriad, and the problems the Boxer Rebellion raises for any account of Chinese colonial modernity in studies of imperialism are legion (Cohen 1997). As preface to this fiction film, then, it is important to note the mélange of myths that have shaped Western attitudes toward China for half a century (Hevia 1997, 132). To give only one example, Chinese actions characterized as atrocities committed against Western missionaries were used as justification for Western military destruction of Chinese temples and shrines, as well as mass slaughter of suspect groups (Hevia 1997, 118, 124). So it is not surprising that a Western-made popular melodrama adapted from the sensational novel written by a missionary's daughter would put mythologies of Chinese atrocities committed against missionaries into further circulation (Wherry 1911). But though *The Red Lantern* adopts the Christian missionary point of view, as we will see, melodrama's staging bares the political and economic conflict in which we also see, to paraphrase Foucault, a colonizing imperial power "opposed to itself" (Foucault 1972, 151).[21]

In taking up the missionary position, so to speak, *The Red Lantern* further illuminates our problem of the modern, since American and British missionaries not only saw their work as companion to capitalist industrial modernization but also saw themselves as moral modernizers of Chinese barbarians, no matter that "barbarian" was also how Chinese described Westerners (Hevia 1997, 118, 130). Note again Jameson's fatal paradox of modernity that produces whatever is unlike as unmodern (Jameson 2002, 211). *The Red Lantern*, closely following the novel, sets up the tension between the traditional and the modern with the example of Chinese female foot binding from which missionaries tried to rescue women. Moral modernizers, as they saw themselves, Christian missionaries were instrumental in the campaign against foot binding, with the height of that campaign, as Dorothy Ko tells us, 1895–98, just before the Boxer revolt (Ko 2005, 15).

From the first sequence of *The Red Lantern* we learn that Mahlee's white father had stipulated that her feet not be bound. Yet, to her Chinese grandmother, her granddaughter's big feet are an abomination, and worse (to the Western audience), the dying woman wants Mahlee's feet cut as sacrifice to placate the gods, setting up complicating actions and delaying obstacles: to cut or not to cut—and consequently the imperative to rescue. An so the film opens with Mahlee attempting to carry out her grandmother's wish. But she of two cultures is torn and hesitates with sword raised; then, by chance she faints and is rescued from self-mutilation by a deaf-mute who carries her to the mission. We later learn that she is has been educated by the missionary family. But her cultural conversion is not complete. Mahlee is still Chinese.

Nazimova's Eurasian Mahlee, pulled two ways, bears uncanny similarity to the American "tragic mulatta" whose white and black blood are at war within her (Carby 1987). Exhibitors were cued to use both the racial divide and paganism to promote the film, as in the suggestions in *Motion Picture News* that hyped, "White blood in Mahlee taught her to live and love, but the yellow forbade her, barred her from the only thing that she wanted—drove her back into paganism—and the mystery of the night" (*Motion Picture News* 1919, 3062). Undeniably, *yellow* is a code word for race, and *mystery* synonymous with *inscrutability*, an old excuse for not attempting to understand Chinese ambivalence toward modernization. Or, *race* coupled with *nation*, explains the inexplicable: Why would a young woman want to be anything other than modern? So "*whose* modernity for *whom*?" we must ask again.

For the Western-educated Chinese, however, colonial modernity was more complicated than Western domination meeting local resistance. As

Lydia Liu explains, the East-West boundary is historically more permeable than we might think, and conditions can be subject to change (Liu 1995, 25). Because many Chinese wanted change, we might better posit China as a society in transition in the first decades of the twentieth century but also make a distinction between rural China and urban Shanghai as associated with the modern girl (Weinbaum et al. 2008, 4). Foot binding, as Dorothy Ko suggests, is best grasped as a microcosm of a distinctively Chinese old-new conflict as the nineteenth century ended. Women, she says, bore the weight of having to both hold over the old and anticipate the new and, thus, she describes practices in this period as characterized by "bind-unbind-bind-unbind" (Ko 2005, 13). Her description of a "lingering in-betweenness, a seesawing motion of time, sentiments, and fashion" (11) may then help us to formulate the contradictoriness of the modern girl. A recent analysis of 1930s Shanghai women's magazines summarizes her dilemma as having to do with "how to be simultaneously modern *and* Chinese" (Edwards 2012, 567).

As a colonial conquest melodrama, *The Red Lantern* is organized around the very paradigm of Western modernization versus Chinese resistance to modernization that Liu finds so rigid and that consequently posed the dilemma that women's magazines intuited. Popular melodrama, weighing in, can be both totally polarized and completely complicated. Why? Because the social enters the popular film as topical tensions, themselves transposed into the delaying obstacles that are structurally requisite to the complicating action that makes the viewing experience so gripping, as in the scene in which mixed-race Mahlee attempts to cut her own feet but fails and does not satisfy her grandmother's dying wish. But the tension here is not only within her but also between the Western point of view and imagined Chinese custom. Put to structural use are the very "against itself" consequences of the colonial conquest of one culture by another: the mixed-race child, the clash of belief systems, the people's resistance to imperial control, and the military reprisal that puts down what one side perceives as uprising against order and the other sees as defense of a higher order. Mahlee is caught between. Consider then the handling of two conventionalized narrative situations that define Western melodrama structure, where situations give rise to crises in which endangered innocence must be first recognized and then rescued, as earlier discussed. First, Mahlee must be saved from the paganism associated with one part of herself at war with the morally modernized other. Second, her innocence will go unrecognized by other characters although not by the audience. Melodrama theory would ask "Who is the innocent victim here?" But Mahlee is also unlike the tragic mulatta of US culture because she is not so precisely divided into two warring sides, "Christian love" fighting "Chinese hate," as the exhibitor urges. Dividing Mahlee *does* provide dramatic structure, for she is first rescued (for the Western viewer) from the superstition of her Chinese grandmother and later wavers between allegiance to her Christian mission side and her Chinese self. But also because Nazimova is playing two roles, it is as though we have four characters: the Chinese Mahlee, the white Mahlee, Mahlee's English half-sister Blanche Sackfield, and Alla Nazimova, popular star actress who is both modern girl and Jewish American immigrant born Miriam Edez Adelaida Leventon in Yalta (Andrin 2012, 13, 24). Only one of these is the endangered innocent—but which one? For this we will finally need melodrama theory.

Further, Mahlee is not the only racially divided character the film uses to complicate the action that threatens Mahlee's innocence: it is the Eurasian Sam Wang who pressures her to side with the Boxers. As a doctor educated in the West, the twisted Wang has his parallel in mixed-race Sylas Lynch in *Birth of a Nation*. Such villains, however, are not torn as the mixed-race female character has historically been, and this is because their mixture simply explains their treachery. But treachery against whom? Critics of *The Red Lantern* accused both Mahlee and Sam Wang of race betrayal, as, for instance, the *New York Times* writer who could not imagine why either could foment an uprising against Westerners when *they themselves were white*: "It is hard to believe that two half-breed Chinese, stamped with the Occident, could have become leaders of the passionately anti-foreign Boxer uprising" (*New York Times* 1919b, 11, Moon 2012, 55). But a closer analysis of the film reveals that Mahlee's apparently "endangered innocence" (the pull of the Boxers) is set against a threat far more devastating for her, as we will see. Although the Boxer fighting against foreign troops in the city streets is a typical delaying obstacle, the more anguish-producing postponement is the white characters' slowness to come to Mahlee's rescue, a delay that sets up the structure to which melodrama has been historically dedicated: "the struggle toward recognition of the sign of virtue and innocence"(Brooks 1976, 28). But is the "innocent" in Mahlee the white European or the Chinese self?

Something else is at stake. Mahlee has been recruited by the Boxers to impersonate the ancient Goddess of the Red Lantern, an incarnation with the power to bring Empress Dowager Cixi over to the cause. In this, Mahlee is made to seem complicit rather than innocent in a callous play on the presumed superstition of Chinese people; but her masquerade serves yet another complicating action in the threat that her unmasking will reveal not only a conspiracy but also another self. Which one? Mahlee continues to vacillate even after she has been recruited to the Boxer cause as the fake goddess. In her last switch of allegiance, she appears to side with the white missionaries who have educated her. But it is finally her white father's refusal to recognize her as his daughter that triggers her decision to side with the Boxers against the foreigner that she finally cannot be. If her father has refused to recognize the Chinese Mahlee as his own, does his refusal not challenge the Christian love versus Chinese hate dichotomy? (*Motion Picture News* 1919, 3). Takeuchi Yoshimi's revised moral hierarchy seems applicable here: "The Orient must change the West in order to further elevate those universal values that the West itself produced" (Takeuchi 2005, 165). And so, from a contemporary point of view, Mahlee and Sam Wang's revolt may be completely understandable as a stand against the hypocrisy of Christian moralism that preached the equality of people in the eyes of God. Most notably, the overseas Chinese did not see race betrayal but objected to the portrayal of educated Chinese characters who embodied "racial antipathy towards westerners," perhaps meaning Sam Wang with his Western medical degree. At the same time, they found the depiction of customs to be "as ridiculous to the Chinese as to Americans" (Kiang, Chen, and Chang 1919b, E14). What they decried was likely female foot binding that seemed barbaric in their eyes, but, to emphasize again, they also denounced the animosity engendered between cultures.

Melodrama has been criticized for rendering questions of epic political proportions as personal. Yet where else do these wars of race and nation finally register but in the intimate familial spheres, home to so much emotional fallout? Why would we expect anything other than that the struggle of the Chinese to rid themselves of foreign invaders, the fate of the Boxer Rebellion, would come down to melodrama's perennial question, "Whose child am I?"

The Classical Score

The classical score is the final angle on our problem—how to situate *classical narrative* relative to *melodrama* on a global sensorium that opens up a space of reception as well as new production. Scholars now agree that, in the United States, because the musical score evolved with classical narrative continuity style, the historiographic point of departure around 1915 is again *The Birth of a Nation*, with the Joseph Carl Breil score the prototype for Hollywood film music into the sound era (Marks 1997, ch. 4; Gaines and Lerner 2001). Most important to grasp about *The Birth of a Nation* model is that it exemplifies the composite score consisting of minstrel tunes, folk music, marches, songs, and popular ballads, held together with Breil's original composition and woven around by the grandiosity of classical symphonic Beethoven, Tchaikovsky, and Wagner (Marks 1997, 143, 145–46). Such composite scores may have represented a mélange of cultures typified by characteristic rhythms and tonalities, although non-Western tonalities were likely parodied for Western listening (Altman 2004, 355). Then again, parodied East Asian music, slipped in "under," could pull the listener in unpredictable affective directions. Although the legacy of eighteenth-century Romantic music is the foundation of classical narrative music in which the strains of the score are subservient to the action, the composite might also produce dissonance or disjuncture and even mismatch between sound and image. Note that one of the premises of the theory of film music is that in its service to the narrative, music is to be unheard yet always threatens to be heard (Gorbman 1987; Buhler and Neumeyer 2014). Significantly, the term *subservient* is used by Sol Klein, musical director for the Crescent Theatre, Bronx, New York, in an interview on the same page as the cue sheet for *The Red Lantern*, published in *Exhibitors' Trade Review* (Marks 1997, 6, 10–11; Rapée 1925). In the published cue sheet, the orchestra conductor—or, more likely, the local pianist—could find a breakdown of all eighty-eight minutes by key action, cued to suggested music. Music editor S. M. Berg, compiling the cue sheet, explains that the use of Japanese as opposed to Chinese music was owing to the scarcity of the latter.[22] The point is relevant, since Mahlee's theme is "A Japanese Sunset," a Jessie L. Deppen ballad that is repeated seven times in the 1919 cue sheet (Altman 2004, 355; Moon 2012, 51).[23] But also, as Michel Chion argues in advancing a theory of "hear-see," in motion pictures, "sound . . . ceaselessly influences what we see" (Chion 2016, 152).

Now, it would be easy to use Mahlee's theme as yet another example of cultural misconception, not only in the Hollywood conflation of Chinese and Japanese cultures, but in the use of musical parody while claiming authenticity. In colonial conquest epics like *The Red Lantern* and *The Birth of a Nation*, however, with the "melos," reinforced by the classical European underscoring, the music takes sides in those decisive scenes where allegiances are sorted out—at the climactic limitation of outcomes when so much hangs in the balance—the fate of nations and the supremacy of one race over another. The classical score, featuring "appropriate" music and deploying musical transition to bridge scenes, is designed to produce continuity out of discontinuity—as a final major chord resolves political as well as tonal discord. Does it always, though? Not with the last note sounded in the performed score of *The Red Lantern*.

Consider *The Red Lantern*'s final scene. Mahlee is dressed in the fake goddess costume with an enormous peacock headdress. Barricaded in the palace under siege, sitting on the throne, she pulls from her sleeve the vial of poison Sam Wang has given her. Her suicide, however, is not explained by the threat of her capture. The title, phonically representing her halting delivery—"Oh, East is East—and—West is West—and Never—the Twain—Shall Meet"—explains her decision to take poison as an escape from the agony produced by the conflict between two races, two peoples, this being a *melodrama of race as much as nation*. The missionary's son, Andrew Templeton, rushes to her side and grabs her hand to kiss it, but it is too late. A close-up shows that he kisses the hand of a woman already dead. Mahlee's white father, Sir Philip Sackville, stands back in the foreground left shielding her half-sister Blanche (also played by Nazimova). An auxiliary theme more pronounced in the novel than the film is Mahlee's unrequited love for Andrew, whose own love for her sister Blanche has been rejected. And in this triangle, it is Mahlee whose love is seen to be higher—the Chinese Mahlee, not the white one—and it is she who is the innocent. For in the melodrama tradition, *it is suffering that denotes the innocent*. The Chinese Mahlee suffers—used by Wang and rejected by white missionaries as well as her own benighted British father.

On the track, the mood music effects are punctuated in the piano's bass chords standing in for the Chinese gong. Mahlee's theme, described as an Oriental andante, is slow and deliberate and, as typical of narrative climax music, moves in levels—up one octave, starting over at the bottom of the next, and slipping from major to minor at the gong stroke—but overall progressing in the major direction as Mahlee, collapsed on the throne, drops the vial of poison and then shudders in death. The piano score registers dissonance in the minor key *yet does not* finally resolve in favor of the major. We expect the classical score, the great resolver of oppositional positions, the accommodator—the arbiter in the standoff between the forces of entrenched power and those subject to it—to mediate between the imperial foreign and local resistance to it—especially in the colonial conquest melodrama. But here it does not. Where is the ameliorating score, we wonder? The film ends with Mahlee's suicide and the piano rumbling in the bass approximation of a Chinese gong. There is neither rescue nor reconciliation but rather an ominous final judgment in a gong sound simulated by a piano.

What was written and produced for export was melodrama, the mode that is internally pulled in so many contradictory directions. With such intimate ties to the social, melodrama, as currently theorized, provides myriad possibilities for intercultural confluence more complex than we have yet to discover. And why do I prefer *melos* over the linguistic implications of the *vernacular* and warn that popular moving image melodrama is unrelated to aesthetic modernism? The terms matter because, in theorizing melodramas of colonial conquest, we need tools with the sharpest political incisiveness. To stress the melos is to listen and to hear, in signs as small yet as resonant as that of a simulated Chinese gong, cultural confluence *and* dissonance—far from home (wherever that may be).

ACKNOWLEDGMENTS

Thank you to Nayoung Aimee Kwon and Zhang Zhen for conceptual input and to Yanfei Song, Briand Gentry, Haneul Lee, Insook Park, and Xinyi Zhao for their contributions as well as to Neil Lerner for the lessons in music theory and to Viren Murthy for citations.

NOTES

1. Thanks to Nayoung Aimee Kwon for this formulation.
2. For another, see Elsaesser (2012, 9–10), on the postclassical, which he calls "classical-plus."
3. Duara (1995, 33–41) lays out the problems with using the European periodization of ancient, medieval, and modern that in addition constructs a Chinese history in a linear mode.
4. Here "melodramas of race and nation" is indebted to Williams (2001) whose subtitle is "Melodramas of Black and White from Uncle Tom to O. J. Simpson."
5. See Zhang (2005, 18–21), for a theorization of a reciprocity between modernism and classical cinema. Hers is also the most fully developed theorization of the vernacular together with modernism as an avant-garde, which, when conjoined in the term "vernacular modernism," has been exemplified by 1930s Shanghai film.
6. Armstrong (1999) reminds us of British modernism's antipathy to mimetic realism that accused literary realism of being "too photographic" in its close resemblance to its object.
7. See Rainey and von Hallberg (1994) at the launch of the journal *Modernism/Modernity*.
8. The recent global modernism movement as part of modernist studies redefines the concept, most relevantly as responsive to the social (Hayot and Walkowitz 2016). The authors reconceptualize a reaction to a range of social changes—capitalism, secularization, modernity—relative to "local conditions of . . . production." The problem with the redefinition of modernism, however, is that in its recruitment for the opposite of what the term historically stood for, the new meaning does not completely cancel the old.
9. For Jameson (2002, 171) the "ideology of modernism" was developed further by Clement Greenberg's commitment to the exclusion of the extrinsic as a defense against hostilities outside the text, most notably exemplified by capitalism.
10. See Yang (2018), Bhaskar (2018), and Airriess (2018). This is not to say that in recent decades melodrama has not been important in the analysis of national cinemas. For Chinese cinema, see Berry and Farquhar (2006, ch. 4), Pickowicz (1993), to give only two of many examples.
11. See Gledhill (2000, 236). This would not be the first time that a critic elevated a Chinese film by means of association with modernism, on which see Yao (1991, 76), who praises *Yellow Earth* for its avant-gardist and "modernist power of critique of Chinese culture and industry," as though the film exemplified political modernism and was not tribute to the socialist realism that the Fifth Generation filmmakers preferred in their Beijing Academy training, on which see Ni (2003).
12. See Gaines (2000b, 107–10) for discussion of the conjuncture between Frankfurt School theory and the Birmingham School of Cultural Studies, as in Stuart Hall's "double movement" of popular culture that does not require us to deny that we are studying mass culture and that also allows us criticality without risking disassociation from "the popular."
13. See Hansen (2012) answering Dudley Andrew's critique of her apparent return to the cinema-as-language position; Bao (2014, 171), acknowledges the connection between "vernacular" and language but sees the term as a "theoretical metaphor" and finds its utility in the model of "cultural circulation" that it offers for which see Bao 2015.

14. Chion (2009, 3) argues that "silent cinema" was not actually "wordless" because there were words, although, since they could not be heard, he proposes the term *deaf cinema*.

15. Koselleck (2004) theorizes this reorientation of the past relative to the future but only in the past three hundred years; see his chapter 14 on the concept of horizon of expectation as a crucial historical category.

16. Morgan (2014, 70), thinks that the theorization is so broad as to ignore essential distinctions, for, following from too automatic a premise, "Every film, by definition, would then be vernacular modernist."

17. See the UK Arts and Research Council project "Colonial Film: Moving Images and the British Empire," accessed October 15, 2020, http://www.colonialfilm.org.uk/.

18. Hansen (2000b, 342) describes cinema as "engaged in the contradictions of modernity at the level of the senses."

19. Bordwell and Thompson (2017) made a commitment to sound in the eleventh edition when Jeff Smith was added as third editor.

20. Thompson (1985, 197, 209) lists Export and Export Films as established in New York in February 1917 and says that in September 1923, the Japanese earthquake that year damaged the Tokyo branch of the company. Fu (2019, 14) explains that, before 1917, US film distribution in China was via London agents.

21. For the question of whether melodrama is progressive or reactionary, see Gaines (2018b, 260), echoing Frankfurt School theory in which this popular form moves both ways, but which, in order to appeal, must offer something to counter the reactionary, that "something" a source of criticality.

22. The two examples of Chinese music given—"Mandarin Dance" and "Chinese Wedding Processional"—are Western typifications referred to as having "Chinese characteristics"; for instance, gong strikes. A violin can imitate a Chinese "fiddle," Berg (1919, 1774) suggests.

23. Working from the 1919 cue sheet for *The Red Lantern*, Belgian Film Archive restorers gathered thirty-six pieces of sheet music. The contemporary DVD track is a compilation of them for piano and organ, including Raymond Hubbell and John Golden's "Poor Butterfly," a 1916 Tin Pan Alley song inspired by Puccini, and Camille Saint-Saëns's *La princesse jaune* (1872), in which an art student is obsessed with a painting of a Japanese woman.

Bibliography

Abel, Richard, and Rick Altman. 2001. Introduction to *The Sounds of Early Cinema*. Edited by Richard Abel and Rick Altman, xi–xvi. Bloomington: Indiana University Press.

Airriess, Hannah. 2018. "Global Melodrama and Transmediality in Turn-of-the-Century Japan." In *Melodrama Unbound*. Edited by Christine Gledhill and Linda Williams, 69–82. New York: Columbia University Press.

Altman, Rick. 2004. *Silent Film Music*. New York: Columbia University Press.

Andrin, Muriel. 2012. "'To Dazzle the Eye and Stir the Heart': Alla Nazimova, 'Star of a Thousand Moods' in *The Red Lantern*." In *To Dazzle the Eye and Stir the Heart—The Red Lantern, Nazimova and the Boxer Rebellion*, 12–24. Brussels: Cinematek.

Armstrong, Nancy. 1999. *Fiction in the Age of Photography: The Legacy of British Realism*. Cambridge, MA: Harvard University Press.

Bao, Weihong. 2014. "'A Vibrating Art in the Air': Cinema, Ether, and Propaganda Film Theory in Wartime Chongqing." *New German Critique*. 41, no. 2 (Summer): 171–188.

———. 2015. *Fiery Cinema: The Emergence of an Affective Medium in China, 1915–1945*. Minneapolis:

Berg, S. M. 1919. "Musical Setting for '*The Red Lantern*.'" *Exhibitor's Trade Review* 5, no. 23 (May): 1774.

Berry, Chris, and Mary Farquhar. 2006. *China on Screen: Cinema and Nation*. New York: Columbia University Press.

Bhaskar, Ira. 2018. "Expressionist Aurality: The Stylized Aesthetic of *Bhava* in Indian Melodrama." In *Melodrama Unbound*. Edited by Christine Gledhill and Linda Williams, 253–272. New York: Columbia University Press.

Bordwell, David, Kristin Thompson, and Jeff Smith. 2017. *Film Art: An Introduction* (11e). New York: McGraw Hill.

Brooks, Peter. 1976. *The Melodramatic Imagination*. New Haven, CT: Yale University Press.

Buckley, Matthew. 2018."Unbinding Melodrama." In *Melodrama Unbound*. Edited by Christine Gledhill and Linda Williams, 15–29. New York: Columbia University Press, 2018.

Buhler, James, and David Neumeyer. 2014. "Music and the Ontology of the Sound Film: The Classical Hollywood System." In *The Oxford Handbook of Film Music Studies*. Edited by David Neumeyer, 21–40. New York: Oxford University Press.

Carby, Hazel V. 1987. *Reconstructing Womanhood: The Emergence of the Afro-American Woman Novelist*. New York: Oxford University Press.

———. 1992. "The Multicultural Wars." In *Black Popular Culture*. Edited by Gina Dent, 187–99. Seattle, WA: Bay Press.

Chen Mo and Xiao Zhiwei. 2004. "Kuaihai de 'Changcheng': cong jianli dao tanta; Changcheng huapian gongsi lishi cutan" [The "great wall" that bridges the ocean: from founding to collapsing; A preliminary study of the history of the Great Wall Film Company]. *Dangdai dianying* [Contemporary film] no. 3: 36–44.

Chion, Michel. 2009. *Film, A Sound Art*. Translated by Claudia Gorbman. New York: Columbia University Press.

———. 2016. *Sound: An Acoulogical Treatise*. Translated by James A. Steintrager. Durham, NC: Duke University Press.

Cohen, Paul A. 1997. *History in Three Keys: The Boxers as Event, Experience, and Myth*. New York: Columbia University Press.

Duara, Prasenjit. 1995. *Rescuing History from the Nation: Questioning Narratives of Modern China*. Chicago: University of Chicago Press.

Edwards, Louise. 2012. "The Shanghai Modern Woman's American Dreams: Imagining America's Depravity to Produce China's 'Moderate Modernity.'" *Pacific Historical Review* 81, no. 4 : 567–601.

Elsaesser, Thomas. 1987. "Tales of Sound and Fury." In *Home Is Where the Heart Is*. Edited by Christine Gledhill, 43–69. London: British Film Institute.

———. 2012. *The Persistence of Hollywood*. New York: Routledge.

Franck, Steth. 2012. "Contextualizing the Red Lantern." In *To Dazzle the Eye and Stir the Heart—The Red Lantern, Nazimova and the Boxer Rebellion*, 4–11. Brussels: Cinematek.

Foucault, Michel. 1972. *The Archaeology of Knowledge*. Translated by A.M. Sheridan Smith. New York: Vintage.

Fu, Yongchun. 2019. *The Early Transnational Chinese Cinema Industry*. New York: Routledge.

Gaines, Jane M. 2000a. "Birthing Nations." In *Cinema and Nation*. Edited by Mette Hjort and Scott MacKenzie, 298–316. London: Routledge.

———. 2000b. "Dream/Factory." In *Reinventing Film Studies*. Edited by Christine Gledhill and Linda Williams, 100–113. London: Arnold.

———. 2001. *Fire and Desire: Mixed Race Movies in the Silent Era*. Chicago: University of Chicago Press.

———. 2013. "Wordlessness (to Be Continued)." In *Researching Women in Silent Cinema: New Findings and Perspectives*. Edited by Monica Dall'Asta and Victoria Duckett, 289–302. Bologna, It.: University of Bologna Digital Library. http://amsactaunibo.it/3814/.

———. 2014. "*4 Months, 3 Weeks, and 2 Days*: Where Is the Marxism in Melodrama Theory?" In *Le mélodrama filmique revisité/Revisiting Film Melodrama*. Edited by Dominique Nasta and Muriel Andrin, 277–91. London: Peter Lang.

———. 2018a. *Pink-Slipped: What Happened to Women in the Silent Film Industry?* Urbana: University of Illinois Press.

———. 2018b. "Moving Picture Melodrama." In *Cambridge Companion to English Melodrama*, Edited by Carolyn Williams, 245–261. London and New York: Cambridge University Press.

Gaines, Jane M., and Neil Lerner. 2001. "The Orchestration of Affect: The Motif of Barbarism in Breil's *The Birth of a Nation* Score." In *The Sounds of Early Cinema*. Edited by Richard Abel and Rick Altman, 252–68. Bloomington: Indiana University Press.

Gerow, Aaron. 2010. *Visions of Japanese Modernity: Articulations of Cinema, Nation, and Spectatorship, 1895–1925*. Berkeley: University of California Press.

Gilroy, Paul. 2011. "Great Games: Film, History and Working-through Britain's Colonial Legacy." In *Film and the End of Empire*. Edited by Lee Grieveson and Colin MacCabe, 13–32. London: Palgrave/British Film Institute.

Gledhill, Christine. 1987. "The Melodramatic Field." In *Home Is Where the Heart Is*. Edited by Christine Gledhill, 5–30. London: British Film Institute.

———. 2000. "Rethinking Genre." In *Reinventing Cinema*. Edited by Christine Gledhill and Linda Williams, 219–43. London: Arnold.

Gledhill, Christine, and Linda Williams. 2018. Introduction to *Melodrama Unbound*. Edited by Christine Gledhill and Linda Williams, 2–11. New York: Columbia University Press.

Gorbman, Claudia. 1987. *Unheard Melodies: Hollywood Film Music*. Bloomington: Indiana University Press.

Hansen, Miriam. 2000a. "Fallen Women, Rising Stars, New Horizons: Shanghai Silent Film as Vernacular Modernism." *Film Quarterly* 54, no. 1: 10–22.

———. 2000b. "The Mass Production of the Senses: Classical Cinema as Vernacular Modernism." In *Reinventing Film Studies*. Edited by Christine Gledhill and Linda Williams, 332–50. London: Arnold.

———. 2012. "Tracking Cinema on a Global Scale." In *The Oxford Handbook of Global Modernisms*. Edited by Mark Wollaeger and Matt Eatough. New York: Oxford University Press. Accessed May 25, 2021. https://www.oxfordhandbooks.com/view/10.1093/oxfordhb/9780195338904.001.0001/oxfordhb-9780195338904-e-25.

Hayot, Eric, and Rebecca L. Walkowitz. 2016. Introduction to *A New Vocabulary for Global Modernism*. Edited by Eric Hayot and Rebecca L. Walkowitz, 1–10. New York: Columbia University Press.

Hevia, James L. 1997. "Leaving a Brand on China." In *Formations of Colonial Modernity in East Asia*. Edited by Tani E. Barlow, 113–40. Durham, NC: Duke University Press.

Huang, Xuelei. 2014. *Shanghai Filmmaking: Crossing Borders, Connecting to the Globe, 1922–1938*. Boston: Leiden.

Jameson, Fredric. 2002. *A Singular Modernity*. London: Verso.

Khoo, Olivia. 2011. *Tokens of Exchange, or the Cook, the Thief, the Wife and Lover: Marginal Asian Characters in 1920s Australian Cinema*. Screening the Past Occasional Papers no. 40. http://www.screeningthepast.com/2011/04/tokens-of-exchange-or-the-cook-the-thief-the-wife-and-lover-marginal-asian-characters-in-1920s-australian-cinema-2/.

Kiang, S., and T. Chen, and C. Chang. 1919. "Plays on China False." *Washington Post*, June 20, E1.

Ko, Dorothy. 2005. *Cinderella's Sisters: A Revisionist History of Footbinding*. Berkeley: University of California Press.

Koselleck, Reinhart. 2004. *Futures Past: On the Semantics of Historical Time*. Translated by Keith Tribe. New York: Columbia University Press.

Lee, Hwa-jin. 2016. "European Film Distribution in Colonial Korea—Focusing on the Case of Towa Shoji. (Yurop yŏnghwa ŭi Chosŏn paegŭp—Towasangsa ŭi sarye rŭl chungsimuro.) *Hyŏndae Yŏnghwa Yŏn'gu* 25: 281–334.

Leyda, Jay. 1972. *Dianying: Electric Shadows: An Account of Films and the Film Audience in China*. Cambridge, MA: MIT Press.

Liu, Lydia. 1995. *Translingual Practice: Literature, National Culture, and Translated Modernity—China, 1900–1937*. Stanford, CA: Stanford University Press.

Marks, Martin. 1997. *Music and the Silent Film: Contexts and Case Studies, 1895–1924*. New York: Oxford University Press.

Mathis, June. 1925. "The Feminine Mind in Picture Making." *Film Daily*, June 7, 115.

Moon, Krysten R. 2012. "The Creation of *The Red Lantern*: American Orientalism at the Beginning of the 20th Century." In *To Dazzle the Eye and Stir the Heart-- The Red Lantern, Nazimova and the Boxer Rebellion*, 42–58. Brussels: Cinematek.

Morgan, Daniel. 2014. "'Play with Danger': Vernacular Modernism and the Problem of Criticism." *New German Critique* 41, no. 2 (122, Summer): 67–82.

Motion Picture News. 1919. "Wonder of Picture Should Be Stressed to the Limit." May 16, 3.

Moving Picture World. 1919. "Handsome Offers Had to Be Turned Down," *Moving Picture World* 24, 1207.

Ni, Zhen. 2003. *Memoirs from the Beijing Film Academy*. Translated by Chris Berry. Durham, NC: Duke University Press.

Pickowicz, Paul. 1993. "Melodramatic Representation and the 'May Fourth' Tradition of Chinese Cinema." In *From May Fourth to June Fourth: Fiction and Film in Twentieth Century Chin*. Edited by Ellen Widmer and David Der-wei Wang, 295–326. Cambridge, MA: Harvard University Press.

Rainey, Lawrence, and Robert von Hallberg. 1994. "Editorial/Introduction." *Modernism/Modernity* 1, no. 2: 1–3.

Rapée, Erno. 1925. *Encyclopedia of Music for Pictures*. New York.

Singer, Ben. 2001. *Melodrama and Modernity: Early Sensational Cinema and Its Context*. New York: Columbia University Press.

Takeuchi, Yoshimi. 2005. *What Is Modernity?: Writings of Takeuchi Yoshimi*. Translated by Richard F. Calichman. New York: Columbia University Press.

Thompson, Kristin. 1985. *Exporting Entertainment: America in the World Film Market, 1907–1934*. London: British Film Institute.

———. 1998. "Narrative Structure in Early Classical Cinema." In *Celebrating 1895*. Edited by John Fullerton, 225–38. London: John Libbey.

Walker, Michael. 1982. "Melodrama and the American Cinema." *Movie* 29–30: 2.

Wang, Yiman. 2013. *Remaking Chinese Cinema: Through the Prism of Shanghai, Hong Kong, and Hollywood*. Honolulu: University of Hawai'i Press.

Weinbaum, Alys Eve, Lynn M. Thomas, Priti Ramamurthy, Uta G. Poiger, Madeleine Y. Dong, and Tani Barlow. 2008. "The Modern Girl as Heuristic Device." In *The Modern Girl around the World: Consumption, Modernity, and Globalization*. Edited by Alys Eve Weinbaum, The Modern Girl around the World Research Group, Lynn M. Thomas, Priti Ramamurthy, Uta G. Poiger, Madeleine Yue Dong, 1–24. Durham, NC: Duke University Press.

Wherry, Edith. 1911. *The Red Lantern: Being the Story of the Goddess of the Red Lantern Light*. New York: John Lane.

Williams, Linda. 2001. *Playing the Race Card: Melodramas of Black and White from Uncle Tom to O. J. Simpson*. Berkeley: University of California Press.

Yang, Panpan. 2018. "Repositioning Excess: Romantic Melodrama's Journey from Hollywood to China." In *Melodrama Unbound*. Edited by Christine Gledhill and Linda Williams, 220–36. New York: Columbia University Press.

Yao, Esther. 1991. "*Yellow Earth*: Western Analysis and a Non-Western Text." In *Chinese Cinema*. Edited by Chris Berry, 62–79. London: BFI.

Zhang, Zhen. 2005. *An Amorous History of the Silver Screen: Shanghai Cinema, 1896–1937*. Chicago: University of Chicago Press.

———. 2018. "Transnational Melodrama, *Wenyi*, and the Orphan Imagination." In *Melodrama Unbound: Across History, Media, and National Culture*. Edited by Christine Gledhill and Linda Williams, 83–97. New York: Columbia University Press, 2018.

JANE M. GAINES is Professor Emerita of Literature and English at Duke University and Professor of Film at Columbia University. She is author of three award-winning books: *Contested Culture: The Image, the Voice, and the Law*; *Fire and Desire: Mixed-Race Movies in the Silent Era*; and *Pink-Slipped: What Happened to Women in the Early Film Industries?* She is a founder of the Visible Evidence conference on documentary.

PART II.
DIVIDED MIS-EN-SCÈNE: COLONIAL CINEMA AND COLD WAR AFTERIMAGES

6. TARZAN/TAISHAN AND OTHER ORPHANS
Taiwan's Melodrama of Decolonization

Zhang Zhen

Abstract

Using a *Taiyupian*, or Taiwanese language film (*Tarzan and Treasure*, Liang Che-fu, dir., Tai Lien Films, 1965) as an entry point, this chapter traces the historical genealogy of the figure of the orphan in postwar Taiwan cinema in relation to the syndrome of "orphan of Asia" made famous by Wu Zhuoliu's (1956) semiautobiographical postwar novel. The orphan condition of the protagonist Hu Taiming in the novel is an allegorical representation of Taiwan's intellectual repression and deformation under coloniality, complicated further by the triangulation between the island and its two parent nations at war with each other, hence the "orphan of Asia." *Tarzan and Treasure* delineates a different orphan condition in postcolonial Taiwan that capitalizes on the trope of orphanhood, offering multiple interpretive and redemptive possibilities. This and other more action-oriented melodramas were made at the peak of *Taiyupian* as a vibrant local and regional film industry and as Taiwan readied itself to take off as a modernized nation in the free world. Whereas Hu Taiming in the novel loses his way and sanity in his futile circuitous journey with no destination, Taishan (Tarzan in Chinese) in *Tarzan and Treasure* is able to recover his native language and return to a state recognized by the United Nations at the time. The stereotypical portrayal of the tribe members in the Malay jungles, however, especially their sexuality, raises the issue of indigeneity in modern national identity construction in general and that of Taiwan in particular. *Tarzan* or the Asian orphan Taishan could serve well as a pioneer figuration for Kuan-hsing Chen's (2010) argument for "Asia as method" (or Asian studies in Asia) in the era of intensified globalization. I would like to supplement his view by adding that, as a historical and theoretical practice dedicated to the social and cultural analysis of base entities beyond intellectual politics on inter-Asian and global horizons, "Asia as method" could be enriched substantially by revisiting film archives in the region and reexamining the intermedia and transnational trajectories of the all-too-important figure of the orphan of Asia.

This chapter is about the orphan figure in post–World War II Taiwan cinema and culture, with a focus on *Tarzan and Treasure* (*Taishan yu baozang*) 泰山與寶藏 (Tai Lien Films, 1965), directed by Liang Che-fu 梁哲夫 (1920–92), a Taiwanese-language film (*Taiyupian* 台語片) that was Taiwan's first Tarzan film (fig. 6.1). It will also consider related films and texts, including fiction and song lyrics. At the outset, the film's title suggests a spin-off of the famous Tarzan franchise from Hollywood, and the hint at a treasure hunt seems to invite more an adventurous experience than a morally edifying melodrama. A closer, contextualized viewing reveals a more convoluted and layered product of Taiwan's film industry and cultural politics under decolonization and the Cold War. I will place this unique film within a genealogy of orphan-themed postwar Taiwan cinema and in relation to the persistent cultural melodrama of the orphan of Asia associated with the island nation to this day.

To link this cinema about orphanhood and decolonization with a broad Sinophone discourse, I will trace the concept of the orphan of Asia from the novel *Ajia no koji* 亞細亞の孤兒 by Wu Zhuoliu 吳濁流 (1900–76)[1] to its contemporary resonance.[2] As the island's sad nickname in the aftermath of its loss of United Nations membership in 1971,[3] it was made famous and widely popular by Lo Da-yu's 羅大佑 (1954–) "Orphan of Asia," likely the most remembered song from his 1983 album, *Masters of the Future* (未來的主人翁).

> Orphan of Asia
> Weeping in the wind
> Red mud stain on her yellow-skinned face
> White terror in her black eyes
>
> Orphan of Asia
> Weeping in the wind
> No one wants to play a fair game with you
> Everyone wants your favorite toy
>
> Dear child
> Why are you crying?
> How many of us are searching for answers to that difficult question?
> How many of us are sighing hopelessly in the dark night?
> How many of us are wiping off tears in silence?
> Dear mother, could you tell us why?

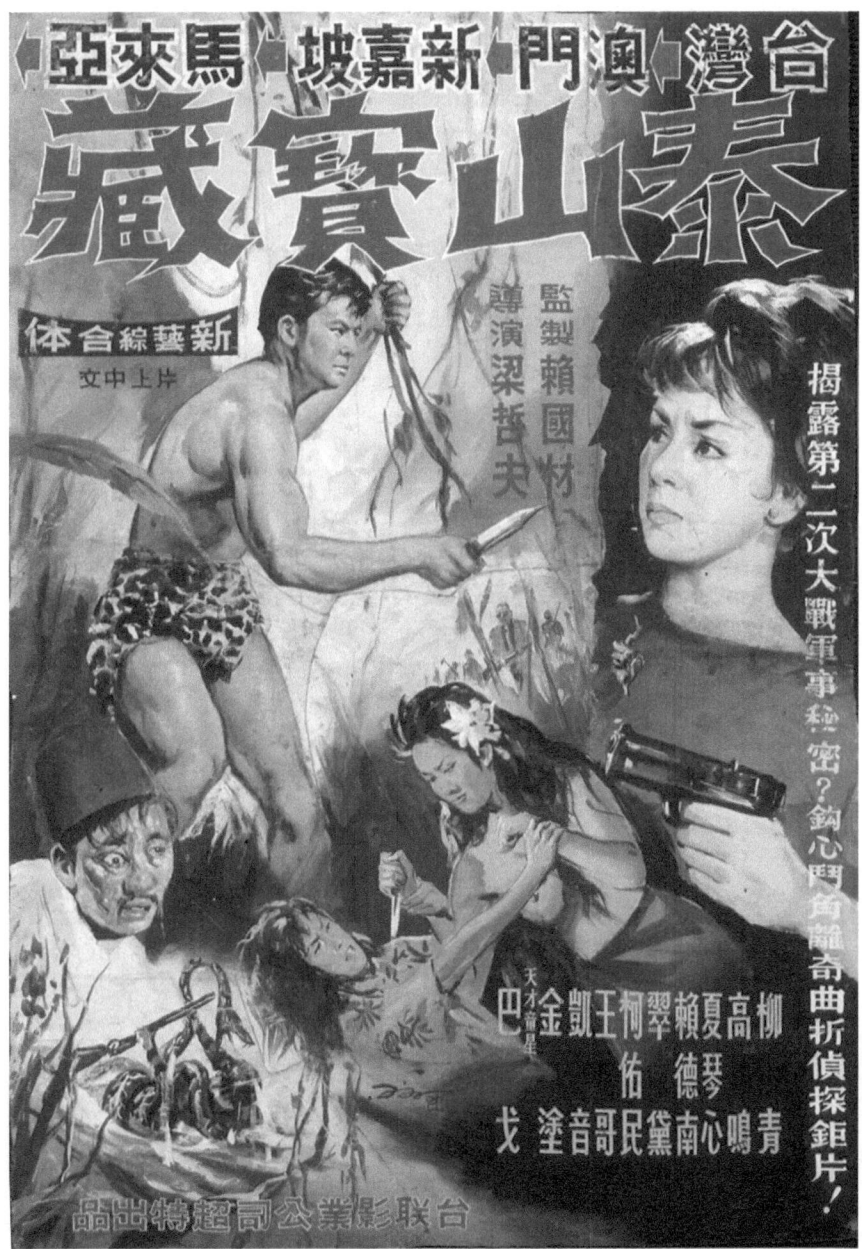

Figure 6.1. Original hand-painted poster (by Chen Tze-fu) for *Tarzan and Treasure* (*Taishan yu baozang*) 泰山與寶藏 (1965). (Courtesy of Taiwan Film Institute)

Lo's lyrics and melody vividly capture the pathos of nationhood as orphanhood and the burden of history. In the Chinese-speaking and Sinophone communities across East Asia, Southeast Asia, and beyond,[4] Lo is the venerated godfather of contemporary Chinese popular music. Among his many enduring works, ranging from love songs to film scores, "Orphan of Asia" is widely seen as emblematic of Lo's passionate commitment as a serious artist concerned with the social and historical problems of our times, in particular Taiwan's national identity. It was adopted as a theme song for Taiwan director Chu Yen-ping's 朱延平 controversial and sensationally successful film, *A Home Too Far* (*Yiyu*) 異域, released in 1990.[5] The film, based on a novel by dissident writer Po Yang 柏楊, offers a visceral cinematic mise-en-scène of the ordeal endured by the surviving members of the ninety-three divisions of the Nationalist Army and their families after fleeing the People's Liberation Army's relentless pursuit in the early 1950s. After a treacherous long hike through the tropical forests across the Yunnan border into Burma, they settled among protective villagers but met with violent suppression by the Burmese government. Some eventually returned to Taiwan, whereas others, disillusioned with the Kuomintang (KMT) regime, choose not to. Lo's song poignantly articulates the feelings of homelessness and hopelessness felt by the orphaned soldiers 孤軍.

The song has been interpreted and staged under various social and political circumstances, such as the aftermath of the June 4, 1989, suppression of the democracy movement in Beijing. It evokes innocence wronged, state violence, and abandonment by the nation that one belongs to and fights for and appeals to a broad demographic beyond Lo's fans. The emotions aroused by the lyrical words and music strike a chord in the hearts not just of Taiwan veterans but also of ethnic Chinese communities in many parts of the world. In the song they find their personal fates inextricably tied to the tragic events in modern histories of China and Taiwan.

Tarzan from the "Treasure Island"

Tarzan and Treasure is also premised on a tale of orphaned soldiers. Other than the obvious reference to the iconic Caucasian Tarzan, the entire story takes place in Cold War Asia, not an imagined colonial Africa. Besides its appeal as a fantastical hybrid genre, the complex backstory involves many locations and relations embedded in wartime and postwar history. Taishan, the Taiwanese Tarzan, lost in the Malay jungle, is in fact the grown-up version of Cheng Da-wei, son of a Taiwanese soldier named Cheng Tien-cheng deployed to the Malay islands by the Japanese during the Pacific War. He and his fellow soldier Fan Chi-ping, from Macau, were involved in interning and concealing a bounty of treasure (gold and US dollar notes) in a mountain cave as the defeated Japanese troops prepared to return home. Years later, Fan dies in Macau and Cheng travels with his son to find the treasure, only to be killed by a venomous snake in front of the cave. Unable to go back to Taiwan on his own, the boy is practically orphaned; he goes native in the jungle and subsequently befriends the local inhabitants (called the primitives [土人] in the film), who treat him as one of their own. Da-wei is cut off from family and Taiwan for fifteen years until his sister Hsiao-hung, now renamed Shu-fen, an independent-spirited and smart modern woman dressed in jeans and boots, decides to find out what happened to her father and brother.

The muscular and oversexualized Taishan is diametrically opposite of the cerebral and celibate Hu Taiming, protagonist in *Orphan of Asia*. As in a large subcluster of orphan-themed films, the melodramatic fate of nature boy Tarzan follows the arc of orphaning for various causes and the final reunion with surviving family members, in this case a sibling and a nephew. The entanglements caused by a reappearing family member after long separation do more than create narrative suspense and complication; they indicate the extent to which the orphan figure embodies the collision of different experiences and temporalities. Shaped by different life experiences and values, the family entanglements in the film are saturated with both emerging and residual forces in sociopolitical transitions. The orphan is thus both a haunting figure carrying repressed memories and histories and a potentially enabling agent as she or he crosses familial, cultural, geographic, and political borders in a series of transpositions and transformations.

Tarzan and Treasure and other more action-oriented melodramas were made at the peak of *Taiyupian* as a vibrant local and regional film industry and as Taiwan readied itself to take off as a modernized nation in the free world. Rather than tear-jerking and heart-rending, a large portion of *Taiyupian* in this second phase gravitated toward the picaresque and carnivalesque ends of action-laden, exterior-oriented "other" melodrama.[6] Liang Che-fu was a prolific director whose output included Cantonese, Taiwanese, and Mandarin productions, but he is best known for his highly popular *Taiyupian*.[7] His films exhibit a wide range of themes and characters: his earlier sentimental dramas, both period and contemporary—such as *Mengjiang's Woman* 孟姜女 (1959), *Mother's Tears* 母淚滴滴紅 (1962), *Last Train from Kao-hsiung* 高雄發的尾班車 (1963), and *Early Train from Taipei* 臺北發的早車 (1964)—playful hybrid genre films such as *Tarzan*, as well as a pair of spy films called *Red Rose Spy* 間諜紅玫瑰 (1965) and *True Rose, Fake Rose* 真假紅玫瑰 (1966). Despite his *waishengren* origin (meaning from the mainland), Liang is lovingly described as a versatile and commercially successful director with a "deep and intimate affinity" for Taiwan grassroots culture, well versed in storytelling traditions of regional operas and folk culture, and adventurous in innovation and experimentation (Liang C. 1994). *Tarzan* is one of the twenty films he made in 1964–65, the peak of his career and that of the *Taiyupian* industry. The film stands out for its transnational geographic coverage and outlandish retake on a Hollywood brand. The plot does not take place in Taiwan, yet the film is entangled with Taiwan's unfinished business of decolonization.

    A widely consumed global popular-culture object, Tarzan, the fictionalized legendary feral child raised by apes, is inseparable from the post-Enlightenment imagination linked to colonialism, the industrial revolution, and capitalist modernity. Since its first appearance in serialized fiction by US writer Edgar Rice Burroughs in 1912, the story has inspired countless sequels, film franchises, comic books, radio plays, television serials, and other media products and has become an "international icon" (Wannamaker and Abate 2012). *Tarzan and Treasure* is closer to the Sy Weintraub productions of the same period, in which the Hollywood Tarzan has become a lone adventurer (no Jane nor "baby" or nuclear family) and speaks broken English, though the monochrome look harks back to the franchises from the silent era and precolor talkies.[8] The Taiwanese incarnation has an unmistakable local and regional look and character, accentuated by the thick Taiyu accent and grounded in an East and Southeast Asian landscape.

    Unlike Hu Taiming in Wu's novel, an intellectual from rural Taiwan who grew up under the intensification of Japanese imperialization that caused him great mental anguish, Cheng Da-wei—who was presumably born after the war and left Taiwan as a boy—does not have Hu's obsession with Taiwan as a spiritual home, nor his self-pity and despair. Da-wei's mother is never mentioned—we assume she is long dead or gone, for his sister grows up under their uncle's foster care. In fact, the story is set entirely outside Taiwan (though obviously it was filmed on location there, as with most low-budget *Taiyupian*). Setting the story away from Taiwan but filming there[9] establishes the island as an off-screen spectral topography of sorts filled with distant memories and haphazard meanings.

    The film's expansive geopolitical topography begins in Portuguese-ruled Macau, a crucial Cold War outpost sandwiched between Taiwan, Hong Kong, and the People's Republic of China. A secretive rendezvous on a noirish street ends in the murder of Da-wei's uncle, who has gone there to find Fan's son and the other half of a map that shows how to get to the treasure cave in Malaysia. Chien Hung-juin, the local mobster head who has orchestrated the murder, kills Fan's son (who is also his assistant). Chien (literally meaning "money") takes the map and his entourage on a bounty-hunting trip through Malaysia. Meanwhile, Da-wei's sister heads with their nephew toward the same destination under the invisible protection of detectives from Malaysia and Macau. The sister, Shu-fen, and the nephew, You-fu, are disguised as aides to the mobster boss, and the beautiful and capable female detective pretends to be Fan's sister and the head detective of Macau wears horrifying makeup as the "monster face" 怪面神, a sharp shooter.

The search for lost kin and buried past illustrates well the dialectic of action and pathos of melodrama (Williams 1998). Shu-fen and You-fu trek through Malaysia's tropical landscape, with the very similar landscape of rural Taiwan as stand-in. They encounter a wild man (野人) wearing Tarzan-style trunks but sporting a clean, sleek haircut as he flies through treetops and appears fully at ease in the animal kingdom (elephants appear in a later scene). At each thrilling turn on the journey, he saves the strangers through last-minute rescues—a life-threatening gigantic snake, the attempted rape of Shu-fen by a fat, lascivious villager in broad daylight, fire-spitting ghosts at night among them. This Tarzan at first seems to be a feral child without language but, after a few encounters with Shu-fen and You-fu, he suddenly begins to speak Taiwanese, as if the long separation from Taiwan and "(Chinese) civilization" has not damaged his memory of his native tongue at all. When Shu-fen asks the hero for his name, he howls, "Taishan" (in Chinese the word also refers to the holy mountain in Shandong province patronized by the Qing emperors). If Tarzan is a "global vernacular" idiom (Hansen 1999) stemming from American literature and Hollywood cinema, Taishan's linguistic and cultural identity prove to be decidedly Taiwanese. As the two teams from Taiwan and Macau respectively reach deeper into the heart of the primitive land, it turns out that the tribal members also speak Taiwanese. It is as though Taiyu functions as a universally intelligible language, akin to the way English as a default lingua franca is used in the African jungles in the Hollywood Tarzan movies.

"Fate's Monstrous Children"

Xiaojue Wang (2013) perceptively reads orphanization in Wu Zhuoliu's *Orphan of Asia* not only as a "trope of the *stranded* condition of the modern subject between Chinese culturalism and Japanese colonialism, between tradition and modernity, but also a narrative strategy that bespeaks the always already *fractured* notions of nation and national culture" (158; my emphasis). Hu Taiming, the protagonist who has a certain biographic affinity to the novel's author, descends from a landed gentry family with distant roots in southern China (Guangdong province) but increasingly finds himself lost between the multiple places where he thought he might have belonged. An educator dedicated to learning, Hu finds his life journey punctuated by a series of schools of various styles and nature: as a young boy, he is sent to a traditional Chinese school by his grandfather and then he attends a modern public school under Japanese colonial administration before becoming a teacher himself in one of those schools fostering imperialization 皇民化. An existential crisis leads to a four-year sojourn of study in Tokyo, where he realizes that, as a Taiwanese, he is accepted neither by Japan nor by his Chinese compatriots. His Taiwanese friend puts it adroitly, "We are deformed—fate's monstrous children" (命中注定我们是畸形儿) (Wu 2006, 98).

Hu Taiming's zigzag journey in search of work and self-realization takes him to another teaching stint in Nanjing, only to become suspected as a spy for Japan in the heat of the national defense movement; he flees back to Taiwan, where he is mistrusted and followed as a suspected spy for China. His subsequent job as a conscripted translator for the Japanese in China and other traumatic events eventually drive him insane. The novel ends on a mysterious note: Hu disappears from the village. Has he drowned himself in the sea? Or has he gone to China to join the resistance, as a Kunming radio station's broadcast in Japanese rumors him to be? It is interesting that the mainland edition's preface insists on interpreting the ending thus: "In the end, [Hu has] overcome the 'orphan consciousness' (孤儿意识) and decides to commit himself to the torrents of the struggle of the masses" (Wu 2009).[10]

Neither Wu the author nor the protagonist Hu is actually an orphan. What, then, is the "orphan consciousness"? Hu loses his beloved grandfather and mother in the course of the unraveling of his life and becomes increasingly estranged from his hometown as he grows into a world-weary intellectual; but his childhood is by and large surrounded by a tightly knit extended family, despite the encroaching shadows of colonial subjugation. Ma Shengmei (2015) sees Hu as "a foundling within the family, within Taiwan's culture, within the Japanese empire," and Taiwan itself as "an island orphanage" (11). Leo Ching (2007) observes incisively, putting Hu's tragedy within the long view of modern world history, "Unlike the Hegelian Spirit, the orphan's itinerary is neither teleological nor triumphant. . . . The condition of the 'orphan' is precisely the impossibility of belonging to the 'family of nations' that undergirds the modern/colonial world system." He concludes, "The orphan remains deferred, detested, and disempowered. For the orphan, modernity/coloniality means, above all, the state of being deprived of subjectivity."

Ma's and Ching's rather pessimistic definitions of colonial subalternity as orphanhood arise from a post–Cold War perspective on Hu Taiming's intellectual and political impotence. His meandering journeys between Taiwan, Japan, and China only make him sink deeper and deeper into the quagmires of colonial modernity and senseless wars. His romantic and sexual desires also become compromised and suppressed as he moves along the hopeless path of defeat and dispossession. Hu was still tormented by his unrequited love earlier in the novel for a female Japanese colleague in the school where they teach, when he realized that interracial free love does not apply between the colonized and the colonizer. His brief marriage with a modern girl of Nanjing ends in misery and separation. For the most part, he prefers to stay in his study reading Chinese classics, when he is not tending to the banana seedlings in his personal little patch of land. The frequent return to his childhood home and rural landscape—and the grandfather and parents who dote on him—whenever he feels injured or abandoned by the large forces of the outside world seems to make him a childlike figure caught up in a recurrent state of arrested development. When this refuge is emptied after the death of his spiritual protectors, which once more makes him practically an adult orphan, the last resort is insanity and disappearance or self-erasure.

Hu Taiming's orphan condition is, for Ching, a colonial allegory of repression and deformation of Taiwan intellectuals, complicated further by the war between its two "parent" nations that leave Taiwan an orphan. His counter strategy, or self-protective mechanism, after repeated failures and betrayals, is turning inward—both the natal rural landscape and his own interiority nourished by Chinese and Western classics. (He reads *Faust* to fill time during his vacuous job at a colonial agency.) The orphan condition for an educated and well-traveled man like Hu might be viewed as passive, but in fact it is a self-conscious theoretical position. He is not literally homeless but nationless, which incapacitates the modern male subject and isolates him on the colonial periphery. The circuitous journeys do not lead to any higher, more promising geopolitical plane for Taiwan or Hu Taiming himself, as with his learning in Chinese, Japanese, and Western languages and cultures, which does not accumulate in a harmonious synthesis and spiritual transcendence. Rather, they seem to have catapulted him into cultural autism and personal madness.

"The Disappearing Image": Postwar Celluloid Orphans

A popular film rather than a serious novel first written in Japanese, *Tarzan and Treasure* stems from a different orphan condition and representation in postcolonial Taiwan that also capitalized on the trope of orphanhood and offers multiple interpretive possibilities. Around the time *Orphan of Asia* was translated and published in Chinese in the early 1960s, Taiwan cinema was experiencing a golden age of sorts, momentarily rivaling and even replacing Hong Kong by mid-decade in its output and exuberant domestic and Nanyang (Southeast Asian) markets. Postwar Taiwan cinema from the mid-1950s to the early 1970s boasted two parallel cinemas (Yeh and Davi 2005), Taiwanese- and Mandarin-speaking cinema. The former was nourished by local popular culture, including the *koa-a-hi* theater 歌仔戲, radio play, and pop music, primarily in the Minnan dialect (Zhang Y. 2013, 1–2n1),[11] whereas the latter was explicitly fostered by the Nationalist regime as the official language. The Taiwanese-language cinema was particularly popular among the 70 percent of the island's population that spoke Minnan, an audience base consolidated by the popular postwar Amoy-dialect (*Xiayu*) films made in Hong Kong for Hokkien-speaking audiences across Asia (particularly Manila, southern Taiwan, and Singapore (Taylor 2013). The Amoy films' popularity stimulated local production of Minnan-speaking films (the two dialects are very similar) (Lee 1997, 125–26). Between 1955 and 1972, more than a thousand Taiyu films were produced, peaking in 1963 with an output of more than a hundred films, though only a fraction of them have been preserved (Liao G. 2001, 13). Taiwan film scholar Gene-fon Liao uses "disappearing images" to describe *Taiyupian*'s neglected place in Taiwan film historiography. Indeed, what Liao sees as a transitional cinema between the film aesthetic and industry practice of primitive cinema and that of classical cinema can also be understood in terms of Taiwan's decolonization and the attendant sociocultural transitions under the Cold War.[12] Although Mandarin replaced Japanese as the national language (*guoyu*) under the KMT regime's authoritarian policy, the Minnan dialect continued to thrive in popular culture, finding its most synthetic form in *Taiyupian*.[13]

At the same time, Taiwan society entered a protracted period of economic expansion and political compression (Chung 1960) and experienced the convoluted consequences of land reform, agricultural modernization, urban development, and the aggressive incursion of American mass culture compounded by US economic, military, and political control of the island nation as an anticommunist frontier. The socioeconomic restructuring and a recovering economy generated a considerable amount of speculative floating capital (游資) that found its way into the nascent, profitable *Taiyupian* industry (Huang 1994).

Early *Taiyupian* with wandering orphans and foster girls (流浪儿, 孤女, 养女) are suffused with a mournful sadness stemming from colonial and postwar experiences under forces beyond ordinary people's control. Scholarship on Taiwan cinema—both *Taiyupian* and the New Taiwan Cinema—has pivoted on sadness 悲情 as a persistent motif articulating Taiwan's colonial and postcolonial condition as an orphaned nation. *City of Sadness* (*Beiqing chengshi* 悲情城市), Hou Hsiao-hsien's widely acclaimed epic of 1990, has likely inspired the retrospective view in scholarship produced in that decade, especially as a Taiyu film made twenty-five years earlier was also called *City of Sadness* (*Beiqing chengshi* 悲情城市) (Lin Fu-di, dir., 1965; Zhang Y. 2013). Hou's 1990 film, narrating the tragic events befallen an extended family during the 2.28 incident (February 28, 1947) and the ensuing White Terror, is a powerful intervention in postwar Taiwan historiography and a critical commentary on the incomplete decolonization under authoritarianism. The observation about the prevalent sadness in *Taiyupian* is validated by the predominance of melodrama, including numerous adaptations from *koa-a-hi* and folktales that are centered on hardship and suffering, separation of lovers and family members and the ensuing tribulations, and women's sacrifice in both colonial (or traditional Taiwan) and postwar periods. Words, songs, and sentiments associated with hardship 苦, sentiment or pathos 情, resentment or complaint 怨, destiny 命, tears 淚 or crying 哭, heartache 心疼, soul-breaking 魂斷, pitiful 可憐, vagabondage 流浪, bidding farewell 送別, and searching 尋 abound and appear in various combinations. Moreover, it is not difficult to find recurring keywords and tropes related to orphanhood and mother-child melodramatic fates in film titles and plots, such as 母子淚 (Mother and Son's Tears, Zong You, dir., 1955), 孤兒怨 (Orphan's Suffering, Hsu Shou-ren, dir., 1958), 慈母淚 (Mother's Tears, Wu Wen-chao, dir., 1958), 孤女報母仇 (Orphan Girl Avenges for Her Mother, Liang Che-fu, dir., 1960), 孤女的願望 Orphan Girl's Wish, Chang Ying, dir., 1961), 流浪三兄妹 (The Wandering of Three Siblings, Shao Lo-hui, dir., 1963), 尋母三千里 (Searching for Lost Mother Across the Country, Shao Luo-hui, dir., 1963), 流浪賣花姑娘 (The Wandering Flower Girl, Guo Nan-hung, dir., 1964), 孤兒哭夜墓 (Orphan Crying by the Grave at Night, Han Wen, dir., 1964), *Orphan Ling Bo* 孤女凌波 (Orphan Ling Bo, Jin Chao-bai, dir., 1964), and more.[14] These empathy-rousing and tear-jerking figures and themes—and the songs that accompany them—persisted in *Taiyupian* until its demise around 1970.[15] In later years, *Taiyupian* appear less frequently and are reconfigured within a changing cinematic and social landscape.

Gene-fon Liao's (2001) mapping of the representational system of *Taiyupian* as an alternative cinema offers a nuanced periodization and generic mapping. He identifies a shift from a prevalent tendency toward sentimental, sorrowful expressions of suffering and the desire to overcome colonial trauma in the 1950s to a tendency toward carnivalesque mass entertainment in the 1960s. My viewing of a number of *Taiyupian* in the Taipei National Film Archive in 2006 and subsequently DVDs that became available later largely confirms this general periodization, though irregularities occur intermittently, and many later films articulate a pronounced hybrid aesthetic and widely mixed sociocultural ethos.

The changing visage of the orphan figure is where the shift seems more visible and consequential. Whereas the screen orphans in the first boom era tend to be young children in search of a lost parent (more often the mother), a film like *Orphan Ling Bo*, based on the real-life story of the eponymous movie actress, follows a longer narrative and life arc into the contemporary time when past conflicts or traumas are resolved and separated family members are reunited (Zhang Z. 2010). Moreover, the melodramatic mode is expanded to include a host of other generic elements, including detective thriller, western, nature adventure, and martial arts films. The early pitiful orphaned children and abandoned women originating from *koa-a-hi* and other opera or folktales are visceral embodiments of the unfinished (to invoke the film *Unfinished Love* 舊情綿綿, Shao Luo-hui, dir., 1962) work of mourning and decolonization, or what Guo-juin Hong terms the "unclean severance" from colonial legacy (Hong 2011, 7). The new generation of liberated teenage and adult orphans such as Ling Po and Tarzan/Taishan, who form mixed kinship ties and communities across a more expansive geopolitical landscape, exemplify, then, an energetic "vernacular hybridity" (Hong 2011, 7) in film genre that also draws and affects an evolving mass culture under the Cold War.

Orphan Ling Bo and *Tarzan and Treasure* are products of the carnivalesque phase of *Taiyupian*, which carries a certain sociopolitical energy not easily contained by the dominant discourse on nation building and anticommunist Cold War ideology, as explicitly articulated in most of the Mandarin-speaking policy films and "healthy realist" films made in the same period. To be sure, the KMT-regime-sponsored Mandarin-language cinema also belabors the motif of orphanhood, as, for example, in *Our Neighbors* 街頭巷尾 (1963) and *Beautiful Ducklings* 養鴨人家 (1964) directed by Lee Hsing 李行 (1930–), one of Taiwan cinema's enduring pillars.[16] These narratives, intertwining the melodramatic and realist modes, usher the female orphan toward the path of healthy assimilation into a new-style family sanctioned by the paternalist Nationalist state embodied by a benevolent foster-father figure, whose northern-China-accented Mandarin points to their origins on the mainland associated with the KMT.[17]

In general, the trope of orphanhood in *Taiyupian* tradition is far more sustained and multifaceted, outlining a parallel landscape of decolonization and modernization that is less predictable and is open to transnational horizons. Many Taiyu films are deeply rooted in local, colonial-era operatic sources and uninterested in portraying the orphan as caught in the binary forces of the two Chinese regimes across the strait or on the island. Although concerned with the breakup of family and love relations and the desire for reunion and recuperation, the films' narratives and formal energy draw from local and regional popular cultural realms, including the Amoy theater and cinema, *koa-a-hi*, folk ballads, radio broadcasts (in Taiyu and other dialects), Japanese popular songs, and sensational social news, dispensing the illusion of or obsession with an intact national sovereignty anchored in the mainland. In other words, although the Mandarin-speaking female teenage orphan (played by the China-born Tang Pao-yun 唐寶雲1944–99) in a colorful healthy realist film like *Beautiful Ducklings* serves well as a national allegory for the KMT-ruled state (albeit stranded on the island province), the tale of a primitive, Taiwanese-speaking Tarzan puts a transnational spin on the colonial allegory of the orphan of Asia as he ventures into the proxy Malay jungles.

Taiwan's Orient

The ostensible global self-positioning is a double-edged sword, however. One side asserts the transnational nature and appeal of golden-age *Taiyupian*, with its markets reaching far beyond Taiwan into many Southeast Asian countries (especially Singapore and Manila, with large Chinese populations of Hokkien origins), where the Amoy-dialect cinema had been popular. These markets proved to be equally desirable as treasure islands like Taiwan, if not more so. The popularity of these two transregional cinemas considerably undermined the dominance of Hollywood by capturing a trans-Asian ethnic spectatorship. The other side reveals, however, a form of settler colonialism that has troubled Taiwanese (Han) national identity since the Qing dynasty.[18] The playful appropriation of the Tarzan meme replicates, if unwittingly, the hegemonic assertion of a linguistic and cultural hierarchy inherent in the Tarzan cultural industry—an Orientalist legacy of colonialism.

There are two levels at which this Taiwan's Orient (after Tanaka's [1995] "Japan's Orient") functions in the film. First, Tarzan/Taishan is heavily coded as a (grown-up) feral child; his smooth-skinned body, muscular legs, and agile, animal-like athleticism are presented alternately in close-ups and long shots as exotic eye candy for supposedly enlightened or civilized Taiwanese (or Taiwanese-speaking) audiences. His jungle-nourished raw energy refreshes the Taiwanese identity he now reclaims. Second, Taishan's beautiful aborigine girlfriend, Samei, is offered as another hurdle, though an enabling one, in the dialectic of pathos and action for recovering Taiwan's lost son, and then an exotic "treasure" to be brought home. (See fig. 6.2.) At first, she mistakes Taishan's yet-unidentified sister for a romantic rival and

Figure 6.2. Romancing the Indigenous: Taishan and Samei. Courtesy of Taiwan Film Institute.

tries to kill her with a dagger. This gives rise to more dramatic complications for temporal delay and suspense building. The disconcerting ambiguity surrounding a possible but not permissible incestuous affection is dispelled in the penultimate scene of recognition, which stages the much-anticipated authentication of proofs of blood kinship and attendant identities. After Taishan recounts how he has ended up in the Malay jungles, You-fu asks him, "So, you are Taiwanese?" "Yes, we are from the same home country," replies Taishan (Da-wei). The siblings show matching birthmarks on their left arms, just as the two halves of the treasure map are at long last pieced together intact. (See fig. 6.3.) After some more action and last-minute rescue scenes, the villainous Chien is subdued and handcuffed by the female Malay detective. The chief detective of Macau tears down his monstrous mask and readjusts his feigned asymmetrical posture—revealing the handsome face of Interpol justice. The war spoils are carried from the cave, but stashes of dollar bills have become worthless dust. Tarzan and Samei get fully dressed (no more exposed torsos and legs) in modern clothing and leave for Taiwan, with the visitors from more civilized parts of Asia. This lowbrow orphan of Asia, lost not to Japanese colonialism and continental Chinese nationalism (as in Wu Zhouliu's novel) but to the entangled business of postwar recovery, returns to his fatherland triumphantly.

The happy ending in family reunion (with the parents' generation entirely gone, however) and intercultural marriage is where further questions of decolonization arise. The film's hybrid-genre characteristics (i.e., detective-adventure-family melodrama) illustrate aptly the transitional nature of *Taiyupian* in a time when Taiwan attempted to establish an autonomous identity as the representative of the free China on the world stage. The receding of the

Figure 6.3. Scene of Reunion and authentication of blood relation ("I . . . I'm your sister Hsiao Hong." "The Same!") Courtesy of Taiwan Film Institute.

mainland further behind the iron curtain of the Cold War and US support of and presence in Taiwan enhanced Taiwan's international and regional significance. But the reconstruction and nation building were slow and painful, and most of the energy and resources of the Nationalist regime had been channeled toward the recovery of the mainland from the Communist rule at the expense of local people's livelihood and cultural development.

Tarzan and Treasure may seem like light entertainment fare at the outset, but it touches on a heavy chapter in Taiwan's recent history. Many Taiwanese and Taiwan aborigine soldiers and workers were stranded in various prisoner-of-war camps or disappeared in Southeast Asia and the Pacific Islands, where they fought for the Japanese.[19] As the film's temporal frame suggests, it took one and a half decades for the young generation to attain adulthood and the necessary resources to embark on the search for missing family members overseas. Apparently born around or after the Pacific War and raised in the Republic of China after the KMT lost the civil war and retreated to Taiwan, the offspring of "fate's monstrous children" find themselves carrying the burden of colonial legacy—hidden war spoils, broken kinship and social relations, and repressed cultural and linguistic memories. "That's why I have been wandering and growing up in this remote mountain," says Taishan (Da-wei), as he concludes his recounting to Shu-fen and You-fu of the ill-fated trip fifteen years earlier.

Taishan is the embodiment of the troubled inheritor of this legacy. As with Hu Taiming in Wu's novel, he, too, experiences a kind of developmental regression, retreating into nature that in fact is not entirely free from the impact of colonialism and war. Whereas Hu loses his way and his mind in his futile, circuitous journey with no destination, Taishan is able to recover his native language and return to Taiwan, his home country. Wu Zhuoliu and his protagonist envisioned for Taiwan an alternative modernity, or "discrepant cosmopolitanisms" (Clifford 1998, 365, quoted Liao G. 2007)[20] in distinction from, or a certain detachment from, Japan and China—two powerful competing versions of Asian modernity that hold sway over Taiwan's destiny.[21] This alternative route to modernity seems realized in a more playful popular expression in *Taiyupian*. The mixed transnational cast of agents composed of professional and amateur, adult and child, fashionable city people and half-naked "primitives" are not spies for either China or Japan but rather are performers of cultural creolization[22] for a widening *Taiyupian* audience and market beyond Taiwan. China is irrelevant to *Tarzan*, and Japan is referred to only through its defeat and withdrawal from its southern advance.[23] In the novel, the Asian orphan consciousness was forged in Hu Taiming's painful vacillation between two imperial traditions and their modernizing ambitions. Taishan/Tarzan, from postwar Taiwan, further removed from colonial times and war memories, is a celluloid orphan with an optimistic spirit and voracious appetite for life. Though an unwitting secondhand victim of Japanese colonialism, he has none of the intellectual trappings and moral anguish that tormented Hu Taiming. He lives in the present, adapting easily to another natural and cultural environment. Even though he is still stamped and proven (through the birthmark) as Taiwanese at the end, his identity is more elastic and immanent, open to contingent forces and relations. Tempered transculturally and cleared of the colonial burden (the sibling renounced the hidden treasure as a curse), the orphan is ready to return to his native land and build his own family and future with Samei, the indigenous Malay woman. Taishan seems to have overcome the Asian orphan syndrome that caused Hu's madness and final departure from Taiwan.

But what about the aboriginal people who adopted and provided Tarzan a community during the fifteen years of his orphanhood? How will he and Samei cope with (reverse) culture shock and the challenges of assimilation in a modernizing Taiwan? The stereotypical portrayal of the tribal members, especially their sexuality, raises the thorny issue of indigeneity in modern nationalist discourse and state building, further complicated by Japanese subjugation of the Han Chinese (*benshengren* and *waishengren* alike), as well as indigenous people in Taiwan. In newspaper advertisements for the 1965 film, Taishan fighting jungle beasts and "beauties bathing naked" in the exotic "Shangri-La" are repeatedly paraded as selling points of the film. The simplistic, complacent attitude toward the tribal people in Malaysia in the film resonates with the historical Chinese treatment—from state policy of conquest and assimilation to popular prejudice and exoticism—of aborigines and ethnic minorities from the imperial time to the present day. As the film is primarily addressed to Taiwan's Hokkienese/Han Chinese population and is shot in Taiwan, reference to the primitives would more immediately invoke Taiwan's own Austronesian tribes and nations (Amis, Atayal, Paiwan, Rukai, Bunun, Taho and Kawalan, Sejiq/Taroko, Pingpu, etc.). The film was shot in Kenting Park 墾丁公園 at the southern point of Taiwan, where many indigenous tribal villagers (Paiwan) live. The "Malay" natural scenery as background in the stereotypical "beauties bathing naked in the river" scene is a brutally convenient representation of using the indigenous to tantalize and entertain, and creating a temporary fictionalized state that is distant and exotic in comparison with the modernized (Han Chinese) Taiwan.[24]

Exploited by a serial colonialism by the Dutch, the Chinese, and then the Japanese (Shih 2013), Taiwan's indigenous peoples have struggled for cultural survival for centuries. Their legal recognition as indigenous peoples or First Nations (原住民族) did not occur until recently, nor did it extend to all.[25] For the various Austronesian nations in the Pacific, including Formosa (Taiwan), as anthropologist Scott Simon (2009) observes, the colonial period is "still far from over" and they "have legitimate human rights grievances against a variety of colonial powers" (55). Although some intermarried with Chinese and sinicized to various degrees, many, including the Amis and the Sejiq/Taroko, remained largely intact and still use their own languages in daily life.

Tarzan and Treasure shows a sympathetic view of the "primitives" through the liminal figure of Taishan and some friendly villagers, but it does not bother to spend much if any of its time and budget on researching the indigenous cultures either in Malaysia or Taiwan. The menacing rapist and jealous girlfriend are demonizing caricatures associated with sex and violence. The generic term *turen* is typical of a sinocentric worldview with regard to the "barbarians" (on a spectrum of "raw" to "cooked"; Fiskesjö 1999). If Hu Taiming felt deeply hurt by Japan's perception and treatment of educated Han Taiwanese like him as second-rate citizens, the indigenous people have been placed on the bottom of the totem pole by generations of colonials, including the Chinese Qing Empire, followed by the nationalist state.[26] To retrieve Taiwan's lost son, the real "treasure," and what he could bring back from the ruins of the Pacific War and a resource-rich Southeast Asia, the transnational detective team undertook a Taiwan-style "Southern Advance" under Cold War conditions. Once the model colony of Japan, Taiwan later graduated as a postwar US model outpost and aid beneficiary in building an anticommunist modern nation in the East in 1965, when it became the designated Retreat and Recovery site for US troops during the Vietnam War.[27]

Tarzan and Treasure was also made that year. Its detective-adventure genre departs from other contemporary films revolving around more "realistic" social life in Taiwan, but the films share a fascination with Southeast Asia not simply as an exotic backward backyard but also as a significant narrative linchpin. Typically, the male protagonist, encouraged by the state's favorable policy on overseas investment, ventures to Nanyang to build his business and career (usually in the rubber plantations), develops romantic relationships with native women, and goes through ups and downs in both business and family, but he eventually returns to Taiwan.[28] *Tarzan and Treasure* mines a different kind of narrative resource there. The tragic war experience and repressed memories of left-behind soldiers in the Pacific islands are now much more distant and selectively repurposed by an exponentially growing Taiyu film industry with a voracious appetite for new material and markets.

"Orphan of Asia" as Method

The Asian orphan Tarzan could serve well as an unwitting pioneer figuration for Chen Kuan-hsing's argument for "Asia as method" (or critical Asian studies based in Asia) in the advent of globalization (Chen 2010). With an emphasis on local and transregional movements, Asia as method decenters the West, northern Asia, and China discursively and geopolitically and pursues the incomplete work of decolonization and deimperialization stalled by the Cold War. I would like to supplement this view by adding that, as a historical and theoretical practice dedicated to the social and cultural analysis of base entities beyond intellectual politics on inter-Asian and global "heterogeneous horizons," Asia as method could be enriched substantially by revisiting film archives in the region (and films scattered around the globe). Retracing the intermedia and transnational trajectories of the all-too-important screen orphan figure and their reconfigurations over time is one productive pathway. *Taiyupian*'s sentimental farewell to Japan and distance from the mainland and the Nationalist regime's Mandarin sensibility, and its disposition to local and regional everyday life, are pronounced indications of a grassroots or *minjian* (民間) form of decolonization and deimperialization. If films like *Tarzan and Treasure* offer an alternative map out of Japanese coloniality and Cold War jungles, the detour through the incorporation of indigenous people and landscape intimates the problematic construction of Taiwan's "orient" on its way to becoming a little dragon of Asia.

In the forest of melodrama worldwide, Tarzan is a peculiar tree or branch of what I call the orphan imagination that illustrates the fertility of the mode and its disposition to transplantation (Zhang Z. 2018). The Asian orphan consciousness of the colonial period articulated by Wu Zhuoliu in Japanese (and then Chinese) and meant for both Japan's and Taiwan's future generations is redirected and reinterpreted in other trans-Asian geocultural terms in the postcolonial and Cold War contexts. An iconic figure of minor transnationalism, the cultural orphan "makes visible the multiple relations between the national and transnational" (Shih and Lionnet 2005). Yet, as melodrama—home to countless screen orphans—the orphan is also vulnerable or open to adoptions, transformations, and appropriations. Some are geared toward progressive democratic aspirations and actions, whereas others reinscribe retrograde cultural and political values. Indeed, the two sides often appear in complex combinations. The multidimensional tale of the orphan of Asia in its various registers and embodiments enables us to reassess the convoluted history of modern Taiwan in relation to Asia and the world anew, as Luo Dayou's song, cited at the opening of this chapter, has brilliantly shown in our time.

Acknowledgments

A NEH Summer Stipend enabled the initial research for this chapter drawn from a larger project on the orphan imagination in transnational Chinese film history. I am most grateful to Taiwan Film and Audiovisual Institute (TFI; previously, Taipei National Film Archive) where I first saw *Tarzan and Treasure* and was now helped with illustrations; and to Shi-yan Chao, Ting-wu Cho, and Ruby Liang for helping to locate valuable material. I appreciate very much the inspiration and support from other Taiwan film scholars, including Daisy Dan-ju Yu, Wen-chi Lin (former TFI director), Chu-chin Wang (current TFI director), Emilie Yeh, Guo-juin Hong, Gene-fon Liao, and Yu-shan Huang. Thanks also go to my fellow panelists and moderator Michael Berry at the North America Association of Taiwan Studies Association (NATSA) Conference, at the University of California–Santa Barbara in 2013, where a partial draft was first presented; to Weihong Bao for inviting me to Shadow History: The Archive and Intermediality in Chinese Cinema Conferences at University of California–Berkeley in 2017; and to Soyoung Kim for co-organizing with me the Trans Asian Migration and Media Symposium, where I presented a revised version, in Seoul in 2018. Nayoung Aimee Kwon was a steady source of encouragement and support during the last stage of my writing and revision.

Notes

1. Wu Zhuo-liu's original name was Wu Jiantian, or Go Daku-ryu in Japanese; another pen name he used was Wu Raogeng. Born in Xinzhu, Taiwan, Wu studied and taught at the Governor's Teacher's College and then spent a year as journalist in Nanjing from 1940 to 1941 before returning to Taiwan. He founded the *Taiwan Wenyi* literary magazine in 1964 and the "Wu Zhuoliu Literature Award" in 1969.

2. Wu Zhuoliu's novel was written in Japanese at the tail end of the Japanese rule on the island (1895–1945). First published in 1946, it was not translated into Chinese and English until decades later. For a brief textual history, see Leo Ching (2007). According to Ching, the novel's title went through many changes. The original Japanese title was *Hu Zhiming*《胡志明》and was later changed to *Hu Taiming*《胡太明》. The 1956 Japanese edition was entitled 亞細亞の孤兒 *Orphan of Asia*, and in 1957 it was published as *The Distorted Island*. Its first Chinese edition appeared in Taiwan in 1962. I use the existing mainland edition edited by 中央人民广播电台对台湾广播部 (1981) and a more recent edition in Chinese published by Hua-hsia Press in Taipei in 2009.

3. Loss of UN recognition was followed by that of Japan in 1972, of the United States in 1979, and of many other countries after that. As of this writing (2018), Taiwan has diplomatic relations with fewer than twenty countries, which are scattered in Oceania, the Caribbean, Africa, and Central America. In Europe, only the Holy See still recognizes Taiwan as the Republic of China.

4. In this chapter and the book project from which it is drawn, I use the two terms "Chinese-language film" in tandem with "Sinophone cinema," following the works of Sheldon Lu (2005) and Shu-mei Shih (2007; 2013), with some flexibility and modification. Shih's conception of "Sinophone" refers to Sinetic languages and cultural productions apart from or on the margins of the geopolitical entity of mainland China, whereas Lu includes them.

5. The film's sequel is dramatically called 異域2:孤軍 (Orphaned army), released in 1993. Between 1999 and 2017, Lee Lee-shao researched and completed 滇緬三部曲 (Trilogy of Yunnan and Burma), a documentary on the subject. See 吳老拍,"泰北孤軍, 心向祖國—中華民國台灣:《滇緬三部曲》影評與導演李立劭專訪" (Wu Lao-pai 2016); Chang, Yen-tuo 張硯拓,「亞細亞的孤兒」背後的真實故事: 紀錄片「滇緬游擊隊三部曲」, 如何修補對家的想像? (Chang 2016).

6. On the action-oriented melodrama in early American cinema, see Singer 2001.

7. Liang was originally from Guangzhou on the mainland. His colorful background includes art teacher, police commissar, and administration in the iron mining on Hainan Island. He moved to Hong Kong in 1950, and there he codirected his first film, *The Miserable Lovers* 苦海鴛鴦 (1956). Thereafter he relocated to Taiwan and allegedly learned the Minnan dialect within six months. He became the famous quick hand in the *Taiyupian* industry. He shifted to making Mandarin films in the late 1960s. Seven of his Taiyu films are extant in full, the most among all Taiyupian directors (Taiwan Film Institute n.d.). On Liang's life and career, see Liang Ch. (1994). For a thoughtful discussion of Liang's pair of train films as melodrama, see Hong (2011, 54–62).

8. Most Tarzan films made before the mid-1950s were black-and-white films shot on studio sets, with stock jungle footage edited in. The Weintraub productions from 1959 on were shot in foreign locations and were in color. For a study of the famous franchise, see Gabe Essoe, *Tarzan of the Movies: A Pictorial History of More Than Fifty Years of Edgar Rice Burroughs' Legendary Hero*. Secaucus, N.J.: Citadel Press, 1968.

9. Taiwan's film censorship policy at the time did not allow plots involving murder crimes committed in Taiwan, thus the fictional location in Macau.

10. Wu Zhuo-liu 吳濁流《亚细亚的孤儿》(1981), 3.

11. Zhang finds *Taiyu* to be a geographic misnomer. He reiterates that it is essentially the same language as Hokkien spoken in southern Fujian across the strait. It has also been called Amoy or Xiayu and deemed related to Holo (Heluo). Taiwanese, strictly speaking, is not a single language but a term both encompassing various idioms on the island and the majority-dialect Minnan as well. In fact, the term *Taiwanese* has a colonial provenance. In 1928 *Taiwanyu* was adopted in place of *aborigine language* (*tuyu*) by the Japanese colonial administration in contrast to Japanese as the island's "national language" (*guoyu*). *Tuyu* was banned in school in 1937 but allowed in radio broadcasts (Chung 1960, 44). For consistency with existing scholarship and vernacular usage, I use *Taiyupian* for Taiwanese-language film.

12. Liao's use of "transitional" is in the sense that *Taiyupian* is a vibrant intermedia or hybrid cinema grounded in vernacular culture that adopted an exhibitionist aesthetic and spectatorial address. But it also incorporated aspects or codes of classical Japanese and Hollywood narrative cinema. Liao

borrowed the terms from Tom Gunning and other early cinema scholars' conceptual periodization on American cinema.

13. The KMT did not suppress *Taiyupian* or other cultural practices in dialects in a systematic fashion, and in fact it promoted their use for disseminating its anticommunist and nationalist ideology. Not a few Taiyu films helped to transmit its ideology, covertly or overtly.

14. Only a small portion of the more than one thousand Taiyu films is extant or in good condition. Even fewer are available for public viewing or commercial distribution in digital format. Since the 1990s, a number of Taiwan scholars and conservationists have been engaged in the recovery and restoration of *Taiyupian*. 《台語片時代》(The Era of Taiyu Film), compiled and edited by the oral history group at the Taipei National Film Archive, includes an annotated list of films in its collection and a comprehensive filmography (297–384). Digitalization has also contributed to *Taiyupian* revival and provided access on DVD and online. On *Orphan Ling Po*, see Zhang Z. (2010).

15. The pervasive tone of sadness in *Taiyupian* owes much to the "crying songs" (*khau-tiau-a*) in *koa-a-hi*. For an anthropological study of the material and affective economy of crying songs in the postwar period, see Silvio (2017). There are many explanations for the decline of *Taiyupian*, including ideological control of the KMT, socioeconomic changes, and technological changes (the popularization of television, and the takeover of color stock in the film industry, because *Taiyupian* thrived on cheap sources of black-and-white film until sources dried up).

16. Lee, originally from Shanghai, moved to Taiwan in 1948 and entered the film industry in the 1950s, taking part in both Taiwanese- and Mandarin-language productions. *Our Neighbors* preceded the healthy realism movement promulgated by the government; it is in black and white and features both Mandarin and Taiwanese. The film exhibits social and aesthetic themes and elements from *Taiyupian*, on which Lee participated as an emerging filmmaker. *Beautiful Ducklings* is, on the other hand, an exemplary film of the new trend and won his first Golden Horse award (best director) in 1965.

17. The fall of the Nationalist regime on the mainland resulted in massive relocation of the Nationalist army to the island. Many of the troops were from the hinterland and coastal provinces like Shandong. The newcomers and their offspring enlarged Taiwan's *waishengren* population. Taiwan's sovereignty remains an issue of contention.

18. A leading advocate for Sinophone studies aimed at decentering Chineseness, Shih (2013) argues for an expanded definition of colonialism to include Qing continental colonialism under the Chinese Empire and settler colonialism in Taiwan and Southeast Asia. Many Chinese settlers in Nanyang (south seas, literally, but meaning Southeast Asia) became "essential coadjutors" of Western colonialism.

19. See, for example, Long Yingtai's 龍應台 famous 2009 nonfiction book 《大江大海》(Big river, big sea: untold stories of 1949), based on oral narratives of many soldiers who endured the pain of separation and abandonment and untold other suffering during and after the war. Many never returned to Taiwan or China, and they perished in camps and jungles.

20. Clifford 1998, 365, quoted Liao G. 2007.

21. Liao Ping-hui (2007) elaborates: "His hermeneutical codes were paradoxically supplied by two metropolitan centers—Japan and China—to which he has no relation; furthermore, it was in the rift between them that his sense of an alternative selfhood developed" (294) and "the more he looked closely at China and Japan, the more alienated he became from both. That was the starting point of his journey into Asian orphan consciousness" (298).

22. *Creolization* is a keyword in Wang Ch. (2017), the most up-to-date, comprehensive, and illuminative anthology on Taiyu film.

23. Japan's southern advance was a crucial component of its Great East Asian Prosperity Circle enterprise, using Taiwan as the gateway to Southeast Asia, for natural resources, labor, and territorial rule.

24. I am indebted to Ting-wu Cho for pointing out this important connection between the shooting location and problematic representation of the indigenous people who live there.

25. According to Simon (2015), the Republic of China has inserted itself into the UN discourse of indigenous rights through a number of legal changes, notably by including indigenous nations into the 1997 revisions of the republic's constitution and then passing the Basic Law on Indigenous Nations in 2005.

26. The Japanese and Chinese states had very similar policies and styles of governing the indigenes, such as forced relocation to plains for easy control and cultural assimilation through education and language (Scott 2009, 56).

27. By 1968, the Nationalist regime's aggressive economic investment in southeastern nations (Malaysia, Singapore, Thailand, the Philippines, and Vietnam) was twice its investment on the island. Cited in Ruby Liang's (Liang P.) well-researched and thoughtful case study of Xin Qi's films in terms the geopolitical hierarchy and subimperial consciousness."

28. Liang P., 389–91.

Bibliography

Chang, Yen-tuo 張硯拓. 2016. 亞細亞的孤兒」背後的真實故事: 紀錄片「滇緬游擊隊三部曲」, 如何修補對家的想像？ [The True Stories behind "Orphan of Asia": How Does the Documentary "The Trilogy of Burma-Myanmar Guerrillas" Revise the Imagination of Home?] *News Lens*. June 18. https://www.thenewslens.com/article/41705.

Chen, Kuan-hsing. 2010. *Asia as Method: Toward Deimperialization*. Durham, NC: Duke University Press.

Ching, Leo. 2007. Review of *Orphan of Asia* by Wu Zhuoliu. Translated by Ioannis Mentzas. *Modern Chinese Literature and Culture*, February 2007. https://u.osu.edu/mclc/book-reviews/orphan-of-asia/.

Chung Hsiu-Mei 鍾秀梅. 2017. 1960 年代台語片與大眾文化的流變 (The transformation of Taiyupian and mass culture in the 1960s). In 百變千幻不思議—台語片的混血和轉化 (Taiwanese-language cinema: history, discovery, transculturalization, boundary crossing, transnationalism, creolization). Edited by Wang Chun-chi 王君琦, 37-57. Taipei: Lien-ching and National Film Archive, 2017.

Clifford, James. 1997. *Routes: Travel and Translation in the Late Twentieth Century*. Cambridge, MA: Harvard University Press.

Fiskesjö, Magnus. 1999 "On the 'Raw' and 'Cooked' Barbarians of Imperial China." *Inner Asia* 1, no. 2: 139–68.

Hansen, Miriam. 1999. "The Mass Production of the Senses: Classical Cinema as Vernacular Modernism." *Modernism/Modernity* 6, no. 2: 59–77.

Hong Guo-juin. 2011. *Taiwan Cinema: A Contested Nation on Screen*. New York: Palgrave Macmillan.

Huang Ren 黃仁. 1994.《悲情台語片》(The sadness of Taiyu film). Taipei: Wang-hisang.

Lee Tien-tuo 李天鐸. 1997.《台灣電影, 社會與歷史》(Taiwan cinema, society, and history). Taipei: Yatai.

Liang Che-fu. 1994. "带场表到台湾"梁哲夫訪問稿 (Bringing shooting script to Taiwan). Film Archive Oral History Group 電影資料館口述電影史小組. Interviewer: Xue, Hui-Ling and Huang, Ting-Fu. Transcriber and editor: Lin, Wen-Pei.《台语片时代》(The era of Taiyupian), 225–42. Taipei: National Film Archive.

Liang Pi-Ju. 2017. 梁碧茹.辛奇電影中的地理參考與次帝國意識 (Geographical reference and subimperial consciousness in Hsin Chi's cinema). In Wang, 百變幻不思議—台語片的混血和轉化, 357–404.

Liao Gene-fon 廖金鳳. 2001.《消失的影像—台語片的電影再現與文化認同》(The disappearing image: Taiwanese-language film's cinematic representation and cultural identification). Taipei: Yuanliu.

Liao Ping-hui. 2007. "Travel in Early-Twentieth-Century Asia: On Wu Zhuoliu's 'Nanking Journals' and His Notion of Taiwan's Alternative Modernity." In *Writing Taiwan: A New Literary History*. Edited by Der-wei Wang and Carlos Rojas, 285–96. Durham, NC: Duke University Press.

Long Yingtai 龍應台. 2009.《大江大海》(Big river, big sea: untold stories of 1949). Taipei: Tianxia zazhishe.

Lu, Sheldon and Emilie Yue-yu Yeh, ed. 2005. *Chinese-Language Film: Historiography, Poetics, Politics*. Honolulu, Hawaii: University of Hawaii Press.

Ma Sheng-mei. 2015. *The Last Isle: Contemporary Film, Culture and Trauma in Global Taiwan*. Lanham, MD: Rowman and Littlefield.

Shih Shu-mei. 2007. *Visuality and Identity: Sinophone Articulations across the Pacific*. University of California Press.

———. 2013. "What Is Sinophone Studies?" In *Sinophone Studies: : A Critical Reader*. Edited by Shih Shu-mei, Chien-hsin Tsai, and Brian Bernards, 1–16. New York: Columbia University Press.

Shih Shu-mei, Chien-hsin Tsai, and Brian Bernards, eds. 2013. *Sinophone Studies: A Critical Reader*. New York: Columbia University Press.

Shih Shu-mei and Françoise Lionnet, eds. 2005. *Minor Transnationalism*. Durham, NC: Duke University Press.

Silvio, Teri. 2017. "Crying Songs and Their Fans: The Material and Affective Economy of Taiwanese Opera, 1945–1975." *positions* 25, no. 3: 269–505.

Simon, Scott. 2009. "Writing Indigeneity in Taiwan." In *Re-writing Culture in Taiwan*. Edited by Fang-long Shih, Stuart Thompson, and Paul Tremlett, 50–68. New York: Routledge.

Singer, Ben. 2001. *Melodrama and Modernity: Early Sensational Cinema and Its Contexts*. New York: Columbia University Press.

Su Chi-heng. 2017. 重访台语片的兴衰起落：黑白底片进口與彩色技术转型 (Revisiting the rise and decline of *Taiyupian*: The import of black-and-white film stock and the transformation of color technology). In 百變千幻不思議—台語片的混血和轉化 (Taiwanese-language cinema: history, discovery, transculturalization, boundary crossing, transnationalism, creolization). Edited by Wang Chun-chi, 59–80. Taipei: Lien-ching and National Film Archive.

Taiwan Film Institute. n.d. "Liang Che-fu." Accessed March 18, 2021. http://www.ctfa.org.tw/filmmaker/content.php?id=575.

Tanaka, Stefan. 1995. *Japan's Orient: Rendering Past into History*. Berkeley, CA: University of California Press.

Taylor, Jeremy. 2013. *Rethinking Transnational Chinese Cinemas: The Amoy Dialect Film Industry in Cold War Asia*. Abingdon, UK: Routledge.

Wang Chun-chi 王君琦, ed. 2017. 百變千幻不思議—台語片的混血和轉化 (Taiwanese-language cinema: history, discovery, transculturalization, boundary crossing, transnationalism, creolization). Taipei: Lien-ching and National Film Archive.

Wang Xiaojue. 2013. *Modernity with a Cold War Face: Reimagining the Nation in Chinese Literature across the 1949 Divide*. Cambridge, MA: Harvard University Asia Center.

Wannamaker, Annette, and Michelle Ann Abate, eds. 2012. *Global Perspective on Tarzan: From King of the Jungle to International Icon*. New York: Routledge.

Williams, Linda. 1998. "Melodrama Revisited." In *Refiguring American Film Genres: History and Theory*. Edited by Christine Gledhill, 69–77. London: British Film Institute.

Wu Lao-pai. 2016. "Orphaned Army in Northern Thailand, Heart to the Motherland—Taiwan." Review of "Trilogy of Yunnan and Burma" and interview with director Li Li-shao. 獨立評論@天下 Independent Opinion@CommonWealth Magazine. July 1. https://opinion.cw.com.tw/blog/profile/304/article/4484.

Wu Zhuoliu 吴浊流. 1981. 亚细亚的孤儿 (Orphan of Asia). 1981. Edited by 中央人民广播电台对台湾广播部 China Central People's Radio Broadcasting Station, Taiwan Department. Beijing: Beijing Broadcasting Press, 1981.

———. 2006. *Orphan of Asia*. Translated by Ioannis Mentzas. New York: Columbia University Press.

———. 2009. 亞細亞的孤兒 (Orphan of Asia). Taipei: Hua-hsia.

Yeh, Emilie Yueh-yu, and Darrell Davi. 2005. *Taiwan Directors*. New York: Columbia University Press.

Zhang Yingjin. 2013. "Articulating Sadness, Gendering Space: The Politics and Poetics of Taiyu Films from 1960s Taiwan." *Modern Chinese Literature and Culture* 25, no. 1 (Spring): 1–46.

Zhang Zhen. 2010. "Ling Bo: Orphanhood and Post-war Sinophone Film History." In *Chinese Film Stars*. Edited by Mary Farquhar and Yingjin Zhang, 121–38. New York: Routledge.

———. 2018. "Transnational Melodrama, Wenyi, and the Orphan Imagination." In *Melodrama Unbound: Across History, Media, and National Cultures*. Edited by Christine Gledhill and Linda Williams, 83–97. New York: Columbia University Press.

ZHANG ZHEN is Associate Professor and Director of the Asian Film and Media Initiative at the Department of Cinema Studies at New York University. She is author of *An Amorous History of the Silver Screen: Shanghai Cinema 1896–1937* (2005) and co-editor of *DV-Made China: Digital Subjects and Social Transformations after Independent Film* (2015). She is completing a new book, *Women Making Waves in Sinophone Cinema*.

7. WHAT IS AN AUTEUR?
Hŏ Yŏng / Hinatsu Eitarō / Huyung between (Post)colonial Indonesia, Japan, and Korea

Thomas Barker and Nikki J. Y. Lee

Abstract

Japanese colonialism in East and Southeast Asia utilized the modern technology of cinema to create and propagate images of Japanese imperial greatness, fidelity to empire, and the benevolence of Japanese rule. Within this apparatus were not only Japanese citizens employed as propaganda officers and *bunkajin* (culture men) but also colonial subjects enlisted to create localized content for various colonial possessions. One such filmmaker came from occupied Korea to Japan to study filmmaking under the pseudonym Hinatsu Eitarō. He would return to Korea to direct the infamous propaganda film *You and I* (Gŭdaewa na, Korean; Kimi to Boku, Japanese, 1941), before departing for occupied Java in 1942 as a *bunkajin*. After 1945, instead of returning home, Hinatsu—who was now known as Dr. Huyung—remained in Indonesia, where he joined the pro-independence movement; after independence, he directed four feature films before his premature death in 1952.

By tracing the life and works of Hinatsu/Dr. Huyung, this chapter puts into question the role of the filmmaker in sustaining colonialism and the possibility of making art and becoming an auteur in a time of colonial subjectivity. Korean history does not remember Hinatsu fondly for his collaborations with Japanese colonialism, but his trajectory after 1945 suggests that a filmmaker could be both a colonial collaborator and a supporter of postcolonial independence. Without a national cinema to call his own, could a filmmaker like Hinatsu ever be considered an auteur? Or will he be relegated to a footnote in national cinema histories, belonging ultimately to none of them?

Introduction

Japanese colonialism in East and Southeast Asia utilized the modern apparatus of cinema to create and propagate images of Japanese imperial greatness, fidelity to empire, and the benevolence of Japanese rule. Within this apparatus not only were Japanese citizens employed as propaganda officers and *bunkajin* (culture men), but colonial subjects were also enlisted to create localized content for various colonial possessions. The legacies of Japanese colonialism on film histories and individuals in various countries continues to evoke questions of collaboration and resistance, shaped by postcolonialism and nationalism. Whereas some filmmakers who worked under the Japanese imperial system such as Kurosawa Akira in Japan and Usmar Ismail in Indonesia were able to become noted auteurs after World War II, other filmmakers have been branded negatively and have been largely forgotten.

One filmmaker who occupied an ambivalent position between colonizer and colonized was a Korean born as Hŏ Yŏng. In the 1920s he moved to Japan to study filmmaking; there, he took the new name Hinatsu Eitarō. He directed the infamous propaganda film *You and I* (Gŭdaewa na, Korean; Kimi to Boku, Japanese, 1941), and not long after that he departed for occupied Java in 1942 as a colonial agent. After 1945, instead of returning home, Hinatsu—who had changed his name again, this time to Dr. Huyung—remained in Indonesia, where he joined the pro-independence movement and, after Indonesian independence in December 1949, he directed four feature films before his premature death in 1952. By using the biography of Hŏ Yŏng/Hinatsu Eitarō/Dr. Huyung, this chapter examines the history and legacy of Japanese colonialism in Asia and the postcolonial nationalist histories that have since been constructed in both South Korea and Indonesia. In particular, this chapter puts into question the role of the filmmaker in sustaining colonialism and the possibility of making art and becoming an auteur during a time of colonial subjectivity. Without a national cinema to call his own, can a filmmaker like Hinatsu ever be considered an auteur, or will he be relegated to a footnote in national cinema histories, belonging ultimately to none of them?

This chapter also shows how Dr. Huyung's position vis-à-vis colonialism changed during his life from colonial subject to colonial collaborator to colonial agent and finally to pro-independence nationalist. Korean history does not remember Hinatsu fondly for his collaborations with Japanese colonialism; but his trajectory after 1945 suggests that a collaborator could also support postcolonial independence. His biography opens new perspectives on the spaces, opportunities, and identities created by colonialism and postcolonial nationalism, moving beyond ideas of ambivalence and the dichotomies of nationalist historiography to assert mobility, self-reinvention, and third spaces as strategies for surviving the tumultuous period of Asian decolonization in the 1940s and 1950s.

Dr. Huyung's trajectory from Korea to Japan and finally to Indonesia and his shifting identifications and actions relate to what Homi Bhabha (1984) has called the ambivalence of the colonial encounter and the subjectivities it produces. In Bhabha's model, the colonial encounter is a binary encounter between colonizer and colonized, usually in the colonized territory. Dr. Huyung's trajectory contrasts in introducing a third space, Indonesia, that complicates the binary encounter of a Korean subject to Japanese colonialization. Indeed, as Japan's empire expanded beyond Korea and China in the 1940s, territories in Southeast Asia such as the Philippines, Malaya, Singapore, and Indonesia [Dutch East Indies] were brought under its rule. Many ethnic Koreans were recruited by the Japanese as soldiers and support staff to service the empire in Southeast Asia.

As this chapter will show, Dr. Huyung allows us to consider the ambivalence of the colonial encounter and how figures like him are remembered in history. Most studies to date that consider Hinatsu/Dr. Huyung focus either on his life before arriving in Indonesia in 1942 (e.g., High 2003; Yecies and Shim 2011) or on his life in Indonesia, especially after 1945 (e.g., Biran 2009; Said 1991).[1] By considering his life in its entirety, this chapter is able to question how nationalist historiography constructs the categories of collaborator or traitor and revolutionary or nationalist in both the Indonesian and the Korean nationalist contexts. Instead, we see how new forms of identity and subjectivity were created under colonialism, how the colonial situation created opportunities for colonial subjects, and what legacy Dr. Huyung's life has left scholars and historians for the study of colonialism in Southeast Asia, national histories, and the history of film.

The Making of a Japanese Collaborator

Dr. Huyung's life was shaped by Japanese colonialism. He was born Hŏ Yŏng (허영) in 1907 in South Hamgyŏng province on the east coast of what is now North Korea, three years before the Japanese annexed the Korean peninsula.[2] He moved to Japan in 1925 at the age of eighteen and, assuming the Japanese name of Hinatsu Eitarō (日夏英太郎), he enrolled in the elite Waseda University in Tokyo to study filmmaking in the school of Film and Performance Arts. In Kyoto, Hinatsu started working at Makino Film Productions as an editor and then as a screenwriter. When Makino Film Productions went bankrupt in 1932, he moved to Shochiku Kyoto Studio, working as a screenwriter and as assistant director under Kinugasa Teinoske. Then, in 1939, he

What Is an Auteur? 165

moved to Shinkō Kinema (in Uzumasa Kyoto).³ Described by film scholar Michael Baskett as an "upwardly mobile Korean colonial youth" (2008, 87), it appeared that from early on Hinatsu had assimilated his Japanese identity and was using it to pursue a career in the film industry. Marked by his fluency in Japanese and his marriage to a Japanese woman in 1936, the language barrier was not a barrier to his cross-ethnic passing. Later evidence suggests he may have been more fluent in Japanese than his native Korean (Kang 2008).

Early in 1937, however, Hinatsu's ethnic identity—being a *Chōsenjin* (Korean)—was revealed when an accident occurred during the filming of *Ōsaka Natsu No Jin* (The summer battle of Osaka, Teinosuke Kinugasa, dir., 1937). An on-set explosion went wrong, damaging historical property, killing one person, and injuring seven others (Nippon Hōsō Kyōka [NHK] 1993, 6). In the subsequent police investigation, Hinatsu was revealed to be a Korean, and in 1938 he was convicted, given a two-year suspended sentence for damage to historical property and misuse of explosives. Although Hinatsu's filmmaking career now looked in doubt, Korean films such as *Han River* (*Han'gang* 한강, Pang Han-jun, dir., 1938) opened in Japan; and actress Mun Ye-bong stayed in Tokyo for the filming of *Military Train* (*Kunyong Yŏlch'a* 군용열차, Sŏ Kwangch'e, dir., 1938), a Korea-Japan coproduced propaganda film. Such events may have turned Hinatsu's attention to an alternative possibility to rehabilitate his own career—directing a Korea-Japan coproduced propaganda film (Kang 2008).

A year later, in October 1939, the Japanese government legalized their policy of controlling film production by bringing all film companies under their control (Kurasawa 1987). That control extended to the Korean film industry when the Korea Motion Picture Ordinance was implemented in the Korean peninsula in August 1940. After the ordinance, in 1942 all film production companies were shut down and merged into one, the Korean Film Production Company, which was put under the control of the Korean Government-General. The system allowed only war propaganda films and films that promoted *kōminka* (imperialization) of colonial subjects to be produced on the Korean peninsula.

To a certain extent, however, such a drastic reformation was on a continuum with the transformation of the film industry from the previous period. Many scholars underscore that the 1930s was the decade when Korean cinema had to reposition itself vis-à-vis *kōmin eiga* (imperial cinema). The Domestic Film Screening Regulation had been in effect on the Korean peninsula since 1934. According to the regulation, domestic films, including Korean or Japanese films, "had to account for more than half of the total meters of film screened at theaters every month from 1937" (Chung 2012, 161). Film scholar

Moonim Baek adds that "though it was grouped with Japanese films under the label domestic films, Korean cinema, as an ethnic cinema distinct from Japanese cinema, was permitted to be distributed in the imperial territories beyond the peninsula" (2015, 71–72). Many Korean filmmakers—in particular the new generation who had worked in the Japanese film industry and returned to Korea during the 1930s—perceived the situation as an opportunity to grow the Korean film industry and to expand its market beyond Korea: to Japan, Manchuria, and territories in Southeast Asia.[4] Japan-Korea coproductions quickly became a norm. The coproduced titles of the period started by selling the local colors of colonized Korea but soon began to promote the imperial government's key colonial policies, such as the Military Volunteer Program and the war mobilization ideology, or *naisen ittai* (Japan-Korea One-Body) (Lee H. 2016, 243–45). With Japanese staff taking key roles in production, and Japanese stars cast alongside Korean stars in leading parts, the coproduction of these Japanese-language Korean films operationalized the assimilation project itself (Lee H. 2016, 245).

You and I, written and directed by Hinatsu, emblematizes the Japanese wartime project. Inspired by the story of Yi In-sŏk—a Korean volunteer soldier killed in action and made an exemplary hero by the Japanese—*You and I* tells the story of a young Korean man who volunteers as a solider for the Japanese, leaves his family and his proud father for the front line, and falls in love with a Japanese woman. In February 1941, Hinatsu visited the Korean Government-General with his draft script and received a fervent response. In consultation with Japanese film critic Iijima Tadashi, Hinatsu then spent much time and effort finalizing the script and lobbying the Korean Forces Command to have his film approved for production (Kim J. 1997).

You and I was not only the biggest-ever Korean film but also—with the full support of the Korean Forces Command, the Korean Government-General and the Japanese Department of the Army—an imperial blockbuster. It was filmed at locations in both Korea and Japan. Most of the filmmaking staff was Japanese, and a Japanese director, Tasaka Tomotaka, was credited as supervising director. The governor-general of Korea, Minami Jirō, made a special appearance (Kim R. 2006, 278). The cast was a mixture of Japanese stars, including Kosugi Isamu and Kawazu Seizaburō, and Korean stars such as Sim Yŏng. For the main character, a Korean military volunteer, Kim Yŏng-gil—who was already a famous actor and opera singer in Japan (known as Nagata Kenjiro)—was cast. The top Korean actresses of the time, Mun Ye-bong and Kim So-yŏng, were also featured, along with Ri Kōran, the biggest pan-Asian female star on the imperial screen of the period. Ri Kōran (whose Japanese name is Yamaguchi Yoshiko) is a Japanese actress and singer who passed as Chinese on- and off-screen and who starred in multiple Japan-Manchuria coproduced propaganda films. Her appearance in *You and I* consolidates the cognitive map of the East Asian Co-prosperity Sphere as projected by Japanese imperialism.

You and I was promoted in ways akin to the marketing conventions of contemporary blockbusters. Other mainstream media platforms were mobilized to help make it the event movie of the time. Among other activities, a radio drama featuring the same cast was broadcast prior to release; major newspapers ran a talk series featuring the administrators of the Korean Government-General, the staff, and the cast; and special music shows were organized for the opening day (Kim R. 2006, 280–81). In this respect, the film's strong performance at the Korean box office can be attributed not just to its full-scale publicity campaign but also to the institutionalized mobilization of group viewing. Although public criticism was muted at the time for obvious reasons, reactions to the film were not all positive (High 2003). It garnered lukewarm responses in Japan, where some reviewers pointed to formal and aesthetic flaws despite its well-intended message (Kang 2008, 68–69). What was at stake for every participant in the project was "performing the imperial subject . . . in front of the gaze of the empire" rather than the quality of the film (Lee H. 2016, 246–49). Lee Hwa-jin states that the production and the promotion of *You and I* were designed to showcase how each participant was dedicated to performing the ideology of *naisen ittai* and to "discipline the audience as the imperial subject" (2016, 249). (See fig. 7.1.)

Echoing Lee, Michael Baskett comments on the film as "a short precis on how to become a model imperial subject whom the Japanese would admire" (2008, 85). Hinatsu, as a Korean who lived in Japan for a long time, projected his own ideal vision into the film. The Korean military volunteer, Kaneko, speaks fluent Japanese with Japanese manners, as acted by Kim Yŏng-gil, who lived in Japan and was married to a Japanese woman. In the film, Kaneko's mentor is Kubo Ryōhei, a Japanese resident in Korea, who loves and understands Korean culture as head of a local museum. Kaneko and Asano Mitsue, a sister-in-law of Kubo, fall for each other, implying the possibility of cross-ethnic marriage. While discussing such a possibility with his wife, Kubo criticizes the colonial system's discriminatory family record law.[5] According to the colonial family record law, even when Koreans changed their names to Japanese ones, their original Korean surnames and family hometowns remained in the official record. The film is not only asking Koreans to be loyal imperial subjects who sacrifice themselves for the empire but also is asking Japanese to accept Koreans as equal citizens of the empire.

Figure 7.1. Production still from *You and I* (1941). Director Hinatsu Eitarō (the figure in the middle) on set. Image courtesy of the Korean Film Archive (KOFA).

In that the main character, Kaneko, can be regarded as a persona of Hinatsu himself, the film embodies his wish to be accepted as a citizen of the empire.

Peter High (2003) suggests that Hinatsu made the film partly to opportunistically advance his film career but also because his psychology was "thoroughly colonized" (309) and he believed in the primacy of the Japanese. Such a thoroughly colonized subject, however, poses a threat to a colonial hierarchy that is based on essentialized differences between the colonizer and the colonized. In *You and I*, Korean characters are not portrayed as inferior to Japanese; they are portrayed as equals. Furthermore, ethnic distinctions are blurred as Korean characters speak Japanese, wear Japanese clothes, and behave with Japanese manners. In particular, the cross-dressing scene in which Mitsue (a young Japanese woman) and Paek-hŭi (a young Korean woman) exchange their clothes undermines such ethnic distinctions and therefore the colonial hierarchy. In addition to such portrayals of Korean characters, the cross-ethnic romance could have stirred anxiety and discomfort among Japanese audiences. Kim Ryŏ-sil argues that "while representing the ideology of *naisen ittai*, there was no other film that expressed the boundary between the two nations as blurred and ambiguous as *You and I*" (2006, 283). The ideology of *naisen ittai* was promoted to mobilize the colonized for the imperial war, but it was not meant to guarantee their equal position as imperial citizens in reality. To judge from the film, Hinatsu appears to have embraced the ideology fully, but his life experience revealed that the ideology extended a false promise. He could not be accepted and respected as Japanese.

A chapter in Ichikawa Sai's (1941) anthology, Ajia eiga no sōzō oyobi kensetsu (The creation and construction of Asian cinema, アジア映画 の創造及建設), presents *You and I* as the ultimate achievement in the development of Korean cinema when it became independent from American influences (Baek 2015). The chapter was rewritten on the basis of an article that was credited to Im Hwa, a literary critic. Baek suggests, however, that, in another article published in 1942, Im attempted to dispute this view (2015, 141–50). Im remarks that *You and I* "simply expresses the view that the army holds about cinema and clarifies the contemporary solutions to the problems that were raised from the controversies surrounding *Homeless Angels* (*Chibŏpnŭn Ch'ŏnsa* 집 없는 천사 , 1941)" (quoted in Baek 2015, 145). Furthermore, Baek points out, Im suggests that the events of the two titles help "envisage the artistic characteristics of Korean cinema, that is, the outline of state cinema [*kokumin*] that will be produced in contemporary conditions of Korea" (quoted in Baek 2015, 145). According to Baek, *You and I* signals to critics like Im a need to reconsider "the distinctive artistic characteristic of Korean cinema" in order to pave a new path for Korean cinema (2015, 147). In other words, while *You and I* registers the inevitable changes in the industrial conditions of film production, Im believes that there is still room to carve out a space for Korean cinema within state cinema (that is, imperial cinema) through "distinctive artistic quality" (Baek 2015, 149–50).

If Im's observations can be extended to Korean filmmakers of the period, can they be said to have carved out their space as Koreans while still making Japanese-language propaganda films? The recent discovery of Korean films of the colonial period caused some embarrassment to Korean film scholars (Kim R. 2006). After all, previous historiographies of Korean cinema had excluded such films from their nationalist narratives by drawing on binary distinctions between collaboration and resistance to judge the relevant filmmakers. The apparent presence of such colonial films demands an alternative framework beyond such binaries (Kim R. 2006; Lee Y. 2008). Filmmakers labeled as collaborators might be excused on the ground that they were forced to make such films as acts of survival or to help secure the further development of the Korean film industry. Yet Hinatsu's situation may not allow such excuses. He volunteered himself without being forced, and the growth of the Korean film industry was not his concern. His position thus exemplifies the complicated ways in which the imperial Japanese film culture exerted attractive power (Baskett 2008). For Hinatsu, that attraction may have entailed recognition as a modern subject—as an imperial citizen—as well as an opportunity to become a notable filmmaker.

You and I earned Hinatsu significant notoriety, and he experienced a backlash from his friends and peers, from Korean nationalists, from critics, and subsequently from historians. A 1997 Korean documentary made about Hinatsu's life described *You and I* as "a humiliating debut as a director" (Kim J. 1997). From available sources, it is hard to discern the definitive reason Hinatsu decided to leave for Indonesia in 1942. Arguably, his move was a logical extension of his already pro-Japanese position and could have been made to advance his career, but it may just as easily have come from a sense of regret and humiliation from having made *You and I*. According to his friend Sasagi Genichirō from the Shinkō Cinema, at his farewell party, Hinatsu sat and drank without saying a word (Kim J. 1997). At the stopover in Kyoto, Hinatsu did not even disembark to visit his wife, son and newborn child. Hinatsu, broken by his experience in Korea, told his friend Sasagi that "he was not going back to Korea but to Southeast Asia" (Kim J. 1997). Moving to Indonesia allowed Hinatsu to escape his past and reinvent himself in a new context, at the cost of becoming a colonial agent in the service of the Japanese Empire.

Hinatsu as a *Bunkajin* in Occupied Indonesia

Hinatsu's life as a colonial *bunkajin* in Indonesia has been covered in detail by Barker (2017), who argued that this period of service to empire incubated a shift in Hinatsu's perspectives, leading to his allegiance to Indonesia and its fight for independence. *Bunkajin* were civilians with expertise in fields such as writing, journalism, film, and theater. They were recruited by the Japanese to run the vast propaganda apparatus necessary to their rule (Kurasawa 1987, 61). Their role was to ensure that the idea of the Greater East Asian Coprosperity Sphere and Japan's role as leader in Asia were accepted by the colonized population (Cohen 2016, 175–76). *Bunkajin* occupied an "influential mediating role between occupier and occupied" (Mark 2010, 349) and "many of them not only promulgated but believed in a conception of the war as one of 'liberation' from Western domination and its evils both for Japan and for Asia" (Mark 2010, 350). For Hinatsu, it was also an ambiguous position, since he himself was a colonial subject of the Japanese who would grow more sympathetic to the Indonesian side, evident by him learning Indonesian and making friends.

In Jakarta Hinatsu was a supervisor in the theater section of the *Keimin Bunka Shidōsho* (Cultural Center) under the auspices of the Sendenbu propaganda agency established in April 1943. Local artists and playwrights were enlisted to work alongside the *bunkajin*. As in other parts of Japanese-controlled Asia, "the Japanese were able to train local technicians in the craft of making films of the highest technical quality while . . . serving their own propaganda interests" (Anderson and Richie 1982, 158; see also Said 1991). Bahasa Indonesia was used in propaganda material to reach as many of the local population as possible, cementing it as the official language of governance for the subsequent modern Indonesian nation (Heider 1991). In April 1943 the Nippon Eigasha was established to produce movies, employing and training many locals in film production (Ramdhan and Pane 2006). Emphasis was given to audiovisual media such as theater, newsreels, film, traditional *wayang* (Javanese puppet theater), and Japanese paper puppetry (*kamishibai*) because they were seen as more effective at reaching the illiterate countryside, where the majority of the population lived (Kurasawa 2015, 256).

The English-language propaganda film *Calling Australia* (Gōshu no Yobigoe), made in 1943, was the first prominent film work by Hinatsu from this period. Hinatsu was assigned to direct *Calling Australia* under the direction of Captain Yamagawa after Kurata Bunjin, who was chief of the Nippon Eigasha, refused to direct the film. According to Okada (2002), Kurata Bunjin refused because it went against the Japanese values of *Bushido* (chivalry) and he preferred instead to focus on education and training. *Calling Australia* depicts Japanese camps for Allied prisoners of war as resembling a holiday camp, with scenes of prisoners playing sports outdoors, putting on a play, and eating steak (High 2003).[6] Directing *Calling Australia* solidified Hinatsu's status as an agent of the Japanese Empire, but it is hard to discern Hinatsu's own position on the film and its content, especially since the task of directing *Calling Australia* was probably thrust on him (Okada 2002). Although *Calling Australia* represented the worst kind of propaganda and is regarded as a "war atrocity" by actual ex-prisoners because of its distortion of the truth of how they were treated (High 2003), the fact that the film was lost until recently and that Hinatsu was not credited with the film meant that he escaped some of the notoriety associated with it.

After *Calling Australia*, Hinatsu was placed in charge of the Perserikatan Oesaha Sandiwara di Djawa (Java Theatrical Play Association), established in August 1944 as an umbrella organization for all theater groups in the country. It is here that Hinatsu would be credited with seven scripts: *Fadjar Telah Menjingsing* (Dawn is breaking, 1944), *Samoedra Hindia* (Indian Ocean, 1944), *Moesim Boenga di Asia* (Blossoming in Asia, 1944), *Pradjoerit Nogiku*

(Soldier from Nogiku, 1944), *Djoedjoer Moejoer* (Prosper honestly, 1945), *Benteng Ngawi* (Ngawi Fortress, 1945), and *Boenga Rampai Djawa Baroe* (New Java medley, 1945), collectively published in the book *Fadjar Masa* on April 26, 1945 (Hutari 2009). Kurasawa (1987, 109–11) also credits Hinatsu with writing *Toeroet Sama Amat* (Following Amat, 1945). His position in the theatrical association seems to have come about because theater groups were multiplying, including Djamaluddin Malik's *Pantja Warna* (Five Colors) and *Bintang Timoer* (Eastern Star) groups. Cohen (2016, 238) describes Hinatsu as an authoritarian figure in his position, and one review of *Samoedra Hindia* calls it "boring" because of its heavy-handed propaganda (Hutari 2009, 111).

Despite the Japanese control of artistic activity, the period of Japanese occupation is seen positively by Indonesian nationalists for the impact it had on the subsequent emergence of an Indonesian national cinema after 1950. Usmar Ismail regards the years of the Japanese occupation favorably, saying that it "created an understanding of the function of film which became extremely useful in efforts to develop a national film industry after independence" (Ismail 1983, 55).[7] In standard accounts of film history, the period prior to 1942 is seen as being purely commercial in its orientation and providing few opportunities in production to native Indonesians (Biran 2009). By contrast, the Japanese actively employed native Indonesians to write and produce cultural works, including films, and provided them with technical education (Biran 2009). The Japanese focus on film as propaganda introduced many young Indonesians to the potential for film as a medium for education directed at the broader population (Kurasawa 2015, 348).

Although Hinatsu played the role of Japanese agent, he also made a positive impression on the Indonesian artists who were recruited into the Sendenbu. Prominent Indonesian author and playwright Armijn Pané recounted meeting Hinatsu after he had been told there was a "good [hearted] theater expert" working in the Japanese censorship office (Pané 1955, 26). Armijn Pané writes, "Later, after the Censor's Office had moved to West Gambir, I got to know him [Hinatsu] as an officer specializing in theater. At that time I didn't consider him different from the other Japanese. One of the Censor officers sneered when I asked, 'I'm here about theatrical production and would like to meet Hinatsu Heitarō,' as that was his name at the time. I didn't understand what the officer had meant. Later, after the revolution, I came to know what the officer had meant by his sneering" (Pané 1955, 26).

This reminder of Hinatsu's Korean origins and thus his inferiority to his Japanese colleagues was no doubt a source of constant acrimony and a reminder that while he worked for the Japanese, he was not considered Japanese. He may have compensated for his inferiority by being "more Japanese than the Japanese" (Cohen 2016, 226), as one acquaintance describes him, although "he did not mix with the Japanese" according to another (Kim quoted in NHK 1993, 25). If Hinatsu occupied an ambivalent position with the Japanese, for the Indonesians he was a sympathetic personality, hardworking and dedicated to the arts.

By 1945, the course of the war was irreversibly heading toward a Japanese defeat. Open warfare, however, had largely bypassed Indonesia, influencing the subsequent independence movement and their fight against the returning Dutch (Ricklefs 1981). It was a crucial time for Hinatsu, for he was witnessing the collapse of the Japanese Empire that had been present for almost his entire life and of which he had once spoken so positively (High 2003). As the other Koreans around him turned against the Japanese, Hinatsu confronted his own Korean identity because he planned to return to Korea with them. Between August and September 1945, he was active in securing the release of eight imprisoned members of the Korean Youth Party for National Independence.[8] As one of the party members recalls, "He tried day and night to get us out of prison" (Kim Sun Gi quoted in Kim J. 1997). Hinatsu joined the Association of Korean Residents in Java, becoming their media officer, and worked to have approximately one thousand Koreans repatriated. He even started to learn Korean in preparation.

Yet becoming Korean again was not that simple for Hinatsu because his past deeds could not easily be forgotten. As Hinatsu himself explained to a friend:

> You [Koreans] all came here [to Indonesia] in a group to work for the Japanese military. But I on my own initiative persuaded the Korean Colonial Government to make *You and I* with the support of the Colonial Military Forces. Everyone knows about *You and I*. Everyone knows that Hŏ Yŏng and Hinatsu Eitarō are one and the same. And in addition to that, my Korean isn't even that good. I'm a Korean who knows almost nothing about Korean history other than what little I studied about in Tokyo. . . . If I returned to Japan now there wouldn't be any jobs for me and if I returned to Korea, I'd most likely be branded a Japanese collaborator. (Baskett 2008, 89)

His fellow Koreans recount the story of a British officer who came and demanded a Korean woman from them, and they were disappointed when Hŏ Yŏng [Hinatsu] did not stand up to him (NHK 1993). Their disappointment turned to anger, and they accused him of being a Japanese collaborator. Their accusations played on Hinatsu's fears that he would be punished when he returned to Korea for having been a Japanese collaborator. Kim Songi, one of the directors of the Korean Residents Association, remembers that

I remember the day he came up to me in tears. He said that he thought he would be understood by his fellow members because they were all in a similar situation. They were also the people who had been living in a foreign county and fighting for the Japanese military as Koreans. But if they didn't understand Hinatsu, who would? I'm sure he was worried about whether he would be accepted by the Koreans in Korea. After that, Hinatsu cut himself off from the Koreans and went with his Indonesian friends. (Kim J. 1997)

Hinatsu had been inspired by the nationalism and dedication of the Indonesians he had worked with in the Sendenbu. Adopting an Indonesianized version of his Korean name and adding the title of doctor, Dr. Huyung left Jakarta for Jogjakarta, where the republican forces had established their temporary government.

Up to this point in his life, it is easy to see how Hinatsu has been understood as an agent of the Japanese Empire and thus a traitor to his Korean origins. Of particular relevance is *You and I*, which marked him as a collaborator according to Korean nationalist historiography. Alternatively, his life can be interpreted as having been driven by opportunism and pragmatism, for which he had to mimic Japaneseness because of the limited opportunities afforded a Korean under Japanese rule. Most English-language accounts of his life stop at this point, seeing his life largely within the Korean-Japanese context. Without considering his life after 1945, such accounts are incomplete and fail to take into account Dr. Huyung's second life in Indonesia. As the next section will show, his life in Indonesia after 1945 creates a very different reading of his identity, his sense of belonging, his position as a colonial subject, and his career as a filmmaker.

A Pro-revolutionary Nationalist

The situation after the Japanese surrender was unexpectedly fortuitous for Dr. Huyung. Although there was widespread resentment against the Japanese occupation, the Japanese were not purged from Indonesia, and the independence struggle focused on fighting the Dutch, who were attempting to reclaim their former colony. Some Japanese and Koreans elected to stay in Indonesia after 1945, including former soldier Yang Ch'il-sŏng, known in Indonesia as Komarudin, who led guerrilla skirmishes against the Dutch. During this interregnum, Dr. Huyung worked to maintain his ties with the artistic community, situating himself as a central figure in the artistic and cultural life of the new republic.

In Jogjakarta Dr. Huyung enjoyed a highly productive period and produced a number of plays in collaboration with Djadug Djajakusuma, renovating and refitting a movie theater (Soboharsono) and a live theater (Seni

Seno) before founding Stichting Hiburan Mataram (Mataram Entertainment Foundation) in 1948. With backing from the Ministry of Information, he established the country's first film and theater schools, called the Kino Drama Atelier (KDA) and the Cine Drama Institute (Cohen 2016). On the enactment deed for the KDA, Dr. Huyung is listed as a high-ranking official in the Department of Information, along with two other signatories from the department, suggesting Dr. Huyung maintained a status in the government of the revolutionary republic similar to his position in the Sendenbu. He was also part of the Berita Film Indonesia (Indonesian Film News) team who produced newsreels for broadcast in theaters.

As a theater supporting the revolutionary cause, the KDA produced and performed plays relevant to the politics and concerns of the day. Their first production was a salutation to the young republic's government, a production called *Drama Reportage Penduduk Jogjakarta* (Dramatized reportage from the residents of Jogjakarta; date unknown). Another KDA production, *Konvoi Penghabisan* (The final convoy, 1949), celebrated the fourth anniversary of the declaration of independence. The comedy *Revue Fantasia* brought the students of the KDA together with famous actors, including Agus Muljiana, Hardjomuljo, and D. Ariffin (Ksatriya Dharma). Posters for the play *Rosina Dalam Taufan* (Rosina in the cyclone; date unknown) to accompany the Indonesian Women's Conference (Kongres Wanita Antar Indonesia) had already appeared during the performance for *Drama Reportage Penduduk Jogjakarta*. In celebration of the 1949 Chinese revolution, the KDA staged the play *Malam Sutji* (Holy night) between October 8 and 10, 1949, after only two days of rehearsal. Expressions of solidarity, celebration, and informative presentations enriched the cultural life of the revolutionary capital and served as propaganda for the revolutionary cause.

Dr. Huyung taught both theory and practice to around fifty students of the KDA, introducing young Indonesians to the disciplines of theater and film through both theory and practice, but this time within a revolutionary context, serving as incubator for many of them in the tumultuous years of the revolution. Experts in literature and the arts gave lectures, and one particular ten-day course brought together Prijono, Katamsi, K. H. Dewantoro, and Dr. Huyung himself to teach students. Students of these lectures and of the KDA included names that shaped Indonesian culture in the 1950s, including Trisno Soemardjo, Kusbini, Usmar Ismail, D. Djajakusuma, and Sri Murtono.[9] Soemardjono, who went on to become one of the great directors and film intellectuals of postindependence Indonesia, was twenty-two years old when he studied at the KDA. He says Dr. Huyung "was the one who taught me what film making is about" (NHK 1993, 35–36). A recent account from *Pantau* magazine contributor Budi Setiyono (2010) calls Dr. Huyung the "filmmaker's teacher" ("guru para sineas").

These activities and eulogies stand in contrast to how Dr. Huyung appears in more general accounts of Indonesian film history. In an interview, film historian and scriptwriter Misbach Yusa Biran said Dr. Huyung was able "to convey to the Indonesian people the importance of movies, through his teaching at the atelier. Until then, people in our country didn't value movies as an art form" (NHK 1993, 35–36). But in Biran's (2009) general history of the Indonesian film industry, recognition of Dr. Huyung's depth of involvement is brief and cursory and he figures as an intermediate figure between the colonial era and independent Indonesia, after which the *pribumi* (natives) such as Usmar Ismail and Djamaluddin Malik became preeminent.[10]

After independence, Dr. Huyung moved to Jakarta and began production on his first feature film free from colonial controls. *Antara Bumi dan Langit* (Between heaven and earth, 1950), written by Armijn Pané, is a love story between Frieda, an Indo (Eurasian) woman, and Abidin, a native, who are reunited after twenty-seven years of separation but who find themselves on different sides of the revolution. (See fig. 7.2.) Their rekindled love, however, is stronger than her betrayal of the revolution, and she is persuaded to join him in the fight for independence. Controversy erupted when preproduction stills showing a kissing scene were released to the press, and protests by a Muslim youth group in Sumatra attacked the film for not being compatible with Indonesian culture. Although not officially banned (though it did cause somewhat of a crisis for the Film Control Board [Harrymawan 1951, 51]), Dr. Huyung delayed the film's release by six months, releasing it as *Frieda* (1950). Armijn Pané, who had been very active in defending the film from critics, was exasperated by the experience and refused to be credited. He dedicates a significant portion of his 1953 essay "Produksi Film Tjerita di Indonesia" (Feature film production in Indonesia) to discussing the case of *Antara Bumi dan Langit*.

As his first Indonesian film, *Antara Bumi dan Langit* is poignant in directly tackling the question of who belongs in the new nation. If it is indeed possible that a film can tell us something about its director, this film suggests that Dr. Huyung was still engaged with questions about his own heritage and sense of belonging in his newly adopted nation. Echoes of *You and I* are also clearly visible in this story. Dr. Huyung was no doubt subject to some suspicion because of his origins and background, just as ethnic Chinese and Eurasians were, and through the film he was able to show that foreigners could also support independence. On the copy of the script held at the Sinematek film library in Jakarta, a handwritten note by Dr. Huyung describes the film

Figure 7.2. Dr. Huyung (*left*) and his cameraman Eimert Kruidhof (*right*) on set making *Antara Bumi dan Langit* (Between Heaven and Earth, 1950). Collection of Sinematek Indonesia, Jakarta.

as being at the center of fierce debate between progressive and reactionary groups.[11] It suggests Dr. Huyung was engaged with the cultural politics of the new nation of Indonesia and his own sense of place within it. In *Antara Bumi dan Langit* Dr. Huyung expresses a sense of political purpose, offering an inclusive vision of Indonesian nationalism in the cultural tradition of what Armijn Pané calls *acculturatie*, or cultural mélange (1953, 89). Multiculturalism was evident, for example, in the crew represented in figure 7.2.

One legacy of Dr. Huyung's experience with *Antara Bumi dan Langit* was his engagement in public debates about censorship and its role in the new republic. In a series of articles published in *Aneka* magazine called "Tjatatan Film" (Film notes), Dr. Huyung questions the role and purpose of censorship (Huyung 1951, 1952a, 1952b, 1952c). Once a film had passed censorship, he reasoned that it should receive institutional backing from the Censorship Board against spurious and reactionary attacks such as those he experienced with *Antara Bumi dan Langit*. Rather than siding with protests, he argued that the Censorship Board should protect filmmakers, who often had little institutional backing or public support. Otherwise, any film could be criticized and forced to be withdrawn, not only causing financial losses for the filmmakers and their investors but also inhibiting the development of the nation and its culture.

Despite these setbacks, Dr. Huyung returned to filmmaking and made three more films that dealt with issues relevant to the new nation. Based on a popular play by Utuy T. Sontani, *Bunga Rumah Makan* (The flower of the restaurant, 1951) received positive reviews for its portrayal of a love story between a pretty waitress and an uncouth male customer. *Kenangan Masa* (Memories past, 1951) told the story of Sumiati, who is engaged to Anwar but becomes jealous of Maria, Anwar's childhood friend. One critical review says the film merely imitates American films and that Dr. Huyung "is unable to uncover the spirit and character of Indonesian people"[12] (*Aneka* 1952). *Gadis Olahraga* (Sportswoman, 1951), a continuation of *Kenangan Masa*, tells how, after the death of her husband, Maria returns to her village to train as an athlete and wins at the 1951 National Athletics Championships held in Jakarta. Using real footage from the championships, *Gadis Olahraga* presents sport both as a means of self-improvement and as a modern institution in national development. Moreover, the central character is a woman, and at the time such a choice was (and still is) a bold and progressive statement to make. Unfortunately, only synopses and brief reviews of these films survive, and the films themselves have been lost.[13]

After producing the four films, Dr. Huyung turned to importing, beginning with the Japanese film *Shina No Yoru* (China nights, 1940). Many regard *Shina No Yoru* as another example of Japanese propaganda, in that it involved a love story between a Japanese soldier and a Chinese woman. It was a hit in Japan because of the actress Ri Kōran and the film's songs (High 2003). Dr. Huyung's decision to import this film may suggest his ongoing attachment to Japan, though it was not uncommon for Japanese films to be imported into Indonesia in the 1950s. The economic reason is obvious, that a film highly popular in Japan could sell well in Indonesia and bring Dr. Huyung capital to continue making films. Or perhaps the film was simply one that made a huge impression on Dr. Huyung, possibly inspiring *You and I*, and he wanted to bring it to Indonesia. The answers to these questions and many others went to the grave with Dr. Huyung on September 9, 1952.

Nationalist Histories and Third Spaces

Dr. Huyung's biography offers a means of interrogating nationalist historiography in both South Korea and Indonesia. In both countries, nationalist historiography, also called a "nationalist paradigm" (Glade 1991), is the dominant frame in which colonial history is remembered and interpreted. Nationalist histories tend to create dualities of temporality, origin, and subjectivity.

Time is divided between before and after independence; individuals are designated according to their allegiance as either prorevolutionary or collaborator and traitor; and foreigners and transnationals are ignored in favor of indigenous figures. Because of his actions and origins, Dr. Huyung has been subject to such discourse, typically falling on the wrong side of nationalist history in both Korea and Indonesia.

In Korea, the distinction between collaborators or traitors and nationalists or victims is particularly pronounced. Hinatsu is a maligned figure in Korean national history for directing the pro-Japanese propaganda film *You and I*. He is seen as a colonial agent and willing collaborator with the Japanese imperial project. By appreciating his trajectory after 1945, however, the much more complicated picture emerges of a man who switched sides as he crossed borders: from colonial subject to colonial agent; from colonial collaborator to revolutionary supporter. The transitions were possible because of Hinatsu's ambivalent position as a Korean working for the Japanese in Indonesia; and as much as he may have tried, he could not erase the fact that he was Korean, and not Japanese.

Dr. Huyung therefore became an example of what Mark (2010, 349) describes as "the full ideological complexity and significance of this [occupier and occupied] interaction." In an earlier study, Ethan Mark (2006), documented the story of the Indonesian Sanusi Pané, who acquired the label of collaborator when his ideas of Asianism became entangled with the pan-Asian vision of Japanese colonialism. Another contradictory trajectory is seen in the figure of antifascist Japanese writer Takeda Rintarō, who on becoming a *bunkajin* in Java became entangled in a web of contradictory political and social ideas (Mark 2014). These portraits challenge the strict duality of nationalist historiography, for it is possible to see that some people were the victims of circumstances that made it impossible to be exclusively a collaborator or resister.

Dr. Huyung offers another model, since he belonged neither to Japan nor to Indonesia. In this, he has much in common with dancer Choe Sŭng-hŭi, who attracted the label of collaborator from the fame and opportunities Japanese colonialism gave her. Sang Mi Park writes that

> Choe rose from relative obscurity to become an East Asian cultural activist on- and offstage who represented the entire wartime Japanese Empire. This did not simply occur out of luck, nor was it the outcome of some helpless collaboration with the Japanese to survive oppressive colonial times. The specific conditions of the 1930s established Choe, who had been no more than a novice in Ishii's dance studio in the 1920s, studying Western ballet with Japanese students, as a prominent figure who was to contribute to the overall cultural clout of the Japanese Empire. (Park 2006, 625)

Choe traveled beyond the borders of the Japanese Empire as one of its Korean subjects and came to represent Korea on the world stage even though she was working as part of a Japanese cultural mission. Dr. Huyung's biography traces a similar trajectory, not simply as a collaborator, but as someone who had to negotiate the compromising conditions that the Japanese Empire created for an ethnic Korean.

Dr. Huyung's biography also complicates the ethnonationalist history of Indonesian cinema, in which indigenous Indonesian filmmakers Usmar Ismail and Djamaluddin Malik are given precedence (Barker 2010). Dr. Huyung is a peripheral figure in the emergence of a postindependence film industry, known more for having produced the first kissing scene in an Indonesian film than for any other contribution he made (see, for example, Indrarto 2013). Usmar Ismail, a contemporary of Dr. Huyung's, was also a native (*pribumi*) and a nationalist and, in keeping with the ethnonationalist foundations of Indonesian nationalism, is privileged over those regarded as foreigners, such as the ethnic Chinese who have often been denied recognition in the foundation of the Indonesian film industry (Setijadi-Dunn and Barker 2010). Dr. Huyung's contribution to the Indonesian film industry, however, challenges the racialized account of Indonesian independence and the history of the film industry.

The mobility, opportunism, and reinvention that shaped Hŏ/Hinatsu/Dr. Huyung's identity also reveal the ambiguities of identity within nationalist historiography. We have seen the ambivalence of his identity as a Korean subject to colonial Japan, and after 1945 he undergoes a process of reinvention signified by his adoption of the title "Dr." Although he graduated from Waseda University, the "Dr." title refers more to his sense of status as a film intellectual and practitioner—his desire to give himself a certain amount of influence and prestige in post-1945 Indonesia. Like Choe in the United States, the third space of Indonesia for Dr. Huyung represented an arena in which this process became possible, allowing him to escape the troubling ambivalence of being a collaborator or traitor and to find belonging in the emerging independent nation of Indonesia where his skills in theater, film, and propaganda were valuable and needed. In this sense, we can see that it was possible for a colonial subject to transcend the stalemate of the ambivalence embedded in the colonial encounter and move beyond the binary logic of nationalist historiography.

Conclusion

Dr. Huyung's biography reveals how enmeshed postindependence Indonesian cinema was in the politics and experiences of colonialism despite often defining itself against colonialism. The 1950s period produced several Indonesian auteurs, notably Usmar Ismail, who has become an exemplary figure of Indonesian national cinema. Such a possibility is denied to Dr. Huyung because of the implications of his background and the ethnopolitics of Indonesian nationalism and the narrow binary of resistance and collaboration. This chapter has shown the possibilities of a different kind of auteur, defined less by his contribution to nationalism or the art of cinema than by a fraught process of grappling with the complexities of identity and belonging under colonialism. Dr. Huyung's difficult position does not excuse him as a propaganda officer, nor should we forget how colonization was a system of subjugation and oppression that denied personhood to the colonized. For some such as Dr. Huyung, the colonial encounter opened pathways to opportunity through which the self could be reinvented and histories could be rewritten and a career in film pursued.

Notes

1. Two Japanese books deal with his life in more complete way: *Shineasuto Kyoei no "Shōwa"* (シネアスト許泳の「昭和」Cineast Hŏ Yŏng's Showa Era) by Utsumi and Murai (1987) and *Ekkyō no Eiga Kantoku Hinatsu Eitarō* (越境の映画監督日夏英太郎 Cross-border film director Eitaro Hinatsu) by Hinatsu Moeko 日夏もえ子 (2011). As both books are in Japanese, they are currently inaccessible to the authors and constitute a lacuna in this research.

2. Sources variously also spell his Korean name as Huh Yung, Huh Yeong, Hae Young, and Hŏ Yŏng. For consistency, Hŏ Yŏng is used throughout this chapter. In some Indonesian sources, his Japanese name is spelled Hinatsu Heitaro. Some records, for example, *Cineast Hŏ Yŏng's Showa Era*, register his birth year as 1908 (Kang 2008, 17–20).

3. According to High (2003, 308), by 1941 Hinatsu had already been working in the *jidaigeki* (period drama) film industry for more than nine years.

4. For further information on such filmmakers and on Japan-Korea coproductions during the late 1930s, see Chung (2012).

5. Among the ten rolls of film that originally composed *You and I*, only the first and the ninth were discovered in March 2009 by the National Film Center in Japan. Kim Ryŏ-sil's analysis refers to the script that was published in a Japanese language magazine in 1941. For further information on this script, see Kim Ryŏ-sil (2006, 283–85).

6. *Calling Australia* was reportedly made in preparation for the planned Japanese invasion of Australia (Baskett 2008).

7. The original reads "terciptanya pengertian tentang fungsi film yang kemudian akan ternyata berguna sekali bagi usaha-usaha membangunkan film nasional di masa kemerdekaan."

8. It is not known who imprisoned them.

9. Associates of the KDA included prominent directors Soemardjono (1927–98), Djadoeg Djajakusuma (1918–87), and R. M. Soetarto (1914–2001), who established the state broadcaster TVRI (Televisi Republik Indonesia), writers and dramatists Utuy T. Sontani (1920–79), Sri Murtono (1916–86), and Trisno Soemardjo (1916–69), future ministers of education and culture K. H. Dewantoro (1889–1959), and Prijono (1905–69), and musician Kusbini (1910–91).

10. The most authoritative English-language work on the Indonesian film industry is Salim Said's *Shadows on the Silver Screen* (1991). Although Dr. Huyung is mentioned in Said's work, the extent and significance of his work is not.

11. A handwritten dedication on the back page of the *Antara Bumi dan Langit* script held at the Sinematek Film Library in Jakarta, written by Dr. Huyung, says, "Mengenai film Antara Bumi dan Langit Kini menjadi pokok perdebatan yg ramai pertengkaran antara Kaum progressief dan reaksionair" (In regard to the film *Antara Bumi dan Langit*, it has become the center of fierce debate between progressives and reactionaries).

12. "dia belum dapat menjelami djiwa dan watak orang Indonesia."

13. Two reels of *Gadis Olahraga* have been found in the Indonesian National Archives. The authors have not been able to view this footage yet.

Bibliography

Anderson, Joseph, and Donald Richie. 1982. *The Japanese Film: Art and Industry*. Princeton, NJ: Princeton University Press.

Aneka. 1952. "Kenangan Masa Preview." *Aneka*, January 31, no. 34: 21.

Baek, Moonim. 2015. *Im Hwa-ŭi Yŏngwa* (Im Hwa's cinema). Seoul: Somyŏng.

Barker, Thomas. 2010. "Historical Inheritance and Film Nasional in Post-Reformasi Indonesian Cinema." *Asian Cinema* 21, no. 2: 7–24.

———. 2017. "Colonial Mobility and Ambiguity: The Life of Filmmaker Hinatsu/Huyung." *TRaNS: Trans-Regional and -National Studies of Southeast Asia* 5, no. 2: 1–19. https://doi.org/10.1017/trn.2017.3.

Baskett, Michael. 2008. *The Attractive Empire: Transnational Film Culture in Imperial Japan*. Honolulu: University of Hawaii Press.

Bhabha, Homi. 1984. "Of Mimicry and Man: The Ambivalence of Colonial Discourse." *October* 28 (Spring): 125–33.

Biran, Misbach Yusa. 2009. *Sejarah Film 1900–1950: Bikin Film di Jawa*. Depok, Indonesia: Komunitas Bambu.

Chung Chonghwa. 2012. "Negotiating Colonial Korean Cinema in the Japanese Empire: From the Silent Era to the Talkies, 1923–1939." *Cross-Currents* no. 5: 136–69. http://cross-currents.berkeley.edu/e-journal/issue-5.

Cohen, Matthew Isaac. 2016. *Inventing the Performing Arts: Modernity and Tradition in Colonial Indonesia*. Honolulu: University of Hawaii Press.

Glade, Jon. 1991. "Collaboration and Resistance: Representations of Colonial Korea." *Studies on Asia* 1, no. 1: 56–65.

Harrymawan. 1951. "Dari Antara Bumi dan Langit ke Frieda." [From Antara Bumi dan Langit to Frieda] *Kentjana* 12: 51.

Heider, Karl. 1991. *Indonesian Cinema: National Culture on Screen*. Honolulu: University of Hawaii Press.

High, Peter. 2003. *The Imperial Screen: Japanese Film Culture in the Fifteen Years' War, 1931–1945*. Madison: University of Wisconsin Press.

Hinatsu, Moeko 日夏もえ子. (2011). *Ekkyō no Eiga Kantoku Hinatsu Eitarō* (越境の映画監督日夏英太郎 Cross-border film director Hinatsu Eitarō). Tokyo: Bungeisha.

Hutari, Fandy. 2009. *Sandiwara dan Perang: Politisasi terhadap Aktivitas Sandiwara Modern Masa Jepang di Jakarta 1942–1945*. Yogyakarta, Indonesia: Ombak.

Huyung. 1951. "Dr. Huyung: Apa jang harus masuk dalam Undang2 Film Baru." *Aneka* 4, no. 2: 17.

———. 1952a. "Tjatatan Film." *Aneka* 7: 13.

———. 1952b. "Tjatatan Film." *Aneka* 8: 22.

———. 1952c. "Tjatatan Film." *Aneka* 9: 20.

Im Hwa. 1942. "Chosŏn Yŏnghwaron" (On Korean cinema). *Maeil Shinbo*, June, 28–30.

Indrarto, Totot. 2013. "Ciuman pertama dalam film Indonesia." *Beritagar*, March 13. https://beritagar.id/artikel/seni-hiburan/ciuman-pertama-dalam-film-indonesia.

Ismail, Usmar. 1983. "Sari Soal dalam Film Indonesia." In *Usmar Ismail Mengupas Film*. Edited by Justin E. Siahaan, 53–66. Jakarta: Sinar Harapan.

Kang In. 2008. *Kŭndae chuch'eŭi singminhwa yŏn'gu: ilche kangjŏmgi sidaeŭi yŏnghwain Hŏ Yŏng-ŭl chungsimŭro* (A study on the colonization of a modern subject: the case of Hŏ Yŏng, a filmmaker of the Japanese imperial period). Master's thesis, Korean National University of Arts.

Kim Chae-bŏm, dir. 1997. *Se kaeŭi irŭmŭl kajin yŏnghwain* (A filmmaker with three names). VHS. South Korea: Shin Dong Panavision.

Kim Kyu-Hyun. 2005. "War and the Colonial Legacy in Recent South Korean Scholarship." *IIAS Newsletter* 38, 6.

Kim Ryŏ-sil. 2006. *T'usahanŭn cheguk t'uyŏnghanŭn singminji: 1901–1945 yŏnŭi Han'guk yŏnghwasarŭl toejipta* (Projecting empire, projected colony: re-considering Korean film history 1901–1945). Seoul: Samin.

Kurasawa, Aiko.1987. "Propaganda Media on Java under the Japanese 1942–1945." *Indonesia* 44: 59-116.

———. 2015. *Kuasa Jepang di Jawa: Perubahan Sosial di Pedesaan 1942–1945*. Depok, Indonesia: Komunitas Bambu.

Lee Hwa-jin. 2016. *Soriŭi chŏngch'i: singminji Chosŏnŭi kŭkchanggwa chegukŭi kwan'gaek* (The politics of sound: theaters of colonial Korea and audiences of empire). Seoul: Hyŏnshil munhwa.

Lee Yŏng-jae. 2008. *Cheguk Ilbonŭi Chosŏn yŏnghwa: singminji malŭi pando, hyŏmnyŏk ŭi simjŏng, chedo, nolli* (Korean cinema in Japanese Empire: the peninsula of the late colonial period, feelings, institutions and logics of collaboration). Seoul: Hyŏnshil munhwa.

Mark, Ethan. 2006. "'Asia's' Transwar Lineage: Nationalism, Marxism, and 'Greater Asia' in an Indonesian Inflection." *Journal of Asian Studies* 65, no. 3: 461–93.

———. 2010. "Intellectual Life and the Media." In *The Encyclopedia of Indonesia in the Pacific War*. Edited by Peter Post, 348–63. Leiden, Neth.: Brill.

———. 2014. "The Perils of Co-Prosperity: Takeda Rintarō, Occupied Southeast Asia, and the Seductions of Postcolonial Empire." *The American Historical Review*. 119, no. 4: 1184–1206.

NHK (Nippon Hōsō Kyōka). 1993. *Life of a Film Director, Eitarō Hinatsu—the National Identity That Arose from the Indonesian Independence Movement* [radio broadcast]. Tokyo: NHK, August 15.

Okada, Hidenori. 2002. "Probing a Void in Documentary Film History: The Rise and Fall of the Nippon Eigasha Jakarta Studio." Documentary Box no. 20. Yamagata International Documentary Film Festival. September 13. http://www.yidff.jp/docbox/20/box20-3-1-e.html.

Pané, Armijn. 1953. "Produksi Film Tjerita di Indonesia, Perkembangannja Sebagai Alat Masjarakat." *Madjalah Kebudajaan* 4, nos. 1–2: 5–112.

———. 1955. "Sedikit Tentang Dr. Huyung." *Kentjana* 21: 26–27.

Park, Sang Mi. 2006. "The Making of a Cultural Icon for the Japanese Empire: Choe Seunghui's U.S. Dance Tours and 'New Asian Culture' in the 1930s and 1940s." *positions* 14, no. 3: 597–632.

Ramdhan, Karta H., and Nina Pane. 2006. *Pengusaha, Politikus, Pelopor Industri Film: Djamaludin Malik; Melekat di Hati Banyak Orang*. Jakarta: Kata Hasta Pustaka.

Ricklefs, Merle. 1981. *A History of Modern Indonesia: c. 1300 to the Present*. London: Macmillan.

Sai, Ichikawa. 1941. *Ajia eiga no sōzō oyobi kensetsu* (アジア映画 の創造及建設 The creation and construction of Asian cinema). Tokyo: Kokusai eiga tsūshinsha.

Said, Salim. 1991. *Shadows on the Silver Screen: A Social History of Indonesian Film*. Translated by Toenggoel P. Siagian. Jakarta: Lontar Foundation.
Setijadi-Dunn, Charlotte, and Thomas Barker. 2010. "Imagining 'Indonesia': Ethnic Chinese Film Producers in Pre-independence Cinema." *Asian Cinema* 21, no. 2: 25–47.
Setiyono, Budi. 2010. "Huyung: Guru para sineas." *Budi Setiyono* [blog], May 4. http://budisetiyono.blogspot.com/2010/05/huyung-guru-para-sineas.html.
Utsumi, Aiko, and Yoshinori Murai. 1987. *Shineasuto Kyoei no "Shōwa"* (Cineast Hŏ Yŏng's Showa era). Tokyo: Gaifusha.
Yecies, Brian, and Ae-Gyung Shim. 2011. *Korea's Occupied Cinemas, 1893–1948: The Untold History of the Film Industry*. New York: Routledge.

THOMAS BARKER is Associate Professor of Film and Television at the University of Nottingham Malaysia. He is author of *Indonesian Cinema after the New Order: Going Mainstream*.

NIKKI J. Y. LEE is Senior Lecturer in Asian Media at Nottingham Trent University.

PART III.
MILLENNIAL HAUNTINGS: RISING GLOBAL ASIAN CINEMAS

8. CINEMA'S COLONIALITY

Takushi Odagiri

ABSTRACT

This chapter deals with two closely related issues. (1) It examines an animation film from wartime Japan, Seo Mitsuyo's *Momotarō: Divine Warriors of the Sea* (1945), along with the documentary theory of Imamura Taihei from the same period, to unpack the complexity of the colonial gaze in the former Japanese Empire. The chapter argues that this multispecific and animalistic film reveals the humanistic foundation of wartime propaganda and that, rather than compare skin colors, the film contrasts the human and nonhuman embodiment of the colonial subject at multiple (conscious and unconscious) levels. The chapter claims that, since racial "epidermalization" (Fanon [1952] 2008) is much less conspicuous in Asia, the phenomenon of coloniality tends to be more Freudian than Fanonian: namely, colonial subjectivity is often unconscious rather than self-reflective. (2) The chapter then shifts its focus to broader contexts, arguing that discourses on colonialism, which tend to emphasize differences (in race, color, ethnicity, etc.), should be rethought vis-à-vis their unconscious underside. That is, coloniality has both its exclusive side (i.e., as differences) and its inclusive (unconscious) side (i.e., as hegemony). Since the phenomenon of coloniality may easily go unnoticed or remain on the level of the unconscious, the colonized may *not* be conscious of their own subjugation. This suggests that discourses on hybridity in today's globalized society may conceal (or even intensify) real problems of coloniality. The chapter investigates the long-term significance of this unconscious, humanistic coloniality, especially its correlation with biopolitical conditions of globalized cultures today.

INTRODUCTION

The goal of this chapter is twofold. First, for the short term, the chapter examines an animation film from wartime Japan (Seo Mitsuyo's *Momotarō: Divine Warriors of the Sea* [1945]), to unpack the complexity of the colonial gaze in

Figure 8.1. The multispecific embodiment of the colonial unconscious. (Seo Mitsuyo, *Momotarō* 1945, digitally restored version [Seo 2016], screen shot.)

the former Japanese Empire. I argue that this multispecific and animalistic film reveals the humanistic foundation of wartime propaganda and that, rather than compare skin colors, the film contrasts the human and nonhuman embodiment of the colonial relationship. The colonial gaze is embedded in the anthropocentrism of the characters' bodies. (See fig. 8.1.) Since racial "epidermalization" (Fanon [1952] 2008) is much less conspicuous in Asia than in North America or some parts of Europe, the phenomenon of coloniality tends to be more Freudian than Fanonian. Second, this humanistic coloniality of the wartime propaganda film has a long-term significance for our time. That is, not only is this entanglement of humanism and colonialism latently with us in the present era, but it also constitutes a biopolitical condition of the globalized culture today. Coloniality should be understood not only as exclusivity (i.e., as differences) but also as inclusivity. In the following, I will discuss these two issues in a few different contexts.

A distinct feature of Seo's *Momotarō* is its biosociological hybridity and equivocality. Humanhood receives a twofold definition in this image narrative. At one (surface and exclusive) level, only the commander, Momotarō, fully belongs to the human species; all the others are depicted either as animals (soldiers of the Japanese troop and native residents) or as demonlike (British soldiers).[1] At a deeper (unconscious) level, however, all the characters behave humanly (e.g., they speak human languages, observe military discipline, and communicate with each other in the manner of human beings). In this sense, even animals or demonlike characters belong to the film's human world, which appears more inclusive. The two-faced humanism of the film resembles what Nishitani (2006) designates as the binary of *humanitas* and *anthropos*.[2] But unlike the latter, in *Momotarō* the duality even cuts across the Japanese troops. The film's anthropomorphism renders the humanity of the soldiers (depicted as various biospecies) ambivalent throughout. Furthermore, it is worth noting that the unconscious humanity (i.e., the humanity at the second, inclusive level) is defined by betweenness, namely, the fact that all the characters are placed in relationality of *between-us*.[3] Specifically, the humanity defined at the second level goes hand in hand with synchronic experiences of a world-historic event. It is this synchronic quality of the film's humanism that resembles the globalized culture today, in which the human world has increasingly become unified and reduced to "the now," a single collective immediacy of the present.[4] The differential geopolitics of colonial temporalities in the past centuries has been fundamentally restructured with the presentism of globalization in our neocolonial era.[5] In this study, I attempt to elucidate this synchronic (unconscious) humanity of both the colonial era and the current century.

Cinema's Colonial Unconscious

In the biopolitical situation of the present era, I would like to think of coloniality as the (Freudian) unconscious.[6] That is, what we observe in colonial history is the tip of the iceberg; coloniality is its hidden underside.[7] (See fig. 8.2.) Here, coloniality *as a structure* should be strictly distinguished from historical colonialism as *instantiations*.[8] I am in alliance with the Jamesonian-Gramscian thesis as discussed later in this chapter. Discourses on colonialism tend to emphasize differences (in race, color, ethnicity, etc.). But this picture of coloniality is fundamentally mistaken.

Why should we guard ourselves against thinking that coloniality is a fully conscious phenomenon? James Rachels provides a possible answer to this question, although from a different angle. His observation is similar to my argument here, though its context differs: his is an observation of everyday prejudice rather than of historical colonialism. Rachels writes, "We feel that we are unprejudiced only because we are unaware of our biases and how

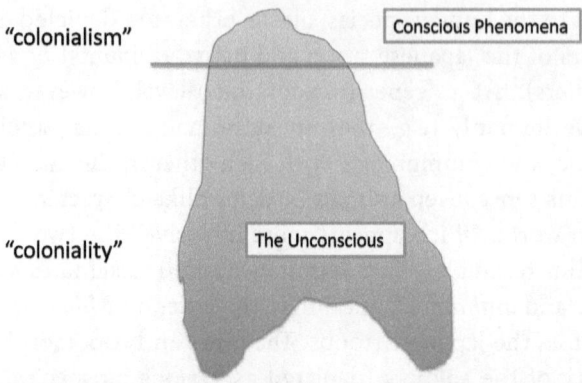

Figure 8.2. Coloniality as the (Freudian) unconscious. Drawing by the author.

they work. This is true not only of bigots but of relatively open-minded people as well. It is a mistake for any of us to think that we are free of bias. Even when we are striving hardest to be objective, prejudices of all sorts can creep into our thinking without noticing it" (Rachels 1997, 199). Rachels provides some concrete examples. "We are familiar enough with prejudice based on race or gender. But those are not the only ways in which we discriminate." For example, there is a body of evidence suggesting that we are prejudiced against shorter people; yet it rarely occurs to us that we are socially biased against shortness (Rachels 1997, 199–200). (More precisely, neither the subject nor the object of this social bias is aware of the existence of such a bias.) A number of other biases presumably can easily go unnoticed—by both the subject and the object of them.

It is even conceivable (although Rachels does not make the claim) that social biases we are not fully aware of can be more persistent and have more lasting effects on our lives than those that have been made publicly observable for us. I would even argue that the former does have more lasting influences. It is far more difficult to contest the biases we are unaware of than the ones we regularly and routinely discuss. Still more difficult is to become aware of them.

Although it is prejudice in everyday living (not specifically coloniality) that Rachels discusses in his essay, it is noteworthy that colonial consciousness (and the biopolitics that underlies it today) can have a similar structure. Rachels observes that a person can (and often does) have prejudice that is unconscious or unnoticed. I believe the same can be said of a group of people with regard to their colonial relations with others; they can colonize (or can be colonized by) another group of people at unconscious levels. Indeed, in the increasingly unified world today, it is possible that many colonial relations go unnoticed or even remain unconscious.

I do not necessarily share Rachels's skepticism,[9] but his observation has a bearing on the present chapter's discussion. It seems important to me that the colonial subject is often (or can often be) an unconscious subject in a similar manner; it is even possible to argue that, when fully colonized, the colonized is not conscious of its own subjugation. (In like manner, consider the possibility that shortness can most deeply influence one's life when social biases against it are unconscious to both oneself and others.[10]) In other words, if the colonized does (or can) reflect on itself as different from the colonizer, there has already been some kind of noncoloniality.[11] To put it another way, the degree of control or subjugation through unconscious coloniality can be just as strong as that of a conscious, explicit bias. In fact, one can observe this unconscious coloniality in the current global consciousness. Very few would call it a colonial enterprise; but the system of subjugation is even stronger and much less likely to be contested.

The colonial unconscious is an essential notion of cultural analysis in the globalized society today, whose populations are increasingly hybrid and intercultural. Even though conscious representations are hybrid, the underlying colonial unconscious remains intact or is even reinforced. Unconscious coloniality may be observed in almost any kind of colonialism; but the notion is even more important in the present age of globalization.

Suppose that there are various ways in which a population can colonize another population, either consciously or unconsciously. Physical violence is probably the most conscious and explicit form of coloniality, but there are other ways. Culturally based colonialism (called "hegemony") is often less explicit, but it can be more powerful and can have long-lasting influences. It is clear to me that cinema's coloniality should be examined on the model of this unconscious form of coloniality. There should be quite many other methods or devices for colonization in between (economic, political, sociohistorical, and so on).

By synchronizing the audiences' experiences across the empire, providing them with the image of hybridity and pluralism, the colonial unconscious created by cinema produces and reproduces desubjectification, an important feature of biopolitics even today. Without relying much on audiences' linguistic capability, film work is often reproduced on a mass scale and widely distributed, which can itself reproduce a sense of sharing a simultaneous history. Throughout most of the twentieth century, cinema has been a lingua franca, a quasi-universal means of communication of the truth (*vérité*) for world populations. It is possible to argue that, historically, film (especially documentary) has played a role similar to that of internet-based social media in the present century. By nature, the lingua franca is a hybrid construct. Its pluralism itself is a device of assimilation.

IMAMURA TAIHEI AND HIS DOCUMENTARY THEORY

Imamura Taihei's wartime observations, which should be considered alongside Seo Mitsuyo's animation work (1945) in the same period, are our starting point in this connection. Imamura is a Japanese film critic of the twentieth century, mostly known for his critical writings on documentary and animation films, which influenced later generations such as Takahata Isao and Suzuki Toshio of Studio Ghibli. As I will discuss later in this chapter, Imamura's documentary theory is closely related to his work on Disney cartoon films. Historically, this duality of his theory has a particular significance in Japanese documentary theory.

Mark Nornes (2003) writes, "The period after the China Incident would become known as the golden age of Japanese documentary film, a time when documentary reached a place of prominence it rarely achieved during any other period in a century of film history" (48). According to him, documentary history during this period was like "a gradual arc from commercial competition to state propaganda, punctuated by the establishment of the Film Law" (70).[12] Both Imamura and Seo were deeply committed both to this complex historical situation and to the shifting stylistics and methodologies of film form.[13]

I would like to construe Imamura's documentary theory as a form of critical theory, much as Horkheimer-Adorno's critique of the cultural industry is also a form of critical theory. In particular, Imamura's dual focus on scientific documentaries and animation films, both of which represent some aspects of cinema's colonial history, reveals an underlying thought on cinema's truth (*vérité*). This duality itself reflects Imamura's nuanced reactions to wartime cultural politics; cinema's *vérité* is its criticality, which should be sought between science (documentary) and self-alienation (animation). In other words, it is possible to construe Imamura's documentary theory as his critical strategy against cinema's coloniality in the political situations of his time. Seo's animation production sits side by side with Imamura's film theory in this sense—especially in their shared critique of documentary, hybridity, and the colonial unconscious. Ultimately, Imamura's theory of documentary has the potential to reveal the colonial unconscious; that is, it can make the colonized conscious of its own subjugation.

Underlying Imamura's treatises on film form ([1938]; Imamura 1991) and animation film (*manga eiga*; [1936], [1941]; Imamura 1991d, 87–103 and 1991a) is his concept of documentariness (Japanese, *kiroku-sei*). Since Imamura's documentary theory preceded the French *cinéma vérité* and North American direct cinema by several decades, one cannot simply conflate his historical situation with the situations of these two lineages. It is, however, still important to think of Imamura's film theory within the overall trajectory of documentary history that culminated in the parallel French and North American versions in the 1960s. In some sense, Imamura's critical theory transcends the methodology of those two movements. His is more focused on cinema's coloniality in itself, that is, the colonial cultural politics of his time and the colonially biased origins of the documentary gaze.[14]

By no means did Imamura equate documentary with objectivity. On the contrary, for him, documentary is a skewed mirror *indicating* some truth. One does need this misleading mirror called documentary, but one should interpret its images carefully. Despite his continuous interest in the physical resemblance (and synchrony) between cinematic images and their object, Imamura seems aware of their fictitious origins.

Imamura's documentary theory, with his graphic imagination, predicted much of what Jürgen Habermas witnessed about a century later—the age of global presentism.[15] From the present-day perspective, Imamura's diagnosis turns out to be largely accurate (especially with respect to the biopolitical conditions).[16] *Documentary synchronizes our eyes*. Its simultaneity permeates our global consciousness today; it produces and reproduces an experience of world history (as if it were happening right in front of our eyes). As is indicated by his repeated usage of the terms *world cognition* and *world history*, Imamura was conscious of film media's potential for global (colonial) consciousness.

Momotarō (1945): Biosociology of Coloniality

What makes Imamura's documentary theory important is not simply its scientific rigor and criticality, but its close correlation with contemporary film production. In light of the historical circumstances of his time (i.e., Japanese imperial expansion), it is natural that theory and practice went side by side in their Brechtian critique.

Around the same time Imamura produced his critiques, Seo Mitsuyo, a legendary animation filmmaker who influenced artists of postwar generations (including Tezuka Osamu), created a few animation films, including *Momotarō: Umi no Shinpei /Momotarō: Divine Warriors of the Sea* (Shochiku Ōfuna Studio, 1945).[17] Regarded as a propaganda film, it was destroyed shortly after the war. Another copy of the film was discovered much later in a warehouse owned by Shochiku and it was digitally restored (Seo 2016).[18] *Momotarō* is now considered to be the first feature-length animation film in Japan (Ōtsuka 2013).

Like Imamura's critical theories, Seo's animation work considers the problem of documentary, which constitutes its important underside. In fact, the film includes a few characteristics that correspond to Imamura's documentary theory. First, the animation in *Momotarō* is, as it were, an allegorical recording of real-time historical occurrences that almost immediately preceded its production. The climax scene, which depicts the Momotarō parachute troop's attack on the island called Onigashima (literally, "demons' island"), is a clear analogy of the fall of Singapore on the real-life battlefields. Second, the work's semidocumentary quality correlates with its character design too. Unlike Disney animation films that exaggerate or caricature animal characters' motions, often to the extent of being nonrepresentational,[19] *Momotarō*'s animal bodies are not "plasmatic" bodies.[20] *Momotarō*'s mimesis is more modest, subtle, and meticulous, presenting animal characters' movements without much exaggeration or distortion.

Despite being based on a popular folk story called "Momotarō (Peach Boy)," Seo's *Momotarō* values documentariness (*kiroku-sei*) as its core method. In other words, *Momotarō* deftly integrates its documentary aspect into its narrative quality. Seo seems to have conceived animation not only as a narrative medium but also as a documentary medium. The cartoon images are skewed pictures of hybridity in themselves. For this reason, one can view *Momotarō* alongside Imamura's treatises; both are complex reactions to the deployment of cinema for the colonial cultural politics of the time.

Momotarō begins with a folktale-like depiction of the (seemingly) perpetual peace of an anachronic time. The opening sequences are set in a rural mountain village near Mount Fuji. Animal habitats in the forest are described in close detail. But the anachronicity (desynchronicity) of the fairly-tale time is suddenly broken by a historic world event—Momotarō troop's attack on Onigashima (the island of demons, *"oni"*), an event analogous to the real-life Japanese attack on Southeast Asia. One should bear in mind that *oni* was a common metaphor for US and British soldiers during wartime. Presumably, the audiences who were informed (to various degrees) of their real-time historical situation could recognize the quasi-documentary quality of the animation. The question is: Does this quasi-documentary style make the audience members feel as if they were sharing the same historical moment with the animal characters in the story, or does it create a strange distance from the narrative event? In other words, does this quasi-documentary create a sense of historical *estrangement* (in a Brechtian sense)?

A newsreel-based wartime documentary titled *Marē Senki Shingeki no Kiroku / Malaya War Record: A Record of the Onward March* (Nippon Eigasha or Nichiei, Japan, 1942) was a pretext for this animation film. The short documentary film was funded by the Ministry of the Army and released a year after Imamura's treatise on cartoon film and a couple of years before the production of Seo's *Momotarō*. The release was shortly after the battle and fall of Singapore, and the film was shown to audiences across Japan and to people of the Japanese Empire in the Southeast Asian region (High 2003, 366–67), apparently in order to claim the superiority or success of the new colonial regime. That is, the documentary seemed to attempt to synchronize its viewers' historic consciousness, although it is not clear how successful it was in achieving that effect.

Marē Senki has a well-known climax scene in the Ford Motor Factory in which General Tomoyuki Yamashita of the Imperial Japanese Army is shown to browbeat British General Arthur Percival into surrendering Singapore (High 2003, 366–67). As Peter B. High points out, the way Momotarō intimidates the opposing officers across the table in Seo's animation looks partially similar to the way General Yamashita browbeats British General Percival in *Marē Senki* in 1942 (High 2003, 367–68; see fig. 8.3). In both narratives, these climax scenes are presented as if they were universal historic events shared by world audiences (i.e., all across Asia)—events that transcended geopolitical differences (within the Japanese Empire). But, in Seo's *Momotarō*, despite this synchronic, collective eye, there is also an otherly gaze that constantly subverts the uniformity of world consciousness. A careful comparison of these scenes in the two films reveals both the conflicting documentariness in the works and cinema's coloniality as its underside.

There is an obvious difference between these films: namely, the biosociological variety in Seo's *Momotarō*. Whereas all the figures in the Ford Motor Factory scene are human soldiers, in Seo's animation, Momotarō is the only human face in the negotiation scene. (In fact, he is the only human character in the story.) The residents of the "Southern Sea" region in *Momotarō* are depicted as various biospecies as well. Yet Momotarō's role in Seo's story is marginal. The narrative description mostly revolves around the four animal characters (a monkey, a dog, a pheasant, and a bear) and their respective biohabitats, all of whom are Momotarō's soldiers.

It is tempting to interpret this multispecific description as a metaphor for the Japanese Empire's multiethnic vision and to see Momotarō as the allegorical voice of the colonial (humanistic) narrative.[21] The film highlights the image of a hybrid population sharing the same historical moment (i.e., the copresence of various biospecies, including animals and demons,[22] in this world-historical event). But what is important here is that the actual construction of the film narrative is far from anthropocentric. Momotarō's marginality in the story is striking, especially if one knows his moralistic

Figure 8.3. Biosociology of the colonial unconscious. (Seo Mitsuyo *Momotarō* 1945, digitally restored version [Seo 2016], screen shot.)

role in the original folktale. His artificial facial expression comes across as a surprise, in contrast to the animal soldiers' smiles and lively behavior. What accounts for this unexpected liveliness in the animal characters (and the reversal of the focal characters)?

Momotarō's role in the film is almost formulaic (to the extent it is even funny); it may cause some audience members to recall Brechtian caricature.[23] This Brechtian critique in the animation film desynchronizes the original gaze of *Marē Senki*. The animalistic images of Seo's *Momotarō* (especially in comparison with *Marē Senki*'s humanism) create a self-alienating distance in the audience's world-historical consciousness. It prevents them from being fully unconscious, from being unconditionally identified with the human protagonist. If coloniality is the (Freudian) unconscious, this heterogeneity destabilizes cinema's harmonious (unconscious) coloniality. Animal characters are spirited, cheerful, humorous, and much more spontaneous and individualistic than one would expect in the folktale version. Occasionally but incessantly, the animals assert for the audience their characteristic animal traits and their differences from the main character, Momotarō (or General Yamashita in the newsreel documentary). As a result, the degree of subjugation in this heterogeneous encounter is much less synchronic than in the Ford Motor Factory in *Marē Senki*.

The multi-layered colonial gaze is embedded in the ambivalent anthropocentrism of the characters' heterogeneous bodies in *Momotarō*. For example, the main character (the monkey), who is a soldier in the Japanese troop, has both humanistic and animalistic appearances. That is, the main character's ambivalent body represents an ethical conflict of the colonial situation in that era, the meaning of which is to be contingently interpreted by different audiences (e.g., by inland Japanese people, residents of the colonized territories, or American and British soldiers).

In comparing *Marē Senki* with Seo's *Momotarō*, one should realize the latter's criticality (or, more precisely, its scientific spirit). The films reveal both the coloniality of documentary and the subjective (colonially biased) origins of its gaze. The marginality of the human leader Momotarō in Seo's film, especially in comparison with the assertive attitude of General Yamashita in *Marē Senki*, creates a sense of self-alienation and brings to light the subjective quality of these synchronic documentaries. The alienation makes one aware that the human commander, who is the apparent voice of the documentary, hides the documentary's subjective (colonial) gaze.

Both coloniality and humanism have the binary structure of inclusivity and exclusivity here. Coloniality, represented through the body (rather than the skin), is expressed in the form of binary humanism. (Put differently, humanism is represented as interspecific coloniality with the binary of inclusivity [harmony] and exclusivity [heterogeneity].) The film's biosociological hybridity makes one aware of this two-fold humanism (i.e., coloniality) implicit in the synchronic history of the era.

This Brechtian critique that underlies Seo's animation film is compatible with Imamura's critical work in the same period. One observes the same critique of wartime humanism in Imamura's treatises. For example, one should consider the following passage about Disney from his "Tōkī Manga Ron": "The popularity of Pluto and Donald is largely due to their behaviors as a dog and a duck; [in their behaviors] everything is contradictory to the human world. Their animalistic actions are their critique of humanity's conventionalized actions" (Imamura 1991d, 100). Imamura did not simply regard wartime *bunka eiga* (cultural films) as accurate "recordings" (*kiroku*) of historical reality; neither did he think of Disney cartoons as photographs in themselves. On both sides of this binary, he seems to have seen some truth (*vérité*) beyond the screen. The act of documentary should be *ethical*; it should create the distance of self-alienation in the audience members' minds, allowing them to see still deeper into the fact. It is possible to regard Seo's *Momotarō* as an act of documentary (recording) in this deeper sense. It is likewise illuminating to read Imamura's treatises on documentary and animation films in this context.

Brecht's Street Scene

The legacy of direct cinema or *cinéma vérité* as we conceive it now is largely an epistemological or methodological one. It has often been debated (in the history of *cinéma vérité*) if and how documentary can achieve its actualities—be it "a fly on the wall" observational methodology or subjective interventions. But rarely is Brechtian critique fully engrained in this discussion of cinema's realism. Perhaps because of the historical circumstances of his time, Imamura's aesthetic resembling *cinéma vérité* is unique in this respect. His frequent references to animation films or, more specifically, his notion of animality (contra-humanity) as discussed earlier ("Tōkī Manga Ron" in Imamura 1991d, 100), attest to this (Brechtian) criticality of his film theory. I shall briefly consider what this criticality consists of, in order to further clarify cinema's unconscious as it seems to be conceived by both Imamura and Seo.

Imamura's cinema theory resembles Bertolt Brecht's dramaturgy on multiple levels. Here are some of their common features: (1) Both Imamura and Brecht were active mostly during the first half of the twentieth century and were generally critical of the advanced capitalism that was emerging in American society; (2) Methodologically, they both held historical materialism and diachronic approaches; and (3) Most important, they both raised fundamental questions about the documentary nature of their respective genres and attempted to create self-alienation in their audiences' minds. Just as Brecht revealed the materialistic basis of classical theater in a capitalist society through his plays and theatrical essays while he was in exile, Imamura's critical eyes captured cinema's coloniality in a nuanced and complex way while he lived in wartime Japan.

One of Brecht's basic models for his epic theater is the street scene, an eyewitness who demonstrates to a collection of people how a traffic accident took place (Brecht 1964, 121). The witness tries to reproduce the accident for people who were not firsthand witnesses. I have discussed this model in detail elsewhere (Odagiri 2019); here I briefly summarize its basic structure in order to explain Imamura's theoretical methodology. Brecht writes, "It is most important that one of the main features of the ordinary theatre should be excluded from our street scene: the engendering of illusion" (Brecht 1964, 122). No one in the scene sees the demonstration as an actual event; the audience members are aware that the eyewitness is neither the driver nor the victim. The theater stops pretending not to be theater. The illusion of its reality never enters the audience members' consciousness and they closely examine the eyewitness's demonstration with their critical eyes, for judicial procedures.

One should note that, despite being a hypothetical scenario, the street scene can itself be conceived as a proto-documentary. The street scene, or Brechtian epic theater in general, is a perfect model for documentary theory. The eyewitness in the "street" scene is functionally analogous to the camera's eye in documentary. In that the purpose and the fictionality of the demonstration are obvious to the audience, the eyewitness (the camera) cannot hide its subjective intentions and interpretations. The illusion of the reality of its images should never occur to the viewers' minds.

This disillusion should constitute *vérité* for both Imamura and Brecht. Although Imamura's reactions to wartime coloniality (and humanism) were more nuanced, his work undermines the (unconscious) illusion of documentary and its subjective origin. Just as Imamura proposed and even anticipated the historical evolution from narrative films to scientific documentaries, Brecht likewise rigorously pursued *vérité* in his theater. Brecht criticized the classical Aristotelian theater for its lack of scientific spirit and its engendering of an illusion. Brecht's model of the street scene not only demonstrates what the epic theater is or should be but also helps to clarify some basic features of Imamura's *cinéma vérité* aesthetics. As I discussed earlier, for Imamura, documentary is a distorting mirror; its images are inseparable from a filmmaker's subjective interventions. It may be true that cinema's simultaneity does not allow any temporal discrepancy between subject and object. But the synchronicity of photographic images with their object does not entail their lack of subjective interventions; on the contrary, the material immediacy of photographic technology often hides or even intensifies its documentary illusion. The camera tends to present its images as if these images possessed certain documentary *truth*. In other words, the existence of the camera itself becomes the colonial unconscious. By theorizing both animation and documentary films with rigorous scientific premises, Imamura illustrates this illusionary (subjective) aspect of cinema's coloniality. Imamura attempts with consistency to rescue the scientific spirit in documentary.

Synchronicity, Hybridity, and the Unconscious

Let me turn to the present century and its neocolonial situation. In 2001, after witnessing the explosion of 9/11 in New York and the slow collapse of the sky-high World Trade Center architecture, Jürgen Habermas compared the impact of this historical world event—an event that took place literally right in front of the "universal eyewitness" of a global public—to that of Hollywood.[24] It was, according to Habermas, "the first historic world event in the strictest sense" (Borradori 2003, 28): the explosion and the collapse were immediately seen through our global consciousness. Or, in fact, Habermas saw it as a more gruesome reality than Hollywood itself. Subsequently, he states that "one never really knows who one's enemy is" (28). It is no longer clear (as it is in Hollywood narratives) who is the real agent of this historic event, nor do we know how to conceptualize it in terms of our ordinary understanding of political agency. The event makes us wonder whether, in the moment in which we conceive the incident as the enemy's attack on our civilization (a commonplace rhetoric in Hollywood, in fact), we might have already deceived ourselves in some important manner.

The present age of *the* world temporality, as Habermas seems to foresee here, is simultaneously the time for the biopolitical system called security.[25] Increasingly, we have become part of the governmentality that treats us not so much as individuals but as a population, the governmentality that has to "arbitrate between the freedom and security of individuals" (Foucault 2008, 66). If everyone ought to be free, no one is allowed to be completely free. As a result, one is forced to partially bracket the very notion of (political) agency. To further think about this worldwide historic age, one needs to consider the third definition of biopolitics developed by Hardt and Negri—what they call "biopolitics as event" (Hardt and Negri 2009, 57–60).[26] Here, an event is defined as desubjectification, which is the "tightly woven fabric of events of freedom" (Hardt and Negri 2009, 58–59).[27] Desubjectification is an important feature of biopolitics today. On the one hand, one's freedom is woven into the nexus of historical world events. On the other, those who are excluded from *the* world are excluded simply for no reason, without any specific causality.

Our consciousness has been synchronized on an unprecedented scale. Consider the fact that nearly every human being has a tablet or a mobile phone, through which they are connected with the worldwide network. World history has been integrated into our material gaze. For the first time in history, humankind has physically shared its global consciousness.[28] Put figuratively, we have become *one eye*. This historical condition (with its global presentism and its image of hybridity) resembles what Imamura described several decades ago—the age of "world cognition" (Imamura 1991b). Imamura writes, "the camera extends its tentacles to every corner of the present earth; its simultaneous vision creates none other than the history of the present" (Imamura 1991c, 267). As he envisaged, the documentary technology of cinema has increasingly permeated all aspects of our everyday lives.

Similarly, it struck Habermas with its collective, immediate, and synchronic quality.

What is the significance of cinema's colonial history for us in the current age of world consciousness? As Fredric Jameson (1998) pointed out some decades ago, cinema is a cultural device for (unconscious) global assimilation, while simultaneously (perhaps deceptively) providing its audiences with a pluralistic worldview. Global cultures today are increasingly hybrid, and this hybridity of globalization (which resembles the biosociological variety in Seo's *Momotarō*) is often seen as a decolonial phenomenon. But what tends to be overlooked in this narrative is that cross-cultural hybridity can conceal its fundamental coloniality. A classical example of this unconscious coloniality is Antonio Gramsci's (2012) concept of cultural hegemony. The complicity of hybridity and coloniality (i.e., hegemony) is ubiquitous both in cultural representations of colonial cinema and in contemporary global cultures. I have investigated documentary film and theory from the colonial period in order to clarify the complicity and would like to extend this investigation to the complicity of our contemporary era.

As against Paul Virilio's (1989) well-known formulation that cinema is war, war is cinema (i.e., war consists "not so much in scoring territorial, economic, and other material victories as in appropriating the immateriality of perceptual fields" [7]), I would like to examine the thesis that cinema is colonial. This thesis consists of a few closely related claims: (1) Cinema's coloniality consists in its presentism (i.e., it consists in the virtuality and immateriality of the synchronic present it creates with its documentary technology); (2) Cinema is the medium whose hybridity often conceals its coloniality; and (3) Just as Virilio regards war and cinema as immaterially constituted, I consider coloniality to be fundamentally an unconscious, rather than a conscious, phenomenon. This thesis—on synchronicity, hybridity, and the unconscious—comes with certain qualifications; but I do consider cinema to be an essential feature of coloniality in our century.

By examining these three claims, thus far I have attempted to think about why moving images have so often been (and perhaps increasingly are) instrumental in expanding cultural colonialism. The key to this question is the documentary (photographic) technology of cinema and its biopolitical consequences. Documentary (often deceptively) provides an instantaneous gaze of world consciousness (Imamura 1991b and 1991c). This synchronic quality of the documentary eye increasingly intensifies our global presentism.

This main thesis of this chapter goes hand in hand with the following supplementary thesis: in its extreme form, a colonial enterprise ends up with the colonization of the future. The empire reigns not only in one's material life, but also in the immateriality of one's future. For some (if not all) of us, the future has become an immaterial territory already colonized through the age of world temporality. If so, are we not entering the stage of neocolonial history *without even knowing it*?

Cinema's Lingua Franca

Postcolonial critique of imperialism sometimes emphasizes the rhetoric of hybridity. But hybridity discourses may conceal (or even intensify) real problems of coloniality. Hybridity is by no means an alternative to cultural imperialism; in some cases, the two terms are synonymous. At the very least, this observation was essential in both Imamura's and Seo's critiques of wartime documentary and the cultural politics underlying it. For example, the animalistic hybridity of *Momotarō*'s climax scene does not foreclose hierarchical distinctions that can be a basis for biopolitical subjugation. On the contrary, it may deftly conceal (and thereby perpetuate) such distinctions.[29]

The binary of the humanistic world—its inclusive and exclusive structure—effectively hides the biopolitical machinery. Thus, the coloniality that underlies this biodiversity is unconscious, rather than explicit. To bring it into a conscious light, one needs to become conscious of the film's documentary illusion (e.g., by Brechtian estrangement). But how should we continue to think about this hybridity *now* if our humanistic gaze becomes increasingly synchronic?

Some two decades ago, even before Habermas in 2001, Fredric Jameson already noted the (potential) synonymity of hybridity and hegemony in the current circumstances of globalization. He contrasts two ways of contextualizing the concept of globalization: communicational and economic. He writes, "If you insist on the cultural contents of this new communicational form, I think you will slowly emerge into a postmodern celebration of difference and differentiation: suddenly all the cultures around the world are placed in tolerant contact with each other in a kind of immense cultural pluralism which it would be very difficult not to welcome. . . . If, on the other hand, your thoughts turn economic . . . what comes to the fore is increasing identity (rather than difference)" (Jameson 1998, 56–57). Jameson regards globalization as a two-sided phenomenon in which cultural pluralism (or hybridity) coexists with the rapid, progressive (economic) assimilation. He regards the latter (economic) aspect as more fundamental. Here I must depart from this Jamesonian picture; like Virilio, I tend to emphasize the immaterial and virtual aspect of this global consciousness over its economic base. But my conclusion is the same as Jameson's: synchronicity ("identity" in the quotation) can often go hand in hand with hybridity ("difference"). In some cases, the latter disguises the former; assimilation is the blind spot of pluralism.

This neocolonial hybridity also resembles certain wartime ethical discourses of imperial Japan. In the 1930s, shortly before Seo's film production, Watsuji Tetsurō ([1937] 1962) wrote a series of texts that examined humanhood as betweenness.[30] His intention was to envision a distinct ethical framework that is not simply based on individualism. Watsuji was probably right in arguing that one should not conceive of ethics *solely* as a problem of individual consciousness. But, despite his moral vision, he apparently fails to see a certain universalism that can accompany betweenness (*aidagara*). Frantz Fanon (2008), for example, uses the term *epidermalization*, rather than *internalization*, phenomena that Watsuji did not fully consider in his ethics. Both terms refer to the (ambivalent and often inevitable) assimilation of the hegemonic values in the mindset of the colonized subject. For Fanon, the assimilation of the hegemonic values takes place at the level of the skin (hence it is called epidermal). In Asian contexts, however, this epidermalization of values has a more complex structure. As discussed previously, because the skin colors (and other racial traits) do not clearly distinguish the "white" from the "black" in Asia (racial visuality is much less conspicuous), one tends to consider the process of the epidermalization less consciously; the phenomenon of coloniality is more Freudian than Fanonian. This imperceptibility of certain differences, which is in fact an underlying condition of Watsuji's concept of betweenness, makes it necessary to investigate the colonial gaze carefully in Asia. But what troubles us now is that this imperceptibility (the Freudian coloniality) is increasingly with us on a global scale.

More specifically, one crucial problem in the present age of world history, presumably an underlying issue for Habermas as well, is the rise of cultural hegemony and a new lingua franca—the problem of what Mizumura Minae calls "the century of English" (Mizumura 2008b).[31] If the system of the last century was characterized by national languages, Mizumura argues, the current century is a return to the previous system, the system of the universal language. But the situation is worse because it is coupled with our unconscious coloniality, created by the worldwide network.

Ever since much earlier than the rise of this universal language, cinema has been far better at cutting across linguistic barriers in an empire's colonial territories. It has been a lingua franca more powerful than any actual language. Moving images have been a vehicle of cultural hegemony in the twentieth century and beyond. Mizumura (2008b) warns that, in the present century, the linguistic and nonlinguistic universality mutually reinforce each other (here her warning is very similar to Jameson's);[32] cinema's coloniality goes side by side with the hegemony of English.[33]

Consider Mizumura's (2008b) attempt to contest this joint coloniality of the present age. In her mind, the issue of coloniality is closely related to the *un*translatability of English. As I wrote earlier in this chapter, the colonial subjects are often unable to see their own subjugation. It is (or can be) difficult for them to see through its real nature. But it is still more difficult to *make* the subjects become aware. Mizumura's book is a rare exception to this rule.

In order to clarify this new historical condition,[34] Mizumura (2008b) refers to her second major novel, *Shishōsetsu from Left to Right* (1995), whose text is a Japanese-English hybrid, with a horizontal (not vertical) textual alignment. But seeing *Shishōsetsu* merely as a hybrid text makes it difficult to realize the underlying coloniality. Hybridity can refer to any kind of mixture: Japanese and English, Japanese and Korean, or Japanese and Polish. Each combination can create a hybrid text. But the hybridity of the *Shishōsetsu* text is special one; as Mizumura (2008a) argues, this particular hybridity (Japanese and English) is untranslatable into English, even though it is translatable to any local language (be it Korean, Polish, or Arabic).[35] Although the hybridity of the text captures readers' conscious attention, the asymmetry between English and all other languages rarely occurs to them.[36]

One should note that, although the rise of cinema predated the system of universality in the current century that Mizumura describes here, this new medium has had the potential of playing a role analogous to that of a universal language for global populations. Moving images do not require translation (or, at least, require less linguistic competence on the audience's side), and they can more easily transcend the linguistic diversity of the colonies. Their function resembles that of the English language in the *Shishōsetsu* text.

In fact, cinema can provide a stronger experience of quasi-universality than any language does.[37] It can reproduce the same unified perspectives for multiple collective audiences (no matter how effective its actual influence has been historically) and therefore can create and recreate a sense of sharing a simultaneous history regardless of their time and space. Many have speculated on this material expediency of cinema and its potential as a colonial apparatus. As Stephen Poland (2016) points out, Imamura foresaw cinema's power to mobilize the masses in the Japanese Empire.

Michael Baskett (2008) showed that Japanese film culture competed with (and eventually replaced) Hollywood in its sphere of influence in the colonies, further evidence of cinema's correlation with the empire's colonial history. Even though, as Poland further notes, in practice there was often interpretative slippage between the Japanese spectator and the spectators in the colonies, the (at least potential) universality of film experience makes it an important locus of a colonial enterprise in the twentieth century and thereafter.

Conclusion

As Imamura would argue, cinema is a hybrid text that often conceals its (inclusive) coloniality. Animals, demons, and humans are presented as hybrid (commensurable) beings, but the untranslatability of *Momotarō* is undeniable.

Just as the image of hybridity hides its underlying coloniality, geopolitical differences disguise the experience of global simultaneity. The fact is that we live in the age of universal, worldwide witnesses. We have become *one eye*. We see world-historical events simultaneously, without any time lag. But this means that in it there is something similar to the system of the universal language synchronizing our gaze. This may be a sign of our perfect coloniality; we are entering a new age of colonialism. If that is the case, how is it possible to think, live, and act otherwise?

The present study has attempted to think about this question through interrogating a historical case of coloniality. Put simply, cinema's coloniality is the unconscious of both cinematic history and the new colonial era of the current century. We have seen an analogous structure of the colonial unconscious in the age of modernism, namely, in wartime film form and theory (of Seo Mitsuyo and Imamura Taihei, respectively). But *our* colonialism has become much stronger and less conscious.

I have argued in this chapter that cinema's coloniality consists in (1) the virtuality (of the present), (2) the hybridity, and (3) the unconscious. Each of these elements deeply characterizes our current century. The (multilayered) geopolitics of colonial temporalities in the past has been fundamentally restructured with globalization in the twenty-first century. That is, the colonial unconscious is no longer observed as temporal differences, for such differences have now lost their historical valence and political force. Does that simply mean that there are no longer colonial temporalities among us or that they have become more deeply concealed (unconscious)? When the future is colonized, the colonized subject becomes an unconscious subject. What Mizumura contested in her controversial essays is this ultimate form of colonization in "the century of English." Jameson alerts us, from an American perspective, about this ultimate colonization (the colonization of the future)[38] when he writes "all history has been moving toward American culture as its apotheosis. But it is rather a matter of whether *we* want that ourselves; because if we can imagine nothing else, then obviously we have nothing to warn other cultures about either" (Jameson 1998, 63, with my emphasis). The historic world event, as Habermas saw it (Borradori 2003), is a symbolic incident that in many ways anticipated our colonial future at the beginning of this century.

Notes

The author would like to extend appreciation for comments and feedback offered by Abé Mark Nornes, Fredric Jameson, Aaron Gerow, Prasenjit Duara, Helen Lee, and Michael Baskett. Previous versions of this paper were presented at Duke Kunshan University on June 9, 2017, and at Yonsei University (Seoul) on June 23, 2017. Unless otherwise specified, all translations from the Japanese in this piece are by the author.

1. Scholars have tended to focus on this multitude (surface) aspect of the film's humanism. For example, observing a threefold structure (Momotarō/animals/demons) in this film narrative, Ueno Toshiya (1991) argues that this threefold scheme represents the imperial hierarchy at multiple levels (116–17). (I owe this point of clarification to Abé Mark Nornes.) Unlike the twofold humanism I present here, Ueno's analysis primarily deals with the manifest differences in the film's biosociology, without considering its inclusive (unconscious) underside.

2. For the two concepts of human beings, *humanitas* and *anthropos*, see the discussion on Nishitani in the introduction to this volume.

3. Watsuji Tetsurō ([1937] 1962) argues in his *Rinrigaku* and other texts that a Japanese term *ningen* (usually translated as "humans") should be distinguished from the Greek term *anthropos*, because the former has two etymological meanings, "humans" and "between humans or between (among) us." The twofold humanism of *Momotarō* resembles the double meanings of *ningen* in Watsuji's hermeneutic writings. That is, humanhood is defined both categorically (as a biospecies) and relationally (e.g., through humanistic communication) in the film.

4. Fredric Jameson (2015) argues that the reduction to the present (i.e., to "the *now*") is the cultural logic of postmodernity and globalization. He calls it "the end of temporality" (105). This aesthetics of "the *now*" (or "synchronic heterogeneity," 119) correlates with the phenomenon of the world synchronicity discussed in the present chapter.

5. In the production processes of the wartime period, a long time gap could occur between locations of production of images and sites of consumption in the order of weeks, months, or even years. For further discussion on this issue, see chapter 1 in this volume. This temporal discrepancy was often a symptom of geopolitical domination. Unlike the internet-based synchronous propagations of images in the current century, the geopolitics of colonial temporalities was differential (rather than simultaneous) in the last century.

6. I partially owe this point and clarification to Walter Mignolo. Mignolo (2017) proposed to distinguish coloniality (as general characteristics of colonialism) from colonialism (as historically specific instances) and to think of the former as the Freudian unconscious underneath what is manifest in the latter. In this chapter, I start with this Freudian framework but give a different meaning to the unconscious; namely, building on this proposal, I further expand the colonial unconscious both in order to clarify the imperceptibility of differences in the colonial gaze of Asia and to undermine the discourse on hybridity in today's globalized society, which tends to conceal real problems of coloniality.

7. This is an antithesis to some existing understandings of colonialism, especially Frantz Fanon's (2008) strict division between the black and white colonial subjectivities. My argument is that the apparent division based on skin colors is merely an instantiation of colonial subjugation,

but it is not the substance of coloniality itself. One should not confuse a cause and an effect. It is coloniality that causes epidermalization, not the other way around.

8. That is, one should not confuse the cause (coloniality) with its effect (historical manifestations of colonialism such as the black-white divide). For example, Fanon oversimplifies the phenomenon of colonialism by focusing on its manifest aspect.

9. In particular, Rachels appears to disregard the generative quality of ethical knowledge (i.e., the fact that our knowledge is fallible in the Peircean sense) in the quoted passage. But it is possible to read his essay as raising precisely this point.

10. As mentioned already, presumably one can more easily contest the biases regularly and routinely discussed among people than the biases of which not many are aware.

11. This is one of my objections to the Fanoninan framework. As discussed previously, the colonial gaze is not always materialized in the way Fanon calls "epidermalization," namely, in the way certain differences capture our conscious attention. Rather, our consciousness of differences is a result (or an aftereffect) of the colonial gaze. Colonialty always escapes our consciousness of it.

12. Nornes (2003) further writes that, in the 1930s, "government participation tipped the balance between support and control in favor of the latter" (48).

13. There was some complex development of documentary methodologies during these several years, especially in *nyūsu eiga* (newsreel films), *henshū eiga* (edited films), and *bunka eiga* (cultural films). For further discussion, see chapter 3 in Nornes (2003). Imamura was responding to this changing situation and the aestheticization of politics during the period.

14. In the present study, I use the term *cinéma vérité* in a broader sense, referring not only to the French *cinéma vérité* but also to the historical legacy of Dziga Vertov and his younger brother Mikhail Kaufman in the 1920s, that is, any styles of documentary filmmaking that interrogate both the truth and the limit of cinematic mimesis, whose origin can be traced back to *Kino-Pravda*. But some historical clarification is in order here. The two lineages that marked a shift in documentary history in the 1960s, the French *cinéma vérité* in Europe and direct cinema in North America, are not identical in their documentary styles. The main difference of their methodologies is that, while the former was interventional, the latter was strictly observational. Those styles and their methodologies were not in place when Imamura was writing his wartime documentary theory. For further discussion of these two documentary movements, see Odagiri (2019).

15. I am referring to Habermas's discussion in Borradori (2003). The use of the term *(global) presentism* is mine.

16. From a historical perspective, it is clear that what underlies Imamura's critique of wartime documentaries and Disney cartoons is his leftist stance. He emphasizes the collective nature of film art (the fact that it is viewed collectively) as compared with the solitary reading of literature, relating this collectivity of film to the commodity fetishism of advanced capitalism ("Tōkī Manga Ron"; Imamura 1991a, 90–91). But what is more important is that his world-historical vision anticipated the biopolitical situation of the present era, and this chapter focuses on this latter aspect of Imamura's criticism.

17. The production of the film *Momotarō* was completed in December 1944, and it was released in April 1945.

18. Shochiku 4K-scanned a 35mm master-positive and internegative that it owned and restored the film in 2K.

19. Although the present study emphasizes the documentary quality of Seo's *Momotarō*, it does not deny other characteristics of animation work of the time, especially the plasmatic aspect of its animal images. In his article on speciesism and neoteny, Thomas Lamarre (2011) calls attention to the plasmaticity of characters in wartime animation. Drawing on Sergei Eisenstein and Ōtsuka Eiji, Lamarre emphasizes plasmaticity as "a move away from representation theory" and explores the materiality of the medium that is "integral to the actual experience and impact of speciesism," the transformation of peoples into nonhuman animal species.

20. For further discussions of the "plasticity" of animation characters' bodies, one should consult Ōtsuka (2003) and Lamarre (2011).

21. As discussed previously, Ueno (1991) interprets the film's threefold biosociological scheme (Momotarō/animals/demons) as representing the multiple levels of the imperial hierarchy. He further argues that the transcendental of the human protagonist is equivalent to what Slavoj Žižek calls "Nation-Thing" (117–19). Despite certain similarities between my interpretation of the film and Ueno's, I disagree with his analysis for various reasons. In particular, whereas I consider the unconscious to be essential for the phenomenon of coloniality, Ueno seems more interested in certain manifest differences in the threefold structure. In other words, he primarily focuses on the surface structure of the film's humanism. This focus on the surface structure is probably related to the fact that he rarely mentions the otherly gaze and animals' lively behaviors. It is also important for me that Ueno misrepresents Kantian transcendental idealism, if not Žižek's Nation-Thing. Because the thing in itself is not an object of our cognition for Kant, one should not simply equate anything empirically observable with the thing in itself. These points, however, fall wide of the present investigation and should be discussed on another occasion.

22. In the animation's climax scene resembling the Ford Motor Factory scene, the officers on the opposing side (supposedly the British) are depicted as *oni* (demons; see fig. 8.3).

23. According to Nornes (2003), the cameraman of *Marē Senki* spontaneously slowed down the running speed of the camera, for the conversation tempo in the real meeting was very slow. Nornes writes, "With the camera running slower, the two men's body movements were accelerated, and the two adversaries were transformed into caricatures" (88). The effect is suggestive (at least for some audiences) of an estrangement resembling Brechtian caricature that was already taking place in the newsreel documentary, but it was made more explicit in the animation caricature of the same scene.

24. Strictly speaking, not every one of us saw this event in New York simultaneously. But the fact that we feel *as if* we saw it right in front of our eyes indicates the peculiar universality and the powerful immediacy of this historical world event, which synchronized global consciousness.

25. I italicize the definitive article *the* in order to emphasize the singular and unified nature of world-historical experiences today and its biopolitical significance. For those who are excluded from *the* world, the unified globalization is nothing but violence.

26. Fredric Jameson also uses the concept of an event in his discussions of the postmodern era (i.e., the age of globalization). Jameson maintains that works of art in the postmodern era are no longer objects but are in fact *events* (Jameson 2015, 110–11). "The installation and its kindred productions are made, not for posteriority, nor even for the permanent collection, but rather for the now, and for a temporality that may be rather different from the old modernist kind" (111).

27. Hardt and Negri distinguish biopower and biopolitics, namely, the power over life and the power of life to resist and determine an alternative production of subjectivity. "Biopolitics as event" is the third definition of biopolitics, as opposed to these two definitions. But, although Hardt and Negri sees biopolitics as event in the creation of new subjectivities, it is not entirely clear how this can be a form of subjectivity.

28. Furthermore, with the historical conjuncture of globalization (global capitalism) and global warming, humankind has inevitably become collectively aware of its deep (species) history, the long historical trajectory that has led to (and will continue for long after) the present environmental crisis. Dipesh Chakrabarty (2012) discusses this correlation of world history and global warming.

29. Thomas Lamarre (2011) makes a similar observation on Tezuka Osamu's multispeciesism. Lamarre writes, "The importance of Tezuka lies in his continuation of the wartime critique of social Darwinism and Western modernity, in conjunction with his adamant discontinuation of the multispecies utopia" (132). According to Lamarre, for Tezuka, "species distinctions are invariably hierarchal distinctions, which only perpetuate segregation, domination, and war" (132).

30. Among many texts by Watsuji, one should consult his *Rinrigaku* ([1937] 1962).

31. The book won the Kobayshi Hideo prize in the following year.

32. Mizumura writes, "The Internet technology has been the last blow to the current situation ... to accomplish this change" [to the century of English] (Mizumura 2008b: 239).

33. Jameson (1998) discusses a similar issue—the coexistence of linguistic and nonlinguistic forms of cultural hegemony in the current age of globalization. He writes, "other languages will never come to equal English in its global function, even if they were systematically tried out" (63) and finds the "formal and also a political" triumph of Hollywood film and North American television programs to be an equally powerful hegemony (Jameson 1998, 62).

34. Critically examining Benedict Anderson's *Imagined Communities*, Mizumura (2008b) distinguishes three kinds of language: local language (*genchigo*), universal language (*fuhen gengo*), and national language (*kokugo*). Prior to the age of national languages, there was a dual structure of local languages and a universal language in each civilization complex. Only a universal language was used to communicate between intellectuals across local regions (mostly in a written format). But in the modern period, the structure changed significantly. National languages were used for intellectual writing in each region (in place of a universal language). A national language resembles the universality of Latin or Greek, but only within boundaries of a region. It functions universally within a nation-state, almost in the same way a universal language operated in the previous era. It was a local practice of quasi-universality. The main issue for Mizumura is that, with the collapse of this previous system (modernity and national languages), we are witnessing the reemergence of the universalist regime.

35. The reason for the untranslatability is clear: the functions of the two languages in the novel are by no means equal. The English text requires no translation for most readers around the globe, but the Japanese has its monolingual limitations. That is, the asymmetrical heterogeneity of this bilingual text testifies to the universality of the English language (which is why the text is untranslatable into English) (Mizumura 2008a; see also Odagiri 2013).

36. This asymmetry is often unnoticeable to language users of the universal language (e.g., native speakers of English) themselves. As Mizumura (2008b: 104–54) writes, users of a universal language often tend to advocate the values of multilingualism or bilingualism. Jameson calls it "blindness at the center," which is, for example, the American "tendency to confuse the universal and the cultural" (Jameson 1998, 59).

37. The coloniality of photographic technology is an important issue for Mizumura's novel too. Mizumura uses photographs in the *Shishōsetsu* text, alongside the two languages (Japanese and English). Just as the untranslatability of the English text attests to its universality, the photographic quality of this book as a whole transcends its linguistic hybridity.

38. Jameson also writes that "Hollywood is not merely a name for a business that makes money." It is, for him, a fundamental (late-capitalist) cultural revolution (Jameson 1998, 63).

Bibliography

Baskett, Michael. 2008. *The Attractive Empire: Transnational Film Culture in Imperial Japan.* Honolulu: University of Hawaii Press.
Borradori, Giovanna. 2003. *Philosophy in a Time of Terror: Dialogues with Jürgen Habermas and Jacques Derrida.* Chicago: University of Chicago Press.
Brecht, Bertolt. 1964. "The Street Scene." In *Brecht on Theatre: The Development of an Aesthetic*, 121–29. Edited and translated by John Willett. New York: Hill and Wang.
Chakrabarty, Dipesh. 2012. "Postcolonial Studies and the Challenge of Climate Change." *New Literary History*, Volume 43, no. 1: 1–18.
Fanon, Frantz. 2008. *Black Skin, White Masks.* New York: Grove Press.
Foucault, Michel. 2008. *The Birth of Biopolitics: Lectures at the Collège de France, 1978–79*. Edited by Michel Senellart. Translated by Graham Burchell. New York: Palgrave Macmillan.
Gramsci, Antonio. 2012. *Selections from Cultural Writings.* Edited by David Forgs and Geoffrey Nowell-Smith; translated by William Boelhower. London: Lawrence and Wishart.
Hardt, Michael, and Antonio Negri 2009. *Commonwealth.* Cambridge, MA: Belknap.

High, Peter B. 2003. *The Imperial Screen: Japanese Film Culture in the Fifteen Years' War, 1931–1945.* Madison: University of Wisconsin Press.

Imamura Taihei. 1991a. *Imamura Taihei Eizō Hyōron* [*Imamura Taihei Image Criticism*]. Vol. 5, *Manga Eiga Ron* [*On Manga Film*]. Tokyo: Yumani.

———. 1991b. "Kiroku Eiga Ron [On Documentary Film]." In *Imamura Taihei Eizō Hyōron*. Vol. 4, *Kiroku Eiga Ron*, 13–29. Tokyo: Yumani.

———. 1991c. "Monogatari Keishiki kara Kiroku Keishiki he" [From Narrative Form to Documentary Form]. In *Imamura Taihei Eizō Hyōron*. Vol. 1, *Eiga Geijutsu no Keishiki* [*Forms of Film Art*], 262–93. Tokyo: Yumani.

———. 1991d. "Tōkī Manga Ron [On Talkie Manga]." In *Imamura Taihei Eizō Hyōron*. Vol. 1, *Eiga Geijutsu no Keishiki*, 87–103. Tokyo: Yumani.

Jameson, Fredric. 1998. "Notes on Globalization as a Philosophical Issue." In *The Cultures of Globalization*, 54–77. Durham, NC: Duke University Press.

———. 2015. "The Aesthetics of Singularity." *New Left Review* 92 (Mar/Apr): 101–32.

Lamarre, Thomas. 2011. "Speciesism, Part III: Neoteny and the Politics of Life." *Mechademia* 6, no. 1: 110–36.

Mignolo, Walter. 2017. Theorizing Colonial Cinemas Workshop, Duke Kunshan University, Kunshan, June 8.

Mizumura Minae. 1995. *Shishōsetsu from Left to Right.* Tokyo: Shinchōsha.

———. 2008a. "Authoring Shishōsetsu from Left to Right." In *The New Historicism and Japanese Literary Studies*. Vol. 4 of *Proceedings of the Midwest Association for Japanese Literary Studies*. Edited by Eiji Sekine. http://minaemizumura.com/Documents/AuthoringAPersonalNovel20080303.pdf. Accessed: April 2, 2009.

———. 2008b. *Nihongo ga Horobiru toki: Eigo no Seiki no Naka de.* Tokyo: Chikuma.

Nishitani, Osamu. 2006. "Anthropos and Humanitas: Two Western Concepts of 'Human Being.'" Translated from the Japanese by Trent Maxey. In *Translation, Biopolitics, Colonial Difference*. 259–73. *Traces: A Multilingual Series of Cultural Theory and Translation*, no. 4, edited by Naoki Sakai and Jon Solomon, Hong Kong: Hong Kong University Press.

Nornes, Abé Mark. 2003. *Japanese Documentary Film: The Meiji Era through Hiroshima.* Minneapolis: University of Minnesota Press.

Odagiri Takushi. 2013. "Subculture and World Literature: On Mizumura Minae's *Shishōsetsu* (1995)." *Japan Forum* 25, no. 2: 233–58.

———. 2019. "Kawase Naomi's Introspective Style: Aesthetic Surfaces of World Cinema." *positions* 27, no. 2 (May): 361–96.

Ōtsuka Eiji. 2003. *Atomu no Meidai Tezuka Osamu to Sengo Manga no Shudai.* Tokyo: Tokuma.

———. 2013. "Bunka Eiga toshite no *Momotarō Umi no Shinpei*." *Mikkī no Shoshiki Sengo Manga no Senjika Kigen*, 241–300. Kadokawa Gurupu.

Poland, Stephen. 2016. "Cinema of Security: Regulating Ethnicity in Manchukuo's Feature Films." Paper presented at the Theorizing Colonial Cinemas Workshop, Duke University, Durham, NC, November 12.

Rachels, James. 1997. "Coping with Prejudice." In *Can Ethics Provide Answers?: And Other Essays in Moral Philosophy*, 199–212. Lanham, MD: Rowman and Littlefield. http://www.jamesrachels.org/.

Seo Mitsuyo. 2016. *Momotarō Umi no Shinpei Kumoto Chūrippu Digital Shūfuku Ban.* Tokyo: Shochiku.

Ueno Toshiya. 1991. "Tasha to Kikai." In *Nichibei Eigasen Pāru Hābā Gojusshūnen*, 92–129. Seikyūsha.

Virilio, Paul. 1989. *War and Cinema: The Logic of Perception.* Translated by Patrick Camiller. London and New York: Verso.

Watsuji Tetsurō. (1937) 1962. *Rinrigaku* [Ethics]. Vols. 10 and 11 of *Watsuji Tetsurō Zenshū*. Tokyo: Iwanami.

TAKUSHI ODAGIRI is Associate Professor of Ethics and Philosophy in the Institute of Liberal Arts and Science and in the School of Social Innovation Studies at Kanazawa University, Japan.

9. A HALLUCINATORY HISTORY OF THE PHILIPPINE-AMERICAN WAR

Khavn's *Balangiga: Howling Wilderness*

José B. Capino

Abstract

The Philippine-American War (1899–1902), a bloody war of conquest that spurred the coming of age of the United States as an overseas empire, has been a recurring subject of narrative films from both countries since the early twentieth century. In Hollywood, the war served as the historical backdrop of numerous pictures, including a 1911 interracial romance featuring Mary Pickford, a 1926 Warner Brothers adventure starring Myrna Loy, and, more recently, the 2010 indie period film *Amigo* by John Sayles. For their part, Philippine filmmakers revisited the war in the decades leading up to and after the end of US colonial rule in 1946. For instance, Lamberto Avellana and Cannes-award-winning director Raymond Red each directed biopics of the "insurgent" leader Macario Sakay half a century apart, in 1939 and 1993, respectively. In 2017 the punk filmmaker Khavn released the first version of his acclaimed feature on the 1901 massacre at the central Philippine town of Balangiga. The event is well remembered in Philippine history but has faded from US memory.

Less than two years into the US campaign in the Philippines, Filipino guerrillas ambushed seventy-eight US soldiers who had occupied their town and forced them into labor. The US army mounted a ruthless campaign of reprisal during which one of its generals ordered his troops to kill all Filipino males above the age of ten and turn two populous provinces into a "howling wilderness." *Balangiga: Howling Wilderness* revisits the incident in a hallucinatory picaresque.

The present chapter discusses the most compelling aspects of Khavn's film and, more broadly, the affordances that experimental cinema offers to the project of a decolonial figuration of history. *Balangiga* uses progressive nationalist historiography as the foundation of its narrative in an attempt to dislodge the historical perspectives instilled by US colonial education and Cold War propaganda. The film also employs the endemic syncretism and polysemy of avant-garde filmmaking to create images that represent the events of 1901 and also evoke other episodes in the history of US empire. The dialectical images in *Balangiga* link episodes across the *longue durée* of US interventionism in the Philippines and elsewhere, potentially enabling a reconsideration of the colonial past and the neocolonial present.

Introduction

In one of the most infamous events of the Philippine-American War, several hundred Filipino guerrillas under the leadership of a small town's chief of police launched a surprise attack at breakfast time on a band of US soldiers. The incident occurred in Balangiga in the central Philippine province of Samar. The assailants included many disgruntled civilians, especially men whom the Americans had detained, forced into uncompensated labor, and virtually starved for weeks on end. To better surprise their foe, some of the Filipino males donned women's clothing and concealed machetes under their skirts. Out for blood, the angry Filipinos slashed, clubbed, and decapitated the US troops for more than twenty minutes, killing more than a third and wounding all but four of the seventy-eight men of the Ninth US infantry's Company C (Couttie 2004, 167). The surprise attack was one of the few truly spectacular successes of the Filipino troops during the war (Linn 1993, 169). Although Filipino troops vastly outnumbered their foreign adversaries, they fared poorly in battle after battle, losing about 20,000 men in contrast to the 4,234 who fell on the US side. Glenn May attributes the lopsided body count to the Filipinos' lack of resources (such as weapons and horses), woefully inadequate training, and the belated decision by their leaders to shift away from conventional warfare to the kinds of guerrilla tactics they had employed to their advantage in Balangiga (May 1983). After the ambush, the Americans destroyed the town, leaving only "the stone walls of the church and a few upright poles" standing (Couttie 2004, 181).

A force of more than four thousand unleashed hell on Balangiga and other places in Samar and nearby Leyte province (Linn 1993, 167). In the first two months of the reprisal, US troops killed 759 guerrillas, destroyed 587 carabaos (water buffaloes), and confiscated 1,662 boats in the area (168–169). Thousands of civilians perished of malnutrition and disease as the US military seized or burned crops and packed townsfolk into small, garrisoned areas that lacked provisions. In what Brian Linn described as one of the "most vicious" (1993, 158) episodes of the war, Brigadier General Jacob H. Smith, commander of the troops in Samar and Leyte, reportedly ordered his soldiers to kill every male Filipino aged ten and over and cause misery to the rest of the villagers (70). At some point in the campaign, US troops seized the three church bells at Balangiga as war booty. Smith's heavy-handed response, including his orders to turn Samar into "a howling wilderness," sparked outrage among anti-imperialists in the United States and eventually forced the military to pull back on their campaign (Linn 2000, 315). The historical episode faded from popular memory in subsequent decades but resurfaced in the 1970s, amid the anti-imperialist fervor over the brutality of the war in Vietnam. In the 1990s the president of the Philippines asked his US counterpart Bill Clinton to return the bells in time for the ex-colony's independence centennial in 1998 (Borrinaga 2003, iii). After impassioned resistance from US veteran groups, the bells remained in place at US military facilities in Wyoming and South Korea. In 2017 another Philippine president—the autocratic Rodrigo Duterte, whose leadership then-President Donald Trump had praised—demanded their return during his state-of-the-nation address. US secretary of defense James Mattis stated in August 2018 that he would grant the request (Ranada 2018). The US government finally returned the bells at the end of that year.

The carnage in Balangiga and the US war in the Philippines are the subjects of the Filipino auteur Khavn's *Balangiga: Howling Wilderness* (2017–18).[1] Khavn (a.k.a. Khavn de la Cruz) has been an accomplished figure in the global avant-garde scene since the late 1990s. After making a handful of shorts on motion picture film, he quickly switched to making feature-length movies in low-cost digital formats (one of the reasons he uses the René Magritte–inspired phrase "This is not a film by Khavn" in his movie credits). His early works include witty, low-budget, and often self-reflexive adaptations of canonical 1970–80s literary material and films, including *Greaseman* (2001), inspired by Anton Juan's monologue about a mentally impaired vagabond, and *Manila in the Fangs of Darkness* (2008), an homage to Lino Brocka's proletarian melodrama *Manila in the Claws of Light* (1975). Equally representative is *The Twelve* (2001), a picaresque shot, as are many of his movies, in Kamias, a lower-middle-class neighborhood in metropolitan Manila known for its upholsterers, secondhand-clothing stores, tire-repair shops, low-end strip clubs, and gay massage parlors. The rambling tale, in which the titular figures evoke the Christian apostles, Snow White's dwarfs, and a grungy mob of Manila street folk, is faintly reminiscent of the satirical and nonsensical wackiness of Euro-American underground cinema (including the Kuchar brothers, early John Waters, and Sidney Peterson), as well as the amateurish skits of Filipino noontime variety shows. In the mid-2010s, Khavn's considerable international following—especially in Europe—enabled him to make narrative picaresques on a much grander scale and with such prestigious collaborators as the Australian director of photography Christopher Doyle and the German auteur Alexander Kluge (*Ruined Heart*, 2014, with Doyle; *Happy Lamento*, 2018, and *Orphea*, 2020, with Kluge).

This later work continues to play with movie genres (such as gangster films) while alternately embracing and deconstructing problematic tropes of cinematic representation. Those tropes include celebrating machismo, making an exotic spectacle of poverty, and fetishizing differently abled or nonconforming bodies (especially persons with dwarfism). In light of his oeuvre, a historical film about the Balangiga massacre was an unexpected choice for Khavn. Mindful of the apparent mismatch between his aesthetics and the ethical challenges posed by the film's subject, Khavn struck a more serious tone than in his other work and, as he put it, employed "the simplest narrative I have ever told on film" (Franco and Dimaculangan 2018). Although exceptional in its instantiation of a historical film, *Balangiga* follows a long line of US and Filipino narrative movies about the colonial war. I shall briefly recount that history in the following section to supply the context for the filmmaker's intervention.

Documentaries and Melodramas of Empire

Several US filmmaking concerns, including the Thomas Edison Motion Picture Manufacturing Company (Edison) and the American Mutoscope and Biograph (Biograph), produced movies about the Philippine-American War throughout the first few years of the conflict, which erupted in February 1899. Tensions had long been running high after the United States disavowed its de facto alliance with the leaders of the Filipino anticolonial revolution against Spain and proceeded to annex the Philippines. Edison's film outfit re-created newsworthy battles, using African American performers as stand-ins for Philippine soldiers. Biograph, for its part, released actuality films featuring the sites and methods of the Philippine campaign, including movies that compared US gunboats to the shabby canoelike vessels that the filmmakers mockingly called Philippine revolutionary leader Aguinaldo's navy. The early films not only exploited the US public's interest in the war but also boosted public support for the occupation of the archipelago. They stoked patriotic feelings with images of Americans outclassing and roundly vanquishing the enemy. Popular and lucrative, the movies of the conflict also gave a shot in the arm to the ailing US film industry, which had already lost its novelty and experienced a steep decline in viewership in just a half-decade of its existence (Rabinovitz 1998).

The war officially ended in 1902 for the United States, but narrative films helped revive public interest in the event during the 1910s and 1920s. Prominent filmmakers, such as Francis Ford and Roy Del Ruth churned out romances and action-packed thrillers set during the long-concluded war. The films, including *The Head Hunters* (1913) and the feature-length version of *Across the Pacific* (1926), portrayed the Philippine populace as a mix of bloodthirsty savages and lecherous mixed-race aristocrats, each one a threat to the virtues of US virgins, the integrity of the white colonial family, the health of imperial business concerns, and US influence and prestige in the East. Such films not coincidentally appeared in the context of extended public debates about the future of the US colonial enterprise in the Philippines. For instance, *The Head Hunters*, which shows a young US soldier rescuing his girlfriend and her father from one of Aguinaldo's military officers, was released a year after William A. Jones, in March 1912, filed the first of several bills in the US Congress calling for Philippine independence (Chu 1982). After the Great Depression, and amid nativist protests against the importation of cheap Filipino goods and labor, the United States saw fit to unload its colony within a decade, setting the date for July 4, 1946.

In the late 1950s, Filipino filmmakers began to revisit the war in a few dozen narrative films aimed at both local and foreign audiences. Most of those filmmakers used the wartime setting to reflect on past and present forms of Filipino nationalism and US imperialism. For example, Eddie Romero made two contrasting features about the war: *The Day of the Trumpet*, also called *Cavalry Command* (1958), a low-budget action film that ends rather laughably with Filipino soldiers and civilians suddenly befriending US troops after witnessing a demonstration of their benevolence; and *Ganito Kami Noon.... Paano Kayo Ngayon?* (This was how we were then.... How are you now?, 1976), a visually sumptuous treatise on Filipino cultural identity set in the transition from Spanish colonialism to the US occupation of the islands.

Raymond Red, a leading figure of the Philippine avant-garde, set his first theatrical feature during the same historical moment. *Sakay* (1993) centers on the eponymous revolutionary figure Macario Sakay, a former theater actor who battled two colonial powers (i.e., Spain and the United States) throughout the northern Philippines. His campaign persisted beyond 1902, belying the US claim that it had contained the Philippine "insurgency" that year rather than around 1906. The timing of Red's film was in itself a nationalistic statement about recent history: it was made two years after the US lease on Philippine military bases was canceled in 1991. Save for a handful of scenes staged and filmed in the style of expressionist theater—mostly brief shots of guerrillas striking martial poses, dancing, and performing rituals—*Sakay* offers a realistic dramatization of historical events and a marked a departure from his experimental aesthetics. In the final decades of the Cold War, filmmakers from the West mainly dealt with the Philippine-American War in documentaries, such as Peter Davis's *This Bloody, Blundering Business* (1975). The latter is a compilation film that, in its satirical treatment of US military interventionism and jingoism in US popular culture, implicitly compares the Philippine campaign to the then-ongoing imbroglio in Vietnam and its coverage in the media.

A much smaller number of movies about the Philippine-American War have emerged since the 2000s, mostly independent productions by Filipinos, such as Sari Lluch Dalena's experimental documentary *Memories of a Forgotten War* (2001). John Sayles's *Amigo* (2006) is a notable exception in its foreign authorship. His film, released in conjunction with a historical novel about the war, centers on a town official who tries to appease two warring foreign powers and protect his constituents from their violent conflict. Apart from remembering the war to US popular memory, Sayles's film implicitly deals with the fate of vulnerable civilians and communities in distant lands whose dwellings and lives were being ruined by the so-called Global War on Terror led by the United States. Jerrold Tarog's *Heneral Luna* (2015) stands out among Filipino-made films about the war for its impressive box-office success. Its earnings of 240 million Philippine pesos in domestic release and more than $200,000 in the United States (Kuipers 2015) were unprecedented amounts for a Filipino historical film (San Diego 2015). Tarog's biopic of a devoted but cantankerous military leader who was assassinated by his compatriots drew sharp rebuke not for its historiography of the war but for an unexpected and unintended reason, namely, glorifying autocratic leaders. Some critics argued—much to the director's chagrin—that the film unexpectedly helped the strongman Rodrigo Duterte get elected to the Philippine presidency (Claudio 2018). *Heneral Luna* also demonstrates other cultural uses for cinematic recollections of the Philippine-American War besides fueling militant critiques of US imperialism. Unlike *Amigo* and other films about the war, Tarog's movie does not emphasize the brutality of the US military campaign, focusing instead on violent infighting among Filipinos. The film suggests that such conflicts, driven by self-interest and willful ignorance, have bedeviled Filipino nationhood from the start and could lead to its undoing.

No fraught episode in Filipino-US relations appears to have triggered the making of *Balangiga*, nor did one unfold amid its December 2017 festival run; but, in both countries, hapless civilians saw their lives imperiled by violence and prejudice. The violence was incited by newly ascendant strongman leaders. Rodrigo Duterte had been prosecuting a ruthless war on drugs that claimed the lives of thousands of adults, including children who were summarily executed by the military and law-enforcement agents. His US counterpart, Donald Trump, demonized non-Caucasian immigrants and either blocked or mistreated refugees fleeing forms of violence that often implicate the United States. Trump also promised a strong military and an aggressively self-centered foreign diplomacy, at some point reviving fears of a nuclear holocaust by quarreling with North Korea and Iran. The spell of violence in both countries may not have directly influenced Khavn's film, but it could have easily resonated with the cinematic reimagining of the brutal war that heralded the US "coming of age" (Jacobson 2001) as an overseas colonial enterprise.

Dialectical Images

In one of his most famous essays, Walter Benjamin (2003a) describes moments of heightened historical consciousness as when an experience or an object makes us sharply aware of uncanny similarities between something occurring in the present and an event from the distant or recent past. On those occasions, we may also become cognizant of the telling disparities between the two episodes. Most important, we might come to appreciate the urgency of sustaining desirable patterns, disrupting an alarming changelessness in society, or radically shifting course to prevent other catastrophes. Benjamin warns us that such moments of lucidity are all too rare and fleeting. He writes, "The true image of the past flits by. The past can be seized only as an image that flashes up at the moment of its recognizability and is never seen again" (390). Those episodes of recognizability occur unexpectedly "in a moment of danger" (391) or what he also calls a "state of emergency" (393). For Benjamin, the struggle against Hitler's fascism was the intolerable state of emergency that should have roused political consciousness and drove the public to action.

Elsewhere in his writing, Benjamin (2003b) uses the term "dialectical image" (403) to name such occasions of recognition and lucidity about the past and its relation to the present. As Eduardo Cadava (1998) notes, Benjamin deliberately uses metaphors from photography (such as flash and image) to characterize arresting moments of recognizability as well as to espouse an "imagistic" conception of "the relationship between a past and a present" (28). The term *dialectical images* did not originally refer to actual pictures but rather to an experience of historical consciousness. That said, I shall occasionally conflate the concept and the objects that illustrate it for the sake of brevity and because unique images (such as Paul Klee's print *Angelus Novus*) famously inspired Benjamin's reflections on history.

Jeffrey Skoller (2005) has written insightfully about the potential of avant-garde films to engender the dialectical recognizability of the past-in-the-present and the present-in-the-past that Benjamin illumines. Skoller cites as examples movies that use footage of historically significant places filmed in the present day to quietly evoke the traumatic past. He also points to experimental compilation films that rework archival footage "in ways that cause them to open onto the present and vice-versa" (xvii). He adds that avant-garde movies can reorient our imaginings of the past by visualizing history in ways that resist the simplistic tendencies of conventional narratives. Whereas mainstream historical films tend to invest in what he calls the "spectacularization" and "literalization of the past" through realistic dramatizations, avant-garde films alternatively deploy "cinematic strategies to consider elements of the past that are unseen, unspeakable, ephemeral, and defy representations not necessarily verifiable through normal empirical means" (xv). Put differently, experimental films can, among other things, not just change the way history is represented but also "signal the aspects of historical knowledge that are occluded, incomplete, and intuited" (xv). He goes on to observe that experimental pictures can offer more nuanced interpretations of the past than conventional historical films by dispensing with the linear storytelling and the rigid cause-and-effect plotting of mainstream narrative features.

Khavn's treatment of the Balangiga massacre uses the historical incident only as a point of departure. The film begins long after the ambush of the US soldiers and amid the campaign to satisfy General Smith's unconscionable directive. The massacre is not depicted, even in flashback. Instead, we find an older man named Apoy Buroy (Pio del Rio) and his grandson, an eight-year-old named Kulas (Justine Samson), preparing to leave Balangiga for a faraway town named Quinapudan while the US reprisal was occurring. We learn that the man's son (and the boy's father) was a guerrilla who has just been killed by the American troops after he took down three of their soldiers. Buroy reassures the distraught child that his mother, who is ostensibly in another town called Biringan, will meet them at their ultimate destination. The two evacuees make the long journey on foot while riding either on a carabao or on a cart pulled by the animal. Encounters with various people break the monotony of travel, but the grandfather deliberately prolongs the slog across the countryside for reasons that will be revealed late in the narrative.

Unlike other films about the war, Khavn's movie counterintuitively eschews the dramatization of military conflicts and political intrigue that characterize both the historiography of the Philippine-American War and the films on the subject. *Balangiga* approaches its historical subject not through dramatic and realistic re-creations of the past but a syncretic mix of allegorical skits, performance art, music and dance, and other cinematic practices characteristic of the avant-garde.

The decision not to represent actual historical figures and incidents nor to film at historical sites are but two indications of the filmmaker's unconventional view of the means and ends of historical representation. *Balangiga* does not espouse what Cadava calls the "'correspondence theory of historical truth'—in which an image corresponds to an historical truth that is the target" (Cadava 1998, 84–85). The film does not equate historical insight with the accuracy of a historical film's simulation of the past. The film's approach does not, however, amount to an unethical elision of history. *Balangiga* engenders an innovative and powerful reckoning with the past precisely by eschewing straightforward re-creations of historical incidents. The film's circuitous and at times uneventful narrative creates ample opportunities for the filmmaker to generate dialectical images of the Philippine-American War through unconventional methods. On several occasions, the film conjures nightmarish premonitions of events that would unfold later in the film, many of which appear to represent Kulas's consciousness. The child's propensity for experiencing traumatic visions motivates the film's oneiricism, but the flamboyant use of surrealist imagery and other devices associated with avant-garde cinema also signal the director's commitment to experimentation.

THE BROWN MAN'S BURDEN

Instead of the sprawling, action-packed, multicharacter plots common to historical films, Khavn loosely structures *Balangiga*, like many of his movies, as a picaresque. The filmmaker depicts the protagonists' journey to a far-distant safe haven through a window-boxed (that is, square) frame that initially evokes the proportions and colors of old postcards but progressively comes to resemble news photographs of wartime violence and death.

The grandfather and boy's journey is decidedly allegorical, and the allegory has many facets. The journey involves three generations of Filipinos: that of Buroy, that of Kulas, and that of Kulas's late father, who appears as a specter and whose fate the other characters discuss at various points in the film. Each generation has carried or continues to bear the burden of surviving Western colonialism. Significantly, the boy's name is Kulas, a name associated with the Filipino everyman and also with the young protagonist of Romero's *This Was How We Were Then*. The fate of patrilineal succession in Kulas's family (and, by extension, among their compatriots) hinges squarely on the child's survival. His untimely demise would put an end to the family's history and, by extension, threaten the survival of the Filipino race.

Early in their journey, Kulas and his grandfather adopt a recently orphaned toddler whom they find alone in a village that had been set ablaze by US soldiers. Kulas names the child Bola (Ball) after the toddler takes a liking to an improvised toy that Kulas assembles out of palm fronds. The child manages to repeat the word for the toy, and the name sticks. Kulas's naming of the younger child after an inanimate object is both an innocent gesture and a reflection of the possibility that he already sees himself and other subalterns like him as bereft of human value, a victim of what Aimé Césaire calls the "thingification" (Césaire 2000, 42) of the native by colonial powers. Kulas's decision to take on the orphan—and another mouth to feed—decreases the already slim odds of their party's survival. The grandfather reassures him, however, that they must do what is right and persevere against all the odds. The toddler's addition to the party is not only an act of solidarity among Filipinos but something of a desperate attempt by the grandfather and Kulas to reconstitute their decimated family. The film thus presents Kulas's family as a stand-in for larger collectives, including their fellow Samareños, other subalterns, and their nation. The animal in the traveling party also comes across as an allegorical figure. The carabao is a native beast of burden that US colonialists historically conflated with Filipinos and the land. Kulas anthropomorphizes their carabao, naming it Melchora, which is the name of a Filipina heroine in the Philippine revolution against colonial Spain. A section of the animal's coat is dusted with blue, red, and yellow powder—colors that correspond to those of the Philippine flag. In short, Kulas's small traveling party is a metonym of the Filipino race.

The group's quest for refuge and survival takes place in a wide range of landscapes: dense forests, stony rivers and, toward the end of the film, a desertlike environment. The latter's endless stretch of sandy gray terrain is an unrealistic depiction of Samar. Indeed, those familiar with recent Philippine history will find the setting reminiscent instead of the ashen landscape of the northern Philippines after the volcanic eruptions of the early-1990s. Indeed, *Balangiga* was filmed on location in Zambales instead of in the central Philippines, where the narrative is set (San Diego 2017). Before and after reaching this arid place, Kulas and his party pass through several nearly desolate villages, some of them still littered with corpses. The villages, which all look alike, are rendered in minimalist and abstract fashion: some of the dwellings lack walls, are only partially roofed, or are little more than bamboo posts and strips nailed together in the shape of huts. The environments that Kulas and his party travel evoke not just the "howling wilderness" Smith and his men created in Samar but also the war-torn Philippine archipelago of the 1900s and the many other places ravaged by the US empire since then.

The allegorical narrative of the multigenerational group's quest for refuge in a treacherous landscape evokes the genocidal effect of the US military's campaign in the Philippines. Scholars estimate Filipino civilian deaths during that period at between two hundred thousand (Welch 1974) and seven hundred thousand (Anderson 2006, 14), with the higher estimate accounting for lives lost from epidemics such as cholera, the plague, and smallpox. The latter figure—if correct—represents a staggering one-tenth of the population at that time. As I shall demonstrate later, there is more to the film's allegory than this one message. For instance, Khavn's decision to focus on children and animals is a statement in itself: it seems to imply that, like the film's narrative, our understanding of the past is similar to a child's fable, partially fictive and largely overdetermined by the lessons we wish to derive for the present.

Figuring the Paths of Resistance

On a couple of occasions, *Balangiga* obliquely represents episodes from the histories of overlapping colonial regimes in the Philippines through spiels of performance art in which prominent artists channel historical figures. In one instance, Kulas and his party happen on a troubadour who seems both mystical and deranged. He is identified in the end credits as Banduria Bandolero, after the *banduria* or banjolike instrument he carries. The troubadour plays discordant tunes while letting out a series of primal screams. With the help of choppy editing and crude camera tricks, Banduria strikes various evocative poses in the blink of an eye. At some point, the corpse of a dead child materializes in front of him and then disappears. The troubadour's dark glasses suggest that he is blind and thus a Homeric figure. The role suits the performer, the famous poet and radio and television personality Lourd de Veyra. His performance foreshadows the demise of the film's young protagonists, mourns the many casualties of a senseless war, and perhaps even signals the insanity brought about by his reckoning of trauma and loss.

Kulas's party has a similar encounter with a ranting, manic figure dressed in a friar's habit (fig. 9.1). The accomplished visual artist, cartoonist, and filmmaker Roxlee (Roque Federizon Lee) plays this eccentric character, named Father Puray. From an improvised pulpit painted with religious iconography in the garishly colorful and simplistic art naïf style, the monk spouts blasphemies and obscenities about Christ and other religious figures. He also appears to masturbate under his robe while invoking the Virgin Mary. Despite what his name might suggest, he is likely not a priest. His disheveled appearance

Figure 9.1. The brief spiel featuring Father Puray (Roxlee) telegraphs the history of millenarian involvement in Filipino anticolonial resistance. (Khavn, *Balangiga: Howling Wilderness*, 2017, screen shot). Courtesy of Khavn.

and the content of his ramblings indicate that he might be a member of the various millenarian movements that worked alongside revolutionaries in subverting the Spanish colonial order and resisting the US occupation of the Philippines. One such sect, called Dios Dios, joined the Filipino troops after the Balangiga incident (Linn 2000, 176).

Although the Filipino elites denigrated the mostly peasant and working-class millenarians for their religious fanaticism and recklessness, they were fiercely committed to the struggle against foreign invaders. Some of these groups forged visions of solidarity, community, and social equality that incited uprisings and offered alternative concepts of Filipino comradeship and nationalism.

Borrowing a term from literary criticism, Skoller illuminates the capacity of avant-garde films to renew the viewer's understanding of the past by "sideshadowing" well-known historical events instead of re-creating them directly. "To sideshadow," he writes, "is to look at what did not happen, as well as what did, what might have happened but didn't, and also what else happened" (Skoller 2005, xxxix). In Khavn's film, the sequences featuring the minstrel and the millenarian "sideshadow" the Balangiga massacre and the famous battles of the Philippine-American War.

First, Kulas and his party's encounters with the millenarian, the troubadour, and several other distressed civilians represent an attempt to center the film's historical narrative on marginal figures rather than on elites and political leaders. The focus on subalterns draws inspiration from efforts by progressive historians to tell Philippine "history from below"—that is, not only to write but to create counternarratives of the past by tracking events, figures, experiences, and texts treated as peripheral in preeminent historical narratives (Ileto 1997). In *Balangiga*, the brief, impressionistic depictions of these subalterns do not take away from their significance, for the film gives no other historical experiences more fulsome treatment, nor are any major historical figures even represented in the film.

Second, the film represents the narratives of these peripheral figures in brief but memorable episodes. The density and brevity of these representations bring to mind Rosenstone's (1995) gloss on the use of "condensation" in the cinematic narration of history. He uses the term as a shorthand for the use of "'fiction' and convention" to "symbolize, condense, or summarize larger amounts of data" than what historical movies can typically represent (70). Khavn's figuration of the minstrel and the millenarian not only condenses hundreds of individuals into two subaltern figures but also telegraphs the nature and significance of the figures' historical roles in momentary gestures, poses, and speech acts rather than in conventionally drawn-out dramatic scenarios. Such condensations invite the viewer to engage more actively in interpreting the film's images and in parsing the historical knowledge that the episodes convey. Viewers familiar with the history of subalterns during the war are called on to draw on that knowledge and to think of how the historical narrative is transmuted and condensed into passing episodes on-screen. Viewers who do not yet possess that knowledge are implicitly prompted to learn more about the war's strange but intriguing players. For the latter viewers, the obtuseness of the episodes might cause annoyance or apathy, but that is a risk that Khavn's films (and other avant-garde treatments of history) take.

The Ugly American

One of the most surprising features of *Balangiga* is its distillation of several years of the Philippine-American War into a couple of episodes featuring a lone US soldier (played by Daniel Palisa) and just a few Filipino civilians, including Kulas and his traveling companions. The first of those episodes is a chamber drama between the soldier and the two Filipino children. After the death of Kulas's grandfather, the eight-year-old assumes the responsibility for leading the journey and caring for the toddler and the carabao. At some point in their travels, Kulas and his party encounter the bedraggled soldier, possibly a survivor of the massacre or a deserter. In a series of brief scenes, the soldier torments the children. He demands a share of their meager provisions and commands Kulas to dance for his amusement. He lifts and—gasp!—shakes the toddler. At some point, he suddenly turns hostile and shoots the carabao. He then points the rifle at Kulas and orders him to butcher the animal. The child does his bidding with great distress, even helping the American cook the meat. But Kulas also engages in small acts of resistance, refusing to partake of the animal and swatting the soldier's hand when he tries to feed the meat to the toddler. After the meal, the soldier ties the children's hands to prevent them from escaping.

The film registers Kulas's and Bola's trauma in several hallucinatory shots. We see images of Kulas eviscerating the animal and then momentarily cowering inside the emptied cavity. In those shots, the animal's entrails are positioned in front of the carcass, literally foregrounding the war's obscene carnage. The film then connects the carabao's death to Kulas's anxieties about his mother's fate. He has a dreamlike vision of his mother in repose and floating on thin air inside a burning shack. Kulas gets over these frightful experiences and visions quickly. He then mounts an uprising, which occurs after the American unties his and Bola's hands. The child picks up his grandfather's scythe and takes a swing at the soldier's legs. Without missing a beat, he seizes the soldier's rifle and shoots him in the shoulder. (See fig. 9.2.) The American retreats. He is not seen again until the film's conclusion. In that second and final appearance, a mob of angry Filipinos pursues and lynches him. From a distance, Kulas and Bola coolly bear witness to his troubles.

The quarrels between the US soldier and the Filipino children are not only allegorical dramatizations of the war but of Filipino-American relations more broadly. The figuration of the natives as children recalls the rhetoric of US imperialists who condescendingly infantilized Filipinos. For example, the US secretary of the interior of the Philippines Dean C. Worcester, who liked to call himself the "great white father" of the indigenous peoples, characterized Filipino nationalists as disobedient children when they were campaigning for independence from the United States. He wrote, "In other words, having brought up a child who is at present badly spoiled, we are to say to the family of nations: 'Here is a boy who must be allowed to join you. We have found that we are unfit to control him, but we hope that he will be good. You must spank him unless you want to fight us'" (Worcester 1914, 961).

Balangiga subverts this imperialistic cliché by having the US soldier routed by a child. Kulas's uprising and the fury of the civilian lynch mob

Figure 9.2. Eight-year-old Kulas (Justine Samson) outwits the American soldier (Daniel Palisa) who bullied and detained him. (Khavn, *Balangiga: Howling Wilderness*, 2017, screen shot). Courtesy of Khavn.

conjure up unexpected visions of native resistance. The US soldier's defeat by untrained combatants indirectly figures not just the ambush at Balangiga but also other successful campaigns against foreign occupying forces. It would be simplistic to regard the fantasy scenario of the once-docile Filipinos trouncing the mighty US imperialist—which, I have argued elsewhere, are quite common in Philippine postcolonial cinema—as a historical lie (Capino 2010). The film's images of victory not only memorialize hard-won battles, they dramatize the sense of hope that has inspired acts of anticolonial resistance in the past and will continue to engender them in the future.

The Intimate and Ubiquitous Enemy

Although *Balangiga* features only one US character, it has more than one figure of US imperialism. In line with the film's creative treatment of history, the second US figure assumes an entirely unexpected form. Early in the film, after Kulas and his grandfather decide to take Bola on their journey, the eight-year-old happens on a mysterious bird that flies past and over him and then settles on the branch of a tree, where it morphs into a birdlike mixed-media sculpture. The film does not name the creature, but the screenplay

Figure 9.3. The mysterious Biringan bird—represented by a found-object sculpture made of American and Filipino components, including a contemporary dartboard—hexes a native toddler and evokes the malevolence of US imperialism. (Khavn, *Balangiga: Howling Wilderness*, 2017, screen shot). Courtesy of Khavn.

labels it the Biringan bird (fig. 9.3), after the place where Kulas's mother has supposedly taken refuge (Khavn and Villamor n.d.).

The creature appears to the children on a few more occasions, mystifying and either upsetting or harming them. Bola is taken ill after one of those apparitions: he develops a rash, his health quickly deteriorates, and he dies. A senior woman whom they meet late on their journey describes the bird that hexed him as a kind of *engkanto* or malevolent spirit.

The woman's designation of *engkanto* associates the bird with Filipino lore, and indeed several mystical birds function as Philippine cultural icons if not national symbols, for example, the Adarna bird and the sarimanok, both of which sport colorful plumage similar to the avian sculpture in the film. The former—which the screenplay compares to the Biringan bird—is known to cause harm, turning humans entranced by its melodious sounds into stone, as Medusa's victims are (Khavn, Gracio, and Villamor n.d., 16). That said, the Adarna bird is known to do favors for virtuous persons. According to legend, it cured an ailing king and ensured that the throne was assumed by a virtuous successor. The Biringan bird, on the other hand, does not cast any benevolent spells during the film.

The forms in which the Biringan bird appears on-screen reinforce its liminal identity between Filipino and American. The sculpture's appearance is minimalist, primitivist, and ramshackle—qualities that can be associated with Philippine culture and with a strain of twentieth-century American art as well. During its first apparition, the creature looks like a cross between a modernist art-naïf sculpture and the contents of a Manila dumpster after the Yuletide holidays. The bird's head is a goat's skull with a mane of gold tinsel and a beak of rolled gold-colored gift-wrapping paper. It has a conical straw hat for a neck and shoulders, and the rest of its body is an egg-shaped wire cage decorated with chicken feathers and American-style Christmas tree ornaments. On its second appearance, the creature no longer sports Christmas décor. Its head is a bare goat's skull with a rosary hanging from its jaw. Its shoulders are made of coconut shells and vegetables and root crops function as its limbs. It still bears embellishments associated with US culture, however, including a contemporary dartboard, a vintage revolver, and a star-shaped sheriff's badge (see fig. 9.3). In both its apparitions, stop-motion animation breathes life into the sculpture. The bird's crude appearance and choppy movement evoke both the primitive magic of indigenous peoples and the basic mechanics of the Western technology of filmmaking.

The sounds heard during the bird's apparitions complicate rather than pin down its identity. A racist and jingoistic ditty sung by US soldiers during the war plays on the film's soundtrack during the creature's second appearance. Several disembodied male voices sing lyrics calling Filipino guerrillas cross-eyed and *ladrones* [agrarian brigands] and enjoining Americans to "civilize 'em with a Krag [rifle]." On another occasion, the creature reads excerpts from the text of President William McKinley's "Benevolent Assimilation Proclamation," the document justifying the US annexation of the Philippines, ostensibly to benefit Filipinos.

Hayden White coined the term *historiophoty* to denote the figuration of history through images, including motion pictures (White 1988, 1193). Some of the advantages of conveying historical discourse largely if not exclusively through pictures rather than words are the richness of their details, the strength of their emotional impact, the complexity of understandings they engender, and the endemic instability and ambiguity of their significance. To be sure, the very same things may also be considered their impeachable weaknesses, especially if one were following the standards and assumptions of traditional academic historiography. In *Balangiga*'s idiosyncratic historiophoty of the Philippine-American War, the mystical Biringan bird is a densely allegorical image of the past that invites creative interpretation. For example, one might read the creature as a figuration of US imperialism. After all, the creature is menacingly ubiquitous and often perceived to be omniscient, like the US spy machine that, not surprisingly, largely came together during the Philippine-American War (McCoy 2009).

Like the enchanted bird, US empire brings various kinds of curses on Filipinos: violent wars, equally murderous exploitation, the theft of national patrimony, and incursions into national sovereignty, among many others. The creature's appearance as a cross between American and Filipino aesthetics supports such an interpretation, for empires thrive not just by imposing their culture on the colonized but by appropriating elements of indigenous culture when needful. If the bird registers to some viewers as an odd variant of the American eagle while others see it—or see it doubly—as an evil manifestation of the Adarna bird, then that ambiguity makes for a unique inscription of US imperialism in the Philippines.

Dialectical Images of US Interventionism

Some of the most polyvalent and emotionally powerful figurations of US imperialism dwell at the very margins of Kulas's story. Twice Kulas and company pass by corpses tied to trees or wooden posts. The narrative does not shed light on the circumstances of their death or hint at the crime's perpetrators. This paucity of narrative information, in addition to the configuration of the ghastly images, invites multiple interpretations. Apart from representing the thousands of civilian deaths during the Philippine-American War, the corpses on the trees evince similar macabre displays at other historical moments. For example, US and Philippine agents involved in anticommunist campaigns in the Philippines during the 1950s famously suspended corpses from trees to spook guerrillas and civilians in restive areas. The Filipino and US counterrevolutionary agents captured the Filipino fighters, executed them, and manipulated the corpses to make it look as if they had been attacked by the mythical blood-and-viscera-sucking *aswang*. Edward Lansdale (1991), the shady CIA operative, described the stunt as follows: "They [the Filipino agents] punctured his [the victim's] neck with two holes, vampire-fashion, held the body up by the heels, drained it of blood, and put the corpse back on the trail" (72). The gruesome spectacle of the desecrated bodies achieved its intended effect. Lansdale's stunt is a well-known tale of clandestine US anticommunist propaganda and military interventionism in the Philippines. The images of the corpses invite another interpretation as well. They recall the Vietnam War, albeit not by way of reality but through a memorable bit of

Figure 9.4. The tableau of desecrated corpses evokes three historic moments in US empire: the Philippine-American War, the war in Vietnam (by way of a similarly composed scene in Coppola's *Apocalypse Now*) and the CIA's antirevolutionary propaganda stunts in the Philippines during the 1950s. (Khavn, *Balangiga: Howling Wilderness*, 2017, screen shot). Courtesy of Khavn.

Francis Ford Coppola's *Apocalypse Now* (American Zoetrope, 1979). A scene from that film shows the protagonists approaching the antagonist's lair by boat and finding decaying bodies suspended from the branches of soaring trees. (See fig. 9.4.)

The villain, a deranged US military officer named Colonel Kurtz (played by Marlon Brando), has been killing suspected communist guerrillas and sympathizers—and the corpses are presumably those of his victims. The suspended cadavers in *Apocalypse Now* and Khavn's film are especially resonant with the Philippine experience—not only because they recall Lansdale's scheme but also because Coppola filmed his movie in that country instead of in Vietnam. Sadly as well, the practice of displaying mangled bodies in anti-insurgency campaigns returned to the Philippines in the late 1980s, in some cases in operations performed by Filipino militia but secretly underwritten by US aid (Wurfel 1988). Such campaigns liberally involved the use of extrajudicial killings—ironically called "salvaging" operations—to suppress political dissidents or opponents. The killers did not hang their victims from trees but often put them on public display to terrify onlookers.

The ability of the images such as those in figure 9.4 to trigger a recollection of temporally distant historical events strongly resonates with Benjamin's (2003a) concept of the dialectical image. More than just suggesting superficial comparisons between historical moments, the dialectical images in Khavn's film may engender a heightened awareness of underlying historical continuities and ruptures, as well as some notion of the still-crucial stakes behind either changelessness or radical disruptions. The inclusion of fictional events in the unwieldy flood of historical associations and resonances is not necessarily problematic. Collective delusions and fantasies, social ideologies and imaginaries, popular memories, and other virtual things profoundly shape actual events and the ways history and public memory record them besides.

Interspersed throughout Khavn's film are other dialectical images that alternately evoke the Philippine-American War and other overseas military interventions led by the United States. One scene dramatizes a premonition of Kulas's in which he finds himself and other children buried up to their necks in sand. In the scene, his mother, distraught or driven insane by trauma, frantically digs up more graves. The scene foreshadows the loss of innocent lives from warfare, sickness, and starvation that occur later in Kulas's journey. At the same time, the scene—minus the Filipina mother—recalls a subset of widely circulated photographs of the Philippine-American War, particularly those that depict US soldiers posing alongside heaping piles of Filipino skulls and bones. Those pictures, which often show the soldiers callously flashing big smiles while standing beside or practically leaning on human remains, index the war's enormous death toll and the US disregard for the lives of civilians in enemy territory. The display of severed heads and other human remains recurs in various US overseas wars, famously prompting censure by the US government during World War II.

Scenes featuring burning fires in *Balangiga* also create dialectical images that represent the Philippine-American War and open up to other episodes of violence instigated by US imperialism. Kulas and his traveling party pass through settlements where conflagrations—likely started by US soldiers—consume dwellings or personal possessions. Such images implicitly represent the fulfillment of Smith's order to burn villages to the ground and make the settlements uninhabitable. The images also recall the similar torching of straw huts and peasant dwellings during the Vietnam War. News footage and documentaries of that war—including *Hearts and Minds* (Peter Davis, 1974)—memorably showed Vietnamese civilians looking on helplessly as US soldiers set fire to their homes.

Balangiga uses fire images less realistically in scenes of the protagonists' demise. In those scenes, Khavn avoids prosaic depictions of the death of Filipino characters, even when caused by uneventful circumstances, such as starvation or illness. The film stages the protagonists' demise poetically: showing the decedents in close-up, with the edges of the shots feathered in a vignette; the images float while superimposed over wide shots of the landscape or other backgrounds. Another layer of imagery appears in the foreground of the frame, featuring large and small flames that rage or flare up as they pass across the screen. The fires rather obviously suggest the characters' life force on the cusp of flaming out. This poetic imagery halts the plot and mourns the untimely death of the Filipinos. By creating such intervals, the film recognizes the value of lives that were taken by the war's instigators, not accurately counted by some historians, or given short shrift in other films about the war.

Along similar lines, Kulas and Bola happen on an area dotted with numerous graves marked by improvised wooden crosses (fig. 9.5). The vision is rendered in a series of shots, culminating in panoramic bird's-eye views that reveal a huge swath of desolate land. The striking image of numerous humble graves provokes yet another reckoning of the Philippine-American War's body count and the magnitude of losses that humanity has sustained from imperialist wars. Counterintuitively, the virtually monochromatic image also recalls the never-ending rows of white crosses on burial grounds for US soldiers. The fallen troops lying in those graves were not only the foot soldiers of empire but also its casualties. No decolonial reckoning of imperialism's history would be complete without a recognition of the damage done by formal and informal empires to their own people.

Regarding the Bells

Khavn's film takes an irreverent approach to the fraught issue of returning the bells taken as war booty by US soldiers. In line with the filmmaker's refusal to realistically dramatize battle scenes and the brutality of war, *Balangiga* portrays neither the taking of the bells nor the debates about their repatriation. The film goes a step further, however, by representing the subject whimsically.

Shortly after they depart from Balangiga, Kulas figures in a series of hallucinatory vignettes involving himself and several bells. It is unclear whether the visions emanate from his consciousness or they represent the filmmaker's highly stylized riffs on the subject of the war booty. Some of the visions portray Kulas inside a belfry equipped, like the church in Balangiga, with

Figure 9.5. The orphans Kulas (Justine Samson, right) and Bola (Warren Tuaño) make their way across an arid landscape dotted with graves in one of the film's evocative images. (Khavn, *Balangiga: Howling Wilderness*, 2017, screen shot). Courtesy of Khavn.

three bells. Khavn films these shots at night, and the light emanating from the belfry's ceiling and floor enhances the dreamlike quality of the images. One of the shots depicts the boy sticking his head inside a bell. The sequence abruptly jumps to daytime scenes filmed in a mostly barren, sandy environment. Three oversized bells with persons whose heads are stuck inside them bump into and bounce off one another as anthropomorphized objects do in performance art or Walt Disney's *Silly Symphony* cartoons. The whimsicality of the episode contrasts with the succeeding image, which takes place in the same setting. A handheld shot follows a rustic torch carried by a person who remains off screen to an unexpected object: a gigantic brass-colored bell sitting on the ground. A tighter shot shows the bell lifting to reveal a young Filipino family cowering inside.

The last image hints at the trauma suffered by Filipinos, but it does not dispense with the stylization and emotional distance that pervades much of the sequence. Rosenstone (1995) writes that one of the functions of postmodern history films is to "approach the past with humor, parody, and absurdist, surrealist, Dadaesque, and other irreverent attitudes" (206). Using a tone and representational strategies familiar to avant-garde filmmaking, the bell sequence in Balangiga provides a distanced and often humorous counterpoint to the tragic incidents in the film. As well, the treatment implicitly deflates the value that Filipino nationalists assign to the bells and the significance of their return by the US government. The film's strangely lit, dancing, and in some cases oversized bells come across as fetishized objects, which underscores the obsession that Filipinos have with the war booty and other fraught symbols of nationalist and anticolonial struggle. The playfully executed sequence demonstrates once more the value of diverting historical discourse from well-trodden routes and of the unorthodox approach to history that the film takes.

On the Road to Nowhere

More than halfway into Kulas's journey, and shortly after he loses his grandfather, he and Bola meet a middle-aged couple at a shack in the woods. The couple offers the children some cassava root and befriends them. Sadly, the couple later absconds with the children's remaining provisions, sneaking out while the young ones are fast asleep. Before their theft, however, the couple tries to give the children a much-needed reality check. They tell Kulas that his proposed destination, Biringan, is not as his grandfather had described. It is not a densely populated town with bright lights and without any cruel Spaniards or Americans; rather, it is a fabled place of spirits from which there is no return. Their advice makes sense, for Kulas's grandfather could never keep his story straight about Biringan. At first, the grandfather conflated it with the similarly named town of Borongan. He later referred to it as a place they should avoid, even if it meant going on a lengthy detour. He then changed his mind another time, characterizing Biringan as a haven that Kulas must seek at all costs. In Kulas's daydreams, Biringan is a mystical place that alternately terrifies and comforts him. He envisions his mother there, along with dead family members and townsfolk, but they are ghostly presences, and some appear disfigured. Kulas represses his doubts about the existence of Biringan and continues his trek to reach the haven "without any Americans." Shortly after making this point, Kulas sees another vision: that of himself and many children playing a game involving a large circle drawn in the sand. The game is similar to that which accompanies the nursery rhyme "Ring a Ring o' Roses" (a rhyme associated with deaths caused by the plague). The other children around the circle instantly vanish, leaving Kulas alone in the desertlike environment. The episode leaves the impression that Kulas's spectral playmates were calling him to the great beyond.

To be sure, Kulas's ill-advised push to find Biringan does not give the couple at the shack an excuse to steal the children's provisions. The couple probably reasoned the pair would die anyway, and the provisions would only be wasted on them. The theft hastens the children's demise: Bola succumbs first, after developing rashes and becoming weak; and then Kulas turns motionless after lying down to rest. Images of other brutally slaughtered animals besides Melchora the carabao foreshadow the children's passing. Before Bola's demise, we see the image of a pig squirming and bleeding while impaled on a wooden stake. After Bola's death, Kulas slaughters a chicken, as if to indirectly punish the mystical bird that cast a spell on the toddler by killing another avian creature. The image of the slitting of the chicken's neck is given a solarized video effect, softening its violence and depicting the act as something more significant than the banal harvesting of animal flesh. Kulas himself succumbs not long after killing the chicken.

Although the narrative suggests that the children's dogged pursuit of the nonexistent destination is a pitiful and misguided tragedy, the film ends with a joyful vision of Kulas finally crossing over into the otherworldly realm he imagined to be Biringan. The child is seen riding on the magically resurrected carabao Melchora before he excitedly alights and crosses the river toward his final destination. We never actually see Biringan, only the picturesque hills toward which Kulas dashes. As upbeat symphonic music swells; the image of the child, the carabao, and the bucolic setting warps, becomes discolored, and then intermittently fills with crudely scribbled drawings of stars, other symbols, and even a few words. The scribbles, rendered in the red, blue, and yellow colors of the Philippine flag, are reminiscent of the ending in Olivier Assayas's *Irma Vep* (Dacia Films, 1996) and other avant-garde films that create text and graphics by scratching off layers of emulsion on motion picture negatives. This self-reflexive ending confirms the notions expressed earlier in the film that Biringan is a nonplace, that empire would keep on claiming many innocent victims, and that the Filipino's resistance and their pipe dream of liberation will endure against all the odds. Khavn scribbles his distinctive neologism *wazak* before the picture fades out. The idiosyncratic coinage reclaims the Filipino word for "wrecked" or "ruined" to denote the pleasure of seeing something blown apart or upended. Indeed, we see nearly everything in *Balangiga* either tragically or gloriously upended by the time closing credits roll on-screen.

The combination of triumphalism and the mourning of innocent death in the film's ending shows that avant-garde cinema is capable of offering certain kinds of radically unexpected, emotionally complex, and polyvalent resolutions that are at times incompatible with the realist aesthetics and conventions of mainstream historical films. The joyful note in the ending does not trivialize death but rather opts to underscore the exhilaration of subjugated peoples finally being liberated or liberating themselves from the clutches of empire.

Praise and Controversy

Balangiga garnered much praise from critics during its summer 2017 premiere as a work-in-progress at QCinema, a festival of independent cinema in Quezon City. Khavn's movie later fetched the best picture trophy from the Manunuring Pelikulang Pilipino, an association of film reviewers and critics, and the most esteemed Filipino body giving awards for motion pictures. The film also won the top prize at the Filipino Academy of Movie Arts and Sciences awards, which until the 1980s was the Philippine counterpart of the Oscars (Lo 2018). This last accolade was unprecedented for a feature-length avant-garde film, making *Balangiga* something of a breakthrough success in winning awards.

Despite its critical acclaim, the controversy that followed the 2018 release of *Balangiga*'s shorter Philippine theatrical version demonstrated that some of the movie industry's influential tastemakers remained incapable of appreciating Khavn's work and avant-garde filmmaking in general. The Cinema Evaluation Board (CEB), an entity tasked by the national government with giving tax breaks to "quality" films, denied the film its stamp of approval (Franco and Dimaculangan 2018). The unfavorable decision rendered the film ineligible for a rebate equivalent to 65 to 100 percent of its amusement tax liabilities. Four of the nine CEB members who reviewed the film voted in favor of granting the incentive, but some of the remaining members blasted the film, calling it "a perverted movie masquerading as high art," "a long, torturous journey with many artsy gimmicks," and a story of "hate, murder, and sexual perversion" (Del Mundo 2018). The CEB's reviewers also expressed their ambivalence about certain aspects of the film that were directly related to the filmmaker's experimentalism. One reviewer described the use of stop-motion animation as giving "pause to the viewer for contemplation, temporarily taking us out of the film." The sentence leaves the reader wondering, however, whether the animation's ostensible effect of "taking us out of the film" is supposed to be desirable. The board additionally gave faint praise to the film's mise-en-scène, describing the cinematography as "more than functional" and the production design as "economical but visually interesting." The use of *functional* and *economical* as pejoratives betrays the board's unexamined bias for the polished look and high production values of commercial films. It also indicates a regrettable lack of appreciation for avant-garde aesthetics and experimental cinema's artisanal mode of production.

Rosenstone (1995) writes that an experimental historical film "opens a window onto a different way of thinking about the past," often pushing back against the unexamined bias for realism and the "demands for veracity, evidence, and argument that are a normal component of written history" (63). Khavn's *Balangiga* accomplishes those goals by departing from the conventional form of historical movies in the Philippines and bucking the prevailing discourse about the US colonial war in the archipelago. Drawing on the resources of avant-garde cinema, progressive historiography, pop culture, and the visual and performing arts, Khavn offered new approaches to a fraught past and historical figuration in the cinema. As I have argued in this chapter, the most compelling aspect of *Balangiga*'s experimentation and syncretic visuals is the potential to evoke not one but several historical moments. The film's dialectical images connect episodes across the *longue durée* of the US formal and informal empire in the Philippines and elsewhere, potentially enabling a critical reconsideration both of imperialism's checkered past and of the analogous modes of oppression that still exist today.

Note

1. The film is available for streaming and download on Vimeo as of fall 2021 at https://vimeo.com/ondemand/balangiga. It is distributed internationally by the French firm Stray Dogs.

Bibliography

Anderson, Warwick. 2006. *Colonial Pathologies: American Tropical Medicine, Race, and Hygiene in the Philippines*. Durham, NC: Duke University Press.

Benjamin, Walter. 2003a. "On the Concept of History." In *Selected Writings: 1938–1940*. Edited by Howard Eiland and Michael W. Jennings. Translated by Edmund Jephcott and Others, 4:389–400. Cambridge, MA: Belknap.

———. 2003b. "Paralipomena for 'On the Concept of History.'" In *Selected Writings: 1938–1940*. Edited by Howard Eiland and Michael W. Jennings. Translated by Edmund Jephcott and Others, 4:401–411. Cambridge, MA: Belknap.

Borrinaga, Rolando O. 2003. *The Balangiga Conflict Revisited*. Quezon City, Philippines: New Day.

Cadava, Eduardo. 1998. *Words of Light: Theses on the Photography of History*. Princeton, NJ: Princeton University Press.

Capino, José B. 2010. *Dream Factories of a Former Colony: American Fantasies, Philippine Cinema*. Minneapolis: University of Minnesota Press.

Césaire, Aimé. 2000. *Discourse on Colonialism*. New York: Monthly Review Press.

Chu, Wong Kwok. 1982. "The Jones Bills 1912–16: A Reappraisal of Filipino Views on Independence." *Journal of Southeast Asian Studies* 13, no. 2: 252–69.

Claudio, Lisandro. 2018. "Sorry, 'Heneral Luna' Romanticized Strongmen." *Esquire.ph*, January 19. https://www.esquiremag.ph/politics/opinion/sorry-heneral-luna-romanticized-strongmen-a1655-20180119-lfrm.

Couttie, Bob. 2004. *Hang the Dogs: The True Tragic History of the Balangiga Massacre*. Quezon City, Philippines: New Day.

Del Mundo, Doy. 2018. "*Balangiga: Howling Wilderness* Graded Zero." *BusinessWorld Online*, August 17. https://www.bworldonline.com/balangiga-howling-wilderness-graded-zero.

Franco, Bernie and Jocelyn Dimaculangan. 2018. "Producer, Director of PPP Entries Lament Grade Zero from CEB." *PEP.ph*, August 13. https://www.pep.ph/guide/movies/28328/producer-director-of-entries-in-pista-ng-pelikulang-pilipino-lament-grade-zero-from-ceb.

Ileto, Reynaldo C. 1997. *Pasyon and Revolution: Popular Movements in the Philippines, 1840–1910*. Quezon City, Philippines: Ateneo de Manila University Press.

Jacobson, Matthew Frye. 2001. *Barbarian Virtues: The United States Encounters Foreign Peoples at Home and Abroad, 1876–1917*. New York: Hill and Wang.

Khavn, Jerry Gracio, and Achinette Villamor. n.d. "Shooting Script of *Balangiga: Howling Wilderness*." Document provided by Khavn.

Kuipers, Richard. 2015. "Film Review: 'Heneral Luna.'" *Variety.com*, November 30. https://variety.com/2015/film/reviews/heneral-luna-review-1201649617/.

Lansdale, Edward Geary. 1991. *In the Midst of Wars: An American's Mission to Southeast Asia*. New York: Fordham University Press.

Linn, Brian McAllister. 1993. "The Struggle for Samar." In *Crucible of Empire: The Spanish-American War and Its Aftermath*. Edited by James C. Bradford, 158–81. Annapolis, MD: Naval Institute Press.

———. 2000. *The Philippine War, 1899–1902*. Lawrence: University Press of Kansas.

Lo, Ricky. 2018. "They are Off and Running!" *Philippine Star*. October 12. https://www.philstar.com/entertainment/2018/10/12/1859229/they-are-running.

May, Glenn A. 1983. "Why the United States Won the Philippine-American War, 1899–1902." *Pacific Historical Review* 52, no. 4: 353–77.

McCoy, Alfred W. 2009. *Policing America's Empire: The United States, the Philippines, and the Rise of the Surveillance State*. Madison: University of Wisconsin Press.

Rabinovitz, Lauren. 1998. *For the Love of Pleasure: Women, Movies, and Culture in Turn-of-the-Century Chicago*. New Brunswick, NJ: Rutgers University Press.

Ranada, Pia. 2018. "After a Century, U.S. to Return Balangiga Bells." 2018. *Rappler*, August 12. https://www.rappler.com/nation/united-states-return-balangiga-bells-to-the-philippines.

Rosenstone, Robert A. 1995. *Visions of the Past: The Challenge of Film to Our Idea of History*. Cambridge, MA: Harvard University Press.

San Diego, Bayani. 2015. "Heneral Luna Earns P240 Million, Breaks Even." *Inquirer* (Entertainment section), October 11. https://entertainment.inquirer.net/180777/heneral-luna-earns-p240m-breaks-even.

———. 2017. "'Balangiga' Bells Ring Again." *Philippine Daily Inquirer*. October 23. https://entertainment.inquirer.net/247342/balangiga-bells-ring.

Skoller, Jeffrey. 2005. *Shadows, Specters, Shards: Making History in Avant-Garde Film*. Minneapolis: University of Minnesota Press.

Welch, Richard Jr. 1974. "American Atrocities in the Philippines: Indictment and Responses." *Pacific Historical Review* 43, no. 2: 233–53.

White, Hayden. 1988. "Historiography and Historiophoty." *American Historical Review* 93, no. 5: 1193–99.

Worcester, Dean C. 1914. *The Philippines Past and Present*. New York: Macmillan.
Wurfel, David. 1988. *Filipino Politics: Development and Decay*. Ithaca, NY: Cornell University Press.

JOSÉ B. CAPINO is Professor of English and Cinema and Media Studies at the University of Illinois at Urbana-Champaign. He is author of *Martial Law Melodrama: Lino Brocka's Cinema Politics* and *Dream Factories of a Former Colony: American Fantasies, Philippine Cinema*.

10. MILLENNIAL VENGEANCE
Park Chan-wook's *Agassi* (*The Handmaiden*) and the Return of Postcolonial *Japonisme*

Nayoung Aimee Kwon

Abstract

Postmillennial Asian cinemas are haunted by repressed memories of colonial and wartime pasts, and these memories have returned with a vengeance. Through a case study of Park Chan-wook's *Agassi* (*The Handmaiden*, 2016) and other contemporary South Korean films, this chapter explores the significance of how once nationally delimited, censored, or invisible images of contested historical pasts are suddenly crossing borders and expanding into a wider and hypervisible global presence through contemporary transnational Asian films. The chapter ultimately asks, What is the broader significance of the return of these transnational twenty-first century cinematic representations of the past in the current geopolitical climate of the rise of Asia and the rise of global Asian cinema?

Introduction

Postmillennial Asian cinemas are haunted by repressed memories of colonial and wartime pasts, and these memories have returned with a vengeance. Through a case study of Park Chan-wook's *Agassi* (*The Handmaiden*, 2016) and other contemporary South Korean films, this chapter explores the significance of how once nationally delimited, censored, or invisible images of contested historical pasts are suddenly crossing borders and expanding into a wider and hypervisible global presence through these contemporary transnational Asian films. It asks these questions: Why are these films about repressed pasts suddenly "returning with a vengeance" now, after such a long delay? What might be the relationship between this recent cinematic phenomenon and broader memory wars in the current geopolitical climate of the rise of Asia and the rise of global Asian cinema (Suzuki 2013)?

The popular period pieces under consideration are part of a broader new wave of transnational Asian cinemas that have been reaching global audiences since the beginning of the twenty-first century. Although prior trends have highlighted one national cinema at a time for an international audience—Japanese films in mid-twentieth century, Hong Kong films in the nineteen seventies, or mainland Chinese films in the nineteen eighties, for example—the transborder scale and scope across and beyond the region in the contemporary moment is remarkable.[1]

Furthermore, what is striking about these colonial and wartime dramas is that their global hypervisibility stands in stark contrast to more than half a century of near invisibility. Before this moment, such films had been seen primarily within the Asian nation where they were produced. But now these colonial and wartime historic representations, which encompass an era that roughly coincides with the two world wars, are crossing borders on an unprecedented scale and in the process are reaching much wider audiences in the region and beyond.[2] The hypervisibility of these films in the postmillennial moment is further noteworthy for its stark contrast with the Western front: ubiquitous images of the world wars from the Euro-American theater have become beloved global cinematic icons, but a severe dearth of transnational images of parallel histories of and about Asia remained.

Of course, nation-centered period pieces or those confined to the nation—either in content or in distribution—have been common throughout this region for decades prior to this era.[3] In fact, only an exceptional few have managed to circulate beyond the borders of any one nation-state, despite the long history of film cultures in Asia that go back to film's very inception.[4] Since the beginning of the millennium, however, we have witnessed a tremendous popular surge of cinematic period pieces crossing borders, unlike prior nation- or region-bound films—in their content as well as in their production, marketing, exhibition, and distribution. These pieces address once-repressed or censored local and regional histories across Asia. Furthermore, once limited to a local spectatorship within one nation, many such recent films have circulated much more widely than previously possible across a region that for decades had been geopolitically and globally divided.

The global prominence of South Korean cinema today offers us one segue into a much wider regional phenomenon, especially when taking into account the unprecedented global recognition awarded to non-English-language films such as Bong Joon-ho's *Parasite* (2019).[5] In particular, we will examine these dynamics via a coincident resurgence of transnational films about the colonial and wartime past that became noteworthy around the beginning of the twenty-first century. A random sampling of films that have emerged since the millennium include *Anarchists* (Yoo Young-sik, dir., 2000); *YMCA Baseball* (Kim Hyun-seok, dir., 2002); *The Good, the Bad, and the Weird* (Kim Jee-Woon, dir., 2003); *Epitaph* (Jung Sik and Jung Bum-Shik, dirs., 2007); *Modern Boy* (Jung Ji-Woo, dir., 2008); *Radio Dayz* (Ha Ki-ho, dir., 2008); *My Way* (Kang Je-gyu, dir., 2011); *Love, Lies* (Park Heung-sik, dir., 2016); *Age of Shadows* (Kim Jee-Woon, dir., 2016); *The Last Princess* (Hur Jin-ho, dir., 2016); *Agassi* (Park Chan-wook, dir., 2016); *Anarchist from the Colony* (Lee Joon-ik, dir., 2017); and *Battleship Island* (Ryu Seung-Wan, dir., 2017). The list seems to expand every year. As we will explore further, it is a significantly noteworthy shift that these contested local memory wars are now being waged ever more visibly and visually through international cinematic screens and for an increasingly wide spectatorship, with little to no time-lag in circulation among disparate distribution sites (Korea Film Council 2017, 7–8, 43).

Return with a Vengeance and Park Chan-wook's *Agassi* (*The Handmaiden*)

Let's turn to a stunning example: Park Chan-wook's *Agassi* (hereafter, *The Handmaiden*). In exploring the transnational cinematic return-with-a-vengeance of once-invisible or repressed colonial memories, we could do worse than start with this film. This visually mesmerizing period piece is directed by contemporary cinema's *enfant terrible* and master of the infamously extreme Vengeance Trilogy.[6] Released to rave reviews for both domestic and international audiences simultaneously—including several prominent accolades at the 2016 Cannes Film Festival, such as the first-ever Vulcan Award given for Art Direction—*The Handmaiden* entices viewers with a voyeuristic peep into an alluring and exotic visual field of early-twentieth-century colonial Korea under Japanese rule. An adaptation of *Fingersmith*, Sarah Waters's 2002 gothic novel of Victorian England, the film retells the tale through a tryptic serial lens of competing and intertwined narratives from the point of view of each of the three protagonists: Sook-hee, a petty thief from the colony masquerading as a handmaiden to a Japanese settler heiress; Hideko, the Japanese heiress who as a child was transplanted from the metropole of Japan to colonial Korea; and "Count Fujiwara," a duplicitous counterfeiter of paintings who is actually a low-born Korean passing as Japanese nobility.

The story opens with Count Fujiwara secretly conspiring with Sook-hee to trespass into Lady Hideko's inner chambers in order to seduce and then swindle her out of her inheritance. Among this shady cast of characters, a sexually charged ménage à trois unfolds, brimming with salacious intrigue

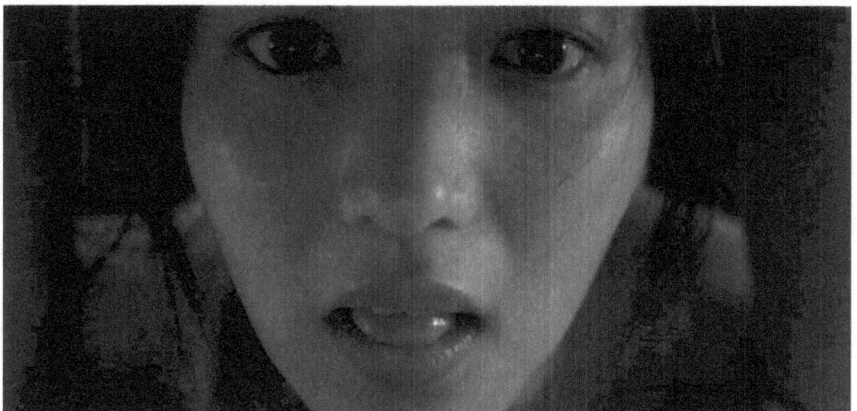

Figure 10.1. Vagina POV shot. (*The Handmaiden*, 2016, screen shot).

and scandalous betrayal. The story development is apropos of Park Chan-wook's bad-boy reputation for flouting taboos and pushing boundaries. Each scene seems more scandalous than the one before. From bondage and sadism to age-old Edo-era ukiyo-e of bestial erotica (with a clever intertextual nod back to yet another startling octopus scene from Park's own 2003 infamous cult classic, *Oldboy*), lesbian cunnilingus, sexual voyeurism, the incest taboo, and what I call Park's signature "vagina POV shot" (fig. 10.1)—there is no shortage of shocking images.

Extravagantly filmed with an anamorphic lens giving meticulous attention to mise-en-scène, every shot is exquisitely framed in a picturesque tableau of sumptuous colors and sensuous textures from a bygone era. Each scene mesmerizes, seduces, and transfixes the audience gaze toward rarely encountered sights and sounds, seeming to dare anyone to avert their eyes from an onslaught of forbidden but enticing visuals. Scene after scene, the film is a seductive ocular assault on social norms and civilized decorum.

Ahistoricity of Historical Dramas

The fact that such a film would garner the fascination for the exotic and erotic from Asia—especially for far-flung global audiences less familiar with and having little prior contact with the film's cultural and historical contexts—is not at all surprising, and in fact quite familiar by now. Edward Said (1978) and others, for example, have meticulously documented the persistent allure that has captured the imaginations of centuries of Western knowledge producers, including writers, artists, politicians, religious figures, and academics, who have built long careers on the reproduction and circulation of erotic-exotic *mis*representations of "the Orient" as Other. It bears noting that this centuries-long process of Othering and misrepresentation persisted despite centuries of actual contact and ample opportunity to learn from mistakes and correct biases. Robert Stam and Louise Spence's (2009) delineation between the irony of having had "contact but no encounter" offers a pithy way of understanding such dynamics of willed racism that refused to truly see the Other as fully human beyond fixed, objectified prejudices despite evidence to the contrary. Why were such racialized prejudices not corrected for centuries? Because unequal power dynamics kept the prejudices in place, for they continued to serve the interests of those who insisted on maintaining the falsehoods.

What may be surprisingly novel from this tired yet still persistent colonial story, and more interesting for our concerns here, is that many aspects of these new historic period pieces, while set in the local historic context, appear just as foreign, exotic, and unfamiliar even to local audiences, who presumably have more proximate historic and cultural knowledge than those situated far away and outside the national border. The case thus may present a more fascinating and complicated psychosocial structure.

Though it is true that local audiences have encountered—actually, even been saturated with—images from the colonial past, in reality, earlier portrayals that have been circulated and consumed widely for decades were severely selective, limited to carefully curated representations with a similar ideological bent. With few variations, they offered a nationalistic, top-down, and censored point of view on the colonial past.[7] These curated monochromatic portrayals from past decades are decidedly one-dimensional in contrast to those that have recently become *hyper*visible in postmillennial films such as *The Handmaiden*. In fact, the new cinematic depictions around the beginning of the twenty-first century are so strikingly fresh that, to a new generation of local filmgoers, they appear to represent a decidedly foreign and exotic past, in contrast to the familiar nation-centered images of the past. In addition, the circulation has changed; for the first time and, after decades of time lag, audiences—at home and abroad—are encountering these sights and sounds of a once-censored and tabooed history simultaneously.

Visualizing Scenes of Taboo

And so, what are these new sights and sounds that audiences both local and global are synchronously encountering anew, and why did it take until the new millennium? Rather than focus on neatly delineated histories, this chapter and this volume build on prior decolonial ethics of engagement with the transborder colonial essence that lies at the very heart of—and buttressed—all modern national histories.[8] The aim of such a perspective is to turn the focus away from divided narratives of both the nation and empire, a one-directional "influence" or "salvation" of the colonizer's onslaught on the colonized and the latter's binary resistance or collaboration as assumed in previous formulations. This chapter, along with the rest of the volume, wagers that for too long, scholars have posited fundamental divides in colonial/modern and colonizer/colonized dyads at the expense of examining actual entanglements of colonial relations and legacies.

To examine these issues, let us turn to Park Chan-wook's *The Handmaiden* as a telling example. From the moment the eponymous handmaiden Sook-hee enters Lady Hideko's grand mansion, we are greeted with an onslaught of sumptuous details of cultural and temporal hybrids of transcolonial modernity—of imperial and colonial cultures (Western, Japanese, Chinese, and Korean, in this case), from traditional to modern, the old and the new, in an era of tremendous confluence and transformation. Making explicit modernity's transcolonial hybridity provides us a border-crossing perspective beyond persistent assumptions about a one-way trajectory from the metropole to the colony.

Sook-hee is immediately assigned a Japanese name, Tamako, by Mrs. Sasaki, who, like many characters, appears to effortlessly code-switch between the Japanese and Korean languages. Mrs. Sasaki explains to Sook-hee that the hybrid building of Western and Japanese architecture she has just entered is the house of the noble Fujiwara clan of Japan. It is occupied by Lady Hideko and her uncle Kouzuki. Gradually, through the peeping eyes of Sook-hee as a new interloper in the household, we find out that Mrs. Sasaki and Uncle Kouzuki are both ethnic Koreans. Once married to each other, Uncle Kouzuki abandoned Mrs. Sasaki and everything else that is Korean—including his own identity—to assimilate into the Fujiwara clan.

Amid this colorfully hybrid context, all things Korean and Japanese, traditional and modern—fashion, food, language and identity, décor, and even sexual and romantic liaisons—seem to blend and intermingle fluidly. This apparently seamless transcolonial entanglement between the realms of colonizers and the colonized, represented in this and other postmillennial films, appears as a natural part of the landscape. What is now being presented as common sense, however, through these new cinematic mis-en-scènes were in fact precisely noteworthy as being decidedly uncommon to what local audiences had long become accustomed to seeing through decades of prior colonial representations. In fact, despite a few exceptions, prior representations of the colonial past had largely been told in black-and-white binary opposition delineating a clear divide between the colonizers and the colonized.

Global cinematic audiences who are already quite familiar with the plethora of films visualizing transcolonial entanglements from elsewhere[9] may be surprised to learn that the very mixture of colonizer and colonized cultures was precisely what had been absented from national cinemas in this local context. It was not that these hybrid scenes and interactions were actually missing from the reality of this colonial context. In fact, as Jun Uchida's groundbreaking scholarship documents, Japanese settlers occupied a formidable population in many major cities in Korea during this time (Uchida 2011). They were indeed an unavoidable and quite prominent part of the colonial landscape.[10]

Like settler colonialists elsewhere, Japanese occupiers reterritorialized their extracted colonial spaces and swiftly inscribed their own cultural imprint through architecture, signage, name changes, and other territorial markings throughout the local landscape. They then reproduced a segregated space of absolutely unequal hierarchy in which the Japanese, much like European colonizers, greedily wrested for themselves dominant positions of power and prime real estate from local Koreans. A striking difference in postcolonial Korea and elsewhere in the region, however, is that this dynamic of transcolonial confluence was deemed as a scandalous and shameful stain on a nation-centered history. Consequently, it was actively censored out and absented in hindsight from dominant postcolonial representations in both official and popular realms. The only exception was a decision to keep intact the vivid portrayal of violence and exploitation by the Japanese toward the colonized. Such violence certainly was pervasive, and in fact undergirded transcolonial relations in this colony as in other colonial contexts of dominance, but what is noteworthy in this case is the herculean effort in the postcolony to erase all other aspects of what was once a substantial presence of the colonizers, including their importation and development of modern accoutrements such as fashion, architecture, and technology within the colony.

In the cultural realm, a formidable degree of censorship was enacted decades earlier to effectively erase the presence of the Japanese and any nuanced representations, including traces of transcolonial modernity, from the postcolonial visual field. The ideological censorship was so extensive that at least two generations of contemporary adult cinemagoers, who had never lived through the colonial occupation themselves, were encountering in the postmillennial films for the very first time sights and sounds of transcolonial encounters that were daily experience for many of their parents' or grandparents' generations.[11]

Furthermore, it is noteworthy not only that these hybrids and intermixtures were finally being seen at all and in greater numbers, but also that they were now visualized in an enticing and seductive manner—yet another unprecedented phenomenon. For example, although global audiences may be familiar with scenes of transcolonial modernity from early-twentieth-century cities such as Tokyo or Shanghai, other spaces in the region signified as national territories were carefully censored of past foreign and imperial influences, especially of alluring representations of modern advancements. What was prioritized and visualized instead was a visual field dominated by scenes of drab, dark, dire situations that in fact deemphasized the rapid technological and cultural transformations that were simultaneously occurring during the era.

Scenes of the late nineteenth and early twentieth century in films—from Euro-America and most notably from Hollywood—often luxuriated in nostalgic optical pleasures of then-new symbols of transcolonial modernity, such as trains, gramophones, department stores, fashion, architecture, and the cinema itself, but many of these visual details were left out or understated in the region's films about the colonial past. North Atlantic cinematic traditions cannot seem to get enough of nostalgic images of the era of the world wars, but in Asia the focus was rather on the dire political and dramatic plotlines and narratives, as well as one-dimensional character representation of good and evil, and everything else was deemed extraneous and faded to the background. The modernity of the colonial era was a sore point for many postcolonial societies, because colonizers used the lure of the modern and its accoutrements to justify their colonial rule over people that they then deemed, by contrast, to be primitive or backward.

Further, in postcolonial Korea, Japanese cultural icons or iconic visualizations of Japaneseness more generally were carefully controlled, censored, and surveilled by the government. Recent Anglophone scholars such as Ted Hughes (2012) and Jinsoo An (2018) have written about this invisibility and about the significance of selective absenting in postcolonial memories of the past. The erasure extends to the present with various Japanese products, including censorship of content and the prohibition of cultural items from importation. In fact, as I discuss elsewhere (Kwon 2015), disavowal of the colonial past stems from the legacies of the valence of colonial relations in the region. In a proximate empire where the racial and ethnic differences between the rulers (Japanese) and the ruled (Korean, Chinese, for example) were barely perceptible to the eye, the boundary between the colonizer and the colonized had to be managed closely (Kwon 2015). Postcolonial education and the mass media served to erase collective memories of broad swaths of now-unwelcome colonial intimacies, mirroring broader geopolitical and economic injunctions that continued long after the end of empire. By contrast, in new postmillennial films, sights and sounds of past transcolonial hybrids reappeared in an enticing and seductive manner, including gorgeous kimonos, elegant furnishings and decor, lush Zen gardens, modern trinkets and new gadgets, and other alluring trappings of a bygone past.

Visualizing the Past

In postmillennial period pieces, the shock of scenes saturated with color, both literally and figuratively, paints the past in a much more robust palette than had been previously seen. To be sure, films set during the colonial and wartime pasts in and of themselves are not new. Both North and South Korean cinemas, for example, since their forced division after 1945 at the behest of emerging Cold War rivalries between the United States and the Soviet Union, have produced a steady stream of such films (S. Lee 2005; Chung 2014). These films, however, were literally and figuratively black and white, and they depicted scenes that were dark, drab, dangerous, and depressing. They also tended to be severely limited in the sights and sounds they propagated in quality, scope, and content.

In fact, such films have historically been so delimited in terms of content as well as their production, consumption, and circulation that they have rarely made an impact beyond their nation of origin. Even for local audiences, most of these films failed to garner popular or critical attention.[12] They were predominantly low-quality, made-for-television fare (or were often slated to swiftly head for the television market) than of high cinematic quality. As for content, they were remarkably persistent and consistent in reproducing or recycling familiar stories of national heroes resisting evil Japanese colonizers, a plotline that became all too familiar for decades. The films nonetheless managed to maintain a local audience because they were trotted out and replayed for mandatory educational screenings during school outings and shown repeatedly during national holidays, such as Independence Day on August 15.

Under such circumstances, it is perhaps unsurprising that there was very little consideration for the reception of an international audience. The local viewership could safely be assumed to share a commonsense familiarity with these orthodox national histories that reinforced messages already taught repeatedly in schools. The trend persisted for decades and became so ubiquitous that it was simply taken for granted as shared common sense and thus unremarkable.

Visualizing the Future

Before we turn to examine in detail some of the major differences in recent film trends, it would be useful to look closely at cinematic examples that came before. Low budgets and correspondingly low production values that appeared in myriad ways were factors that limited the market to local audiences. As many have discussed, the obvious propagandistic nationalism of the films was another factor. I would like to build on these observations to consider the extent to which restriction to a domestic market built alternate realities of the past.

One effect was on the film's content. The storytelling rarely ventured into novel territory but instead tended toward didacticism heavily laden with familiar nationalist ideology and repeated the same old stories in the same old ways. The most popular genre for that type of messaging was, perhaps unsurprisingly, melodrama that set up dualities of good versus evil, with mourning instrumental music in the background tugging at heartstrings. The overall ambiance tended to be dark and dreary, aligned in tone with a standardized nationalist story focused on the suffering of the colonized people and their collective struggles against all odds.

As for location shoots, these films were shot locally, focused on the devastating exploitation of the Korean landscape, limited in scale to small villages and hamlets. Prison cells and other clandestine and confined spaces were de rigueur in depicting the claustrophobic atmosphere of colonial violence and terror. Confined spaces best conveyed the suffocating and shady exploitations in the colonial system. A commonly repeated trope was the plundering, transformation, or destruction of a familiar and idyllic rural village by the infiltration of colonial foreign land grabs and speculation. The limited scope of the spatial landscape also symbolized the lack of mobility facing the colonized at this time; peasants and tenant farmers were particularly vulnerable to the vicissitudes of imperial land grabs, which severely curtailed the mobility of the colonized people, especially of peasants, who were both tied to and dependent on the land but who were then displaced from that very land by colonial plunder, left with no place to go.

Peasants and other common folk came to stand in as common symbols for the suffering nation as a whole.[13] Heroic male figures were cast to resist, bravely if tragically, the Japanese colonizers and broader exploitative forces. The increasing absence of male figures was yet another dominant narrative structure, a result of either their death or their departure—through exile, imprisonment, conscription, or other colonial and wartime exigencies.

For the most part, in this melodramatic structure, characters were divided along a clear-cut binary: heroes versus villains, Koreans versus Japanese; and the two sides were neatly segregated and rarely intermingled except to represent conflicts and clashes between them in the story arc. Colonial collaborators, such as the local police deputy or brokers and overseers of imperial economic speculation and transactions, for example, sometimes stood in as villains doing the bidding of Japanese colonialism. They blurred the neat dichotomous national boundaries, but their characterization consistently represented cartoonish evil incarnate that ultimately did not depart from the master storyline of good versus evil.

PRODUCTION DESIGNS AND OTHER BACKDROPS

The flattened, two-dimensional patterns were not only limited to commonly repeated character archetypes; the limits were also manifest facially on the screen surface, at times quite literally. In his important recent book, *Parameters of Disavowal*, film historian Jinsoo An (2018) astutely analyzes a telling scene in one of Im Kwŏn-t'aek's films from the 1970s. In the film *Genealogy (1978)*, observes An, the grandiose Western-style baroque building of the colonial governor general, in actuality a formidable concrete architectural mammoth, was represented by a shabby two-dimensional painting in the backdrop as the plot thickened in the foreground. In a melodramatic film deeply imbued with that era's heightened sense of emotions, it is striking that the production design of even such an actual grandiose colonial structure was flattened out and made so bland to become almost invisible on screen. The limits of the film's low-budget production may have been more influential than the possibility of a veiled political gesture, but the end result minimalized the visual impact of what had once occupied the lived space as an intimidating, grandiose colonial structure.[14] It is also significant that these structures that had once iconically symbolized Japaneseness were relegated to the margins or entirely outside the screen's mise-en-scène. This effort is perhaps most iconically symbolized by the literal demolition of the gargantuan concrete structure of the former governor general building, a decision marking the sixtieth anniversary of liberation in 2015, at the height of South Korea's globalization fever—which then had to undergo a ghostly techno-resurrection in computer-generated imagery for other postmillennial colonial films such as *Modern Boy* (Jung Ji-woo, 2008).[15]

Boundaries between inside and outside, as represented by the placement of this colonial structure outside the window frame beyond the main scene of narrative action, also symbolized a general dichotomy between Us and Them, which was consistently maintained throughout these films. Such binary divides were repeatedly reinforced through divided framing devices that segregated the national Self from the imperial Other. Those characters who were permitted to cross back and forth across these boundaries were typically depicted as traitorous collaborators who betrayed the greater good of the nation and were ultimately punished for their transgressions.

Likewise, in these films from the 1940s onward, Japanese settlers in colonial Korea were rarely depicted, or were erased from these representations.

Japanese characters were reduced to minor roles, and when they appeared at all, they were played by Korean actors, with minimal to no Japanese language skills or training. Even if the productions had wanted to cast Japanese actors for these roles, they would have been hard-pressed to find them, since no talent exchange was permitted anyway.

Younger generations of cinemagoers who had not directly lived through that era would be challenged to see in these representations how the settler Japanese population had actually inhabited major Korean cities in quite substantial numbers. In fact, in per capita terms, they were one of the largest populations of settler colonialists. But when Japanese settlers were represented at all, they were not given any depth of character or substantial plotlines. They were relegated to playing the requisite role of the evil colonialist, often stroking stereotypically sparse mustaches while plotting their evil deeds.[16]

Along with the rigid boundaries between the colonizer and the colonized, the linguistic landscape was predominantly Korean. This may seem unsurprising, in that the films mainly focused on colonial Korean characters. However, the actual reality of the draconian assimilatory language policy that had been in place, intruding into the everyday lives of the colonized people—even into the private spaces of daily living—was rendered invisible or inaudible. Audiences rarely heard the Japanese language spoken in these films, and they especially did not hear Korean characters speaking in Japanese.

The films' monolingual linguistic landscape was not in keeping with what actually happened. The generations that lived through the era would have found the film representations distant from the reality of their lives. For younger generations, however, the majority of cinemagoers in contemporary South Korea, who have no direct experience nor knowledge gained through historic studies, the linguistic reality simply would not have registered in watching these earlier filmic re-presentations. The actual past would be in effect unrecognizable for the new generation as a result of the postcolonial audiovisual silencing and erasure that had been enacted selectively to divide the present from the past. The erasure exacerbated the divide between generations of filmgoers, and the past appeared as a distant and foreign territory for younger audiences. As we shall see in the next section, the depth of such ideological divisions had far-reaching consequences for decades to come.

Divided *Waesaek* (Japan Color) and Postcolonial Color Lines

At the beginning of the last century, W. E. B. DuBois cogently diagnosed the problem of the twentieth century to be its racist division (DuBois [1903]

1993). Building on this important framework, Heonik Kwon (2010) added that by midcentury DuBois's analysis could be extended to the global cold war color line of the new world order. Around the world, the political color Red was Othered, vilified, and violently exterminated with a virulence akin to racist hate. In the superpower metropolitan center of the United States, the ideological witch hunt of McCarthyism is a particularly noteworthy example. But this globally recognized example pales in comparison to the mass state violence that was fomented in the newly decolonizing world. That such violence and exclusions were enacted and exacerbated by the superpowers' manipulations of local divisions in the very name of freedom, democracy, and anticommunism is a deep irony that subsequent generations have yet to reckon with. The violence was based on fears triggered by the rising influence of socialist and communist thought around the world in the wake of decolonization. The lure of such political ideas for those within newly decolonizing societies as they struggled to break free from the yoke of centuries of colonial oppression should be unsurprising. What is remarkable is the length of time it took—more than half a century—for the world to begin to have basic access to archives that would reveal how the anti-imperialist stance of the emerging powers of the United States and the Soviet Union in the name of liberation from colonization had been used instead to consolidate new imperialist structures. In the case of the United States, the manifest motivation was to preserve the decolonizing world from falling over to the Other side. The underlying goal, however, was to secure the allegiance of the decolonizing world in alignment with new imperial power dynamics and security interests. Sociopolitical divisions already extant within the newly decolonizing and war-torn chaos of the so-called third world were being instrumentalized to form these new allegiances.

Ever-deepening divides were exacerbated within already bifurcated and volatile societies reeling from decades of colonial rule. Divide-and-conquer strategies set the stage for a proliferation of midcentury superpower partitions and proxy wars, the violent extent of which were still being heavily censored and occluded into the next century. Here, I would like to build on prior scholarship to examine how the color lines were pluralized as Cold War divides overlapped with and consolidated postcolonial divisions. I shall then turn to how such divisions proliferated in ever-new forms of erasures and continued to have deep implications, including the cultural realm of film, in how the past would be reinvented, circulated, and remembered for decades into twenty-first-century, postmillennial Asia.

By mid-twentieth century, what was an already deeply rooted *colonial divide* became even more entrenched with the superimposition of the new

Cold War divide in the postcolonial aftermath. The confluence of the two divides was then conflated for generations, confounding a path toward untangling the two, and challenging ways to understand and address their relationality, differences, and mutual impact. At the height of the global Cold War and after decades of mutual dis-recognition and ever-yawning geopolitical divides, the occasion of normalization in 1965 of diplomatic and economic relations between Korea and Japan appeared to signal an openness for a reconciliation. Politicians on both sides framed the movement as an opportunity to move beyond a deeply contested past between the former colonizer and the former colonized, with the potential of opening up political, economic, and cultural exchanges. Until then, there had been many restrictions, as we have seen thus far, including how images of the colonial past in the postcolony were strictly confined to representations within national boundaries.[17] After Japan was defeated by the Allied Powers, inaugurating an end to Japan's colonization of Korea, the postcolonial government imposed an official ban on Japanese cultural imports in the postcolony.[18] The bilateral treaty of 1965 proposed to normalize political and economic relations between the former colonizer and the former colonized for the first time since the end of colonial rule.

Around the time of the treaty signing, Korean cultural producers advocated more open border policies, including cultural collaborations with Japan. The possibilities of opening up South Korea's markets to Japanese imports, however, unleashed a heated debate on how best to police the impending influx across the border of yet another divided color line, that of *waesaek* or "Japan color."[19] A mass-media panic revealed a deep-seated public anxiety about yet another form of infiltration and takeover by Japan. The fear was of imperialism by other means—through the production of economic and cultural dependencies by way of an influx of advanced technologies and other enticingly well-made commodities and technologies.

An article serialized in a major daily newspaper, titled "Japan Trouble" (*Ilbon t'ŭrŏbŭl*), for example, encapsulates the broader atmosphere of the time. The article warned of the "Three S Policy" through which geopolitical dominance was being waged in the contemporary moment. The Three S's were "sports, speed, and screen," and the writer warned against the negative infiltration of cultural contents and products—such as spectator sports programming, automobiles, and film and television shows—into the impressionable hearts and minds of contemporary South Korean consumer-citizens, especially of young people, through market liberalization.[20]

Not all imports from Japan were frowned on or outright prohibited. For one, cultural products with ambiguous origins were welcomed with open arms. These were products whose national or cultural "color" of origin as Japanese were not as apparent or those whose "Japan color" had been diminished or erased. Famous examples were science fiction or fantasy-themed manga or anime such as *Astro Boy*, *Mazinger Z*, and *Doraemon* or those set in Western contexts, such as *Candy* (rural Michigan), *Heidi, Girl of the Alps* (Swiss Alps), and *The Rose of Versailles* (France). These and numerous other examples with "colorless" content had a much easier time passing through border patrols.

Dubbing was an increasingly popular technique for presenting foreign-language content to local audiences, and dubbing over Japanese-language materials was seamless and unremarkable and was practiced as business as usual. In contrast, as Yi Chiwŏn (2015) notes, in print matter the written form of the Japanese language proved to be a particularly irksome target of censure and censorship. And as Jinsoo An (2018) cogently examines, many such efforts to open borders on the cultural front were met with draconian refusals or active censorship or were subject to inconsistent policies and practice. In the film industry, for example, films such as *Daughter of the Governor General* (*Ch'ongdok ŭi ttal*, Cho Kŭngha, dir., 1965) or *Happy Solitude* (*Haengbokhan kodok*, Shin Kyŏng-gyun, dir., 1963), which featured Japanese actors and location shoots, were censored and refused distribution permits (An 2018).

Dubbing as Silencing, Coloring as Erasing

What the permissible commodities had in common, in contrast to others deemed impermissible, was a distinct audiovisual absence—including silencing and erasure—of any sights and sounds of cultural origins, specifically that of Japaneseness or Japan color.[21] In other words, audiovisual dubbing over or washing out of Japan color served a function beyond the seamless translation across cultures. Rather than the standard purpose of translation to render or mediate another culture into visibility, here the tools of translation were deployed for exactly opposite ends—accommodating or facilitating a culture's very erasure and silencing (Nornes 2007).

When possible, traces of Japan color were selectively censored out in order to permit their passage across national borders. For example, anime and manga were especially amenable in that the content was relatively easy to doctor with a few strokes of the pen to erase any traces of Japan color before they were released for broadcasting. Japanese character and place names were simply translated into Korean ones. Questionable cartoon panels that might cause offense were censored by literally coloring out images or backgrounds that were deemed too Japanese (as showing too much Japaneseness). For example, a panel with a kimono might be colored over to localize it into a monochromatic image that approximated a culturally neutral or ambiguous fashion style. Once Japanese products were thus effectively rendered colorless of their background and delinked from signifying Japan, the content was not only imported freely but became so desirable and popular that they soon reached beloved iconic status and had an impact on the hearts and minds of Korean youths for generations to come.

It is interesting to note that anxieties about *waesaek* were triggered not just by the most obvious and usual suspects of images such as samurais and geishas that visually flaunted and exhibited the mark of Japan in such a clear and obvious way. Aural traces also became an issue: the spoken and written Japanese language certainly, and traditional instruments like the shamisen, would be obvious targets, but even the sounds of popular contemporary music became problematic. Popular music became a particularly sensitive arena for rooting out traces of Japanese influence, albeit with a great amount of inconsistency. For example, the popular old-style music genre called t'ŭrot'ŭ, with ambiguous hybrid origins including Japan (although the name derives from the fox-trot), became a regular object of contention and often the target of frequent calls for boycotts and bans. Even some songs that were produced and sung by popular Korean artists were suspected of incorporating too much Japanese color and were at times heavily censored or closely monitored. The (in)famous case of popular icon Yi Mi-ja's song "Dongbaek Agassi" (Miss Camelia), and even songs like "Pusan-hang" (Pusan harbor) sung by beloved crooner Cho Yong-p'il were particularly memorable targets of condemnation for allegedly exhibiting too much Japan color.[22]

Subimperial Alignment and Counterfeit Reconciliation

As seen in the previous discussion, during the height of the global Cold War, not all Japan color was the same. A divided color line appeared between *waesaek* that could be permitted across the border and openly visualized on the surface and *waesaek* that was impermissible or was repressed to the subterranean and invisible realms once it was permitted entry. This *waesaek* color line fundamentally revealed a coexisting contradiction between simultaneously saying yes and no to Japan color in the postcolony.

The apparently ambivalent reaction turns out in fact to be a perfectly lucid response to a structurally instituted contradiction that had triggered the so-called bilateral Normalization Treaty in the first place.[23] As declassified archives have since revealed, it was ultimately the need for a united Cold War front against a perceived common enemy of communist politics that was imposed top-down by the third-party security interests of the United States in the region that pressed for a treaty (Cha 1996).

In the name of a veneer of normalization that prioritized political and economic interests, the former colonizer and the former colonized were pressed into realignment with one another as subimperial partners or allies under the aegis of the US nuclear security umbrella.[24] Further, as long suspected and only recently confirmed in declassified documents, the normalization enforced a premature alignment between the former colonizer and the former colonized and it actively suppressed any true reckoning of the colonial past—in other words, at the very expense of, rather than as a genuine opening toward, a true historic reckoning.[25] The divides engendered a fundamental and long-lasting contradiction between what could be visualized openly and what had to remain repressed. The division between what was manifested above and what remained latent below mirrored the broader geopolitical contradictions and hierarchies embodied in the actually fake or counterfeit reconciliation that, in fact, further entrenched Cold War divides.

It is worth noting that this divided logic continues to have consequences. Even today, there is no widely circulated understanding about the historic realignment between Korea and Japan and the United States in all three countries. An ordinary US, Korean, or Japanese citizen may have little idea how these former enemies suddenly came to be friends, because much of the convoluted and divided history is not taught in our schools with any consistency at any level and has remained all but invisible in popular culture.

Uncanny Convergence of *Waesaek* (Japan Color) and *Japonisme*

In the present context, after decades—no less than half a century—of visualizing a nationally divided and delimited reality in the postcolony, an altogether new shade of Japan color began to rise to the surface on cinematic screens with the millennial turn.

Cold War superpowers had suddenly descended on the region in the midst of the chaotic evacuation of the Japanese colonialists, superimposing the divided logic of the Cold War onto the immediate postcolonial aftermath. The result was a parallel and overlapping coexistence of deeply divided postcolonial sentiments toward Japan and the colonial past with the virulent exclusionary practices toward the political color red imposed by new Cold War ideologies. As Ted Hughes (2012) has shown, the double exclusions from the postcolonial body politic coexisted in parallel persistence for decades; just as the political color red was being vigilantly ousted from the body politic during these years, so too was the color of Japan. In the case of the developmental state's postcolonial memories about Japan, we have seen how these divided contradictions were manifest in even literally coloring over Japan

Figure 10.2. Japanese- and Western-style hybrid architectural structure. (*The Handmaiden*, 2016, screen shot).

color to make it invisible, even as Japanese commodities and cultural products were imported with open arms.

In contrast, around the beginning of the twenty-first century, new postmillennial films began depicting Japan and the past era of Japan's colonization in much more dynamic, ambivalent, and complex ways. The new visibility of Japanese characters and transcolonial interactions—including romantic relations, nuanced storylines, vibrant images of colonial modernity, and even the reemergence of coproductions and collaborations with Japanese production companies and actors—is noteworthy particularly because they had been unavailable or were severely curtailed for decades, in past cinematic representations since the colonial era ended.[26]

Amid the sudden outpouring of new films that made Japan much more visible and complex, Park Chan-wook's *The Handmaiden* is especially striking.[27] In captivating cinematic visuals, the film captures the colonial past in a rich palette of gorgeous colors, offering variegated cultural mixtures, from traditional to modern and from Korean to Japanese to Western.

The house of Fujiwara and its well-groomed grounds are a breathtaking surfeit of transcolonial cultural entanglements. In fashion and furnishing, decor and architectural details, audiences are treated with a charming mix of cultures and temporalities. (See figs. 10.2–10.4.) Against such a gorgeous backdrop, a cast of attractive characters and bodies are entangled in a scandalous ménage à trois that crosses taboos of class, gender, and ethnoracial divides.

Furthermore, more than any of its contemporaries, *The Handmaiden* sutures content and form in Park Chan-wook's cinematic style; it uses its scandalous themes to offer a probing, full-frontal postcolonial gaze directly

Figures 10.3 and 10.4. Shot-reverse shot of the transcolonial architectural structure. (*The Handmaiden*, 2016, screen shot).

into the complex psychic allure of a taboo colonial past. The shocking queer love story against all odds between Lady Hideko and her Korean handmaiden Sook-hee, which seems to subvert all inherited boundaries and conventions, appears as an especially fitting vehicle to explore psychic entanglements. Hideko and Sook-hee's salacious rebellion, especially against the evil patriarchs Uncle Kouzuki and the self-styled Count Fujiwara, is heightened by scenes of explicit homoerotic intimacies as well as ethnic, gender, and class cross-dressings and masquerades that flout social norms. With the colonial past in general and Japanese culture and Japanese characters in particular, depicted by Park in alluring, even desirable ways, *The Handmaiden* seems to further subvert familiar conventions and overcome past censorship.

The most scandalous and taboo parts are the instances of Japan color—images of stereotypical Japanese culture. In the postcolony, such images, especially when depicted in a positive light, were vociferously condemned and even outright outlawed and had therefore been erased or made invisible for decades.

The film, however, appears to highlight and even flaunt these visuals that had been rendered unfamiliar—almost foreign and exotic in the local context. Upon its release to local audiences, *The Handmaiden* garnered controversy around the question of whether it exhibited too much Japan color in a positive light.[28] What makes it even more scandalously fascinating for contemporary global viewers is the all-too-uncannily familiar form of imperial encounter—of Japonisme—through which this once taboo Japan color seems to have returned to global audiences.

Japonisme, as seen in *The Handmaiden* and other contemporary films, follows the style of an age-old European imperialist pastime—that of commodifying and collecting objects from Japan as symbols of exotic Otherness or colonial kitsch. In *Japonisme and the Birth of Cinema*, Daisuke Miyao (2020) makes the important point that the circulation of Japonisme actually involved a much more complex two-way conversation (7). It seems commonsensical now to point out how Japanese artists and culture had a profound influence on many European artists and their highly valued works. Vincent van Gogh, Édouard Manet, and Claude Monet are just a few European artists who learned from Japanese artists and artworks in developing new techniques, styles, and forms. Further, Miyao's book newly documents Japonisme's little-known yet significant influence on early cinema's form and style.

In this chapter, I am focusing on how in Japonisme—*despite* the undeniably influential role Japanese artworks and artists played in the development of some of the best-loved and most widely recognized masterpieces of art and cinema as documented by recent scholarship—their contributions were historically devalued and unrecognized even by the very artists who were most profoundly indebted to them. This dynamic, of course, persisted because of the unequal circuits of transcolonial cultural traffic and blithe imperial disregard. In the absence of an ethical engagement, imperial artists and consumers had the power to reduce whatever they came into contact with from other cultures to what I call elsewhere exotic objects of colonial kitsch rather than as properly appraise, acknowledge, and value them (Kwon 2015, chapter 5). In fact, the artists who created the works were rarely acknowledged by name.

Critics, including Jeong and Jeong (2017), An (2018, esp. his epilogue), and several others (such as Kim K. 2011) have pointed to the appearance of exoticized Japonisme in other recent films, such as *Epitaph* (*Kidam*, Jung Sik and Jung Bum-shik, dirs., 2007). In *Epitaph*, the trope of the Japanese colonial era as exotic and erotic is again taken to extremes in depictions of madness and necrophilia, punctuated by a dream wedding sequence that pays aesthetic homage to iconic scenes of Japonisme from Kenji Mizoguchi's

1953 film *Ugetsu monogatari* (*Tales of Ugetsu*). What seems further worth noting for our purposes here is the unexpected mirroring of Japonisme as a timeworn imperialist pastime—with what we have been discussing so far of taboo postcolonial desire in Cold War–era Japan color.

Here we see an uncanny convergence of taboo desires in what at first glance appears to be mutually oppositional historic points of view—the postcolonial gaze of Japan color and the imperial gaze of Japonisme. The two gazes may seem contradictory—Japanese cultural symbols as imperial Other in the case of one, as colonial Other in the other—but, in fact, they uncannily mirror one another via a shared ambivalent structure of disavowal. Both exhibit a similarly complex fantasy of exotic and erotic desire, taboo, and resentment toward the same object of the gaze: imagined Otherness of Japanese culture. Of concern here is the question of what the significance might be of such a convergence of once competing gazes in contemporary, postmillennial Asian cinema—as the uncanny return of the imperial gaze as a postcolonial revenant via Park Chan-wook's cinematic lens?

Local and Global Cinematic Traffic of Gazes

What appears as an asynchronous or anachronistic convergence between the global imperial gaze of Japonisme and the local postcolonial gaze of Japan color in Park's *The Handmaiden* is most strikingly and immediately recognizable when the film descends spatially, from the main hybrid Western-Asian architectural structure on the ground level into the subterranean space of Uncle Kouzuki's secret lair. The rest of the film has stepped back in time into 1930s Korea under Japanese colonial rule, stunningly visualized with all the trappings of transcolonial modernity, and the scenery is set apart both spatially and temporally yet another degree and seems to go even further backward in time.

With its tatami floors, fusuma doors, and tokonoma displays, floor-to-ceiling shelves lined with Edo-era Shunga tomes, calligraphy scrolls, bonsai evergreens, and decorative folding panels, the space is visually marked wall to wall as a descent into an altogether Other space of Japaneseness. Kouzuki's study is marked as a pure, timeless pastness of traditional accoutrements, while appearing frozen and fixed as unchanging and seemingly untainted by any trace of transcolonial encounters—whether imperial West or colonial Korea. (See figs. 10.5–10.9.) The film's alternate space is cinematically marked off as a divided color line of a distinctly different chronotope, set apart from the rest of the film's transcolonial mise-en-scène—in time and space—via decor, fashion, and architecture, all reminiscent of a bygone era of a Japan that no longer exists in reality.

Figures 10.5, 10.6, 10.7, 10.8, 10.9 Hideko performs before tuxedo-clad gentlemen audience. (*The Handmaiden*, 2016, screen shot).

Figures 10.5, 10.6, 10.7, 10.8, 10.9 (*continued*)

The film's award-winning art director, Ryu Sŭng-hŭi, explained in an interview how many such scenes were designed after thorough location scouting in Japan—a luxury that was not permitted for decades for reasons discussed earlier (Kim S. 2016). The semblance of pure Japaneseness, like the object of ideology of Japan color and Japonisme, is, of course, not based on reality but is a construct of the imagination—here, Uncle Kouzuki's.[29] His desire for Japan has been so strong and absolute that he has surrounded himself with all things Japanese. We the audience, however, know that this is all counterfeit, much like Kouzuki's new identity itself: no matter how hard he tries to assimilate as a Japanese subject, the object of his desire is elusive, and he remains nothing but a fake, like the counterfeit books he is trying to sell to his customers.

The entire space, though visually stunning, is marked not only as a space of exotic Otherness but as one of inauthenticity or the counterfeit, heightened by memories of trauma and perversion. For Hideko, for example, the daily ritual crossing into this Other space is marked by traumatic repetition, exhibited literally through bodily symptoms, nerves, and anxiety. We peep through flashback sequences that show us how since childhood Hideko had been compelled, sometimes with corporal punishment, under Uncle Kouzuki's tutelage in this subterranean space, to practice recitations from old erotic texts. It was the duty of Hideko—and before her, it had been the duty of her aunt, until the aunt's suicide by hanging from a cherry blossom tree outside Hideko's window—to perform these readings before an audience of gentlemen patrons.

When Hideko performs here, the camera zooms in for an extreme close-up of her gaze, then pans to reverse shots of each of the men looking back at her. She appears to perform *mise en abîme* for two sets of audiences: for the diegetic audience (within the film) of Kouzuki and the male collectors suited in Western tuxedos and for extradiegetic, global cinematic audiences—exhibited in full ceremonial kimono, Nihongami geishaesque coiffure (fig. 10.7), while kneeling on a tatami floor surrounded by Japanese-style decor.

Ventriloquizing the male narrative voice and playfully eyeing the gentlemen audience, Hideko reads aloud from erotic texts, including famous Shunga stories by Katsushika Hokusai, and at times performs shocking scenes with the aid of an adult-sized wooden puppet (fig. 10.9).[30] The purpose of the performance is presumably to seduce the visibly aroused men into parting with their riches and acquiring Uncle Kouzuki's rare books for their own fetishistic collections, but also to seduce the global cinematic audiences beyond the film's diegetic frame as well. Such scenes seem to present a striking visual reenactment of Japonisme's imperialist transactional performance that had once been on display for the Western gaze. By the look of it, Hideko's performance seems to be a repetition or mimicry of a stereotypical performance of Japonisme that had circulated during the nineteenth century exclusively for Western audiences. What is significant now, in *The Handmaiden*, is how this point of view has been counterfeited and appropriated by Park—the postcolonial auteur—to converge simultaneously onto a fully fleshed-out cinematic embodiment for twenty-first-century local and global cineasts alike.

Perversion, Subversion, and Counterfeit in the Postcolonial Imperial Gaze

In lieu of a conclusion, I would like to explore the lingering question of how contemporary audiences might view the significance of contemporary South Korean film's appropriation of the age-old imperialist gaze. In our reading thus far, Japan, the former colonizers, and their culture appear to be relegated to the position of exotic colonial kitsch to which colonial Korea was historically subjected and objectified by Japan's own imperial gaze. How do we understand the convergence of once taboo Japan color with that of a Japonisme that is newly flaunted for a global audience, in particular in the postmillennial moment? In the loosening of Cold War ideologies that has finally lifted a geopolitical injunction against a historic reckoning, is this a delayed manifestation of postcolonial ressentiment? In other words, is it a postponed manifestation of a desire for postcolonial vengeance against the former colonizer through the iconography of Japan, depicted as a perverse and erotic object of Otherness?

Yet the possibility of a straightforward revenge is complicated by several factors here. Though Japan color at its most heightened climax is certainly pictured in this film as contemptuous, depraved, and perverse, it is simultaneously represented as multiple desirable objects of attraction. Also, Kouzuki, the colonized interloper and a counterfeit Japanese himself, is the character depicted in the worst possible light, while other authentic Japanese characters like Hideko are pictured as alluring objects of desire and even as heroically subverting patriarchal confinement. Also, a very real possibility exists that, for many contemporary global audiences, any nuanced visual differences between Korean and Japanese cultures and their complex historic entanglements may not be legible, because most cultural cues are presented as decorative backdrop, erased of any historical or ideological significance. For most global viewers, then, the visualization of Asian exotic erotica in this film may not differentiate between Korea and Japan. In the gaze of the global consumer, the two may be conflated as signifying an all-too-familiar, age-old, generalized exoticized gaze on the "Orient" in toto, rendering any possibility of postcolonial revenge ambivalent at best.

It does seem worth noting in the end that many of these scenes of Asian erotic exotica are painted in an over-the-top, perversely exaggerated manner. They are rendered farcical, even cartoonish, and therein may exist a sliver of an opening to an ironic postcolonial reading. Such an alternative or queer reading may be in extradiegetic tension with the film's diegetic exhibition of a straightforward imperial mimicry akin to Kouzuki's homosocial counterfeit antics for his gentlemen audience. Is there a trace of a postcolonial subversion or queering of a familiar imperial gaze—one that travesties the very power dynamics of global cinematic circuits? Is there room for self-reflexive irony about the global film circuit in which postcolonial or Third World auteurs are often pressed to self-consciously commodify a (self) exoticized culture, in exchange for global recognition? Such a dynamic may be akin to—and yet offer a twenty-first-century complication and departure from— what Rey Chow, an early Anglophone critic of contemporary East-West dynamics, had diagnosed decades ago in the preliminary exotic-erotic foray of fifth-generation Chinese filmmakers into the limelight of the global cinematic circuit.[31] To be sure, a similar critique had been likewise aimed at Japanese directors such as Mizoguchi and Kurosawa further back during the mid-twentieth-century version of Japonisme as well. Perhaps such competing and repetitive global cinematic desires are embodied, even unwittingly, within Park Chan-wook's manifest and latent convergence of style and content—exhibiting an uncanny *untimeliness* in the film's iconic moments of once-repressed historic revenants. Through *The Handmaiden* and other such postmillennial Asian films, global audiences may glimpse a deeply postcolonial ambivalence—of a simultaneous subversion *and* perversion—of an all-too-familiar and all-too-taboo desire of the imperial gaze at the cusp of the new rise of global Asian cinema.

Notes

1. This phenomenon is not unidirectional and extends to coproductions and other transborder enterprises in and beyond Asia. Christina Klein (2003) labels it an "Asianization of Hollywood and Hollywoodization of Asia." See also Pugsley (2013).

2. It is interesting that one of the few notable exceptions, for example, include the North Korean film *Kkot p'anŭn ch'ŏnyŏ* (Flower girl, 1972) which garnered tremendous popular following outside the nation in China and beyond. From critics and scholars to fans, many local and global cineasts have contributed important analyses of these recent films, from various angles. See, for example, Kim Kyung Hyun (2011), especially ch. 2; Kyoung-Lae Kang (2015); Kevin Michael Smith (2017); Michelle Cho (2015); Ch'angho Yun (2018); and Moonim Baek (2012).

3. In the case of South Korea, for example, an entire category of "liberation films" (*kwangbok yŏnghwa*) came out in the 1940s, such as *Hurray for Freedom* (*Jayu Manse*, Ch'oe In-kyu, dir., 1946), *Hometown Liberated* (*Haebangdoen nae kohyang*, Chŏn Changgŭn, dir., 1947), *Martyr Yun Ponggil* (*Yun Ponggil ŭisa*, Yun Pongch'un, dir., 1947); *Before and after Liberation* (*Tongnip chŏnya*, Ch'oe In-kyu, dir., 1948), *Martyr Yu Kwansun* (*Yu Kwansun*, Yun Pongch'un, dir., 1948). The standard narrative of these few examples has been canonized within the nation but is little known beyond. See Yi Yŏngil ([1969] 2004), 214–24, and S. Lee (2005).

4. A revelation that emerged from the contemporary rise of these historical representations, especially circulated for wider global audiences, was just how limited such representations of the colonial and wartime pasts about the region had been until then, not only within the local context within the region, but in global cinematic histories as well.

It is not uncommon for traumatic or unsavory histories to emerge into the limelight only after decades of being repressed or buried. The delayed structure of postcolonial or postimperial memories in particular is also a well-known phenomenon. The long delay in the case of East Asia and the Asia-Pacific front, however, is remarkable when juxtaposed with the simultaneous histories from the European front. Films depicting parallel histories in Euro-America—from the 1930s to the 1940s—are ubiquitous. Even before the war ended, films about the two world wars began to be released and have by now become classic fare in western film histories *Casablanca* (Michael Curtis, dir., 1942) is but one iconic example, and new films continue to be produced yearly. *Dunkirk*, Christopher Nolan, dir., 2017), *Darkest Hour* (Joe Wright, dir., 2017), and *1917* (Sam Mendes, dir., 2019) are just a few recent examples. The few exceptions were limited in their focus on Euro-American fighters, prisoner-of-war stories, Japanese atrocities such as the Nanjing massacre, or the story of

Euro-American subjects such as *Sands of Iwo Jima* (Allan Dwan, dir., 1949) and *Bridge on the River Kwai* (David Lean, dir., 1957). In stark contrast, it is only in recent years that we see a significant rise in globally circulated representations of the Pacific front from the period. Within the region, most previous representations, as in the case of South Korea explored in this essay, were limited to local audiences and highly nationalistic in representation. Bruce Lee films and Hong Kong *wuxia* more generally were exceptions largely because of remarkable distribution plans.

5. In the case of China, a few well-known recent examples include coproductions such as Ang Lee's *Lust Caution* (*Si jie*, 2007) and *Flowers of War* (*Jinling shisan chai*, Zhang Yimou, dir., 2011). An interesting point is that *Parasite* embodies repressed memories of yet another empire in the region—that of US imperialism. Closer analyses of the overlapping legacies of multiple imperial entanglements warrant further examination elsewhere.

6. The films that have come to be widely known as the Vengeance Trilogy are *Sympathy for Mr. Vengeance* (CJ Entertainment, 2002), *Oldboy* (CJ Entertainment, 2003), and *Lady Vengeance* (CJ Entertainment, 2005).

7. Recent studies have provided important new explorations on the extent of film censorship in South Korea. See, for example, Hanguk (2016). It is worth noting that it was not until the new millennium that South Korean and international audiences would have access to some of the controversial films made during the colonial and wartime era. Several scholars were able to explore such newly unearthed colonial-era films, especially ones developed with the collaboration of the Japanese film industry and those apparently supporting the imperial cause. See, for example, Yecies and Shim (2011) and Fujitani and Kwon (2012).

8. See volume introduction.

9. *Passage to India* (David Lean, 1984), *Indochine* (Régis Wargnier, 1992), and *L'Outremer* (Brigitte Roüan, 1990) are some noteworthy examples of films reenvisioning Europe's vast colonial ventures.

10. A contemporary tourist to many former colonial territories in Asia, Africa, and Latin America, for example, may also be familiar with the uncanny encounters with leftover territorial imprints of settler colonial cultures, in architecture, monuments, ruins, and street names. All empires, once they forcibly took over a territory, unfailingly and proudly made grand caninelike habits of avidly marking their newly attained territories with visible claims of ownership.

11. The encounters of the earlier generations were more frequent, of course, in the cities than in more remote rural areas.

12. Jinsoo An (2018) discusses the films' poor critical reception. See, especially his chapter 4.

13. See Prasenjit Duara (2003) for similar examples from another context.

14. Such awkward production choices are not limited to one particular scene in this film. Another such striking image occurs when the gaffer is visible in the diegetic frame.

15. For a news retrospective on the demolition, see "Chosŏn ch'ongdokpu ch'ŏlgŏ sŏnp'o 1995" (Proclamation of the governor general building demolition 1995), *MBC News*, March 1, 2019. https://www.youtube.com/watch?v=uoDTcw_kh1I.

16. The stereotypical moustache appeared in contemporary news in a controversy over the moustache of the US ambassador to South Korea. Some South Korean citizens apparently were offended by how this official of Japanese-American descent was sporting facial hair that harked back to facial fashion from the colonial era. I would like to thank my father for drawing attention to this contemporary moustache-gate. See Justin McCurry. "U.S. Ambassador's Moustache Gets Up South Korea's Nose," *The Guardian*. January 16, 2020.

17. Many scholars have documented how, in postimperial Japan, there was a noteworthy absence of any acknowledgment of its imperial and wartime past. See, for example, Conrad (2014).

18. After the overthrow of Syngman Rhee's presidency, a slight window opened up, but that closed after a brief period.

19. The Sino-Korean character "Wae" used as a reference to Japan had derogatory origins going back centuries with connotations of dwarvism and barbarism based on the presumed small stature and lack of culture of island neighbors.

20. "Ilbon t'ŭrŏbŭl: Pŏnjinŭn Ilbon Mudŭ, 6" ("Japan trouble: expanding Japanese mood," part 6), *Donga ilbo*, February 6, 1964. https://newslibrary.naver.com/viewer/index.nhn?articleId =1964020600209201002&editNo=2&printCount=1&publishDate=1964-02-06&officeId=00020 &pageNo=1&printNo=13009&publishType=00020.

21. Again, local color of Western locations and cultures were not considered to be a problem.

22. Celebrity singer Yi Mija laments in an interview that "It was tremendously painful when 'Dongbaek Agassi' was banned based on accusation of exhibiting too much *waesaek*." Kim Hyeyun, *Sŭt'a T'udaei* (Star today), December 10, 2019. https://www.mk.co.kr/star/hot-issues/view/2019/12 /1031435/. In an interesting sidenote, Yi Mija sang the title song for the aforementioned controversial film *Happy Solitude*.

23. The Cold War dynamic of saying yes and no to Japan was decidedly different from contemporary versions of "the nation that can say no" movement that has been rising in contemporary Asian politics. See Chen (2010) for the significance of this rise in Japan, Taiwan, and elsewhere in the region. Most recently, "No Japan/No Abe" boycotts extending to all forms of exchanges, cultural, economic, and political, have challenged bilateral relations in the region and are a symptom of rising power plays in Asia.

24. See Chen (2010) and J. Lee (2010) for cogent analyses of the new parallel status of Korea and Japan as subimperial powers beneath the US imperial security umbrella.

25. The case of the comfort women exposes how investigations were actively silenced by the three governmental powers in order to move the treaty forward.

26. *Lost Memories 2009* (Lee Si-myung, dir., 2002) and *Rikidozan* (Song Hye-sung, dir., 2004) are some noteworthy examples of such postmillennial collaborations.

27. Some other striking recent films about the colonial era, such as *Dongju* (Portrait of a poet, Lee Joon-ik, dir., 2016) and *Hangō: Yu Kwansun Iyagi* (A resistance, Cho Minho, dir., 2019) have been filmed in stylistic black-and-white aesthetics as well.

28. Many fans and detractors via fan sites and reviews have taken vocal stands on both sides, and the director himself was compelled to comment on the complex feelings related to the Japan color issue and dispute the accusations. See, for example, Jo Yeon-kyung, "'Handmaiden' Director Park Chan-wook Speaks about Controversy over the Color of 'Complex Emotions,'" *Newsen*, https:// www.newsen.com/news_view.php?uid=201605141900271110.

29. Art director Ryu Seung-hee explains how she wanted to add an interior Japanese garden to convey a heightened sense of Kouzuki's admiration for all things Japanese (Kim S. 2016).

30. In one scene, a close-up of the erotic octopus scene from Hokusai's "The Dream of a Fisherman's Wife" (1814) is featured prominently.

31. Jeong and Jeong (2017) directly apply Chow's critique from more than two decades ago to their reading of Park's *The Handmaiden*, but what I am arguing here is that there are fundamental differences in the regional dynamics of mutual and competing positionalities and relationalities that require an updated critique in the postmillennial moment.

Bibliography

An, Jinsoo. 2018. *Parameters of Disavowal: Colonial Representation in South Korean Cinema*. Berkeley: University of California Press.

Baek, Moonim. 2012. "The Beautiful, the Lame, and the Weird: Three Types of Colonial Heroes in Contemporary Korean Films." *Review of Korean Studies* 15, no. 2 (December): 7–32.

Cha, Victor. 1996. "Bridging the Gap: The Strategic Context of the 1965 Korea-Japan Normalization Treaty." *Korean Studies* 20: 123–60.

Chen, Kuan-Hsing. 2010. *Asia as Method: Toward Deimperialization*. Durham, NC: Duke University Press.

Cho, Michelle. 2015. "Genre, Translation, and Transnational Cinema: Kim Jee-woon's 'The Good, the Bad, the Weird.'" *Cinema Journal* 54, no. 3 (Spring): 44–68.
Chung, Steven. 2014. *Split Screen Korea*. Minneapolis: University of Minnesota Press.
Conrad, Sebastian. 2014. "The Dialectics of Remembrance: Memories of Empire in Cold War Japan." *Comparative Studies in Society and History* 56, no. 1 (January): 4–33.
Duara, Prasenjit. 2003. *Sovereignty and Authenticity: Manchukuo and the East Asian Modern*. Lanham, MD: Rowman and Littlefield.
DuBois, W. E. B. (1903) 1993. *The Souls of Black Folk*. New York: Knopf.
Fujitani, Takashi, and Nayoung Aimee Kwon, eds. 2012. *Transcolonial Film Coproductions in the Japanese Empire: Antinomies in the Colonial Archive*. In *Cross-Currents: East Asian History and Culture Review* 1, no. 5 (December): 1–169. https://cross-currents.berkeley.edu/e-journal/issue-5.
Hanguk yŏngsang charyowŏn, ed. 2016. *Hanguk yŏnghwa sok kŏmyŏl chedo* (Censorship policies in Korean film). Seoul: Korea Film Archive.
Hughes, Theodore H. 2012. *Literature and Film in Cold War South Korea: Freedom's Frontier*. New York: Columbia University Press.
Jeong Ch'ang-hun and Jeong Su-wan. 2017. "Singminji shigi yŏnghwadŭlŭi sangp'um mihak ideologi pip'an" (Representation of the colonial period in contemporary Korean films and merchandise aesthetics). *Inmun K'ŏnt'entch'ŭ* 45, no. 6: 33–58.
Kang, Kyoung-Lae. 2015. "Kyung Sung: Cinematic Memories of the Colonial Past in Contemporary Korea." *Camera Obscura* 30, no. 3 (90): 27–59.
Kim, Kyung Hyun. 2011. *Virtual Hallyu: Korean Cinema of the Global Era*. Durham, NC: Duke University Press.
Kim Sŏng-hun. 2016. "Ryu Ryu Sŭng-hŭi misul kamdogi malhanŭn *Agassi* pot'o coment'eri" (Photo-Commentary by Agassi's Art Director, Ryu Sŭng-hŭi), *Cine21*, June 6. http://www.cine21.com/news/view/?mag_id=84314.
Klein, Christina. 2003. "The Asia Factor in Global Hollywood." *YaleGlobal Online*, March 25. https://yaleglobal.yale.edu/content/asia-factor-global-hollywood.
Korea Film Council, ed. 2017. *Korean Cinema 2016*. Seoul: Korea Film Council/KOFA.
Kwon, Heonik. 2010. *The Other Cold War*. New York: Columbia University Press.
Kwon, Nayoung Aimee. 2015. *Intimate Empire: Collaboration and Colonial Modernity in Korea and Japan*. Durham, NC: Duke University Press.
Lee, Jin-kyung. 2010. *Service Economies: Militarism, Sex Work, and Migrant Labor in South Korea*. Minneapolis: University of Minnesota Press.
Lee, Soon-jin. 2005. "Singminji kyŏnghŏm kwa haebang chikhu ŭi yŏnghwa mandŭlgi" (Colonial Experience and Filmmaking in the Post-Liberation Aftermath). *Taejung Sŏsa Yŏngu* [Popular Narratives] 11, no. 2: 105–43.
Miyao, Daisuke. 2020. *Japonisme and the Birth of Cinema*. Durham, NC: Duke University Press.
Nornes, Abé Mark. 2007. *Cinema Babel: Translating Global Cinema*. Minneapolis: University of Minnesota Press.
Pugsley, Peter. 2013. *Tradition, Culture, and Aesthetics in Contemporary Asian Cinema*. Farnham, UK: Ashgate.
Said, Edward W. 1978. *Orientalism*. New York: Vintage.
Smith, Kevin Michael. 2017. "Vicarious Politics: Violence and the Colonial Period in Contemporary South Korean Cinema." *Asia-Pacific Journal* 15, Issue 12, no. 3 (June 15): 1–25.
Stam, Robert, and Louise Spence. 2009. "Colonialism, Racism, and Representation: An Introduction." In *Film Theory and Criticism*. Edited by Leo Braudy and Marshall Cohen. New York: Oxford University Press: 751–766.

Suzuki, Tessa Morris. 2013. *East Asia beyond the History Wars: Confronting the Ghosts of Violence.* New York: Routledge.
Uchida, Jun. 2011. *Brokers of Empire: Japanese Settler Colonialism in Korea, 1876–1945.* Cambridge, MA: Harvard University Asia Center.
Yecies, Brian, and Ae-Gyung Shim. 2011. *Korea's Occupied Cinemas, 1893–1948: The Untold Story of the Film Industry.* New York: Routledge.
Yi Chiwŏn. 2015. "Hanil munhwa kyoryu wa pan'Il nolli ŭi pyŏnhwa" (Korean-Japanese cultural exchange and changes in anti-Japanese sentiment). *Hanguk kwa Kukchae chŏngch'i* [South Korea and International Politics] 31, no. 88 (Spring): 119–50.
Yi Yŏngil. (1969) 2004. *Hanguk Yŏnghwa Chŏnsa Kaejŏng Chŭngbop'an* (History of Korean cinema, revised edition). Seoul: Tosŏ ch'ulp'an Sodo.
Yun, Ch'angho. 2018. "A Study on Space Map through Gender's Power Relationship—Focused on Park Chan-wook's 'Handmaiden.'" *Journal for the Moving Image Technology Association for Korea* 6: 77–93.

NAYOUNG AIMEE KWON is Associate Professor in the Department of Asian and Middle Eastern Studies and the Program in Cinematic Arts at Duke University. She is Founding Director of the Asian American and Diaspora Studies Program and Co-director of the Andrew Mellon Games and Culture Humanities Lab. She is author of *Intimate Empire: Collaboration and Colonial Modernity in Korea and Japan* and editor (with Takashi Fujitani) of *Transcolonial Film Coproductions in the Japanese Empire: Antinomies in the Colonial Archive.*

INDEX

allegory: allegorical characters played by Na, 59; in *Balangiga: Howling Wilderness*, 17, 222–224, 227, 231; in *Beautiful Ducklings*, 151; in *Momotarō*, 196–197; in *Orphan of Asia*, 139, 147; in *The Red Lantern*, 112; representations of Taiwan's plight through, 15, 139, 147, 151

anachronistic space and time, 30, 38, 196, 262

animation: anime, 256; Disney, 194, 196, 199, 235; Great Wall Film Company productions, 103; Imamura's critical writings on, 75, 194, 197, 199–201, 209n16; *Momotarō: Divine Warriors of the Sea*, 16–17, 189, 190–191, 194, 195, 196–199, 203, 204, 207, 208nn1–3, 209n17, 209–210nn19–23; of Seo Mitsuyo, 16, 189, 194, 195, 196, 198, 200, 207; stop-motion in *Balangiga: Howling Wilderness*, 230, 238; Studio Ghibli, 194

anthropos and humanitas, 2, 7, 19–20nn8–9, 191, 208nn2–3

archives, 1, 4, 6, 7–8, 11, 15, 140, 156, 254, 257

Asia as method, 15, 139–140, 156

asynchronicity, 25–30, 39, 41–43

audiences: Asian films for proletarians and farmers, 61; Asian theaters run by Western traveler-entrepreneurs, 99; censorship and control of films shown to, 100, 101, 104–105, 166–167, 246, 247–248, 250, 253, 256, 268n7; Chinese, 104, 108n12; Chinese Film Censorship Committee, 105; "condensation" to facilitate viewer engagement, 226; disinterest in, 217–218; of documentary films, 42, 83, 197, 199, 201; "fascinating cannibalism" of colonial, 60–61, 101; film language and audience understanding, 71, 75–76, 82, 115–117, 193, 196, 197, 198–199, 206, 245, 250, 264, 265; filmmakers' inability to control responses of, 41–42, 78; film theory discussions of, 13, 68, 70–71, 74–76, 83–84, 86; global, 106, 112–113, 118–119, 203, 243–245, 248, 249, 261, 265–267, 267–268n4; government attempts to instruct or train, 78–80, 84, 101, 104, 106, 168, 193; Hays Code and MPPDA, 101, 106; Im Hwa on Korean, 59–60, 80–81, 82, 88n8; imperialist mythmaking and propaganda presented to, 19n6, 26, 37, 40, 41, 62–63, 101, 106–107, 122–123, 125–126, 168, 197, 217, 245–246; internalization in, 68, 70–71, 86–87; Japanese, 57, 58, 63, 78, 169; Korean, 57–60, 75–76, 82–85, 246, 250–251, 253, 255, 256, 261, 265, 267–268n4, 268n7; Korean films' appeal for colonial, 57–59; Korean workers' reactions to *The Engagement*, 82; Koriyama's attitude toward Korean, 60, 81; local versus international, 9, 43, 101–102, 198–199, 206, 218, 245–246, 250–251, 261, 267–268n4, 268n7; as major concern among film theorists, 74–75, 81–87, 87n4, 88n8; Malayan, 11, 41–42; Manchurian, 76, 79, 87n1; newsreels shown in theaters, 176; overseas Chinese reactions to *ruHua pian* films, 99–102, 104–107, 122; O Yŏng-jin on importance of externalizing, 68, 83–87; O Yŏng-jin's theory of shock and surprise, 76, 85–86; participation of viewers watching *Arirang*, 59; popularity of cinematic period pieces with, 243–244; popularity of Korean films with, 167, 255; popularity of melodrama with, 79, 114–115, 118–123, 126, 143, 149–150; popularity of Na's films with, 57–60, 63; popularity of orphan-themed films with, 143, 147–151, 156–157; popularity of Taiwanese films with, 143, 148, 151; popularity of *Taiyupian* films with, 143, 154, 156; popularity of Tarzan films with, 140, 144–145, 150, 156–157; popularity of Western cinema with colonial Asian, 94, 96, 104, 112, 118; as proletariat for socialists, 57–58, 61, 81–82; responses to and resignification of films by, 2, 9, 41–42, 59, 74–75, 78–80, 82, 83, 85, 116–117, 200–201, 206–207, 210n23; *ruHua pian* films shown to American, 103–104; "sideshadowing" to facilitate

273

understanding, 225; Taiwanese, 148–149, 151, 158–159n12; unpopularity of proletarian films with Japanese, 57, 58; visceral reactions of, 79, 93, 97, 104–105, 107, 114, 230–231; "voice of the home" as influence on, 118–123, 128

auteur, 163, 164, 182, 216, 217, 265, 266

avant-garde cinema: *Balangiga: Howling Wilderness*, 17, 215, 222, 225–226, 236–239; contributions of Khavan to, 216; Hansen on modernism and, 116; *Sakay*, 218–219; Skoller on, 215, 221, 225–226; surrealist imagery and oneiricism in, 222; as tool for reinterpreting historical knowledge, 221, 225–226; tropes and devices of, 17, 222, 238–239; Zhang on modernism as avant-garde, 131n5

Balangiga: Howling Wilderness (2017): avant-garde devices used in, 17, 215, 219, 222, 225–226, 236–239; characters in, 221, 222–227, 236–237; "condensation" in, 226; cultural icons in, 229–231; historic situation that inspired, 214–216, 221; imagery of, 215, 222, 225–235, 237, 239; Khavn's contributions to, 17, 214, 216–217, 221–222, 224–226, 233–235, 237, 238, 239; mise-en-scène in, 17, 223, 230–236; picaresque structure of, 222; plot of, 221, 222–228, 234–238; "sideshadowing" in, 225–226; stop-motion animation in, 230, 238; treatment of history in, 17, 215, 217, 221–223, 224–226, 228, 231–234, 235–236, 239

Balázs, Béla, 51–52, 62

Barlow, Tani, 95, 98

Benjamin, Walter, 17, 31, 220–221, 233

betweenness (*aidagara*), 191, 205

biopolitics: biopolitical conditions of global culture, 189, 191, 209n16; desubjectifying power of global cinema and, 193, 195, 203; as event or desubjectification, 202; Hardt and Negri on, 202, 210n27; system of security and subjugation and, 202, 203, 210n25; unconscious, humanistic coloniality of global, 189, 190, 204

Birth of a Nation (1915), 111, 118–119, 121, 122, 123–124, 127, 128, 129

Brecht, Bertolt: Imamura's cinema theory compared to that of, 195, 200–201; pursuit of *verite* by, 201, 204, 210n23; Seo's animated film theory compared to that of, 196, 198, 199–201

camera: cameramen, 31, 43n1, 99, 178, 210n23; camera use in *Mar ē Senki*, 196–197, 199, 210n23; intermediating role between reality and screen presentation, 28, 29, 31; subjective intentions and interpretations of, 29, 32, 202, 210n23; as tool for establishing cinematic reality, 27, 32, 84, 201, 202, 210n23, 224, 265

capitalism: British imperial reorientation from colonialism to, 31; capitalist modernity, 28, 131n8, 144; Christian missionary work as complement to, 125; exclusion or economic displacement of indigenous peoples by, 25, 34, 35, 38, 39; global spread from the West of, 27, 35, 48, 200, 210n28; Hollywood as tool and symbol of Western, 94, 95, 107n1, 116, 209n16; socialist fight against, 48, 60, 94; as ultimate goal and global future, 27, 31, 32, 34, 35, 39

censorship: Asian censorship of negative colonial memories, 1, 2, 18, 242, 259; cinematic allegory as tool to avoid, 59; colonial censorship of local voices, 1, 6; film burning, 105; Film Censorship Committee guidelines, 104–105, 158n9; foreign films censored as being *ruHua*, 103–104, 105; *The Handmaiden* as challenge to Korean, 259–261, 268n7; Hays Code, 106; Japanese censorship of Korean cultural media, 65n2, 243; Japanese imperial censorship office, 173; Korean censorship of negative colonial memories, 242, 246, 248–249, 256–259; Korean censorship of *waesaek* ("Japan color"), 255, 257, 258–266, 269n22; nationalist Chinese government censorship of *ruHua* films, 99, 104–105; power of censorship to misrepresent reality, 243, 246, 248, 249, 259–261, 268n7; public debates in nationalized Indonesia regarding, 177–179; public censorship of *ruHua* films, 97, 103; Regulations for Film Censorship (*Dianying jiancha fa*) (1930), 104; Western Cold War censorship in Asia of Communist ideologies, 258–259

China: Boxer Rebellion, 103, 111, 112, 123–124; Chinese nationalism, 93; coloniality and modernity in, 95, 112, 126; decolonization and nation-building in, 14, 92, 93; effect of protests against *ruHua pian* on Chinese nationalism, 97, 101, 103–107; fragmented colonization of, 95, 96, 97–98, 104, 108n5, 121; Hollywood misrepresentations of, 13, 100, 101, 123–125; indigenous populations of, 154–155; Japanese invasion of (1931), 104, 165, 194; Kuomintang (KMT), 104–107, 150,

153; as major film market for the West, 93, 94, 106, 112, 132n20; as market for Japanese films, 96; Mandarin language, 142, 143, 148, 150, 151, 156, 158n7, 159n16; participation of overseas Chinese in nationalist dialogs, 100–103; People's Republic of China, 98, 144, 176; Qing Dynasty, 93, 102, 151, 155, 159n18; Republic of China, 93, 98, 99, 104, 153, 158n3, 159n19, 160n25; Sinitic languages in, 158n4; Taiwan, 142, 152, 154, 159n21, 160n25; warlord strife in, 93; Western missionaries in, 111, 112, 124–125; Wu Zhuoliu's *Orphan of Asia* (*Ajia no koji*) (novel), 139, 140, 145–147

China-humiliating films. See *ruHua pian* (China-humiliating films)

Chinese cinema: aesthetic disagreements between Chinese critics and overseas Chinese, 99–103; Brodsky's Asia Film Company (*Yaxiya yingxi gongsi*), 99; confluence of Western cinema with, 122; early role of Western travelers-entrepreneurs in, 99, 100; emergence of, 93, 98–101, 106–107; entanglement of Chinese nationalism with, 93, 98–99, 104–107; films to counter Western *ruHua pian*, 104–105; government intercession in, 104–107; Great Wall Film Company (*Changcheng zhizao huanpian gongsi*), 103–104, 108n10; Hong Kong filmmaking, 99, 144, 148, 158n7, 243, 267–268n4; Lu Xun on Western exploitation of China, 93; *The Motion Picture Review* (*Yingxi zazhi*), 100–101; *Orphan Chicks in the Snow*, 122; Shanghai filmmaking, 79, 99, 103, 105, 108n12, 116, 122, 131n5; *Yellow Earth*, 131n11; Zhenzhen Society, 103–104

cinema: film theory, 70–79, 82–86; as form of thought and theorizing, 74–75, 85; O Yŏngjin on importance of audience to, 83–87

cinéma vérité, 17, 193, 194–195, 199, 200–201, 209n14

Cold War: anticommunist propaganda, 150, 215, 254, 258; breakdown of viewpoints and borderlines, 4, 254; film settings, 142, 144; interfering influence on Asian decolonization of, 155, 156–157, 219, 250, 254–255, 258; modernism as postcolonial Cold War product, 115; postcolonial Korea, 18, 254–258, 269n23; postcolonial nation-building in East Asia, 148, 152–153; postcolonial Taiwan, 14–15, 140, 142–143, 146–148, 155, 156; postimperial Japan, 255; US-orchestrated Normalization Treaty, 255, 257–258, 269n24

collaborations: Chinese filmmaking, 99; collaborators as traitors, 165, 175, 180, 181, 182; colonial-Japanese, 15, 16, 83, 164, 170–171, 180–181, 268n7; film characters that embodied complexities of, 251–252; of Hinatsu/ Dr. Huyung, 15–16, 163–171, 174–176, 180; Khavn's cinematic, 217; *Miles Away from Happiness*, 3; postcolonial, post–Cold War transborder cinematic, 255, 259, 269n26; scholarly collaborations around cinema, 4, 6, 8, 10, 15; transborder, 3; wartime cinematic, 3

colonial documentaries: asynchronous nature of, 25, 29, 43; colonial historicism that characterizes, 27–31, 39–40; as depictions of what should be rather than what is, 26–29, 38–40, 43; *Five Faces of Malaya*, 30–43; imagined past posited in, 27; myth-making tools of, 11, 25; propagandistic purposes of, 28; race-time in British, 11, 26, 31–32, 38, 40, 43; *Voices of Malaya*, 25, 43

colonial historicism: assumptions regarding time and progress, 27, 28, 29, 30; asynchronic character of, 26; cinematic tools for fabricating, 11, 25; colonial documentary, 26–30; mythology inherent in, 11, 42; power of reality to undermine presentations of, 26, 38, 39, 40

colonialism: assumptions of controllability of the colonized, 50–51, 60; assumptions of technological progress and social evolution, 11, 25, 38, 51, 249; British, 12, 30–31, 35, 155; Chinese, 155, 159n18; colonial gaze, 16, 189–190, 199, 208n6, 209n11; damage to colonizers and the metropole from, 51, 57, 231–232, 234; Dutch, 35, 155, 165, 174, 175; epidermalization and, 16–17; filmmaking and cinema as tools of, 1–2, 5, 7, 11, 16, 18–19n4, 25–26, 29, 31, 42, 92, 94–95, 119–121, 151, 163–164, 193–194, 203; globalization as, 193–194, 201–204, 207; historicism as tool of Western, 27, 38; humanism as complement to, 190; impact on development of film theory, 13, 70–87, 96; Japanese, 15, 155, 163–164; of Japanese socialists, 51–52, 54–56, 59–62; modernity as product of, 25, 27, 38, 63, 65, 249; oppression as inherent to, 5, 48, 51, 57, 63, 69, 96, 180, 182, 248–249, 251, 253–254; Othering as tool of, 12, 17, 30–35, 49–50, 60, 69, 189, 191, 208–209nn7–8, 223, 246; Portuguese, 35, 144; propaganda and publicity to legitimize, 25, 30, 37–38, 40, 49–51, 73, 77, 119, 124, 163–164, 230, 249; reality

Index 275

versus myths of, 38–40, 42; Spanish, 217, 218, 223, 225, 236; stereotyping as tool of, 30, 38, 49–51, 57–58, 60; subcolony and semicolony, 97–98. *See also* imperialism; metropole; Othering; racism

coloniality: of cinema, 17, 193, 194–195, 203, 205–207; colonialism versus, 208n6; cultural hegemony, 203; differing manifestations of, 16, 92–93, 189–194; epidermal colonialism versus, 16, 189–190, 191–192, 205, 208–209nn7–8; "everydayness" quality of, 20nn13–14, 191–193; hybridity, 203–204; Imamura on, 16–17, 194–195, 200–201, 204; impact on development of film theory of, 17; inclusive and exclusive qualities of, 189–190, 193–194, 199, 203–204, 207; intertwining of modernity and, 95, 98, 146; in Japanese Empire, 16–17, 139, 146, 156, 189–190; nationalism as reaction to, 93, 94–95, 102–103; ongoing and renewed forms of, 10, 18, 189–190, 193, 203, 207; of photographic technology, 211n37; repressive, deforming nature of, 15, 18, 19n7, 139, 146; Seo on, 16–17, 196–199, 204, 210n21; as unconscious, hidden aspect of colonialism, 16–17, 20nn13–14, 189–194, 203–206, 210n21. *See also* consciousness and unconsciousness

colonial modernity: Barlow on, 95; as concept of Othering, 117, 125; depicted in colonial documentaries, 31; depicted in *The Handmaiden*, 259, 260; formation of Chinese cinema culture as response to, 92–93, 106–107, 112, 125–126; global coloniality and, 95; making of Others as unmodern, 117; power hierarchy inherent to, 95–96, 105; progress toward, as depicted in *Five Faces of Malaya*, 26, 30–41; race-time spectrum of, 11, 30, 31, 38, 40, 43; reality versus, 38–41; scholarship on, 19n8; transcolonial modernity, 247–249, 262

colonized: actual entanglement of colonizer and, 247–248; challenges and transgressions by, 52, 55–56, 61–62, 80–82, 96, 121, 168–170; cinema as tool for making the colonized conscious of subjugation, 194; collaborators and navigators, 163–166, 170, 180–181; damage sustained by the colonized through colonizer control of technologies, 6; face of the colonized projected through cinema, 32–35, 51, 52, 57–60, 121; internalization by the, 68–70; Khavn's cinematic treatment of sufferings of the, 222–237; prolonged damage to the colonized following departure of colonizers, 5–6; protagonist Hu Taiming as embodiment of damaged, 145–147, 153–154; protagonist Mahlee's plight as victim of colonization, 125–130; stereotyping of, 31–35, 41–42, 44n6, 47, 49, 52–57, 61–65, 81, 96, 168–170; struggle for liberation among peoples, 48, 50–51; unconscious aspect of being, 17, 68–69, 189, 191–194, 205, 207; unruly populations, 12, 40–42, 50–51

colonizers: appropriation of indigenous cultural elements by, 231; assumptions in response to resistance, 49–51, 61; assumption that colonized are uncivilized, 31–35, 47, 50–51, 53–54, 61; capitalist orientation of Western, 27; challenges to hierarchical thinking and behaviors of, 39–40, 41–42, 44n6, 52–57, 61–65, 81, 96, 168–170; entanglement with colonized by, 164, 171–173, 247–248; extraction of resources by, 6, 7, 36; "fascinating cannibalism" toward colonized of, 60–61, 63, 261–262, 264–267; Japanese challenges in identifying, 50, 249; Japanese intellectual positioning between Asia and the West, 13, 70, 72–73, 86; limited knowledge of the colonized by, 6; reterritorialization of taken space by, 248, 251; unliberated state of, 51, 57, 80

Communism: actions by United States to prevent spread of, 148, 155, 231–232, 254, 257; Chinese Communist Party, 98; Japanese Communist Party, 49, 54; KMT efforts to recover mainland China from, 153, 159n13; Korean Communist Party, 49, 54; Marxists and Marxism, 48, 54, 114; as political option for decolonial nationalists, 48, 231. *See also* Socialism and Socialists

consciousness and unconsciousness: Benjamin on "dialectical image," 220–221; cinema's unconscious, 200–201, 207; creation of coloniality through colonial documentary, 16–17, 201, 203–204; as dual aspects of colonial subjectivity, 189, 193, 194, 198, 208n6; as dual aspects of prejudice, 192–193; epidermalization, 16, 19n8, 69, 87, 189, 190, 205, 208–209nn7–8, 209n11; global collective consciousness, 193, 195, 201–202, 204, 210n24; global collective unconsciousness, 6, 193, 201–205; hegemony, 71, 98, 193, 203–206, 211n33; repression, 1, 2, 5–7, 11, 15, 16, 18, 19n8, 51, 57, 139, 156, 242, 243, 244, 257, 258, 267. *See also* coloniality

critics: absence of film theory for Japanese imperial critics, 7; American criticisms of *The Red Lantern*, 127; criticisms of Na's films by Korean socialists, 59; discussions of Na's work among Korean and Japanese, 57–60; failure of Japanese to define Japanese film style, 71; favorable global reception of *Flower Girl* (*Kkot p'anŭn ch'ŏnyŏ*), 267n2; film criticism versus film theory, 72; Imamura Taihei, 17, 194–195, 199–200; Im Hwa, 52, 55–57, 59–63, 65–66n6, 76, 80–82; influence of the West on Asian film, 14; Iwasaki Akira on Hollywood movies, 94, 107n1; Japanese imperial film, 12, 51, 57; Korean socialist Alliance of New Film Artists, 59; Koriyama Hiroshi, 57–58, 60, 61; politicizing role of Marxist, 48; poor critical reception of Korean postcolonial films, 250, 268n12; power to resignify film, 2, 9, 51; reactions of Chinese critics to Chinese films made overseas, 102; reactions of Chinese critics to *ruHua pian* films, 13–14, 92, 93, 97, 102, 104, 106; reactions of Filipino critics to *Balangiga: Howling Wilderness*, 238; reactions of Filipino critics to *Heneral Luna*, 219; reactions of Indonesian critics to *Frieda* (*Between Heaven and Earth Antara*) (*Bumi dan Langit*), 177; reactions of Korean critics to Japonisme in twenty-first century films, 261; reactions of Korean critics to *You and I*, 16, 171; reactions of Malay critics to *Five Faces of Malaya*, 40. *See also* film theory
cultural hegemony, 189, 193, 203, 204, 205–206, 211n33

decolonization: in China, 14, 92, 93, 104–105, 107; misreading of hybridity as, 203; role of film in, 93–96, 104, 121, 140, 148–149, 214–215, 234; scholarship on, 20n10; in Taiwan, 140, 144, 148–150, 152, 156; violence as by-product of, 234, 254
desubjectification, 193, 202
direct cinema. *See cinéma vérité*
discrimination: anthropos and humanitas, 2, 7, 19, 19–20n9, 191, 208; as inherent in colonialism, 191; Japanese discrimination against Koreans, 168–170; Japanese discrimination against Taiwanese, 155; unconscious, 191–193. *See also* racism
Disney, 194, 196, 199, 209n16, 235
documentary films: *Asian Americans*, 19n6; asynchronous time of colonial, 11–12, 25–30, 31, 39, 41–43; *China (Chung Kuo/Cina)*, 108n4; documentary time, 27–30, 43; documentary "truth," 201; *Five Faces of Malaya*, 30–43; historicism of colonial, 27–29; Imamura's documentary theory, 194–195; *Marē Senki*, 196–199, 210n23; realist mode, 26, 27, 28, 30, 40; subjective nature of, 195; *This Bloody, Blundering Business*, 219; *Voices of Malaya*, 25, 43
Dr. Huyung. *See* Hŏ Yŏng
DuBois, W. E. B., 107, 253–254

editing: conventions, 114; documentary that creates realistic mythology, 25, 26, 28, 31, 32–33, 35–36; film, 31, 62, 209n13; stock jungle footage used in Tarzan films, 158n8; style of Na Un-kyu, 60
education: *bunkajin* (well-educated men), 15; educated protagonists, 125, 127–128, 146, 147, 155; film as tool for education and emotional reeducation, 14, 92, 93, 101, 104, 107, 172, 173, 249, 250; seepage of cultural-political ideas into, 95–96, 215, 249, 250; as tool for cultural assimilation, 160n26
epidermalization, 16, 19n8, 69, 87, 189, 190, 205, 208–209nn7–8, 209n11
eroticism. *See* exoticism
ethnic groups: Austronesian tribes and nations (Taiwan), 154–155; colonial attitudes toward and management of, 17, 25, 30–31, 44n6, 49–52, 124–125, 154, 167, 168, 193–194; coloniality in colonized subjects, 17, 169–171, 177, 180–182, 191–194; colonial perceptions, depictions, and stereotyping of, 25–26, 28, 30–35, 47, 49, 54, 57–61; cross-ethnic passing, 166, 181; ethnographic documentaries, 32–40; ethnographizing of the colonized, 32–40, 47, 49, 52–54, 57–59, 65, 189; ethnonationalism, 39, 43, 44n6, 95–96, 97, 99, 105–107, 142, 181–182; "fascinating cannibalism" toward, 60–61, 260; group loyalties within, 42; Hokkienese/Han Chinese (Taiwan), 154–155; Malays (Malaya), 33, 34–36, 38–39, 40, 41–42, 44n6; in Manchuria, 78; nationalist inclusivity of, 39, 47; Orang Asli (Malaya), 32–33, 35; Paiwan (Taiwan), 155; physical blurring among, 169, 249; recruitment of colonialized to serve imperial Japan, 165; resistance of, 39, 78, 118–121, 126, 128, 130; responses to being stereotyped, 41–42, 52, 55–57, 61–63, 65; segregation, 42, 44n6; socialist inclusivity of, 47–48, 49, 54, 60, 78; Temiars (Malaya), 31–33

Index 277

Europe. *See* West
exclusivity and inclusivity: as binary aspects of coloniality, 189, 190; contradictory nature of colonial inclusivity, 47; exclusivity as colonial differences and heterogeneity, 190; in humanism, 199; inclusivity as colonial harmony, 199; Indonesian nationalist multiculturalism, 178; in *Momotarō: Divine Warriors of the Sea*, 189–191; portrayals of Soviet empire as ethnically inclusive, 47–48; realities of socialist cultural inclusivity, 49, 54, 57, 61–62, 65, 80–82; in *Storm over Asia (Potomok Chingis-Khana)*, 47–48
exoticism: erotic, voyeuristic exoticism of East for West, 18–19n4, 32, 151, 154–155, 245–246; exotic-erotic in *The Handmaiden*, 244–245, 259–260, 264–265, 266, 269n30; of historic cinematic pieces to local audiences, 246, 261; Japanese use of Korean *kisaeng* figure, 12; Korean use of Japonisme, 261–262, 264–266; Rony on "fascinating cannibalism" of, 60–61; as tool for Othering, 155–156, 217, 261, 266. *See also* "fascinating cannibalism" behaviors

Fanon, Frantz: concept of "epidermalization," 16, 19n8, 69, 87, 189, 190, 205, 208–209nn7–8, 209n11; on internalization of Western values by the colonized, 68–69, 87, 205; *The Wretched of the Earth*, 68–69
"fascinating cannibalism" behaviors, 60–61, 63, 261–262, 264–267. *See also* exoticism
film: camera, 27–29, 31; carnivalesques, 143, 149, 150; confluence of Asian and Western filmmaking, 122; dubbing, 256–257; editing, 25–26, 28, 31–36, 60, 62, 114, 158n8, 209n13; female ingénue as iconography of Hollywood close-up, 12; film cultures, 2, 9, 10, 12, 18n1, 59, 68, 71, 77, 81, 86, 92, 93, 96–99, 107, 170–171, 206, 243; montage, 35, 38, 62–63, 74, 87–88n7; nationhood, colonialism, and postcoloniality in Asia, 94–95; picaresques, 143, 214, 216, 217, 222; Pure Film Movement (Japan), 76, 80–81; realist mode, 26, 27, 28, 30, 40, 118, 150, 151; silent, 9, 59, 108n12, 117, 119, 121, 122, 132n14, 144; technology, 27–28; Virilio on cinema as war, 203, 204
film export-import: Asia as global export market for silent films, 9; Asian refusal of objectionable Hollywood films, 122, 123; *The Birth of a Nation*, 118–119; classic Hollywood narrative films, 113, 118–121; Export and Import Films, 112, 123, 132n20; export of US cinema, 111, 113; Hansen's first-global-vernacular paradigm, 113–114, 116, 145; Hollywood's assumptions about overseas markets, 112, 118, 122–123; "horizon of reception," 117; import-export paradox, 112, 113–114, 116; Japanese commodification of Korean *pullyŏng sŏnin* films, 63; melodramas, 114, 117–118, 122, 130–131; *The Red Lantern*, 112, 118, 121–123; Shanghai-made films exported to United States, 103
film narrative: of *Agassi (The Handmaiden)*, 244, 246–247, 252; audience responses to, 41–42, 78, 122, 123; of *Balangiga: Howling Wilderness*, 215, 217, 221–226, 231, 237; colonial, 30–42, 111; counternarratives, 225–226; of *Five Faces of Malaya*, 30–42; narrative suturing in documentaries, 11–12, 25–26, 27, 31, 32, 35, 38, 39; of race and nation, 14, 111, 114, 118, 128, 131n4; Western narratives about imagined Asia, 2, 42
film theory: absent for Japanese imperial critics, 7, 68; alignment with universality, 70, 72; attempts to conceptualize nature and functions of cinema, 70; colonialism and, 12–13, 68, 70, 72, 75–77; contributions of Nishida to, 7; disagreements over Japanese film style, 71–72; discussions of internalization of cinema by spectators, 70–71, 75–76, 78; discussions of montage, 62–63, 74, 81, 87–88n7; discussions of spectatorship and role of audience, 70–71, 74–79, 82–86; early twentieth century discussions of cinema, 74; *Film Criticism (Eiga hyōron)*, 77; film criticism versus, 72; film form and, 72; Imamura's documentary theory, 75, 194–195, 199, 200; Im Hwa on, 75–76, 80–82; Japanese imperial, 13, 73–74, 76, 77, 87n2; Korean, 80–84, 86–87; Osaki's concept of "random thoughts on cinema" (*eiga manso*), 74; O Yŏng-jin on importance of surprise and shock, 76, 82–86; Pure Film Movement in Japan, 76, 80–81, 87; realism in Japan, 84; relationships between Asian and Western, 14, 70, 72–76; roundtable discussions of Korean (*zadankai*), 77, 87n3; self-privileging by imperialist Japanese theorists, 77–78; on subjective, indexical nature of documentary, 27; Terada on absence of Japaneseness in Japanese film theory, 74, 76; theory of face of Balázs, 51–52; Tosaka Jun, 20n13, 73, 74–75;

Western, 14, 20n11, 72; written by colonial subjects of imperial Japan, 75–84, 86–87. *See also* critics
first global vernacular, 113, 116, 145
Five Faces of Malaya (documentary; 1938), 30–43
future: imperial assumptions of progress and time, 27, 28, 29, 31, 32, 39–40; imperial fictionalized past and, 26, 31, 42–43; modernity and capitalism as assumed goals, 27, 34, 38; orientation of globalization toward, 117, 132n15; power of coloniality to colonize a person's, 203–204, 207

Gramsci, Anonio, 20n13, 203
Great Britain: Balfour Declaration (1926), 31; British Empire, 8, 11–12, 28, 34, 41, 44n5, 48, 119; British missionaries in China, 125; British modernism, 131n6; colonial documentary as tool for legitimizing British imperialism, 26, 28, 31–37, 40, 132n17; *Empire and Film* and *Film and the End of Empire* (two-volume essay collection), 8; *Five Faces of Malaya*, 25–26, 30–43; Gilroy on British Empire films, 119–120; imperial occupation of Malaya by, 11; *Malaya*, 25; Ottawa Conference (1932), 31; propaganda touting benefits of modernity and technology, 34–35, 37–38; propaganda touting colonial cosmopolitanism, 25, 30–31, 35, 40, 44n6; racism and Othering of colonized peoples by, 30–31, 36, 38, 44n6, 44n14; reorientation from colonialism to modernity, 31; Strand Film Company, 25, 43n1; *Voices of Malaya*, 25, 43. *See also* West
Great Wall Film Company (*Changcheng zhizao huanpian gongsi*), 103–104, 108n10
Griffith, D. W., 111, 118–119, 121, 122, 123–124, 127, 128, 129

Habermas, Jürgen, 95, 195, 201–203, 205, 208
The Handmaiden (*Agassi*) (2016): as adaptation of *Fingersmith* (novel), 244; characters in, 244–245, 247, 260, 262, 264–265; divergence from colonial and Cold War Korean cinema, 242–243, 245–246, 248–251, 259–260; imagery of, 244–245, 247, 259–265; Japonisme in, 258, 261–262, 264, 265–267; plot of, 244–245; in postmillennial global cinema, 243–244, 246–248, 250, 259, 265, 266, 267–268n4; as study in repressed coloniality, 18, 242, 244, 246, 267, 267–268n4; *waesaek* (Japan color)

in, 253, 255–262, 264, 266, 269n28; work of Park Chan-wook, 244–245, 259–261, 262, 265, 267, 269n28
Hansen, Miriam, 95, 98, 113–114, 116–117, 131n13, 132n18, 145
hegemony: coloniality and, 189, 203, 205; cultural, 203–206, 211n33; as culturally based colonialism, 193; hybridity and, 204; as imperial tool for Othering the colonized, 71, 98; as reflection of sociopolitical assumptions in cinema, 106, 151
Hinatsu Eitarō. *See* Hŏ Yŏng
historicism. *See* colonial historicism
historiophoty, 230–231
Hollywood: as filmmaking style debated in Asia, 72, 78, 81, 84; early confluence with Asian cinema, 14, 122, 144–145, 151, 158–159n12, 267n1; Hollywood film product as "first global vernacular," 113–114, 116, 145; melodrama as primary export of, 113–114, 118; popularity of films in colonized countries, 72, 94, 111, 112, 113, 206–207; production of films misrepresenting China, 13, 105–106, 122; prototypical film music, 118; then-now depictions of modernity in films, 249; vision of Otherness, 14, 52, 94, 106, 111, 112, 129, 140, 144–145; war films, 214; as weapon of global capitalist exploitation, 94; world colonizing power of cinema, 94–95, 113, 116, 140, 211n33, 211n38, 249
Hŏ Yŏng: absence of formal national cinema and, 16; activities in support of Indonesian independence, 175–176; activities to repatriate exiled Koreans, 174–175; *Calling Australia* (*Goshu no Yobigoe*), 172; collaborations with imperial Japanese, 15–16, 167, 171–172, 180; cross-ethnic passing, 166, 173; education and early filmmaking career, 165–166, 182n3; employment as *bunkajin* in colonized Indonesia, 164, 171–174; filmmaking career as auteur damaged by politics, 167–171, 172–173, 177–182; Korean censure of, 16, 163, 164, 165, 171, 180; as thoroughly colonized imperial subject, 169–171; transformations into Hinatsu Eitarō and Dr. Huyung, 15–16, 19n8, 163, 164, 165, 182n2; work in support of Indonesian independence, 164; work with Sendenbu and Java Theatrical Play Association (Perserikatan Oesaha Sandiwara di Djawa), 172–173; *You and I* (*Kimi to Boku*), 16, 76, 163, 164, 167–171, 174, 175, 180, 182n5

Index 279

humanism: coloniality and, 16, 20n14, 189; entanglement with colonialism, 190; exclusive-inclusive aspect of, 190, 199, 204; humanistic foundations of wartime propaganda, 189, 190, 199, 201; hylomorphism, 20n12; in *Momotarō: Divine Warriors of the Sea*, 191, 197, 198, 199, 208n1, 208n3, 210n21

hybridity: assimilation as by-product of, 204–205; in bilingual intertitles, 108n12; capacity of cinema to hide coloniality through, 204–207; capacity to conceal or intensify coloniality, 189, 193, 202–203, 204; as cultural imperialism, 203, 204; of globalized society, 193, 202–203, 204, 207, 208n6; in *The Handmaiden*, 247–248, 249–250, 259, 262; hybrid genre films, 142, 143, 150, 152, 158–159n12; lingua franca as hybrid construct, 194; linguistic, 206; in *Momotarō*, 190, 204; Seo's filmic commentary on, 194, 196, 197, 199, 204; of *Shishōsetsu from Left to Right*, 206, 211n37; of Tarzan and Taiyupian films, 143, 150, 152, 158n12; of *t'ŭrot'ŭ* musical genre, 257

images: actions by overseas Chinese to correct derogatory, 101, 103–104; America derogatory images of Chinese, 99–101, 104; American imperial greatness projected by, 217–218; animated, 190, 196; audience rescripting of, 41–42; in *Balangiga: Howling Wilderness*, 17, 215, 222, 226, 227, 228, 230–239; Benjamin on "dialectical image," 220–221, 232–233; Brecht on interpretation of, 200–201; British imperial greatness projected through, 30–31, 37, 39; censorship of and protests against, 97–107, 242, 246, 255–257; cinema designed to counter negative, 101–105; cinematic colonialism through, 203–208; contrived, 16, 27–29, 31, 40, 19n6, 201; dialectical, 17, 215, 220, 222, 231–234, 239; documentary as orchestration of, 28–31, 195–196, 201; eroticized, 12, 245, 260, 261–262, 266; exoticized, 18–19n4, 32, 151, 154–155, 217, 244–246, 261–262, 264, 266; in *Five Faces of Malaya*, 33, 34, 36, 37; globalized, shared, 193–194, 201–203, 205–207, 246; in *The Handmaiden*, 242, 245, 259–261; Im Hwa's redefinition of Nakano's racialized, 52–57; Japanese imperial greatness projected through, 15, 163–164; Japanese stereotyping of Koreans as *kisaeng* and *pullyŏng sŏnin*, 47, 49, 54; Korean postcolonial control of Japanese-related, 242, 246, 255–257; in *Momotarō: Divine Warriors of the Sea*, 196–199, 209n19; montage, 35; moving, 117, 130, 203, 205, 206; music for melodramas, 129; Na's presentation to Korean audiences of reflective, 84; nationalist censorship of derogatory, 99–102, 104–105; O Yŏng-jin on relationship of viewers to cinematic, 83–86; power to transcend linguistic diversity, 193, 205–206, 230–231; race-time of colonial documentaries, 11, 30–38; racialized, 12, 101, 125, 217; reintroduction of delimited, censored, or invisible, 242; Rony on "fascinating cannibalism" of, 60–61; of *ruHua pian* ("China-humiliating films"), 92, 99–101; time delay between production and presentation of, 208n5; as tools to educate, 104–105; Western images of World War II, 243, 249. *See also* propaganda

Imamura Taihei: animated film theory of, 199–201, 209n16; anticipation of *cinéma vérité* and direct cinema by, 195, 209n14; Brecht's cinema theories compared to those of, 200; on cinema as form of thought and theorizing, 75, 85; on coloniality of cinema itself, 195, 200, 201, 207; contributions to Japanese film theory, 16–17, 74–75, 84, 85, 87n2, 189, 194–195, 199–202; documentary theory of, 189, 194–195, 199–201, 204, 209n13, 209n16; world cognition and world history theories of, 195, 202–203, 206, 209n16

Im Hwa: arguments against biased Japanese representations of Koreans, 52, 55–57, 80; arrest and renunciation of politics (1934), 80; arrest in Chongno (1931), 53; challenge to Japanese segregationist ideas, 62, 65, 81; criticisms of Na Un-kyu, 59–61; "On Several Tendencies in Korean Cinema" (essay), 52, 61–63, 80–81; "The Pier of Yokohama under the Umbrella" (poem), 52, 54–57, 61; poems and literary criticism, 65–66n6, 68, 75–76, 80–82, 88n8, 170; poetic response to Nakano's poem, 52, 55–56, 61; responses to Japanese culture producers, 12, 13, 52, 61–63, 65, 80–82; response to Koriyama Hiroshi's essay, 52, 61–63, 80–81; on socialist film history in Korea, 61–63, 76, 80–82

immigrants: Chinese laborers in Malaya, 30, 35–36; demonized by Trump, 220; diasporic Chinese, 30, 33, 35–36, 99–102, 105, 106, 108n9; displacement of indigenous peoples in Malaya by, 25, 31, 33, 35, 36, 39; Europeans and Americans in Asia, 30, 31–32, 35, 37–38, 44n14, 125, 248; expulsion of Koreans from

Japan (1929), 52, 54, 55; Indian, 31–32, 33, 35, 36, 42, 44n14; Japanese in Indonesia, 175; Japanese in Korea, 248, 251, 252–253, 255, 258–260; Koreans in Japan, 50, 56, 164; land grabbing and speculation by, 251; missionaries, 99, 100, 111–112, 124–125, 127–128

imperialism: American, 17, 94, 215–218, 229, 231–233, 254–255, 268n5; in *Balangiga: Howling Wilderness*, 221–224, 226–228, 230–236; British, 8, 28, 35, 38, 44n6; Chinese, 154–155; cinema as tool of, 9, 29–32, 35, 47–48, 79, 94, 111, 116, 166–171, 217–218; Cold War, 253–255, 257–258, 269n24; colonized peoples and places designated as primitive and inferior, 11, 12, 16, 29–32, 35, 48, 50, 72–73, 76–77, 81, 94, 99–103, 125, 146, 154, 261; cultural, 111, 204; dominance of imperialist viewpoints and interpretations, 1, 2, 6, 9, 13–14, 18, 19n6, 71, 73, 75–77, 94–107, 124–126, 166–167, 218; Dutch, 35, 155, 165, 174, 175; "fascinating cannibalism" behaviors of, 60–61, 63, 261–262, 264–267; French, 18n2, 98; hegemony as integral to, 98, 189, 193, 203–206; hierarchy as fundamental to, 26, 50, 75, 80, 95, 169, 204, 208n1, 210n21, 210n29, 248; Hollywood, 111–113, 118–123; impact on filmmaking and cinema, 9, 70–74, 92–93, 98–106; imperialist gaze, 18, 68, 72–75, 262, 265–266, 267; intra-Asian socialist alliances to combat, 12, 80; Japanese, 12, 15, 48, 50, 53, 69, 75–78, 80, 86, 144, 154, 163, 164, 165, 168; metropoles, 13, 29–30, 31, 51, 68, 71; missionaries, 99, 111, 112, 124–125; Portuguese, 35, 144; postimperial reactions, 2, 5, 9, 249, 255–257, 262, 267–268n4, 268n5, 268n17; prolonged postimperial damage to ex-colonies, 6, 7, 9, 156, 239, 255–258; propaganda to legitimize, 15, 28, 29, 37–38, 124, 163, 166–170, 254; racism and prejudice as fundamental to, 11, 12, 16, 50, 125, 144, 146, 218, 254; in *The Red Lantern*, 124–128, 130; resistance by colonized intellectuals, audiences, and subalterns to, 38–39, 41–42, 52, 75, 76, 78–83, 124, 215; resource plunder, 6, 7, 37, 124, 251; Spanish, 217, 218, 223, 225, 236; in *Storm over Asia (Potomok Chingis-Khana)*, 47–48; transcolonial filmmaking and cinema, 3, 9–10, 70–74, 78, 96–97; transcolonial relationships within empires, 4, 5, 247, 261–262, 265; universalist claims of, 72–73, 76–77, 80, 86; Western imperialism in China, 97–98; Western imperial modernity, 72–73, 75–77, 126; *You and I*, 167–171. *See also* colonialism

indigenous peoples: cinematic portrayals and stereotyping of, 32, 139, 154, 159n24; colonial taxonomizing of, 30, 32, 38; exploited by outsiders, 155, 215; forced relocations of, 160n26; Han Chinese, 154, 155; imperial Othering of, 154; indigeneity and nationalism, 15; of Malaya, 25, 32–33, 38; Orang Asli of Malaya, 32–33; portrayed in *Five Faces of Malaya*, 32; portrayed in *Tarzan and Treasure*, 154, 155, 156; as POWs, 153; recognition as First Nations, 155, 160n25; state subjugation of aborigines and ethnic minorities, 154; of Taiwan, 154, 155; Temiars of Malaya, 31, 32

Indonesia: activities of Nippon Eigasha in, 172; Bahasa Indonesia used for Japanese propaganda, 172; Berita Film Indonesia (Indonesian Film News), 176; Cine Drama Institute, 176; contributions of Dr. Huyung to Indonesian independence movement, 16, 163, 164, 171, 174, 175, 176, 178, 182n2; contributions of Dr. Huyung to Indonesian theater, 172–173, 175–176; Dr. Huyung as *bunkajin* in Indonesia, 171–174, 180; Dutch attempts to retake, 175; Indonesian cultural leaders, 176; Jakarta, 172, 175, 177, 178, 179; Japanese colonialism in, 164, 165, 171; Jogjakarta, 175–176; Kino Drama Atelier (KDA), 176, 182n9; Koreans and Japanese remaining in postimperial, 175, 180

Indonesian cinema: benefits of Japanese occupation to, 173, 181–182; contributions of Dr. Huyung to, 16, 19n8, 164, 174, 176–179, 181, 182n2, 182n10, 183nn11–13; Djamaluddin Malik, 173, 177, 181; Sinematek Film Library, 183n11; Soemardjono, 176; Usmar Ismail, 164, 173, 176, 177, 181, 182

internalization: as colonization of the mind, 12–13, 68; of colonizer's values, 68–69, 205; difficulty in demarcating internal and external colonial influences, 70, 82–83; epidermalization versus, 69; of film language or style, 71, 82, 86; lingering character after colonial occupation, 4; spectator, 71, 78, 86

Ismail, Usmar, 164, 173, 176, 177, 181, 182

Jameson, Frederic: on assimilating power of cinema, 203, 206; on globalization, 204–205, 207–208, 210n26, 211n33, 211n38; on modernism, 115, 131n9; on modernity as concept of Othering, 117, 125; on synchronicity, 204–205, 208n4

Japan: battle and surrender of Singapore (February 8–15, 1942), 196–197, 199; *bunkajin* (culture men), 163, 164, 171–175; Cold War influences on, 254–255, 257–259, 269n23; colonial challenges to hierarchical thinking of Japanese intellectuals, 52, 54–57, 61–65, 80–82, 168–169; colonial collaborations with, 167, 168, 182n4, 268n7; colonial collaborators with imperial, 15, 16, 83, 165, 170–171, 175, 180–181, 182; erasure of memories of Empire and wartime in, 268n17; expulsion of Koreans (1929), 52, 54, 55; Great East Asian Co-Prosperity Circle of the Japanese Empire, 159n23, 168, 171; Hirohito, 53, 54; as imperial metropole, 47, 48–49, 51, 63, 76–78, 81, 86, 96, 166–167; intellectual growth in imperial, 7, 12, 20n13, 48, 73–77, 205; invasion of China by, 104, 165, 194; Iwasaki on film as Western propaganda, 94; Japan color (*waesaek*), 253–259, 261, 262, 264, 266, 269n28; Japanese Empire, 12, 16–17, 18n3, 49–51, 68, 69, 72, 146, 171, 172, 174, 175, 180–181, 189, 190, 197, 206; Japonisme, 258–262, 264, 266; Kanto earthquake, 50, 56; *kisaeng* (professional entertainer) as Japanese stereotype for Korean females, 12, 47, 49, 51; Kyoto School, 76, 81; massacre of Korean immigrants (1923), 50, 56; occupation of Indonesia by, 164, 165, 171; occupation of Korea by, 47, 98, 144, 247–248, 252, 255, 259–260, 262, 265–266; occupation of Manchuria by, 78, 168; occupation of Philippines by, 77–78; occupation of Taiwan by, 48, 146, 154, 155, 156, 158n2, 159n21, 159n23; planned invasion of Australia by, 172, 182n6; *pullyŏng sŏnin* ("malcontent colonial Koreans") as Japanese stereotype for Korean males, 47, 50–52, 57–58, 60; racism in imperial, 49, 50, 54, 60, 63, 154, 160n26; socialists in, 12, 47–49, 52, 54–55, 57, 59–63, 65; *The Source Material* guide, 50; treason case of Pak Yŏl and Kaneko Fumiko (1923), 56–57, 65n4; US-orchestrated Normalization Treaty, 255, 257–258, 269n24; Watsuji on humanhood as betweenness, 205, 208n3, 210n30; writings of Nakano Shigeharu, 52, 54

Japanese cinema: animated films, 189–190, 194–200, 209–210nn19–23; audience as concern of government and theorists, 78–79; *bunka eiga* (documentary cultural films), 83, 194, 199, 209n13; contributions of Imamura to, 16, 73, 74–75, 85, 189, 194–195, 199–202, 203, 206–207, 209n13, 209n16; contributions of Sasa to socialist, 48; contributions of Seo, 16, 189–190, 194–199; film theory in imperial Japan, 7, 13, 20n11, 70–79, 81, 84, 86–87, 194–195; imperial propaganda films, 15, 163–164, 167–171, 172, 173, 194; Japan-Korea coproductions, 167; Kurosawa Akira, 164, 267; *Malaya War Record: A Record of the Onward March* (*Mare Senki Shingeki no Kiroku*), 196–197, 210n23; *Marē Senki*, 196–199, 210n23; *Momotarō: Divine Warriors of the Sea*, 189–191, 194, 196–200, 203–204, 207, 208n1, 208n3, 210n23; montage in, 62; *Proletaria Eiga*, 47, 48; Proletarian Film League of Japan (Prokino), 80; Pure Film Movement, 76, 80; socialist cinéastes, 48–49, 57–58, 62–63; Terada on absence of Japaneseness in Japanese film theory, 74; Tezuka Osamu, 195, 210n29

Japonisme, 261–262, 264, 265–266, 267
Joseon. *See* Korean cinema

Khavn, 17, 214, 216–217, 221–222, 224–226, 233–235, 237, 238, 239
kisaeng (professional entertainer): as objects of Japanese control, 51; as stereotypical of Korean females, 12, 47, 49, 51
Korea: Alliance of New Film Artists, 59, 61, 62; censorship of negative cultural memories in, 242, 246, 248–249, 256–259; Chōsen Film Company, 83; colonial Korea as film market for Japan and the West, 84, 86, 96; Japanese-Korean socialist interactions, 47–49, 52–54, 60–63; Japanese occupation of, 47, 98, 244, 248, 252, 255, 262, 265–266; Japanese use of *kisaeng* to stereotype Korean females, 12, 47, 49, 51; Japanese use of *pullyŏng sŏnin* to stereotype Korean males, 12, 47, 49–52, 54, 57–58, 60, 63; massacre of Korean immigrants in Japan (1929), 50, 56; North Korea, 59, 165, 220, 267n2; public concerns over *waesaek* ("Japan color") 255–257, 258–266, 269n22; treason case of Pak Yŏl and Kaneko Fumiko (1923), 56–57, 65n4; US-orchestrated Normalization Treaty, 255, 257–258, 269n24

Korean cinema: *Arirang*, 51; audiences of, 243, 244, 245, 246, 247–249, 250, 251, 253, 256, 259, 261, 264–267, 267–268n4, 268n7; censorship and erasure, 252–253, 255–259, 268n7; Chōsen Film Company, 83; contributions of

282 Index

Im Hwa to, 54–56, 61–63, 80–82; contributions of Na Un-kyu to, 51, 57–60, 63, 64; contributions of O Yŏng-jin to, 13, 68, 82–87; contributions of Park Chan-wook to, 242, 244–245, 247, 259–265, 267, 269n28; coproduced Korean-Japanese propaganda films, 166–167, 182n4; Domestic Film Screening Regulation (1934), 166–167; *Epitaph*, 261–262; experiments montage, 62; film theory development, 54–56, 61–63, 80–87; *Flower Girl*, 267n2; *Genealogy*, 252; *The Handmaiden*, 18, 242, 244–267, 269nn28–31; *Homeless Angels (Chibŏpnŭn Chŏnsa)*, 170; Hŏ Yŏng (Hinatsu Eitaro/Dr. Huyung), 163–182; internalization, subjectivity, and externalization, 70, 71–72, 75–76, 78, 86; Joseon (Korean colonial cinema), 96; Korean workers' reactions to *The Engagement*, 82; Kōriyama's article on, 57–63, 65, 80–82; "liberation films" (*kwangbok yŏnghwa*), 267n3; melodramas, 251–253; *Modern Boy*, 252; *Parameters of Disavowal* (book), 252; postcolonial, 246, 247–252, 256–257; postcolonial Japonisme in, 258, 261–262, 264, 265–267; prominent films of twenty-first century, 243–244; *Sinsidae*, 83; socialist cinéastes, 59–63; *waesaek* ("Japan color"), 255–257, 258–266, 269n22; *You and I (Kimi to Boku)*, 16, 76, 163, 164, 167–171, 174, 175, 180, 182n5

Kōriyama Hiroshi, 12, 13, 52, 57–63, 65, 80–82

Kuomintang (KMT): disillusionment within Nationalist Army toward, 142; involvement in eradicating *ruHua* films, 104, 106, 107; language policy of, 148, 150, 159n13, 159n15; work to establish positive image of nationalist China, 105

labor and laboring masses: assumptions of British in Malaya, 30, 32, 35–39; as basis for Socialist unity and solidarity, 48, 52, 55, 58, 61, 65; capitalist, globalist function of colonial, 35–38; Chinese immigrants in Malaya, 35–37; colonial ethnic hierarchies of, 38; enlightened laborers in Eisenstein's *Bronenosets Potemkin (Battleship Potemkin)*, 62; Filipino immigrants in the United States, 218; forced labor of Filipinos by US occupying forces, 214, 215; Great East Asian Prosperity Circle of Japanese Empire, 159n23; immigration into colonies of, 33, 36, 38; Korean workers' reactions to *The Engagement*, 82; role of ethnic labor under colonial pluralism, 30; subsistence labor, 35; Taiwanese stranded in Japanese POW camps, 153; Tamil immigrants in Malaya, 37

language: allegory in protagonist Hu Taiming, 147; Amoy (*Xiayu*) dialect, 148, 151, 158n11; association of social status with, 44n18, 82, 145, 151; Bahasa Indonesia, 172; biased representation as product of limited knowledge, 6; cinematic bilingual intertitles, 108n12; competition in cinema between action and, 13, 68, 71, 75–76, 86; cross-ethnic passing through fluency, 50, 166; dialect groups and sociopolitical loyalties, 42; dubbing, 256–257; English, 172, 211n33, 211nn35–37; film as universal, 51, 62–63, 113, 116–117, 131n13, 193, 205–206; government fostering of specific languages, 148, 150, 160n26, 172, 253; Hokkien, 148, 151, 154–155, 158n11; Im Hwa on cinematic, 80–82, 172; influence of language of the metropole on film theory, 71, 80–82, 86–87; Japanese film language, 70–71; Japanese-language Korean films, 167, 170, 182n5; lingua franca, 145, 193–194, 205–206; local, national, and universal languages, 211n34; Mandarin, 108n4, 142, 143, 148, 150–151, 156, 158n7, 159n16; Mandarin-language cinema, 148, 150, 159n16; in melodrama, 114, 116–117; Minnan dialect, 148, 158n7, 158n11; Mizumura's *Shishōsetsu from Left to Right* (novel), 206, 211nn34–37; non-linguistic speech, 75–76, 82, 86; Sinitic languages, 158n4; speech acts, 75–76, 81–82, 226; Taiwanese-language cinema, 148, 159n16; Taiyu, 144, 145, 158n11; *Taiyupian* (Taiwanese language film), 14, 139, 140; translatability and untranslatability, 206–207, 211n35, 211n37

Lee, Jinhee, 49–50

Liang Che-fu, 14, 139, 140, 143–144, 149, 158n7

Lu Xun, 77, 94, 95, 97, 108n3

Malaya: *Bangsa Melayu*, 39; *Five Faces of Malaya*, 30–43; Kuala Lumpur, 25, 37, 41; Malayan Emergency (1948–1960), 43; Malays, 33, 34–36, 38–39, 40, 41–42, 44n6; Orang Asli, 32–33, 35; Temiars, 31–33

Malaysia, 32, 144–145, 154, 155, 160n27

Manchukuo, 13, 68, 76, 78, 79

Manchuria: five most prominent ethnic groups in, 78; intellectuals on Eurocentric film theory, 75; Japanese colonial presence in, 75, 76, 78; Manchurian Film Association, 3; spectatorship in, 71

Manchurian cinema: appeal of gloomy melodrama to Manchurian audiences, 76; colonial audience reactions to Japanese films, 87n1, 96; influences of Shanghai and Japanese cinema on, 79; Japanese-Manchurian co-produced propaganda films, 168; Korean films shown in Manchuria, 167; Zhou on, 76, 79, 87n5

melodrama: action-oriented, 122, 158n6; for addressing social issues, 115–118; *Aizen katsura*, 79, 87, 120–121, 123–128, 130; *Balangiga: Howling Wilderness*, 215, 221–237; *The Birth of a Nation*, 111, 118–119, 121, 122, 123–124, 127, 128, 129; capacity to reflect and generate emotion, 114, 126, 128, 145, 149; as cinematic tool of colonialism, 111, 117–121, 123–125, 217–220; classicism versus, 112–114, 116; of colonial conquest, 111, 112, 114, 118–123, 126, 129–130; contributions of Griffith to, 111, 118–119, 121–124, 127–129; contributions of Liang to, 143–144, 158n7, 158–159n12; cultural dominance of, 114, 116; export of modernity through, 117; film melodrama theory, 111, 114, 118, 126–127; formulaic character of, 115; as Hollywood export, 117–118; iconic and acoustic signs in, 117, 118, 121–122, 128, 130–131; innocence in, 114, 123, 126–127, 130; Japanese, 79; *Manila in the Claws of Light*, 216; melodramatic rhetoric, 114, 116–117; as *melos*, 118, 129, 130; modernism as counteraesthetic of, 114–116; musical scores, 128–131; narrative continuity structure of, 111, 114, 121, 126; narratives of race and nation, 14, 111, 114, 118, 120–121, 123–124, 128, 130, 131n4; as old, mass-oriented modality, 115, 116, 117–118, 130, 132n21, 216; *Orphan Chicks in the Snow*, 1; *Orphan Ling Bo*, 149, 150, 159n14; orphan-themed films, 143, 156–157; postwar Korean, 250–252; *The Red Lantern*, 123–131; Shanghai-produced, 79; silent melodrama produced by both East and West, 122, 130–131, 131n10; *Taiyupian* (Taiwanese language film), 15, 139, 143, 145, 149–150; *Tarzan and Treasure (Taishan yu boazang)*, 139–140, 143–145, 151–152; Tarzan films, 156–157

melos, 118, 129, 130

metropole: colonial assumptions regarding distance from, 29, 30–31; divisions between colony and, 9, 18–19n4, 29; film theorists and, 13, 57–63, 65, 68, 69, 71, 75–78; inhabitants as victims of colonialism, 51; internalization of colonizer's gaze by colonized, 68, 69, 73, 168, 209n11; laboring masses as link to colonies, 48–49, 52; racialized imperial gaze of, 16, 32–39, 68, 69, 190, 195, 199, 265–266; transcolonial nature of Asian colonial cinema that belied colonialism, 17, 18–19n4, 247. *See also* colonialism

Mignolo, Walter, 20n10, 95, 98, 208n6

mise-en-scène, 17, 142, 238, 245, 252, 262

missionaries, 99, 100, 111, 112, 124–125, 127–128, 130

modernism: British, 131n6; counteraesthetic nature of, 115–116, 131n9; global, 131n8; Jameson on, 115, 131n9; melodrama versus, 114–116; vernacular, 29, 93, 95, 113, 116

modernity. *See* colonial modernity

modernization: association of melodrama with, 117, 119; capitalist encroachment on the indigenous, 38, 125, 126; China's dilemma, 112, 125, 126; colonial aggression portrayed as, 121; defense of customs or territory as resistance to, 50–51, 119, 125, 126; political modernization as goal of colonialism, 33, 121; as tool of colonial reformers, 37, 51; Westernization as, 37, 40, 126, 148

Momotarō: Divine Warriors of the Sea (1945): behaviors of characters in, 190–191, 197–199, 210n21; biosocial hybridity in, 190–191, 197–199, 203, 204, 207, 208n1, 208n3; commentary on *Mar ē Senki* in, 196–199, 210n23; film narrative of, 196–198; folk story of "Momotarō" ("Peach Boy"), 196, 209n17; Seo's animation work, 17, 195–196, 199, 209n19; Seo's use of documentariness, 16, 189–190, 194, 196–197, 199–200, 204; setting of, 196

Mongolia, 47–49, 78

montage, 35, 38, 62–63, 74, 87–88n7

Nakano Shigeharu, 52–54, 57, 60, 61, 63, 65, 65n2, 80

narrative film: Asian vernaculars in, 151, 156, 158–159n12; avant-garde film versus, 221, 225–226; Chinese cinema, 99; classic Hollywood, 72, 78, 111, 113–114, 116, 118, 121, 200, 202; complication and suspense, 114, 125–128, 143; continuity style, 113, 114, 121–122, 128, 129; documentaries, 11, 25–26; Korean postcolonial, 250–252, 267n3; melodrama versus narrative causality in, 114, 118, 121, 126; music, 121–122, 128–131; narrative continuity, 113–114, 116, 118, 128–131; orphan figure, 147–151; picaresques, 143, 214, 216, 217, 222; Seo's animated *Momotarō*, 190, 196–199, 203, 208n1; spectacle versus narrative in, 85, 123–124; wartime settings, 123–124, 142–143, 196, 214, 215, 217, 218, 249

nationalism: Chinese, 93–94, 99, 152, 153, 159n13, 159n17, 160n27; collaborators and traitors in nationalist historiography, 164–165, 170–171, 175, 179–181; cosmopolitan cultural, 74; ethnic and race-based, 39, 41, 42, 43, 54, 93, 99, 156, 181; Filipino, 215, 218–219, 225, 227, 236; government attempts to shape cinema and its uses, 99, 104–106, 150, 159n13; government fostering of specific languages, 148, 159n13; Indonesian, 164, 165, 173, 175, 177–182; Korean and South Korean, 54, 164, 170–171, 179–180, 267–268n4; life trajectories that challenge duality of, 164–165, 175, 177–180; Malay, 39, 41, 42, 43; national identity, 14, 15, 78, 93, 139, 142, 151; nationalist cinema of Na Un-kyu, 80; nationalist struggles, 26, 215, 218–219, 224–225, 227; nation-building, 14, 92, 93, 94, 96, 98, 99, 104, 107, 122, 150, 153; postcolonial, 164–165, 254–256; as reality that contradicted colonial documentaries, 26, 38, 41, 43; role of cinema in discourses involving, 92–96, 99, 170–171, 177–178, 181, 215, 218–219, 224–226, 235–236, 246–252, 256–257, 267–268n4; selective memory of, 164–165, 170–171, 246–252, 267–268n4; subjugation of minorities and indigenous people as by-product of, 154, 155, 160n26

Na Un-kyu: *Arirang*, 51, 58; cinematic roles of, 57–59, 63, 64; as cinematic symbol of unruly *pullyŏng sŏnin* for Japanese socialists, 12, 47, 51–52, 57–58; contributions to Korean cinema, 57–60, 76; dislike of Korean socialist intellectuals for, 59–60; *A Ferryboat without an Owner (Imcha ŏmnŭn Narutpae)*, 63, 64; *The Field Mouse (Tŭlchwi)*, 58; Im Hwa on, 59–60, 61; Kōriyama on, 57–58, 60–61, 80–81; O Yŏng-jin on, 84; *A Soldier of Fortune (P'unguna)*, 58

neocolonialism. *See* West

newsreels, 83, 103, 104–105, 172, 176, 196–198, 209n13, 210n23

Nishitani Osamu, 2, 7, 19, 19–20n9, 191, 208

North Korea and North Korean cinema, 59, 165, 220, 250, 267n2

Orphan of Asia (Ajia no koji) (novel; 1946), 139, 143, 144, 145–148, 153, 154, 155, 158n2

orphans and orphanhood: allegorical use by Wu, 14–15, 139, 145–146, 159n21; in *Balangiga: Howling Wilderness*, 223, 227–229, 234–237; Ching on *Orphan of Asia*, 146–147, 158n2; homelessness of stranded Nationalist Army soldiers and workers, 142, 153, 156, 158n5; Lo's "Orphan of Asia" (song), 140, 142; *Orphan Chicks in the Snow*, 122; "orphan consciousness" of non-orphan, 146–147, 154, 156–157; *Orphan Ling Bo*, 149, 150, 159n14; *Orphans of the Storm*, 122; postcolonial Taiwan as orphan nation, 15, 139, 140, 142, 146–147, 148–149; Tarzan orphan in melodrama, 156–157; Tarzan/Taishan character of, 139–140, 143, 147, 151, 152, 154; in *Taiyupian* and postcolonial Taiwanese cinema, 14, 139–140, 143, 148–151, 156–157

Othering: assumed by colonial hegemony, 71, 98, 151, 189, 205; Balázs's theory of Othering the face, 51–52, 62–63; cinematic exotic-erotic aspect of, 18–19n4, 32, 151, 154–156, 261–262, 264–265, 266–267; Cold War political Othering of Communist red, 150, 215, 254, 258; colonial commodification of colonized cultural artifacts, 261; colonial documentary cinema and, 195; coloniality, 189, 193, 209n8, 209n11; filmic representation, 101, 199; imperial Othering of indigenous peoples, 154; of Koreans by Japanese imperialists, 47, 50–51, 57–60, 63, 65, 80–82; Kōriyama on Othering the face of Na Un-kyu, 57–59; objectifying aspect of, 217, 265–266; Rachels on unconscious prejudice and bias, 191–193; unequal power dynamics that sustain prejudice and racism, 246; violence against civilians under Duterte, 219–220; violence against immigrants and refugees under Trump, 219–220; willed racism and prejudice, 101, 245–246. *See also* colonialism; racism

O Yŏng-jin: on cinematic powers of surprise and shock, 85; contributions to Korean cinema of, 82–86; on externalizing viewers, 13, 68, 76, 83–87; "General Issues of Korean Cinema" ("Chosen eiga no ippanteki kadai"), 83; on Japanese film theory, 83–84, 86; on primacy of the audience, 83–85

Park Chan-wook, 244–245, 259–261, 262, 265, 267, 269n28

Index   285

Philippine cinema: *Balangiga: Howling Wilderness,* 2, 221–238; Cinema Evaluation Board (CEB), 238; contributions of Khavn to, 17, 214, 216–217, 221–222, 226, 233–235, 238–239; contributions of Red to, 218–219; *The Day of the Trumpet (Cavalry Command),* 218; Filipino Academy of Movie Arts and Sciences, 238; films about Philippine-American War, 17, 214, 218–219; *Heneral Luna,* 219; role of Sawamura in recognizing, 77–78; *Sakay,* 214, 218–219

Philippines: activities of Duterte in, 216, 219; activities of Sawamura while in, 77–78; American racism toward Filipinos, 215–218, 223–224, 227, 230, 233; Balangiga Massacre (1901), 214–216; bells of Balangiga church controversy, 216; contributions of Sakay to freedom for, 219; cultural icons, 229–230, 231; exploitation of Filipino civilians by US soldiers, 215; Filipino death and property damage from invaders, 33, 215–216, 219, 224, 233–234; Filipino struggles against invaders, 33, 219, 223, 225, 226, 228, 231–232; independence, 218; Japanese imperial presence in, 165; Leyte province, 215–216; Manila, 148, 151, 216; Nationalist Chinese government investments in, 160n27; Philippine-American War, 17, 223–224, 230–231; Samar province, 215–216, 223–224; Spanish imperial presence in, 219, 223; *This Bloody, Blundering Business,* 219; US CIA counterrevolutionary violence in, 231–232; US Cold War presence in, 218–219, 231–232; US imperial presence in, 214–215, 223–224, 230, 231; US-made films set in Philippine-American War, 218, 219; US-made wartime films about Philippine-American War, 217–218; volcanic eruptions in, 223

picaresques, 143, 214, 216, 217, 222

postcolonial environments: censorship in, 18, 249; cinema in, 14–15, 16, 19n8, 139, 147–149, 156–157, 163, 228, 253; Cold War's influence on, 254–255, 258–259; in *The Handmaiden,* 259–267; Indonesia, 19n8; Korea, 19n8, 248–249; memory erasure and repression of colonial presence, 1, 2, 5, 18, 248–249, 253–255, 267–268n4; scholarly discourses, 4, 10, 18, 19n8, 27, 31–32, 43n3, 68–69, 94–97, 111, 164–165, 204, 254; Taiwan, 139, 147, 148–149; turmoil left in wake of colonialism, 6, 9, 254–255

power: of the audience, 83–84; of cinema, 84–85, 92, 101, 107, 112, 116, 117, 118, 193, 205, 206; control and transmission of knowledge as function of, 6, 13, 18, 71, 73, 77, 81, 95–96, 254; to represent subjective perceptions, 92–99, 106, 107, 112, 246; unequal dynamics between colonizers and colonized, 2, 6, 7, 39, 42, 154, 155, 219, 248, 261; uneven dynamics of capital, technology, and geopolitics, 2, 9, 35, 69, 81, 95, 98–99, 105, 171, 254, 258

prejudice. *See* Othering

proletarian cinema: Alliance of New Film Artists (Korea), 61; as basis for Socialist solidarity, 49, 61, 65; Im Hwa on, 61–62, 76, 80–81; Kōriyama on, 81; *Manila in the Claws of Light,* 216; as mode of philosophy, 75; *Potomok Chingis-Khana Storm over Asia,* 47–48; *Proletaria Eiga* (Japanese journal), 47, 48; Proletarian Film League of Japan (Prokino), 80; Pure Film Movement, 76, 80; Sasa Genjū, 48–49; *Shinko Eiga* (Japanese journal), 57; unpopular with Japanese audiences, 57, 58

propaganda: American *ruHua* films as, 101; British imperial, 37, 38, 41; *bunkajin* (cultured, well-educated men) as propagandists for Japan, 15, 163, 164, 171; *Calling Australia (Goshu no Yobigoe),* 172; *China Nights (Shina No Yoru),* 179; colonial documentaries on, 26, 28–31, 34, 41, 42; colonial subjects as propagandists for Japan, 15, 163, 164; destruction of *Momotarō: Divine Warriors of the Sea* as, 195; *Five Faces of Malaya,* 30–43; Greater East Asian Co-Prosperity Sphere, 171; Hinatsu Eitarō/Hō Yŏng/Dr. Huyung, 15–16, 163–170, 180–182; humanistic aspect of wartime, 189, 190; *Indian Ocean (Samoedra Hindia),* 172–173; Indonesian revolutionary propaganda in Jogjakarta, 176, 181; Iwasaki's article "Film as a Means of Propaganda and Agitation," 94, 107n1; Japanese film *You and I (Kimi to Boku),* 16, 163, 164, 167–171, 174–175, 180, 182n5; Japanese focus on film as, 173, 194; Japanese-Korean co-produced film, *Military Train (Kunyong Yŏlch'a),* 166; Japanese-language films made by Korean filmmakers, 170; Japanese-Manchurian coproduced films of Ri Kōran, 167–168; Japanese use of Bahasa Indonesia, 172; Korea Motion Picture Ordinance (1940) to promote war, 166; Korean postcolonial nationalist film, 250–251; Lansdale murders and mutilations as, 231–232; *Malaya War Record: A Record of the Onward March (Mar ē Senki Shingeki no Kiroku),* 196–197, 210n23;

Oriental Song of Victory (Tōyō no gaika), 77–78; O Yŏng-jin on national policy films, 83–84; Sawamura and, 77–78; Sendenbu agency established by Japan in Jakarta, 172; US Cold War anticommunist, 215, 231. See also images

pullyŏng sŏnin ("malcontent colonial Koreans"): extension of the concept, 50, 51, 54, 57; Im Hwa's responses to, 52, 55–57, 61, 80; Japanese appropriation of to justify colonialism, 51, 54, 63, 65; in Japanese socialist cultural productions, 47, 49, 52–54, 57, 61, 65; Jinhee Lee on use of, 49–50; Kōriyama's use of, 57, 61; Nakano's use of, 53–54, 61; Na as embodiment of, 47, 49, 51; Pak Yŏl and Kaneko Fumiko, 56–57; predictable, controllable aspects of, 50–51, 63; as stereotype for Korean males, 12, 47, 49, 54, 63

race-time: asynchronous character of, 26, 40, 43; colonial modernity as apex of the spectrum, 31, 35, 38; as creation of colonial documentary, 11, 26; as defined by Nadine Chan, 11, 26; in Five Faces of Malaya, 30–38

Rachels, James, 191–193, 209n9

racism: Across the Pacific, 218; American and European racial prejudice, 100–101, 106, 108n4, 111, 118–119, 122–123, 125–129, 181, 218, 230, 245–246, 253–254; attributions used in place of physical traits, 49–50; Birth of a Nation, 111, 118–119, 123–124; The Birth of White Australia, 118; China (Chung Kuo/Cina), 108n4; colonial conquest cinema, 114, 118–119, 121, 123–129; of colonial race-time, 11, 25–26, 30–32, 35, 38–43, 125–126; of colonial racialized hierarchies, 1–2, 7, 19–20n9, 30–32, 37, 69, 111, 118–119, 129, 189, 249; epidermalization, 16, 19n8, 69, 87, 189, 190, 205, 208–209nn7–8, 209n11; exoticized, gendered Other as product of, 12, 19n6, 19–20n9, 30–32, 51–52, 60–61, 63, 69, 95, 101, 107, 118–119, 123, 125, 190, 248, 261; Five Faces of Malaya, 11, 30–38; The Head Hunters, 218; in humanitas-anthropos dichotomy, 1–2, 19n8; internalization, externalization, and, 87; Japanese assumptions about Koreans, 47, 49, 52–54, 57–60; Korean responses to Japanese, 51–52, 54–57, 61, 65; of Kōriyama, 57–58, 60–61, 65, 81; massacre of Koreans in Japan, 50, 56; of Nakano, 53–54, 61, 103, 117, 121–128, 130; pullyŏn sŏnin and kisaeng stereotypes, 12, 47, 49–51; "Rain Falling on Shinagawa Station," 53–54, 61; The Red Lantern, 103, 117, 121–128, 130; segregation, 42, 62, 248, 251, 252; The Source Material and, 50; Thief of Baghdad, 94; unconscious, 61, 108n4, 191–192; Welcome Danger, 94, 104, 105, 106; willed 124, 227, 233, 245–246. See also colonialism; discrimination; Othering; stereotyping

The Red Lantern (1919): Boxer Rebellion (1898–1900) setting of, 103, 111, 112, 123–128; as colonial conquest melodrama, 126, 129; conflict between traditional and modern in, 125–126; as fictionalized impression of Asia and Asians, 112, 122, 124–125, 129; homage to Birth of a Nation, 118–119, 124; as impetus for growth of Chinese film industry, 123; Mahlee as embodiment of larger sociopolitical conflict, 117, 121, 123, 125–128, 129–130; musical score for, 128–131, 132n23; narrative progression in, 121; novel on which film is based, 111, 112, 124, 130; racism and bias in, 117, 121, 122–123, 127, 130; ruHua pian designation by Chinese in America, 103, 117, 122, 123; theater showings of, 122, 123; "voice of the home" appeal of melodrama, 118, 123

repression. See consciousness and unconsciousness

ruHua pian (China-humiliating films): China (Chung Kuo/Cina), 108n4; Chinese-American filmmaking and, 103–104; Chinese cinema's expenditure on films to counter, 104–105; Chinese dignity damaged by, 13, 92, 93, 104–106; Chinese film industry growth and, 92, 98–99, 100–101, 103, 107; Chinese overseas students' responses to, 101, 102–103; Chinese protest against Western-made, 93, 97, 99–106; Chinese racial-national identity and, 93, 104–105; complicity with Western imperialism, colonialism, and racial prejudice, 94, 101, 105–107; Film Censorship Committee decrees (1931), 104–105; The First Born, 103, 123; For the Freedom of the East, 101; The Hatchet Man, 105; Lu Xun on protests against, 94, 97; Outside the Law, 101; political upheavals in China coinciding with, 93, 97–98; power politics of representation and, 92, 93, 104–107; The Red Lantern, 103, 122–123; Regulations for Film Censorship (Dianying jiancha fa) (1930), 104; Shanghai Express, 105; Thief of Bagdad, 94; Welcome Danger, 94, 104, 105, 106; Xu Hu's response to, 102

Russia, 48, 78, 96

semicolony, 95, 98, 116, 124
Seo Mitsuyo, 16–17, 189–190, 194–197, 199–200, 204, 209n19
Shanghai: as early filmmaking center, 99, 103, 105, 108n12, 116, 122, 131n5; influence on Manchurian cinema, 79; as semicolony, 95; as symbol of modernity, 126
silent film, 9, 59, 108n12, 117, 119, 121, 122, 132n14, 144
Singapore: fall of (February 1942), 196, 197; Japanese occupation of, 165; as model of Western modernity, 25, 35, 37, 43n1, 112, 148, 151; Taiwanese investment in, 160n27
Skoller, Jeffrey, 215, 221, 225–226
Socialism and Socialists: Alliance of New Film Artists, 59, 61, 62; filmmakers and critics, 57–59, 61–63, 80–82; global intellectual impact of, 254; Im Hwa's response to Japanese comrades, 52–53, 54–56, 61–62, 80–81; Japanese self-perception as center of Asian, 48; Japanese socialist movement, 47–49, 51–52, 54, 60–62; Japanese use of Korean actor Na as symbol, 51–52, 59–61; Japanese use of Korean *kisaeng* image, 12, 47, 49, 51; Japanese use of Korean *pullyŏng sŏnin* image, 47, 49–52, 54, 57, 61, 65; Korean Socialist response to work of Na, 59, 61; Kōriyama and, 52, 57–61; Marxism and Marxists, 48, 54, 114; misalignment of Japanese and Korean comrades, 12, 48–56, 62, 65, 80–81; Moscow's global centrality, 48; *Musanja*, 54, 61, 65n2; Nakano and, 52–54; *Proletaria Eiga*, 47–48; Proletarian Film League of Japan (Prokino), 80; Sasa on colonial cinema, 48–49; *Shinko eiga*, 57, 80; socialist internationalism, 52; Socialist realism, 131n11. *See also* Communism
South Korea: General Government Building (Seoul), 252; nationalism, 164, 179–180, 268n16; Normalization Treaty, 255, 257–258, 269n24
South Korean cinema: appropriation of Japanese imperialist gaze by, 265, 266; contemporary, 18, 242, 243, 250, 253, 265, 267–268nn3–4; *Pak Yŏl*, 56; *Parasite*, 243; postcolonial film censorship, 267n4, 268n7
Soviet Union. *See* Union of Soviet Socialist Republics (USSR)
Spain, 217, 218, 223, 225, 236
spectators. *See* audiences
speech acts, 75–76, 81–82, 226
stereotyping: of Chinese during the Boxer Rebellion period, 103; in *The Handmaiden*, 260–261, 265; of Japanese by postcolonial Korea, 253, 268n16; of Koreans through *pullyŏng sŏnin* and *kisaeng* imagery, 12, 47, 49–51, 54, 57, 61, 63; of Malayan peoples in *Five Faces of Malaya*, 15, 31–38, 44n14, 139, 154–155; of Mongolians in *Potomok Chingis-Khana*, 47–49. *See also* racism
Storm over Asia (*Potomok Chingis-Khana*), 47–49
subjectivity. *See* colonized
synchronicity, 201–204, 208n4

Taiwan: Amoy (*Xiayu*) dialect, 148, 151, 158n11; Austronesian nations and tribes of, 155; Chinese imperialism and settler colonialism in, 139, 142, 151, 159n18, 159n21; Cold War's coinciding with postcolonial modernization in, 15, 143, 144, 148, 152–153, 155, 269n23; contributions of Lo, 140, 142; February 28, 1947 incident and White Terror, 149; Great East Asian Co-Prosperity Circle of the Japanese Empire and, 159n23; Hokkienese/Han Chinese of, 154–155, 158n11; indigenous populations and national identity of, 139, 153, 154–155; intellectual repression and deformation of colonial, 15, 155; Japanese imperialism in, 48, 146, 154, 155, 156, 159n21, 159n23; *koa-a-hi* theater, 148; Kuomintang (KMT), 104–107, 142, 148, 150, 159n13, 159n15; loss of United Nations membership, 140, 158n3; Mandarin fostered by Nationalist government, 148, 150, 156; *minjian* decolonization and deimperialization of, 156; Minnan dialect, 148, 158n11; Nationalist government priorities, 152–153; orphaned Nationalist Army of, 142, 153, 156, 158n5, 159n19; orphan figure in Taiwanese culture, 140, 146; as Orphan of Asia, 15, 139–140, 147, 152–153, 157; "Orphan of Asia" (song), 140, 142, 157; Po Yang (dissident writer), 142; war between China and Japan that affected, 140, 142, 147, 153–154; Western placement on Cold War anticommunist frontier of, 148, 152–153; Wu's *Orphan of Asia* (semiautobiographical novel), 139, 144, 145–147, 153–154, 155, 157–158n1–2
Taiwanese cinema: Amoy- and Minnan-language films, 148; censorship policies affecting, 158n9; *City of Sadness* (*Beiqing chengshi*), 149; contributions of Lee to, 150, 159n16; contributions of Liang to, 143–144, 158n7; flourishing postwar state of, 148, 151,

154; *Home Too Far* (*Yiyu*), 140; Japanese film style influences, 71; Liao on *Taiyupian* and, 148, 149, 158–159n12; Mandarin-language films, 148; melodrama in, 15, 143, 145, 149; *minjian* decolonization and deimperialization of, 156; motifs of sadness and orphanhood in, 148–149, 159n15; New Taiwan Cinema, 148–149; orphan figure in, 14–15, 139, 140, 143, 147, 149, 150–151, 154; *Our Neighbors*, 150, 159n16; Taipei National Film Archive (Taiwan Film and Audiovisual Institute), 149, 157, 159n14; Taiwanese-language films, 148; *Taiyupian* film industry, 139, 148, 149; *Tarzan and Treasure* (*Taishan yu baozang*), 140, 142–145, 147, 150; Tarzan/Taishan figure in, 14–15, 142–143, 150, 151–157. See also *Taiyupian* (Taiwanese language film)

Taiyupian (Taiwanese language film): *Beautiful Ducklings*, 150–151, 159n16; *City of Sadness* (*Beiqing chengshi*), 149; contributions of Liang to, 143–144, 158n7, 158–159n12; creative phases of, 143, 148, 149, 158–159n12; "crying songs" (*khau-tiau-a*) of, 159n15; film output of (1955–1972), 148, 159n14; industry peak of, 14–15, 139, 143, 148; keywords and tropes in, 149; KMT tolerance of, 159n13, 159n15; local culture's influence on, 151; melodramas of sadness and sacrifice, 149; *minjian* decolonization and deimperialization, 156; Minnan dialect's popularity in, 148; motif of sadness in, 148–149, 159n15; neglected in Taiwanese cinema, 148, 159n15; orphanhood in, 14–15, 139, 140, 143, 147, 149, 150–151, 154; *Orphan Ling Bo*, 149, 150, 159n14; post-1970 films, 149; revival of, 149–150, 159n14; *Tarzan and Treasure*, 14–15, 139–147, 150, 151–157; transnationality of, 151, 152, 154, 156, 158–159n12, 159n22. See also Taiwanese cinema

Tarzan and Treasure (*Taishan yu baozang*) (1965): as carnivalesque *Taiyupain*, 143, 147, 150, 153; comparison to *Orphan of Asia* and its protagonist, 139, 143–144, 147, 153–154; as detective-adventure film, 144–145, 155–156; Hollywood heritage underlying, 140–141, 142, 144; indigenous peoples' plight in, 154, 155; melodramatic character of, 143, 144–145, 151–152; orphan allegory in, 14–15, 139, 142, 143, 147–148; protagonist, Taishan/Cheng Da-wei, 15, 142–143, 145, 151–153; settings, 144–145, 155; symbolization of Taiwan in Taishan, 15, 150; Taiwan's Orient in, 151–156; in *Taiyupian*, 143, 150, 154, 155–156; work of Liang, 14, 139, 140, 143–144, 149, 158n7

Tarzan films: Hollywood-produced, 140, 142, 144, 145, 151, 158n8; Taiwan's Taishan, 14–15, 139–141, 142–144, 145, 147, 150, 151–152, 153, 154, 156

technology: cinema as technology of knowledge, 6; cinematic, 60, 85, 92, 97, 99, 159n15, 163; control over ideas and their dissemination through, 6, 11, 15, 92, 93, 97, 106–107, 163, 202–203, 248–249, 255; in documentary filmmaking, 11, 26, 28, 30, 202–203; media and communication, 14, 26, 38, 159n15, 210n32; Nishida on, 20n12; photographic, 201, 203, 211n37; unequal acquisition among countries of, 2, 6, 9, 92, 99, 106, 248, 249

Terada Torahiko, 74, 76

Thailand, 95, 160n27

theater: Amoy, 151; backgrounding of human face in, 52; Brecht's contributions to, 200–201; Cine Drama Institute, 176; Greek, 116, 201; Hinatsu's/Dr. Huyung's participation in Indonesian, 171–176, 181; Indonesian, 171–176; Japanese use of *bunkajin* and, 171–173; Java Theatrical Play Association (Perserikatan Oesaha Sandiwara di Djawa), 172; Kino Drama Atelier (KDA), 176; Sendenbu propaganda agency in colonial Indonesia, 172, 173, 175, 176; street scene model, 200–201; Taiwanese *koa-a-hi*, 148; *vérité*, 201; *wayang* (Javanese puppet theater), 172

Thompson, Kristin, 112, 113, 121–122, 132n20

time: asynchronous time of colonial documentary, 11–12, 25–30, 31, 39, 41–43; Chakrabarty on, 27, 210n28; colonial temporality, 11, 26, 27, 28, 30, 39, 43; desynchronicity in *Momotarō*, 196, 198; documentary time, 27–30, 43; event-based dualities of, 179–180; global presentism, 195, 202, 203; logic of "the now," 208n4, 210n26; race-time, 11, 26, 30–38; synchronizing of experiences of world audiences and, 193, 195, 202–203, 205, 207, 208n5, 209n16, 210nn24–25, 210n28; Western historical time, 27

Tosaka Jun, 20n13, 73, 74–75

transcolonial relations: colonizer and colonized cultures, 247–248; in contact zones, 2, 7, 9, 11, 12, 14, 96–97; *The Handmaiden* as reinterpretation of past, 18, 242, 244–267, 269nn28–31; inequalities, 5, 7, 13, 261; modern cinema's reinterpretation of, 247–249; resignification of film by, 2, 4, 5–6, 9, 10, 14,

Index 289

17, 18, 96–97; transcolonial film productions, 3; transcolonial modernity, 247, 248–249, 259, 260, 262; transcolonial nature of Asian colonial cinema, 18–19n4
transnational media, 14, 15, 92–93, 96, 106, 144, 150–151, 154, 156–157, 242–244

unconsciousness. *See* consciousness and unconsciousness
Union of Soviet Socialist Republics (USSR): Cold War with US, 250, 254; depictions of Soviet imperial inclusivity, 47–49; Soviet montage, 62, 63; *Storm over Asia (Potomok Chingis-Khana)*, 47–49
United States: American cinematic mythology and propaganda, 99–100, 122–126, 217–218; American racist and exploitative behaviors, 124–126, 215, 220, 223, 227, 230, 233; *Amigo*, 219; anticommunist activities of, 148, 150, 155, 231–232, 254; *Asian Americans* (PBS documentary), 19n6; Balangiga massacre by American soldiers, 215–216; Cold War against Communism, 155, 215, 218, 219, 231–232, 250, 254, 257–258; films in support of Philippine-American War, 217–218; imperial presence of, 17, 214, 215–220, 227, 230, 231, 233, 268n5; Normalization Treaty orchestrated by, 255, 257–258, 269n24; Philippine-American War, 17, 214, 215, 218, 224, 225, 230, 231; *This Bloody, Blundering Business*, 219; Vietnam War, 155, 233; worldwide export of American films, 94, 111–112, 122. *See also* West
universalism: confusion of the universal with the cultural, 211n36; as critique of Japanese imperial fascism, 80, 81; as critique of Western aspirations, 13

Veil of Happiness (France; 1923), 102
vernacular modernism: colonial modernity versus, 29, 98; Hansen's theory of, 95, 98, 113, 116; as tool for challenging colonial power, 116
Vietnam, 94–95, 98, 102, 155, 160n27, 216, 219, 231–232, 233
viewers. *See* audiences
violence: American massacre of inhabitants in Samar and Leyte provinces, 215–216; Balangiga massacre (1901), 214, 217, 221; by British-Americans and Chinese in China, 103, 111, 112, 123, 124–125, 127–128; Burmese government persecution of orphaned Nationalist Army, 142, 158n5; Chinese tong wars, 100; against civilians under Duterte, 219–220; expulsion of Korean activists from Japan, 54, 55; February 28, 1947 massacre and White Terror, 149; Filipino retaliation against US military exploitation in Balangiga, 215; against immigrants and refugees under Trump, 219–220; by Lansdale to intimidate Filipino communist sympathizers, 231–232; loss of lives through imperialist, 231–232, 234; massacre of Koreans in Japan (1923), 50, 56; race war as topic of melodrama, 118–122; Western violence in 1890s China, 124. *See also* wars and conflicts
Virilio, Paul, 85, 203, 204
voice-over, 11, 25, 26, 31, 35, 41, 78, 108n4

war films: Asian-made, 214, 267–268n4; *The Day of the Trumpet (Cavalry Command)*, 218; documentaries about wars, 219; global popularity of Asian, 243; *Storm over Asia (Potomok Chingis-Khana)*, 47–48; wartime documentary, 9, 16–17, 196–197, 199, 233; Western-made, 18, 214, 217–219, 231–232, 243, 267–268n4. *See also* wartime films
wars and conflicts: Boxer Rebellion (1899–1901), 103, 111, 112, 123, 124–125, 127–128; cinematic depictions of death and damage from, 219, 231, 233, 234; Cold War-incited proxy in Asia, 254; depicted in melodramas, 118–122; government censure of images, 233; loss of Taiwanese in POW camps, 153; Malayan Emergency (1948–1960), 43; Miki on wartime coloniality, 20n14; Pacific War collaborators and proponents, 83, 169–172; Pacific War front of World War II, 41, 44n6, 142, 153, 155–156, 174, 267–268n4; Philippine-American War (1899–1902), 17, 214, 215–217, 219, 221–222, 225–226, 231–234; as products of imperial policies, 6, 94, 120–121, 223–224, 231, 233; psychological damage from, 9, 15, 18, 153, 156, 159n19, 224, 242, 255–256, 267–268n4, 268n16; Russian Civil War (1917–1922), 48; Taiwan and Taiwanese, 139, 140, 147, 153–154, 155; Vietnam War (1955–1975), 216, 231–233; wartime imperial film network in Asia, 3, 180–181; wartime propaganda, 77, 166–167, 169–170, 172, 189–190, 196–197, 199, 210n23; World War II, 83, 233, 255. *See also* violence
wartime films: Asian-made, 18n3; audience as concern of, 78, 82–87; *Balangiga: Howling Wilderness*, 214–215, 221–238; cinema

290   Index

during times of war, 16–17, 18, 71, 118–122, 207, 208n5, 243, 268n7; films set in wartime environments, 17, 142, 214, 218–219, 243, 250–253, 267–268n4; Imamura's wartime observations, 194–195, 199–201, 204, 209n14, 209n16; *Mar ē Senki* newsreel documentary, 196–197, 199, 210n23; *Momotarō: Divine Warriors of the Sea*, 189, 196–200, 204, 209n19; wartime imperial film network in Asia, 3, 180–181; *You and I*, 167–170. *See also* war films

Watsuji Tetsuro, 205, 208n3, 210n30

Welcome Danger (1929), 94, 104, 105, 106

West: Asian market for Western films, 84, 93–94, 96–98; Balázs's theory of the face, 51–52; capitalism, 32, 38, 48, 94; challenges to Western stereotyping and misrepresentation, 13–14, 39–40, 92–94, 97, 99–104; *cinéma vérité* and direct cinema, 209n14; colonial ideas of history and progress, 19–20n9, 27, 30, 35, 37, 131n3, 265; colonial racism, racialized hierarchies, stereotyping, and Othering, 13, 19–20n9, 30–31, 51–52, 69, 95, 101, 107, 118–119, 123, 190, 248; confluence of Asian and Western cinemas, 116, 122; East-West hybridity, 247, 252, 259–260, 262, 265; "fascinating cannibalism" behaviors of Western consumers, 60–61, 63, 261; imagining and exoticizing of Asia by the, 18–19n4, 69, 111–112, 122–126, 128–129, 245–246; melodrama's popularity in Asia, 118–121, 129, 150; socialist alliances in Asia as response to Western imperialism, 12, 83; Western film thinking and theory, 14, 20n11, 70, 72–77, 86; Western imperialism in Asia, 37, 92, 94, 97, 98, 124–125, 222, 268n9; Western modernization and modernity, 32, 37–38, 95, 96, 111–112, 117–118, 125–126, 210n29, 247; Western neocolonialism in Asia, 13, 68, 70, 73–74, 191, 201, 204, 205, 215; Western values viewed as universal, 69, 72–73; West-to-East movement of film technology, 69, 92–93, 98–100, 107, 108n12. *See also* Great Britain; United States

Williams, Linda, 113–114, 116, 131n4

workers. *See* labor and the laboring masses

Wu Zhuoliu, *Orphan of Asia* (*Ajia no koji*) (novel; 1946), 14–15, 139, 140, 144, 145–146, 152, 153–154, 156–157, 157n1, 158n2, 159n21

You and I (*Kimi to Boku*) (1941): Hinatsu's making of, 167–170, 174, 175, 182n5; Im Hwa on, 170; as imperial propaganda film, 16, 163, 164; in Korean filmmaking, 170; negative responses to, 16, 76, 163, 164, 167, 171, 174, 175, 180; portrayal of Korean and Japanese characters as equals in, 169

Zhou Guoqing, 76, 79

www.ingramcontent.com/pod-product-compliance
Lightning Source LLC
Chambersburg PA
CBHW030103170426
43198CB00009B/474